BRICK BY BRICK

BRICK BY BRICK

*The Biography of the Man Who Really Made
the Mini - Leonard Lord*

MARTYN NUTLAND

authorHOUSE®

AuthorHouse™
1663 Liberty Drive
Bloomington, IN 47403
www.authorhouse.com
Phone: 1-800-839-8640

Published by AuthorHouse   10/01/2012

ISBN: 978-1-4772-0318-7 (sc)
ISBN: 978-1-4772-0317-0 (e)

Library of Congress Control Number: 2012908033

CONTENTS

To, Barry Walker, who could have, should have and would have written this book and my ever-supportive wife, Dolores, who has 'lived' with Leonard Lord for 25 years.

ACKNOWLEDGEMENTS

To Bob Burlington, Austin ex-apprentice and lifelong Longbridge devotee whose unceasing research and investigation helped tremendously.

To his friend, Paul Fox, whose panache when delving into the registers of births, marriages and deaths enabled me to piece together Leonard Lord's early life and family background. Also for Paul's visits, on my behalf, to museums, archives and sundry other locations.

To two of Lord's surviving relatives, Guy Breeden and Mrs F A Q Blundstone. The former, Lord's grandson, for agreeing to write my foreword, and for Mrs Blundstone's recollections of my subject.

To the late Barry Walker who helped start the 'ball rolling' by his own interest in Leonard Lord and for his contribution to my knowledge of Austin commercial vehicles. Also to Barry's circle of contacts, especially Chris Smart for many contributions but particularly sifting the archive after Barry's untimely death and processing dozens of Mrs Blundstone's pictures. In addition, my thanks to Ian Elliott.

To Geoffrey Rose OBE, who, again, sadly, never lived to read the book and especially to Bill Davis and Bernard Johnson. Bill Davis, as deputy managing director of BMC knew Lord at board level and as the senior surviving executive of the company showed me great kindness in sharing anecdotes and memories. Bernard Johnson received his indentures from Leonard Lord personally and was of immeasurable assistance on the technical details of Austin vehicles. And to all the other ex-Longbridge apprentices who shared their expertise and memories—Tony Ball MBE and Jon Nightingale with their knowledge of sales and administration; Roy and his late wife, Josephine (Jo), Dunnett (née Harriman) for their recollections of George Harriman and Jo for her memories of family life in the Lord household; Major Haynes with his experiences of the engineering department, introduction of computers and the Austin Works in general; Vaughan Hatton who researched Lord's one time home (Lambury) near Limebury Point; Norman Milne for statistics and observations; Bob Myers who worked on production development and Mike Sheehan whose knowledge extends from the pedal car factory at Bargoed through a period at Land Rover to involvement with BMC overseas.

In addition my gratitude to Austin/BMC personnel, who were not apprentices, and other individuals from the 'Longbridge family'—Godfrey Coates, whose late father, George, had been with Herbert Austin since the early days and spent a lifetime at the Works my thanks for his reminiscences. Also, the late Aubrey Edwards, for his knowledge of the company's publicity machine; Ingrid Greening for her wide-ranging memories; Geoff Iley, of Morris, MG and BMC quality control and to Paul Ragbourne long-term colleague of Bernard Johnson in engineering development who helped with information on Lord's secretarial arrangements and other personal details.

To Ralph Clarke in South Africa for sharing with me his recollections of Lord and the operation of the Austin plant in that country and to Ron Sheldon who patiently facilitated that input.

Of vital importance to my research was the contribution of Dick Etheridge Junior who, with enormous magnanimity, unstintingly shared his late father's record and reminiscences of the industrial disputes at Longbridge in the 1950s and 60s. This previously unpublished material is of tremendous value in recounting the life of Leonard Lord and I am deeply indebted to Dick who continues to be a guide and mentor.

On the club scene, my thanks to David Whyley of the Austin Counties Car Club whose encyclopaedic knowledge of post-War Austins was of great help. To Chris Garner of the Pre-War Austin Seven Club for his support and enthusiasm; to Tony A Osborne of the Federation of Austin Clubs, Registers and Associations; Jim Stringer of the Vintage Austin Register for his wise counsel and also Bob Wyatt MBE president of that organization. In addition, to the members of the Daimler and Lanchester and Singer owners' clubs while not forgetting the Morris Register and the help given me by their historian the late Harry Edwards and Register member, the late Geoff Creese. But especially to Malcolm Jeal of the Society of Automotive Historians in Britain and former member of the Veteran Car Club of Great Britain's dating committee who provided me with chapter and verse on Leonard Lord's involvement with the VCC. Also to Malcolm's former colleague on the dating committee and motoring historian, Anders Clausager, for his encouragement.

In addition, and very importantly on the Morris and Wolseley front, my thanks to Norman Painting, leading historian of Morris Commericial Cars and an expert on the early years of Wolseley. To Ian Grace for other help in this area and to Peter Seymour whose contribution both directly and through his excellent books was an invaluable source of information on Lord, The Nuffield Organization and aeronautical matters.

Also, in the aircraft world, to Les Whitehouse of the Boulton Paul Association for his extensive correspondence with me on Boulton Paul Aircraft Limited. To Bernard Shaw for his additional guidance and his willingness to check my aeronautical history. Also in this field to Gerard Ferris.

To genealogist Patrick Stokes who researched Lord's trans-ocean voyages in minute detail.

To Timothy Richards, an ordinary enthusiast, for his encouragement and the many snippets of interesting information he forwarded. In similar vein to my friends Kelvin Price and Michael Loasby and to Stuart Ulph who took the time and trouble to read the section on the Murray Jamieson racers and give me his view.

To Paul Rogers, BBC Radio *Archers'* historian, for fascinating and generous input associated with Leonard Lord's passion for that programme.

I would also like to extend my thanks to the staff of HRH the Duke of Edinburgh's private office for pursuing relevant matters with Prince Philip on my behalf.

Also to the staff of Birmingham Museum and the National Motor Museum, Beaulieu. In addition, to The Guild of Motoring Writers for their help in identifying the correspondent 'Cambrian'.

To Robert Orford of the Oxford undertakers, Cowley and Sons, who took the time and trouble to research the details of Leonard Lord's funeral.

And last but not least to my wife, Dolores, who has put up with me and Leonard Lord for the last quarter century!

If, by oversight I have omitted any organization or individual from this list I sincerely apologize. No discourtesy or ingratitude is intended. I am extremely endebted to every one of the people who have helped me with this work.

This book has received funding from The Society of Authors' Foundation which provides support for historical biography. It is administered by The Society of Authors which is an organization devoted to protecting writers and representing their interests. I am grateful to the Foundation and the Society for honouring me with a financial contribution to the costs of a work such as this.

FOREWORD

As someone not directly involved in the motor industry, but from a family that had extensive interests in the component manufacturing side, I was flattered to be invited to write a foreword to this book. My principal qualification has to be that I am Leonard Lord's grandson but over and above that relationship, someone who remembers him with both enormous affection and respect.

In recent years the way my grandfather has been maligned by, and the subject of much misinformation from not only a number of motoring journalists, but also so-called 'historians' and commentators in the wider media, has become increasingly unacceptable.

I am delighted, therefore, that this book, although it takes a 'warts and all' stance, will go a long way towards correcting the record and firmly establishing the breadth of Leonard Lord's achievement and its huge significance on the national and industrial scene.

In saying this I have to emphasize that this is not a 'car book' in the accepted sense. The setting is, of course, that world, yet students of sociology will find a tremendous amount of interest as will anyone concerned with military history and the national and political scene from the 1920s until the early 60s.

The writer suggests that Leonard Lord was the greatest British industrialist of the latter half of the 20th century. Whether or not that is true it is my hope that by the closing pages of this book the reader will be able to make an accurate, but above all, fair assessment of the man's contribution to the nation.

GUY BREEDEN
Berkshire, UK
2010

Author's Note

This is a unique book. That is not the conceit it may seem. The uniqueness is in the number of people, from industry and beyond, who, given the opportunity, have wanted to add their brush strokes to a realistic portrait of the man most of them recognize only as the father of the British Motor Corporation.

Leonard Lord was immensely more than that. Yet he remains an unsung hero. One of, if not the greatest exponents of British industry when the nation's manufacturing sector was second only in significance to that of America.

In recent decades Lord, largely as a consequence of his no longer being alive, and that when he was, his life was closed and private, has become an all-too-easy scapegoat for the ills and ultimate demise of the United Kingdom's motor industry.

His reticence makes the task of the biographer difficult. In some cases the available sources are limited. Others may now wish to expand or disagree with my assessment. I welcome the discussion. Meanwhile I give you the real Leonard Lord.

INTRODUCTION

In her biography of Jacky Fisher, an admiral as great as Nelson, some say greater, Jan Morris describes how she came to write an account of the great sailor's life. *"Although he died six years before I was born he has been one of my life's companions"*, she says. Casual sight of a photograph in the late 1940s was her first acquaintance. The chance acquisition of a set of his memoirs followed. Endless correspondence with former shipmates, relatives and acquaintances, with women who adored him and men who detested him, ensued. The cuttings, files and books accumulated. *"I cherished the project in my heart for the better part of a lifetime,"* says Morris.

Her book, *Fisher's Face* (Random House), was published in 1995. The story of a man who was a great Englishman, a disgrace to his uniform, a manipulator, a hobgoblin, a damned Socialist, a crook, a paragon of kindness, a *parvenu*, a cad, a genius, a fraud, a delight. I came to Len Lord in a similar way to Jan Morris coming to Admiral Fisher.

Somewhere in my late teens or early 20s I fell upon the quote: *"We're not in business to make bloody motor cars; we're in business to make money"*. It was attributed to a man whose name I had only seen in ancient, back numbers of the *Austin Magazine*, and then only vaguely noted—Leonard Lord.

To this day I could not tell you if *'we're not in business to make motor cars but to make money'* is a Lord original. Certainly, something similar was being quoted to recruits at Rolls-Royce in Derby as late as the 1960s.

'Why is Rolls-Royce in business?'

'To make the world's best aeroplane engines, sir'.

'Wrong'.

'To develop the most advanced aero engine technology, sir'.

'Wrong . . . to make money!'

Although I don't know whether the utterance is unadulterated 'Lord' it stuck with me, colouring my very perception of business and of life itself. Other statements clung, snowball-like, to this first flake: *'Make proper cars and you don't need salesmen'*; *'If the door's not open, kick it open'*; and the rather less inspiring, *'I'm going to take Cowley apart brick by bloody brick'* and *'what are those buggers down on the farm* (Morris—my insertion) *doing?'*.

Here was a man, who, if nothing else, was colourful. Someone eminently quotable in an industry where, if you set aside Royce's, *'whatever is rightly done, however humble, is noble'*, and Ford's, *'you can have any colour as long as it's black'*, seemed singularly devoid of aphorisms. I became a motoring correspondent and my interest in Lord grew—the secondary school boy who rose to be a captain of industry and had led a company I had revered since childhood—'the Austin'. Sparse facts were beginning to attach themselves to those first anecdotal flakes.

I discovered the Morris Motors years, realized I had found the man who gave us the Morris Eight then quarrelled with William Morris, departed and was to say he would take the business apart brick by brick. I grew to appreciate his impact on immediately pre-War Austins and became familiar with the term 'Lord look'. I was conscious of his presence at Longbridge during the dark days of WWII, suspected much, but could prove very little.

He grew in stature as I came to appreciate his role in the merciless battle for dollars in the late '40s.

I reeled at the brazen decisiveness of a man who set the Mini on course to become one of the best known and best loved cars the world has ever known. Yet I was frustrated there was apparently no biography of this hero. Moreover, my peers in motoring journalism seemed to be obsessed with two utterly unimportant aspects of his life. That he swore a lot and smoked a lot. This struck me as a remarkable indictment of those who purport to be serious commentators on the motor industry, and indeed, the economic and industrial history of the Western world.

Admittedly, there was plenty in print, much of it banal, whole *tranches* of it anecdotal and a great deal highly questionable. Just as Jan Morris cherished the desire to tell the story of Fisher, like any journalist worth their salary, I harboured a wish to correct the injustices heaped upon Lord.

It is scandalous that history should remember a man who achieved so much, not only in the motor industry but on the industrial scene as a whole, primarily as a cigarette-puffing foul-mouth. It is easily arguable that Lord was the most important British industrialist of the latter half of the 20th century and that without his influence the end of the nation's car making would have come 40 years earlier than it did. Yet these two points seem to have become incidental to the trivia.

All that said, I am more fortunate, for obvious reasons, than Jan Morris. I have no romantic illusions about Leonard Lord! Some of what he did in the late 1940s and in the '50s, towards the end of his career, did indeed contribute to the collapse of the British motor industry. Even so, this has to be viewed in context, with the benefit of hindsight, and acknowledging that in many instances a person's greatest strengths are also their weaknesses.

Writing in *The Automobile* magazine in December 2007, motoring journalist, Jonathan Wood, suggests that Miles Thomas, whose path crossed that of Lord on more than one occasion, was: '*the best leader the British motor industry never had*'. The point is, of course, hypothetical and purely academic. Miles Thomas *wasn't* the leader of the British motor industry; Leonard Lord was. And how!

Yet this is a story of, to broadly quote something yet to come and that, at this stage, will mean little to the reader—'*relentless energy, arrogance, a domineering nature, furious temper, ruthlessness, impatience and a single-minded devotion to business*'. It is also a story of strained parenting, a traumatic childhood and in various arenas, sex and sexual ambivalence. That is the story of one section of the British motor industry and, in a way, of its destruction.

It is, also, of course, a story of a cancerous, debilitating, industrial relations infrastructure and of thwarted vision, of courage and determination.

We must take all that on board, while recognizing that for far too long it has been a case of 'anything goes' for many of those who have written or spoken about Lord. A piece of misinformation here an irrelevant or misleading anecdote there. That said, to write about the man with any degree of authority is difficult. Most of the people who worked alongside him in positions of authority are dead and, for whatever reason, he covered his tracks extremely well. Indeed, to chart this life may be more difficult than examining that of a Pepys, one of the Tudors, or any number of characters that have been dead for hundreds of years; rather than less than 50.

Such is the challenge we now face.

CHAPTER ONE
HOPE BUT NO ANCHOR

She was strikingly beautiful; stark naked and rode through the streets bareback.

The legend of Lady Godiva is one of two things most people know about the city of Coventry in the English Midlands. The other is that it was once an epicentre of the nation's motor industry; home to such universally acclaimed makes as Daimler, Jaguar, Alvis and Riley.

It would be convenient if we could cite as another well-known fact that the conurbation was the birthplace of Leonard Percy Lord. The reality though is different. The story of Lord's upbringing there is fragmented, complex and difficult to assess. Born in Coventry he certainly was, to Emma (*née* Swain) and William Lord, on November 15, 1896. Emma was four years Lord's senior and Leonard was the younger of two children. What has been previously documented is Mr Lord was superintendent of Coventry's public baths—just one, in reality.

The history of this facility dates back to 1742 when a small cold water wash house was established by private enterprise. By 1820 it had been expanded into a much bigger undertaking in Smithfield Street. However, the type of baths William Lord would have known were corporation run and first appeared in Hales Street in 1852. Such was the craving for cleanliness, and indeed the public health need, of the citizens of Coventry, that 2,000 of them passed through the waters on opening day.

Greater capacity came in 1891, but the work of those architectural doyens of the nation's public baths and wash houses, Henry Spalding and Alfred Cross, was not yet for Coventry. Not the towering facades and elegant windows of their Hampstead, Marylebone or Camberwell designs. The facility William Lord oversaw had been intended as a Wesleyan chapel but converted by Francis James, an entrepreneur from Wolverhampton, who had previously provided baths for Halifax and Nottingham.

The 22 foot frontage was on the west side of Priory Street and the building extended back for about three times that distance. Back-up water tanks were housed in the roof, part of the first floor was devoted to a flat where the Lords would have lived and Leonard was born, while the fire-proofed basement housed the boiler and laundry equipment. The first class bathers had changing rooms on the ground floor while their less affluent counterparts went upstairs to what had been designed as the upper gallery of the church, supported on ornamental iron pillars.

The hot rooms themselves were communal, offering three temperature ranges: from 130-140° Fahrenheit, through 160-190°, to 200-240°. There was also a vapour bath and a very hazardous-sounding electric bath.

Mr Lord, working from eight to eight, would have collected the money in a lobby just beyond the public entrance, issued the tickets, directed the clients to the appropriate sections, ensured it was women only on Wednesday, seen that the chiropodist was on hand and, no doubt, complained to his Emma about the vagaries of the 100 cell battery for that 'electric dip'.

Another structurally extravagant building was Wheatley Street Schools. It had been opened in 1893 and accommodated a total of 1,228 pupils; at that time, in three streams, from infants, through elementary, to senior. It was here the young Leonard received his early education, but whether or not he was ever actively aware of his father's ultra respectable, stable, lower middle class employment is not clear. By the time the boy was attending Wheatley Street, William Lord would have been hatching plans for a change of direction. When his son was old enough to start senior school, on August 22, 1906, the family address was *The Hope and Anchor* public house at 17 Whitefriars Lane, just to the north east of the city centre, near where the workhouse then stood and today the Ringway looms.

Why William Lord took the licence in preference to continuing in what we can only imagine was a regular, respected and not uncomfortable role is a mystery. It is, of course, the whim of many, when they feel a certain financial security, to run a pub and play mine host. Albeit, not usually in a city centre. Or the old adage of 'the grass being greener', with the actuality far removed from the dream, could equally well have applied. Or indeed, it could have been something quite different. An inheritance perhaps, or circumstances within the extended family or something different again. But this is supposition. And anyway, is it relevant to our story?

I think it is.

On the basis that early experience affects all our lives as does the quality, or otherwise, of our parenting. I believe this period impacted on Lord, not least because *The Hope and Anchor* venture was, as we shall see, not an unqualified success. This would not have been the romanticized inn of Noyes's *'Highwayman'*, more that of George Moore's *Esther Waters*. The living quarters were normally upstairs with split level accommodation on the ground floor, the ceilings of which would not have been much higher than a tall man's head.

Often there were three bars. The parlour, a semi-private area for special customers where spirits could be served from a mahogany wotnot; the public bar, and an area called the jug and bottle which we might liken to an off-licence and selling beer by the pitcher.

The parlour and public bars were often separated by a silk or velvet curtain and in addition to the landlord and his family it was common for a serving girl and a pot boy to have lived there amid the sawdust-spread floors.

For Leonard Lord, school now meant 'the Bablake'. There is some debate as to the exact origins of that august Coventry establishment. But a good case can be made for its roots dating from 1344 when Queen Isabella gave land in the countryside at Babbelak for the building of a church. This may have been to salve her conscience over her involvement in the gruesome murder of her husband, Edward II, whose homosexuality, somewhat understandably, did not please the French princess. In any event, it seems likely that by the mid 1360s her church of St John had assumed an educational role, possibly at the behest of the Black Prince, Isabella's grandson, and on additional land given by him.

Such charitable acts kept the school going until 1563 when Thomas Wheatley, a former mayor of Coventry, handed it much of a bizarre windfall. According to a rather unlikely story, Wheatley had ordered some steel wedges, or maybe that should read widgets, from Spain. The couriers of the day misdelivered the consignment and he received instead a crate of silver ingots whose rightful destination proved impossible to establish. Troubled by this situation, Wheatley resolved not to profit from the mischance and spent his gain on good works. Thus the school was able to provide board, clothing and tuition, significantly as far as we are concerned, *for poor boys that wished to become apprentices.*

Although little is known about Bablake in the 17th and 18th centuries it was still holding true to these traditions in the 19th and 20th. That is undoubtedly part of the explanation as to why Lord transferred there in 1906 instead of moving into the senior stream at Wheatley Road. Bablake shrank to just one pupil in 1824, but by 1870 headmaster Henry Mander had turned it into a flourishing institution. It was against this backdrop that the scene was being set for the life and training Leonard Lord enjoyed.

William Lord died on November 26, 1911, of cirrhosis of the liver and a duodenal ulcer. He was 44, Leonard barely 15. William Lord's daughter, 22-year-old Annie, registered the death. The popular perception is that the first complaint results from alcohol abuse. Although this is broadly true, it can also emerge, after a long period, in sufferers from the blood-borne virus hepatitis C—although this form of the infection had not been identified in 1911—and the latter can be contracted from nothing more sinister than a transfusion of infected blood. However, on the circumstantial evidence, I think we must conclude William Lord, now officially a licensed victualler, drank himself to death.

From a note on Leonard Lord's school record card dated August 1, 1909, we learn the boy's fees are to be paid in their entirety by Coventry Education Committee. This funding is then renewed every year until the end of his schooling in the summer of 1913. Thus it would seem affairs at *The Hope and Anchor* were not going well. At first the support was just one shilling per week (5p) eventually rising to 3s 6d (17.5p). Of the 322 pupils attending with Lord, 87 were financed either by scholarship or what we might term social support.

It follows that with the death of her husband and in a harsh male-dominated environment, it would have been virtually impossible for Emma to continue at *The Hope and Anchor*. So uncomfortable, perhaps, that the period has been air-brushed from family history altogether, not least by Leonard Lord. Emma and her children moved a little further north to 305 Foleshill Road. But we need to ask, did anything positive from Whitefriars Lane move with the boy? Although the value is debatable, it is possible that there his colourful turn of phrase was first implanted in those over-size ears pressed, along with that statuesque nose, to a bedroom wall or surreptitiously encroaching on a raucous adult world. We can even surmise that some of his forthrightness and sure-footedness was engendered in similar circumstances.

The Doomsday Book spells what Leonard Lord knew as Foleshill, 'Fulkeshill'. Later documentation renders it Folkshull. But all versions are a corruption of 'folk's' or 'people's hill'. In one form or another it would have been known to Lady Godiva, who we met briefly at the start of the chapter. Her husband, Earl Leofric, was lord of the manor and it is thought it was her ladyship who built the 11th century church of St Lawrence there. George Eliot lived on the southern edge of the area from 1841-49 and the weaving village of Tipton in her novel *Middlemarch* is probably Foleshill.

Until the beginning of the 18th century the hamlet was predominantly an agricultural settlement but, gradually, single hand loom weaving developed as, quite literally, a cottage industry. The opening of James Brindley's 38-mile Coventry canal, begun in 1768, and the Coventry and Nuneaton branch railway line in 1850, gave the activity a boost. At the time of the weavers' strike of 1860 6,430 of the 8,140 people in the parish and 30,000 of Coventry's total population were involved in making silk ribbon, chenille and black crepe, a coarser form, popular at the time for female funeral wear and over the long mourning periods of the age.

In part, the strike arose when workers at the Courtaulds mill in Halstead, Essex, downed shuttles in a bid to get a share of the 1000 per cent increase in profits the company had seen since 1830. But in Coventry it was more to do with preserving protectionist policies. Needless to say, when home supplies were no more, foreign ribbon flooded the market and the industry was crippled. At least 2,000 jobs were lost in Foleshill alone. Those that could, got out. Into better trades in Coventry itself, typically watchmaking; or to Birmingham, Leicester, Lancashire and sometimes North America. Many who were left went hungry.

However, it was not the end of silk weaving in the district. In 1862 William Stevens stepped in to alleviate the crisis by inventing and manufacturing the Stevengraph, a silk weave bookmark with an illustration relating to the subject of the volume in which it would be used. We might consider these the height of kitsch, but they were popular at the time and in 1882 W H Grant opened a mill, in Lockhurst Lane, to make a range of similar items. Grants were still operating in the late 1930s. John and Joseph Cash's business, with its roots as far back as the 1840s, exists to this day making some of the items on Torrington Avenue, Coventry, that made Coventry famous. Their most noteworthy product, developed around 1870, was labels for school uniforms. No doubt it was such tags Emma sewed into her son's and daughter's school clothes.

In 1904, perhaps ironically, but certainly of great importance to this story, Courtaulds arrived on the Foleshill Road and established a factory that would make them world leaders in the production of artificial fibre. One of the plant's various claims to fame was that in 1924 a 365 ft chimney, reputed to be the tallest in the land, was added. Even single hand loom weaving, the term distinguishing it from machine or factory processes, survived, to an extent, into the '20s. A 1927 issue of the *Coventry Standard* carried a short feature on an elderly couple still producing silk ribbon by this method.

Perhaps even more important than the continuation of silk weaving was that other industries were establishing themselves in the district. Brickworks along the canal; the Arthur Herbert company, that claimed to be the largest machine tool maker in the world and could justifiably argue that access to equipment like its capstan lathes was one of the reasons the automotive industry came to Coventry in the first place, and, of course, just off Foleshill Road itself, car maker Riley.

A complexly structured operation, Riley had been producing bicycles, engines and the odd car from 1890 but vehicle production in the accepted sense did not start until 1913. That the factory was rented from a wealthy entrepreneur named Lancelot Pratt will become of some relevance later when we find this gentleman closely associated with William Morris.

In little over a century, Foleshill had changed from a sleepy agricultural hamlet to a sprawling urban community that was the most heavily industrialized in Coventry. Growing up there, Leonard Lord would have been acutely aware of the manufacturing scene and would have seen, and heard at first hand, all the ramifications including those that surrounded labour relations. However revealing that may have been, there was more poignant enlightenment—watching his mother struggling in reduced circumstances.

By the time Leonard Lord arrived at Bablake the school had moved from its ancient site in Hill Street to splendid new premises at Coundon, opened on October 20, 1890. It still occupies them. The headmaster of the day was Joseph Innis Bates; his second in command Francis Humberstone and the matron the formidable Miss Cramp. No doubt Lord was one of the boys who quipped that Miss Cramp herself had been founded in 1560.

The buildings Leonard knew were of York and Corsham stone in the Gothic style to the design of Giles, Gough and Trollope of Craven Street, The Strand, London. The budget set by the trustees was £16,000 all in, which was not an onerous sum as they owned several farms and three public houses. It would be intriguing if one was *The Hope and Anchor* but this is not the case, the hostelries in question being *The Board Tavern* in Cross Cheaping, *The City Hotel* on Broadgate and Cow Lane's *The Bablake Boy*.

The new school could accommodate around 400 boys, 40 of whom would have been boarders. As a day boy, Lord would have made his way through the main door in a tower with battlements and surmounted by a clock. He would have said his prayers and attended communal events in the great hall with its block floor, hammer beam roof and tracery windows with tinted glass.

But probably of more interest to him were the impressively equipped chemistry laboratory and indeed the metalwork workshop that had been added in 1894 at the back of the headmaster's house, and the physics lab, which came in 1896. The metalwork room featured a forge and anvil and in Lord's day was under the control of a teacher named Frank Morgan.

The facilities just described suggest an emphasis on technical and practical training and this reflected Bablake's desire to become what was termed an Organized Science School. This was a phenomenon embodied in Liberal MP William Forster's 1870 Education Act. It sought to provide more technical and clerical staff for industry and was to a format agreed with the national Department of Science and Art. Such schools had to devote more than half their timetable to scientific subjects with the remainder spent on manual work, extra maths or art of 'a kind that would be of value to industry'. Thus it becomes even clearer why Leonard Lord was not continuing his studies at Wheatley Road but sat in the 40-strong classes at Bablake, tolerating longer days and shorter holidays than at comparable schools.

As an Organized Science School Bablake would have been a 'halfway house' between an elementary and the city's King Henry VIII Grammar School. This led to a certain amount of controversy. The first pupils came, like Lord, from the elementary system and found Bablake true to its traditions—providing '*an opportunity for families of modest means to have their sons educated to a level fitting for apprenticeship to a trade*'. Two thirds of Lord's classmates would have been the children of artisans, shopkeepers and clerks, only a tiny percentage having a parent listed as 'professional' or 'independent'. Even the Humberstone prize for character and scholarship and intended for someone proceeding to higher education, took account of the parents' financial standing.

In the main the intake was of modest talent and in Lord's day only required a boy to read well, write a letter on a simple subject, correctly spelled with sound grammar, and for him to be able to 'work sums'. Yet emphasizing the technical seems to have been a success and it was not uncommon for Bablake pupils to pass the Department of Science and Art exams in an impressive selection of subjects such as chemistry, mathematics, magnetism and electricity, solid geometry, geometrical drawing, physiography, mechanics and sound, light and heat, freehand model drawing and perspective.

There were tensions though between headmaster Bates, who himself had a scientific bent and had taken a degree in geology in 1898, and the school inspectors appointed by the charity commission. They felt the syllabus was too biased. In 1906, right at the start of Lord's Bablake education, they said the course was '*more restricted than is usual in a school denominated secondary*'. They found the standards of English low with many boys inaccurate and uncouth of expression—an observation we ourselves may heed! French was taught, but badly, and the inspector concluded that a Bablake boy would be '*at an initial advantage in a workshop or machine shop but not fitted for further advancement.*'

Some of what has been written about Leonard Lord suggests that he had a debilitating inferiority complex. If that is the case it might give us an insight into some of his personality traits. And what has been written here about Bablake may help us understand any feeling of inadequacy.

'*Lord, a bitter man, with a huge inferiority complex*' is the observation of Martin Adeney in *The Motor Makers* (Collins 1988) while Graham Turner in *The Leyland Papers* (Eyre and Spottiswoode 1971) says '*Lord was both crude in speech and manner and the victim of an inferiority complex*'. Barney Sharrett in *Men and Motors of the Austin* (Foulis 2000) relies on an anecdote from Longbridge works manager, Joe Edwards, about Lord's supposed discomfiture in the presence of royalty in 1955, quoting Edwards as saying: '*Lord had an enormous inferiority complex*'. Peter Seymour on the other hand describes Lord in *Wolseley Radial Aero Engines* (Tempus 2006) as being '*intensely proud of his humble origins*'!

There are harsh judgments here and maybe we should confront bitterness and/or a sense of inferiority at this early stage in our story as it is only now, the latter at least, could have formed.

If Lord was bitter at this point in his life it must have been over the death of his father, the fact that he and his mother and sister were left in an impoverished state and he was suffering the humiliation of having his schooling paid for by an outside agency. The resentment may have been compounded by a feeling that it was folly for his father to have relinquished stable, worthy, employment to take a pub.

Some of this could well have prompted a sense of inferiority and if we take Seymour's view that '*he was intensely proud of his humble beginnings*' and Miles Thomas's that in a new job he could be proud of his authority '*almost to the point of arrogance*', we do, perhaps, detect an inversion of the inferiority complex, an over compensation and, indeed, much else besides.

On this same count we might briefly quote an item, by an unacknowledged writer, in *Motor* magazine for September 23, 1967. '*Mr Lord finished his formal education early . . .*' This is untrue. Lord passed through all the grades at Bablake from form one to the upper sixth. In fact, Peter Burden, who wrote the excellent history of the school—*Lion and the Stars*—has commented that the boy's stay was '*a long one for those days*' and as archivist, he is in a better position to judge than anyone.

Yet did Lord himself, preoccupied with, and embarrassed by, perceived—certainly not actual—educational inadequacies, take to 'down-scaling' his time in school. It would be the obvious excuse although he would have done better to utter a favourite quote of his deputy headmaster: '*Education is what is left after everything that has been learnt is forgotten*'.*

What is of additional interest is that there was a pupil-teacher scheme in operation from Bablake. Senior boys were paid a small amount to give four-days-a-week instruction in the city's elementary schools, only the fifth day being spent at their own desks. So it may have been back to Wheatley Street for Leonard Lord in a bid to bring a few extra pence into the household coffers.

We will return later to the closeness of the relationship between Leonard Lord and his mother, which was undoubtedly forged during the Bablake years and at 305 Foleshill Road. But for the moment, and it is why I examined in some detail the history of single hand loom weaving in the area, we need to pose the question as to whether Emma Lord was involved in this activity or something closely associated with it. It is logical that she would have been.

---

* This has been variously attributed to Erasmus, the 15th/16th century humanist, the writer Bernard Shaw and 18th century statesman, Lord Halifax.

Historically, the textile scene had been vexed; woven with restrictive and sharp practice. At the root of the problem was the dependence of the cottage industry, made up of individual craftsmen assisted by family members, on tariffs to protect them from foreign imports. With such barriers in place there was no incentive to develop new designs or adopt the latest machinery. The Dutch engine loom (contrary to the description, this was not a powered device, simply a multi-function machine) and the later Jacquard equipment could have revolutionized the industry and made a factory system viable, but the independent producers would have none of it.

Another impediment was middle men called 'small masters'. They contracted work to the cottage operators but rode rough-shod over both employment and pricing agreements. Thus a struggle between factory and cottage continued for decades until ultimately the whole industry collapsed.

Whether or not Emma Lord was involved in silk weaving, and although the most acrimonious conflicts were several decades before she could have been, she and the whole of Coventry would have been aware of the history and have an opinion. It is beyond doubt that Leonard Lord would also have had a view on what were essentially production engineering and policy issues—both areas that were to become the essence of his genius.

It is eminently understandable that as Lord embarked on his career, then began to take on ever more senior roles calling for authority and presence, he did not wish to delve into the spit and sawdust of *The Hope and Anchor*. One might be tempted to conclude that one of the reasons we have such a sketchy overall impression of him is that throughout his life there was much about '*his humble beginnings*' he sought to obfuscate.

We now have an adolescent who owed little to anyone but his mother and himself. Who was going to have to 'kick those closed doors open' and as he developed in that industrial crucible that was the Foleshill area of Coventry, maybe he was embittered and angered by many things he saw.

Chapter Two
TURN OF THE WORM

Leonard Lord passed the University of London's Matriculation examinations in June, 1913. This was no mean achievement for someone of his background and upbringing and in the light of the hardship he had suffered.

By now Annie was recently married, to a machine tool salesman called Benjamin Blundstone. Although his roots were in the north of England, the couple lived in Coventry—at 27 Spencer Avenue—and it is interesting to note, purely as an aside, that Benjamin's father, of the same first name, had taken out a patent on a pneumatic tyre in 1891 in association with a Joseph Moseley. At the time, Mr Blundstone was managing the India Rubber Company's factory in Manchester and although he was dead by the time of his son's marriage, Annie had chosen an affluent spouse.

Leonard Lord's qualification would have entitled him to attend university, an option he declined. The reason is almost certainly that he felt the family finances on Foleshill Road could not support higher education and, of course, this can be a classic recipe for resentment and bitterness. Instead, Lord joined Courtaulds Ltd as an apprentice engineering draughtsman. Conveniently, the plant was on the street where he lived and during his time there—from August 1913 to December 1915—he would train in the drawing office for two years and the engineering workshops for six months. He was paid just 4s 6d a week (less than 25p).

As to how or why the position with Courtaulds materialized we can only speculate. A mundane, but very likely explanation, is that this major and prestigious employer had contacts with Bablake School and at the end of the academic year touted for apprentices, what later sixth form pupils might have called the 'milk round'.

Another possibility, and the reason that I explored in some detail the ribbon making industry in Coventry, is that Emma Lord was, indeed, involved in the textile trade. She may have been formally employed or undertaking finishing work at home. In any event, there would have been a large number of, mainly female, employees within her circle. It is conceivable it was suggested to her that there were good opportunities for a young man within the perimeters of the giant Courtaulds plant.

We may now challenge that Leonard Lord had a destiny specific to any one field of engineering. That anonymous story from *Motor*, referred to earlier, suggests that he decided '*it was in the motor industry that his future lay*'. This is convenient, if not glib, journalistically. Yet, if that was really the case, there was Riley just off Foleshill Road and a firm of such worldwide acclaim as Daimler had been in the city since 1896.

Yet, what is perhaps very much a part of Leonard Lord's greatness is that he was *not*, essentially, a 'motor man'. Often he was the man for the hour; the only man who could do the job; but he was not someone steeped in automotive lore or, in the early days, with an obvious passion for vehicles. It was his breadth of understanding, particularly of mechanical engineering, which enabled him to achieve what he did.

Ever the diligent worker, while at Courtaulds he studied at Coventry Technical College for the City and Guilds of London Institute certificate in mechanical engineering which he passed in 1914 at the premier grade. Simultaneously he was teaching night school there in higher mathematics, often to students much older than himself. Again, this employment was needed for extra cash. Lord himself admits, quoted by Peter Seymour in *Wolseley Radial Aero Engines*, it was to keep his mother *'in comfort and provide her with little luxuries'*.

The few shillings accrued weren't going to keep Mrs Lord in much comfort and the statement, curtailed by Peter King in *The Motor Men* (Quiller Press 1989), to: *'buy little luxuries for my mother'*, is probably nearer the mark.

In any case what small treats there were, were short-lived. In a fit of rage Lord threw a wooden blackboard scrubber at a pupil who annoyed him, was justifiably admonished by the administration, and would have realised that in whatever direction his destiny lay, it was probably not education.

Lord's period at Courtaulds is interesting and, I would suggest, relevant to his later life. The Courtauld family came to England from France at the end of the 17th century to work as gold and silversmiths in London. It was not until as late as 1775, when George Courtauld was apprenticed to a silk 'throwster'—a term for spinner—in the Spitalfields area of the capital, that an interest in textiles developed.

Eventually George's son, Samuel, set up a business in Essex and, impatient with traditional methods, mechanized his factory to make silk mourning crepe for the Victorians. By the 1870s, with 3,000 workers on the payroll, Samuel Courtauld and Company had become one of the biggest firms in the British silk industry and Courtauld himself was drawing the fabulous income of £46,000 per annum. But as we saw in Chapter One, the business was volatile and by the turn of the century, with the company now under the management of Henry Greenwood Tetley and Paul Latham, the technology was on a plateau with profits falling.

However, three new processes were under development—none of them by Courtaulds. As Count Hilaire de Chardonnet realised in France, the way forward was with regenerated cellulosic, or man-made fibre. The Germans were trying a similar approach but the simplest technique, known as the viscose process, had been invented, in London's elegantly leafy Kew suburb, by Charles Cross, Edward Bevan and Clayton Beadle.

It involved dissolving cotton or wood cellulose with a selection of chemicals, then using dilute sulphuric acid to convert the treacle-like yellow substance back to pure white cellulose. It was the latter that could be spun into fibre. Tetley bought the British rights, patented in 1892, on July 14, 1904, for £25,000. The Foleshill factory was built in 1905 and started spinning in mid 1906. By 1913, the year Lord joined, it was producing more than 1,339 tons of rayon a year and had also bought the American licences and established a plant there.

But the methodology Tetley had acquired with such enthusiasm was unreliable and inconsistent. In the early days 75% of the output was waste and it was the job of the chemists and engineers in Coventry and Essex to correct this and help Courtaulds towards an ordinary share capital of £12m by 1920 and the status of the world's largest producer of rayon. This is an excellent example of production engineering turning potential disaster into record breaking profitability, and while it would be ludicrous to suggest that Leonard Lord took any practical part in the process, he must have been acutely aware, when in both drawing office and workshops, of the drama that had been enacted and of its crucial importance.

It is beyond doubt he learnt such lessons well. Far better than had many of those who were later to surround him. It was of Tetley, who died in 1921, that it was said, he was of: '*relentless energy, arrogant, domineering, of furious temper, ruthlessly impatient with a single-minded devotion to business*'! Perhaps the traits were contagious. Not least the arrogance, because it is claimed—I have to admit rather unconvincingly—that when asked by a senior manager at Courtaulds what he wanted to do when he completed his apprenticeship, Lord replied: '*sit in your chair*'! It's just one more of those quotes for which there are no witnesses and sound very much as if they may have been invented by Lord himself!

In December, 1915, Leonard Lord moved from Courtaulds to the Coventry Ordnance Works Ltd in Red Lane to continue his training. The two most likely explanations for the transfer are, a sense of patriotism, amongst the management at the fibre makers, where much of the work was suitable for women, and who, therefore, were happy to allow a particularly talented young man to move into an industry that would have a direct bearing on the war effort.

Or, it may be, that devoted to his mother as he was, Lord realised that sooner or later conscription would be on the cards and although he was the principal breadwinner in the Foleshill household, at 19, single and fairly fit, being called up would be hard to avoid unless he was in a reserved occupation. Compulsory service actually arrived in 1916 as it became apparent the million volunteers that had joined the forces by January 1915, in response to General Kitchener's recruitment pleas, were insufficient to feed the carnage at the Front.

As they lay in their beds on the night of July 23, 1916, and all through that summer week, Leonard Lord and his mother would not have been able to hear the gunnery barrage on the Somme, as, when the wind blew from France towards Hampstead Heath, their compatriots in London could. But along an 18-mile front 1,537 British guns blazed as did as many French. The British fired 1,723,873 rounds. When this futile exercise was over and the battle proper began, nearly 60,000 of the nation's soldiers fell, dead or wounded. It was the worst day in the history of the British army.

'Coventry Ordnance' would have built some of the artillery that had raged. The company was part of a fraught and acrimonious munitions industry where a clutch of companies had struggled for years to persuade the services, and especially the world's navies, to buy their wares. Rather appropriately, it had been captained from 1910-1914 by Sir Reginald Bacon who had been the commander of the very first dreadnought battleship.

The concern was established five years before Bacon came on board by a consortium of shipbuilding firms that included John Brown and Cammell Laird. It sought to break the dominance of Vickers and Armstrong-Whitworth and to that end had designed a 5.5 inch naval gun and developed a 37 mm weapon that was the first modern auto cannon (an automatically loading heavy machine gun). They also made aeroplanes, producing 700 in WWI, plus 100 each of tanks and anti-aircraft guns. There was a second factory in Scotstoun, Glasgow.

Their greatest claim to fame, though, was the design and production of siege howitzers for the British, and subsequently allied, armies just like those that fired that July on the Somme. This is of significance to our story. 'Coventry Ordnance' had begun with a 9.2 inch model in 1913. It had a sophisticated variable recoil mechanism and a range of about six miles, depending on the version. The prototype, nicknamed 'Mother', was in action in France as early as October 1914 and a total of 512 were supplied, but largely by arch rival Vickers.

A 15 inch variant was developed from the 9.2. Developed in late 1914, and used by the Royal Marine Artillery, it fired shells weighing over 25 hundredweight and was intended to destroy deep fortifications. However, the range was relatively short and the Coventry firm lost out as the army turned to a 12 inch version that Vickers started producing in August 1916, then to railway mounted howitzers of the same calibre. The predictable decline in demand for arms after the armistice saw the Coventry Ordnance Works fall on hard times and it failed in 1925.

Lord worked in the heavy workshops and tool rooms. It must have represented a spectacular change of scale after Courtaulds. Some of the equipment used had been sourced in continental Europe and America. There were milling machines with 36 foot diameter tables, used for machining the enormous ring gear fitted to naval gun turrets. Useful insight as that undoubtedly was, the most valuable experience for Lord was making the acquaintance of Carl Engelbach and seeing him at work.

Charles Richard Fox Engelbach, always known as Carl, was in charge of that all-important howitzer production. He was a London boy, born in Kensington, and, by coincidence the son of a War Office clerk of Huguenot descent but with Jewish undertones. He had been sent to boarding school in Southport, although the justification for this locale remains something of a mystery. The most likely explanation is links to, or contacts within, the town's flourishing Jewish community. That apart, Carl Engelbach grew into a gentle, sensitive and cultured young man.

When he was 16 his godfather presented him with the considerable sum, for 1893, of £1,000. He very wisely spent it securing an indentured apprenticeship at Armstrong-Whitworth in Newcastle-upon-Tyne, rather than taking up the professional singing career that had been offered by the D'Oyly Carte Opera Company, back in the capital.

Armstrong-Whitworth were a major engineering manufacturing company dating back to the mid-19th century and now produced ships, aeroplanes, railway locomotives and subsequently cars. When firmly established there, Engelbach specialized on the automotive side and in 1902 cut his teeth on the Roots & Venables car that Armstrong-Whitworth were contracted to build. Rather auspiciously, perhaps, his grandfather's first name was Gottlieb—as in Daimler!

Although now lost in the mists of time, the Roots & Venables is an interesting make. Like Engelbach himself, it had its origins in London and used an oil engine. They first emerged in 1896 as a tiller steered three-wheeler and at the time were one of only four British marques on the market. The others were Daimler, the Coventry Bollée and Petter dog-cart, but of course, two of those—the Daimler and the 'Bollée'—were essentially foreign brands.

'Roots' had difficulty actually making the car and after a period employing BSA to do so, turned to Armstrong-Whitworth. There Engelbach would have watched over three models, a three horsepower rear engined machine and two forward powered cars of four and seven 'horse' respectively. While he was attending to all this, Engelbach affirmed the more esoteric side of his character and married, in 1902, Florence Ada Neumegen. She was an artist with Spanish connections, but living in Newcastle.

She painted in a vigorous style with strong gouts of colour, the texture of cream, spreading across the canvas. The style was to grow in popularity during the '30s and continued through the next decade. Florence's speciality was flowers and her work was good enough to be hung in temporary exhibitions at London's Royal Academy.

Engelbach, for his part, soon had to undertake the production of the Wilson-Pilcher, another London make that had come to Armstrong Whitworth under similar circumstances to those of the Roots & Venables. It was also an interesting machine with a horizontally-opposed engine coupled to a four speed epicyclic gearbox with, naturally, a clutchless change. Englebach looked after production of a four cylinder and a big four litre, powered by a 'square'* flat six.

By now he was manager of the motor side of the business and, as the Wilson-Pilcher died, launched, in 1906, Armstrong-Whitworth's own make. This necessitated a major reorganization of the Works and Engelbach aspired to produce a comprehensive range of cars at the ambitious rate of 6,000 vehicles a year. His confidence was not matched by management and he left just before the outbreak of WWI.

At some point during his career at Armstrong Whitworth, Engelbach had joined the Royal Naval Voluntary Reserve, which was formed in 1903 from civilians. In 1914 he was called to active service but it was soon realised his talents would be better employed elsewhere and he was posted to 'Coventry Ordnance'.

Hopefully, this brief profile gives a picture of the man Lord was to encounter. Carl Engelbach was acclaimed as the best production engineer in Britain and Lord was privileged to work under him. He was also, primarily, a 'motor man' and it was almost certainly from Engelbach that Lord would gain an introduction to the motor industry and its potential. Without pre-empting the story, it is worth noting that Lord was to encounter Engelbach again, much later in both their careers, but the circumstances were less positive.

While at The Coventry Ordnance Works Ltd Leonard Lord rounded off his formal education by passing the Board of Higher Education examination in machine construction and drawing. As with his 'City and Guilds' qualification he passed with distinction. Perhaps inspired by something, or many things, Carl Engelbach had said, it is now, in 1919, that Lord first enters the world of car building, albeit for an amazingly short time!

To quote a snatch of doggerel derived from *The Vicar of Bray*: '*And whosoever king may reign, he still will own a Daimler*'. And it was for the royal car maker that Lord departed the ordnance works. Engelbach could well have recommended this manufacturer, hailing from the dawn of motoring, in preference to the other local player—Riley—who were insignificant by comparison. At the time, Daimler were based in Sandy Lane, in the Radford district of the city, a little to the west of Foleshill. They would have been making a 30 and a 45 horsepower model, the latter with a six cylinder sleeve-valve engine.

Interesting innovations had followed the return of peace including a steel frame on which coachbuilders could mount their bodies in readiness for fitting to a chassis, rather than having to wait for the arrival of the actual running gear. Less importantly there were concealed radiator caps, believed to be the first appearance (or non-appearance!) of this feature on a British car.

Leonard Lord went to work in the toolroom. To get there from Foleshill Road he would just have had to cut through Cash's Lane, walked along Witherington Road and then into Sandy Lane. Of the environment he would have encountered Brian Smith, in his definitive book on Daimler, *The Daimler Tradition*, (Transport Bookman Publications 1972) says: '*In the foundry laboratory, qualified chemists were engaged in blending metals, in heat treatment, evolving the best iron and steel for the particular use to which it would be put whilst in the research and chemical departments other chemists tested to the utmost limits the products of their creative work. Tests for hardness, impact tests and ingenious methods of finding out the fatigue resisting properties of all the metals used were undertaken and in conjunction with the results of chemical analysis, the use of the correct materials for all purposes was scientifically guaranteed*'.

---

*   Bore and stroke of the same dimensions.

He goes on: '*The Daimler Company had early appreciated the fact that a high standard of machine shop practice was necessary—hence the development and equipment of the Daimler toolroom to a standard of efficiency superior to anything existing elsewhere. Tools of such accuracy and precision were used that Daimler craftsmen were able to work to the finest limits of toleration (sic) and moreover, many of the master gauges issued during the war through The National Physical Laboratory to the many other factories producing aeroplane engines, were products of the Daimler tool room. A particular branch of tool room activity was the cutting of the Daimler/Lanchester* type worm gears.*

'*When the ratio of the gear had been settled, it was a four months' job to develop a set of tools from the master hob. The intricate tools were hand made and from these a master set of gears were produced and these would be retained for comparison throughout the production*'.

On the basis of Smith's account alone one would conclude that Daimler was about the best engineering centre in the land and anyone fortunate enough to be offered a job would gain invaluable experience and be on the threshold of a remunerative and satisfying life-long career. So why was Lord only there for eight weeks?

We have to suspect that at this point in his own career—he was 23—he was not temperamentally suited to the job and perhaps he never would have been. Any question about Lord's technical competence can be confidently set aside but he was a quick tempered and impatient man of action. We can imagine that in the rarefied atmosphere of those Sandy Lane toolrooms, being involved with long-serving, painstaking craftsmen, taking 16 weeks to produce a set of gear cutters, where everything was highly prescriptive, would have caused him to explode—at Foleshill Road if not in the workshop!

Jon Box served his apprenticeship at Daimler and subsequently worked in a wide variety of motor industry jobs including at Standard Triumph, Land Rover and TVR. He is now a regular contributor to the Daimler and Lanchester Owners' Club magazine, *The Driving Member*. He says of this period: '*The Daimler toolroom would not have been somewhere where Lord could have his own way. It does not surprise me he was soon on the move and looking for something where he could have much greater control*'.

Thus, an outstanding opportunity had come too soon.

On the other hand, Lord may have viewed his next job, as general manager of The Jig Tool and General Engineering Company Ltd, in his native city's Hertford Street, as a chance he could not afford to miss. It was, after all, promotion to a position of authority where he would much more readily be able to be his 'own man', while the work itself would have given him a much broader perspective than that at Daimler. As he would have said: '*If the door's not open; kick it open*'.

'Jig and Tool' were a modest engineering company employing 50 people to make small machines and assembly jigs. Lord's time there was highly successful because when he left in September 1920 he had full responsibility for the shops and had applied, on July 18, 1919—application 13,158—to become a graduate member of the Institution of Mechanical Engineers.

For those not familiar with that august body, it is the bastion of engineering excellence in the UK, numbering among its ranks such luminaries as Sir Nigel Gresley of locomotive fame, John Thornycroft from the world of marine engines and commercial vehicles and Frederick Henry Royce. The conditions for entry are both stringent and complex. Lord was safely clear of the

---

*   This is slightly misleading. F W Lanchester was a pioneer of worm drive. He became a consulting engineer to Daimler in 1909 and Daimler adopted this method of final drive. Lanchester as a manufacturer did not become part of Daimler (aka BSA) until 1931.

minimum age of 21 but he needed to pass the Institution's own associate membership exam or hold a qualification it recognized. His City and Guilds pass should have sufficed. He would also need to prove he had received regular training as a mechanical engineer.

To move on to full membership, which he gained in 1927, he would have to have reached the age of at least 30 and apart from the required formal qualification, show that he had '*attained a position of such eminence in the profession, or in the direction of engineering work, as to qualify him, in the opinion of the council, for the distinction of membership*'. Lord never presented a paper to the Institution. Neither was he published on any subject. We might conclude, therefore, that his letters were more for status than out of dedication to his profession, but it is obvious that he had the wherewithal to realize that his standing as a MIMechE would give him influence and help pave his career path.

Lord moved from The Jig Tool and General Engineering Company to the east London firm of Messrs Holbrook and Sons* at 44 Martin Street, Stratford. At the time Holbrook were famous for a range of high quality lathes. They concentrated on medium sized models but also made a 3.5 inch centre height (16.5 inches between centres) precision machine. It was basically to the 1862 design of the American company, Stark, and was a scaled up watchmaker's type.

This miniature Holbrook was intended both for skilled operators turning one-off parts and for small-batch production. An unusual feature, designed for the latter process, was a counter shaft that enabled stopping, starting and speed changes to be made by pressing pedals that operated through wire links.

The firm lasted into the 1980s but by then was owned by the giant Coventry company, Arthur Herbert.

Lord, impressively, was chief engineer in charge of a 150-strong workforce and after just six months became general manager with responsibility for both the machine shops and drawing office. He remained with Holbrook for 20 months leaving in the spring of 1922. This was after his marriage, on July 16, 1921, to Ethel Lily Horton. The service was conducted by the Reverend Basil Littlewood in Coventry's 12th century Holy Trinity Church. Its 230 ft spire is still one of the city's landmarks. It seems reasonable to assume the move from Holbrook back to Coventry was prompted by Lord's change in marital status.

Ethel was the daughter of George and Mary Clarice Horton (*née* Overton) from Coventry's St Peters Street. It no longer exists. She was born on June 19, 1896, when the family lived at 33 Colchester Street, so was almost an exact contemporary of Lord. Mr Horton at the time of Ethel's birth was a cycle machinist, but by the time of his daughter's wedding was noted as simply being employed in the motor trade. We might speculate that he worked at Riley, who, in the early 1890s, were, of course, cycle makers, and that as Riley and St Peters Street were a 'wheel's turn' from the Foleshill Road, Lord, in the broader sense, had married 'the girl next door'.

What is even more interesting is that on the marriage certificate, William Lord is recorded as a 'cabinet maker, deceased'. There is no evidence available to support this and we can only guess that Mr Lord trained in this skill at some point before he took the job at Priory Street baths. However, what *is* clear is that his son wished to conceal the fact his father had ended his days as a pub landlord. That may have been for reasons of personal embarrassment, or, unnecessarily in

---

*   For the figures on his *curriculum vitae* to be correct Lord must count the September of his joining Holbrook to be a full month, thus he must have left 'Jig and Tool' at the very beginning of September 1921 to give the 20 months of employment at Holbrook he also quotes.

the light of his own achievements, to enhance his social standing in the eyes of his in-laws! The ploy, though, was not uncommon.

The young couple made their first home in Priory Row, just around the corner from the public baths where Leonard Lord had been born.

Between joining Courtaulds in August 1913 and leaving London in the spring of 1922—a period of seven years and eight months—Lord changed jobs four times. There are various references to him having worked in 'engineering' in Peterborough. Probably, these all emanate from a reference to that effect in *The Times* newspaper's obituary. However, the consensus of opinion is that Lord was never employed in or around the Cambridgeshire town.

Yet, on the basis of there being 'no smoke without fire', we need to recognize that Peterborough was an important engineering centre at the relevant time and a possible explanation is that Holbrook were suppliers to one or more of the companies so engaged, or, the London firm had a presence of some kind there. Even discounting any activity in Cambridgeshire, those four moves in under eight years—even less if you allow for the restrictions on mobility of an apprenticeship—is a fairly volatile work pattern.

The move to Coventry Ordnance Works Ltd in December, 1915, we may put down to his wishing to avoid the likelihood of being conscripted into the Armed Forces. The move from that company was undoubtedly due to the very sensible realisation that, with no, or very few, civilian initiatives, unlike Vickers and Armstrong Whitworth, 'Coventry Ordnance' was a dead end.

The switch to Daimler in 1919 can thus be attributed to 'career advancement' and we have an explanation for his very short stay at the prestigious car maker. Again, the transfer to The Jig and Tool and General Engineering Company. Ltd. can be seen as professional progress and similarly the move, in September, 1920, to Holbrook and Sons in London.

But mobility at this level, at that time, is unusual. Admittedly, there was a brief post-War boom when the job market had buoyancy and fluidity. Even so, unemployment in 1919 stood at 3.5 per cent of the total workforce and after a very brief recovery in 1920 had soared to 11 per cent by 1921. By contrast, for the fortunate few who could get such a position, it was also the era of the 'job for life' culture—in banks, in the public sector, on the railways—placings to be fiercely guarded.

So do we see the emerging character of Leonard Lord? At first glance, advancement meant more money and he and his mother would benefit from increased financial security. Yet, is there more to it than that? Was there a restlessness, something to prove, over and above the dictates of normal ambition? Did his impatience, if not his temper, get the better of him in some of these situations? Of course, we now have no way of knowing. But maybe Leonard Lord was looking for something. And maybe that something was himself.

CHAPTER THREE

THE FRENCH CONNECTION

Whatever Leonard Lord may have been looking for, he found something of significance in 1922 when he joined the Coventry Works of Hotchkiss.

That April day changed the course of automotive history.

The company was originally the creation of an American designer called Benjamin Berkeley Hotchkiss, who had been born in Watertown, Connecticut, in 1826. While working in the family engineering business he became passionately interested in firearms, but having failed to interest the American government in his ideas, he decided to move to France in 1867. He set up shop on the Route de Gonesse, in the ancient township of St Denis, just north of Paris and, with its magnificent basilica, the traditional burial ground for the kings of France.

There he strove to perfect a truly automatic machine gun and although Hotchkiss himself died in 1885 his loyal team strove to finesse the concept, had done so by 1892, and in 1897 the 'Hotchkiss gun' was adopted by the French army. It was air cooled and combustion gas operated and in the run up to the First World War was modified and improved until, as that other great exponent of the machine gun, Hiram Maxim, said, enabled '*these Europeans to "cut each others' throats" with greater facility*'.

Yet to help Hotchkiss et Cie become one of the most important engineering companies in France, diversification was necessary. Around the turn of the century the firm took the very important step of manufacturing major components, like crankshafts, for some of the leaders in the embryo motor industry, including Panhard et Levassor and de Dion Bouton. By 1903 they were making complete engines then, spurred on by two motor dealers, Mann Overton in London and Fournier in Paris, started building complete cars.

The début model was based on the Benz-derived Simplex, but reworked by Georges Therasse who Hotchkiss had brought in from Mors. These early cars had a proliferation of ball bearings in their engines and of course the trend-setting 'Hotchkiss drive'. The latter, which was the dominant transmission system during most of the 20th century for front-engine-rear-drive vehicles, used an open transmission ('propeller') shaft attached by universal joints to the gearbox at one end and the differential at the other, having the axle located simply by parallel leaf springs.

By 1910 Hotchkiss were turning to smaller cars and this policy was accelerated by the Agadir crisis of 1911. This was a tripartite squabble centred on Morocco, with France and Germany as the major protagonists. In any event, it all led to a crisis of confidence for long term international stability, not least in the motor industry. Here Hotchkiss's cars continued to be reduced in size. Of course, none of it really mattered, because in 1914 the automotive scene, as so much else, was to change for ever.

In the first few weeks of the Great War, 180,000 German troops tore through Belgium, brushing the shores of the English Channel. By now they were on foot or horseback, but had crossed the Rhine in 500 trains made up of a total of 25,000 wagons. It seemed it might be, as the Kaiser had predicted: *'Paris for lunch, dinner in St Petersburg'*. Once out of the Low Countries the Imperial army swung south. There was chaos in Paris. The banks were besieged. Tens of thousands of reservists from the male population had barely hours to reach the Gare de l'Est and board the trains that would take them to meet the invader.

Today, St Denis is a vibrant, bustling, multi-cultural, community, bordering the railway along which the expresses thunder to the Gare du Nord. It is the insignificant last station on their long hauls from the north, ignored by nearly everything but commuter trains. In 1914 it was the very first place in France the Germans would have encountered an engineering facility of any significance—the arms and motor works of Hotchkiss.

What no one could envisage was that on September 5, with the Germans 35 kilometres from Paris, 600 Renault taxi cabs would spill out their soldier passengers beside the river Marne to add weight to Joseph Joffre's French forces. The casualties over the next five days would be appalling. But the invasion was stopped. For the moment, briefly, the Germans had been broken and defeated.

A proportion of the management had already fled from Hotchkiss, intent on establishing a satellite works in England. They chose Gosford Street, Coventry, and machines and workers were moved from St Denis. The company began manufacturing their famous machine gun and, possibly, armoured cars, of which they had had an impressive type since 1909.

When, eventually, the armistice was signed, on November 11, 1918, in *Wagons Lits* dining car 2419 ('Pullman' carriage in British parlance), in the Forest of Compiègne, little more than 30 kilometres north east of Paris, the armaments industry collapsed. Virtually overnight.

There were spectacular sufferers; not least the Austin Motor Company at Longbridge in Birmingham. But also Hotchkiss et Cie on Gosford Street. We cannot be sure whether the St Denis firm's managing director, American, Laurence Benet, was one of those who came to Britain in 1914 to set up the auxiliary factory, but there is no question he was on English soil in 1919 to use his skills on behalf of his British cohorts, Henry Ainsworth and A H Wilde, who had run the factory throughout the war, and aid their recovery from the dearth of work that beset the company.

Benet, with a somewhat liberal interpretation of both the English language and the nation's culture, concluded that a likely place to find work in exchange for labour might be the 'labour exchange'. At that organization's offices, thanks to one of those incredible accidents of history that shape the course of the world, he met an administrator who was both imaginative, informed, and could interpret his caller's 'take' on the situation. And thus that character, who was to have such an enormous influence on Leonard Lord's life, first appears on the scene. William Morris.

In a moment we will need to examine Morris, because although this work makes absolutely no pretence at assessing Morris's role in the British motor industry or United Kingdom society in general, we can never understand Lord unless we know much of Morris.

Returning to the Coventry Labour Exchange for a moment; it was the official there who suggested that Morris Motors, in not-too-distant Oxford, might be looking for an engineering firm who could build motor car engines and that may provide useful employment for the idle hands at Hotchkiss.

And it is here we must digress to look at the man who was to become Lord Nuffield—not the nation's greatest motor man, but certainly its best known charitable benefactor.

William Richard Morris had a 'good war'. Thereon hinges his business success. Therein is a pivotal element in the story of Leonard Lord.

Morris had a fundamentally different approach to engineering and vehicle production than Herbert Austin, or, say, Henry Royce. Austin believed that a motor car factory should be a self contained unit in which practically all the elements involved in the construction process—engines, radiators, gearboxes, rear axles, chassis frames, even the raw metal contained in them—were manufactured or processed in-house, then finally brought together in the finished product. That was how quality was controlled and maintained. Royce worked largely in the same way but the detailing was finer. For example, pre-WWI, Rolls-Royce would have made its own carburetters and magnetos.

Morris was an assembler of other people's output. '*There is no point in producing any article yourself which you can buy from a concern specializing in the work.*' Contemporary business associates said of him: '*His best asset was his nice appreciation of price and costs. Basically he was a buyer and a very acute* (possibly '*astute*'—this author's hypothesis) *buyer indeed. Anything he bought, he bought at a very keen price, and he would get it in the end. The basis of Cowley is buying, not manufacturing*'.

'. . . *Morris always had second sight. He liked to think of himself as an engineer, but really he was a prince of commerce, because he had an instinct to know what the people wanted, to know what the next man was thinking, a buying capacity and so on. Those gifts were much greater than his engineering ability, although that was not small*'. As a consequence Morris had not the genius of Austin or even Ford. Yet it was this very thinking that left him so well placed at the end of the Great War.

Austin, for his part, had poured equipment into the conflict—7,000,000 shells, no fewer than 2,000 aeroplanes and as many two/three ton lorries, 480 armoured cars and close on a total of 1,000 ambulances, staff cars and vans. Such was the production capacity at Longbridge, often employing machines Austin had designed himself, that output of eight inch howitzer shells, weighing 175 pounds each, reached 15,000 a week and peaked at an amazing 15,500. Between the spring of 1914 and 1917 a relatively small car factory, with 2,638 people on the payroll, mushroomed to an enormous works employing 20,000 men and women—as many as were employed there in the 1960s. Huge new machine and process shops had been constructed around the original site, many of them at government expense.

Morris had virtually no manufacturing capacity at the motor works he had established at 100, Holywell Street in the Longwall district of Oxford. His material contribution to the war was hand grenades from around July 1915, machining trench howitzer bomb cases and, from 1916, the assembly of a sinker for naval mines. This was a device that was jettisoned with the charge and then, as it plummeted to the sea bed, payed out and subsequently locked the securing hawser so the mine was located at a pre-determined depth. Morris methodology increased output from the 40 a week the craftsman at *HMS Vernon* in Portsmouth were capable of producing, to an ultimate total of 2,000 over the same period—output in excess of what was needed!

So it was that when peace returned, the Receiver was soon to be at Longbridge and W R Morris looked to the future with optimism. Morris had wanted to be a surgeon and maybe that tells us something about the direction of his benefaction in later life. But his medical ambitions were thwarted by a decline in the family's finances. It is easy for us to leap to a comparison with Lord, who, at approximately the same age, we strongly suspect, would have liked to have furthered his education at university but for the aftermath of the circumstances at Whitefriars Lane and those continuing on Foleshill Road.

To make such a connection though would largely be an error. Morris's father, Frederick, although diminished in health, gave his full support to his son and so did the mother, who was not physically strong herself. The boy began his career as an apprentice in a bicycle shop but soon walked out to start his own rival business in 1893. Likewise he failed to pursue for more than two classes a course in engineering and design at the Oxford Schools of Technology, but was soon trading as '*W R Morris Practical Cycle Maker and Repairer of 48 High Street and James Street* *Oxford. Sole maker of the celebrated Morris cycles*'. '*The celebrated Morris "cycles*' 'was, in fact, one machine made for a gentleman of ample proportions called Pilcher who was rector of the local St Clements church and who had commissioned a huge bicycle based on a 27 inch frame.

Morris soon entered the field of motor cycles. Of interest, as far as we are concerned, is that the castings for the one horsepower engine were bought in for final machining at 'Longwall'. By 1902 he was buying complete de Dion Bouton engines.

From 1904 until 1912 Morris's principal activity was as a garage proprietor and participant in various peripheral automotive enterprises such as the private hire of cars and operating a taxi service. But in 1912 he was ready to announce his 'own car' at the London motor show. It had an engine from Coventry supplier White and Poppe and one of their gearboxes. The rear and front axle came from E G Wrigley and Company in Smethwick, west of Birmingham, and so, probably, did most of the gearbox. The wheels were from the highly respected firm of Sankey, the chassis frames travelled from Belgium and the bodies arrived from Oxford coachbuilders Raworth.

This was the Morris Oxford. Some 1,500 sales were anticipated and White and Poppe were asked to organize for 50 engines a week. Meanwhile, a second, slightly larger model, called the Cowley, was in the pipeline. White and Poppe had no surplus capacity for the 14.9 horsepower power unit needed. Morris turned to America and the Continental Motor Manufacturing Company in Detroit for the engines themselves and to other firms Stateside for the gearboxes, transmission and other items of running gear.

Continental had entered the world of motorization around the same time as Morris, when Chicago engineer Ross Judson and his brother-in-law, Arthur Tobin, built a twin cylinder engine based on a Mercedes design. As orders flooded in they set up a company called 'Autocar' but the name was the same as an existing firm so the enterprise was re-christened 'Continental', because they thought it suggested 'European quality'.

In 1905, lured by incentives put in place to compensate for the demise of the logging industry, Judson and Tobin moved to Muskegon on the shores of Lake Michigan. By 1907 they were building for Studebaker at the rate of 1,000 engines a month. Then, in 1911, Hudson came through with an order for 10,000 units and Continental shifted to Detroit to be close to their factory. They went on to build for more than 100 makes of automobile, including such top flight names as Auburn and Stutz and such household ones as Willys. The Muskegon plant continued, but making bus, lorry and industrial engines. Eventually Continental went over to producing aircraft power plants.

Morris had called on Continental in 1914 to a somewhat frosty reception. They had been caught out previously by entrepreneurs from Britain placing orders then welshing on the deals and were inclined to be wary. However, the visitor returned home with drawings for an engine that could be built for £25 against White and Poppe's price for a similar unit of £50. Consternation abounded and eventually Morris returned to America with Hans Landstad, White and Poppe's

---

*   This was his parents' address in Cowley St John.

chief draughtsman, to see how this wonder was worked! Landstad did, in fact, go to work for Continental, and in a semi-formal capacity acted as Morris's liaison officer, advising on what would be required when the engines arrived in England and on what parts would need to be sourced locally. He remained in Detroit until the prototypes came off test, returning home in December 1914 to the pleasing Christmas present of a job at Morris.

Even now, matters did not run particularly smoothly. Continental only extracted an order for 1,500 engines. That was William Morris's revision of the number he thought he could utilize, as opposed to the 6,500 he originally envisaged would be needed to cover the first two years of Morris Cowley production. Then, as the war began to bite, it became increasingly difficult to deliver the stock and the first engines did not come through until September 1915. All this was compounded by the imposition of McKenna duties, so named after Sir Reginald McKenna, the British Chancellor of the Exchequer between May 1915 and December 1916. He placed a duty of 33% on motor car imports and dulled the attraction of an engine costing, by now, $85 (about £17.50 at the exchange rates of the day) plus insurance and freight charges. Finally, Continental decided they didn't want to bother with a motor suitable only for a light car and that they would be unable to place with manufacturers in America. However, they were prepared to sell Morris the drawings and some of the tooling.

The way out of this situation, as suggested by that perspicacious gentleman at the Coventry Labour Exchange, was for Morris to have Hotchkiss build his engines. The supply came on stream in September 1919, Hotchkiss using adapted gun making machinery and having resolved quality issues associated with the proprietary cylinder block castings they received.

As an aside, there is a bizarre story that around 1920, Hotchkiss were contemplating going into production, in England, with their own car. It was to have used a 1,080 cc air cooled, overhead valve, V-twin engine with a three speed gearbox fitted into, of all things, a Morris Cowley chassis! It *is* just possible there were one or more Morris chassis at Gosford Street that had been used experimentally when engine production for Morris Motors was getting underway and one of these formed the basis for a now forgotten Hotchkiss.

The new relationship between Hotchkiss and Morris was not as happy as it might have been. Throughout 1920 and '21 the French firm had built up engine production from a faltering total of 60-odd in 1919 to slightly more than 200 a week by the beginning of 1922. Morris wanted guarantees of between five and six hundred which was about twice what Hotchkiss were able—or wanted—to supply. The reasoning was the French company were again building their own cars in France and to pursue a policy of investing capital that could be better used at home was unappealing. Thus Morris resorted to the course of action he nearly always adopted—he bought into the company. And with it, of course, he acquired Leonard Lord.

A fairly 'scratchy' partnership between Morris and Hotchkiss continued for about 12 months. The latter were represented on the board of the reorganized company and as a consequence would have access to engine developments. This, not unreasonably, irked William Morris. The cars from St Denis at the time were in an AF, AH, AL series and although available in the UK were much larger than the Morris and could hardly be construed as competitors.

Nonetheless, William Morris wanted to sever all connection and in May, 1923, he bought out the French interest altogether.

It is impossible for us to know what Leonard Lord said in his application to Hotchkiss et Cie in the opening months of 1922. Indeed, his own version, which is a little unlikely from a 'newly married' with a wife to support, was that he knocked on the door looking for whatever job was going. Whatever the circumstances, there would have been an interview at Gosford Street with Ainsworth, Wilde, or their chief engineer, Herbert Taylor—perhaps all three.

We can conclude that Lord was an ideal candidate but it is not entirely clear what exactly his position was. Some sources have him as assistant chief engineer, but Frank Woollard, who entered the company as general manager and became Lord's immediate boss, described him as machine tool engineer. This makes perfect sense. What was now Morris Motors Engines Branch was being restructured. Ainsworth and Wilde (in charge, you will remember, during the war) were not required by William Morris and left for Hotchkiss in St Denis to become manager and chief engineer respectively.

Among those who remained was works manager George Harriman—'old George'. He was the father of the George Harriman who headed the British Motor Corporation after Lord and about whom we shall obviously have much to say. As it happened 'young George' started an apprenticeship at 'Morris Engines' in 1923.

General Manager, Woollard, had been the 'designer'—although this was never officially his title—at E G Wrigley and Company (again, you will recall, makers of axles and transmission parts for the Morris Oxford) and had advised Morris on the purchase of Hotchkiss before being given his post at Gosford Street. Taylor, a talented man of diminutive stature, went on as before as chief engineer.

What Lord brought to the picture was the sound production engineering practice he had witnessed at Courtaulds, a thorough grounding and recognized qualifications in general engineering procedures, and the broadness of mind and flexibility to understand that when facilities were not available at home they could often be imported from abroad. He had witnessed this at the Coventry Ordnance Works Ltd. He also had the considerable skill necessary to design machinery himself. *And* he had worked in munitions, Hotchkiss's cornerstone. A bonus in the latter case was working alongside—'Coventry Ordnance' again—a man who was, arguably, the best production engineer in the land—Carl Engelbach.

Perhaps most important of all, at least from a personal standpoint, was that in less than one, highly active, decade Leonard Lord had firmly laid to rest that negative from the Bablake inspectors that a boy would be '*at an initial advantage in a workshop or machine shop but not fitted for further advancement*'.

Frank George Woollard was a Londoner and advanced through that most thorough of engineering routes, the railway workshops, to his post at Wrigleys. He arrived there as chief draughtsman in 1910, progressed to chief engineer and then assistant managing director. In WWI, as the military tank was developed and Wrigleys began producing its gearbox, Woollard ensured the quantities required for these machines were available. His presence at Wrigleys and involvement in making parts for Morris is the basis for the link to the Cowley industrialist.

The denouement, of course, is Frank Woollard taking over at Gosford Street with the brief to double engine production, from the same floor space and as rapidly as possible. The significance to the story of Leonard Lord, who was already at Morris Engines, is we are now seeing him at work alongside some of the best production engineers in the world, holding his own and at 27 years of age making incredibly bold decisions about his employer's way forward.

Herbert Taylor's basic philosophy was the product should be the focus of the processes in its manufacture. This meant that rather than moving, say, a cylinder block from machine shop to machine shop to be bored, faced, drilled or whatever, the machinery should 'go to the component' to carry out the various operations. This is the theory behind the transfer machine.

We will need to look at this equipment in greater detail later. But, for the moment, suffice to say, it is multi-functional plant, which can adapt to different procedures on a component while the part itself needs to have minimal mobility for those actions to be carried out. Such machines were to be essential if Morris was to achieve the production volumes and thus price levels he sought. Put another way, the success of Morris Motors, indeed its very survival in this most crucial period of the company's history, depended to a large degree on the success of transfer machines.

The set-up at 'Engines Branch' was, in all practical terms, the work of Lord.

To briefly place matters in context. The British motor industry had shared in a short, general trade boom, immediately after WWI. But by 1920 this had collapsed and at least half of the country's 90 car manufacturers were in serious financial difficulty. William Morris believed that the situation was caused by too high prices for the cars themselves, the materials that went into them and the labour to put it there, compounded by low output that prevented the industry capitalizing on what demand existed. Consequently, in February 1921, he took the astonishing step of slashing his prices. The four-seater Cowley came down from £525 to £425, the two-seater dropped £90 to £375, there was £25 off the more up-market Oxford and the coupé variant of that model dropped £80. These measures immediately stimulated sales. They started to soar towards the 1,000-plus vehicles a week that would be leaving the dealerships by 1925. The Morris had become Britain's best-selling car, but obviously everything depended on the output being there in the first place.

The transfer machine that Woollard had made to Taylor's design was 181 feet long, weighed 300 tons and had 53 work stations where just 21 men pushed buttons to convert a raw casting into a finished cylinder block in a total of 224 minutes—or one off the line every four. The trouble was the buttons that operated features like the limit switches, which ensured a component stopped in exactly the right spot for the next process, relied on pneumatics, hydraulics and electrics. And, quite frankly, although the concept was brilliant the execution was flawed. Lord was asked to resolve the problem. It took three weeks deliberation but when the solution came it was earth-shattering and somewhat fazed management when they were told the machine should be scrapped!

To quote Woollard in a 1955 article for *Motor*: '*Even general managers can't execute such a* volte face, *tantamount to admitting that we have spent a vast sum of money on a mistaken policy*'. What Lord was actually suggesting was that the root problem was the control systems of the day were not up to the job of governing the automatic movements (the 'transfers' themselves) of the cylinder blocks. The answer was to convert the one vast machine back to individual stations. He further argued there would be no cost penalty because sourcing a milling or boring machine from a traditional supplier would only provide an extremely expensive piece of equipment, most of whose functions were not required, while those that *were* needed were already admirably contained in the in-house design.

Lord had costed his revision to the last detail and could prove its efficacy. This is interesting. He has a reputation for being reckless over cost analysis to a point where he would eventually debilitate BMC. Clearly this is not the case.

Lord's plan for the transfer machine at Morris Engines was implemented with spectacular results. Engine output rose over six months during 1923 from the 300 a week Hotchkiss were just about capable of producing, to 450; then to 600 by the turn of the year. By mid-1924 production had reached 800 with 1,200 a week projected for 1925 with still further increases forecast. Over that initial six months—300 engines to 450—the manpower needed dropped from 3.1 to 2.7 per unit.

It should be acknowledged though, the final rises quoted were helped by doubling floor space and installing more equipment including extra transfer machines. One of these was for the complex task of machining gearbox casings and was designed in its entirety by Lord, the first of its kind in the world. Some of these machines were still in use in 1955. It had taken Leonard Lord three weeks to devise a dramatic solution to the problem with the original transfer machine. Yet he could work much faster and, into the bargain, show his level of commitment. When Morris Engines needed four heavy-duty milling machines and attempts to source them either at home or abroad failed, Lord was given the task of producing a design that could be manufactured within the works.

He began work in the cramped drawing office at Gosford Street but progress was slow and on a Thursday morning he sought Woollard's permission to take the job home with the promise it would be completed by the following Tuesday. By Monday afternoon he had not only produced beautifully executed isometric projections of the machines themselves, which subsequently performed perfectly, but a layout for the whole work area.

One last episode from Morris Engines is worth recounting. It does not have the momentous impact on production as the work on the transfer machines, or the ingredients of dexterity, design skill and devotion that surround the 'mills', yet it illustrates extremely well Lord's imagination, ingenuity and directness of approach.

Not surprisingly, the equipment inherited from Hotchkiss was French and as a consequence, not only were the threads to the metric standard, but the bolt heads as well. This caused a problem for fitters and machinists equipped with imperial tools. Lord's strikingly simple expedient was to make or modify the fasteners so they retained metric threads but had imperial heads.

William Morris was so impressed with Lord's work that in 1927 he moved him to the Wolseley Motor Company, a bankrupt concern he had acquired from the Receiver in January of that year. Thus Taylor, Woollard and Leonard Lord parted company. They would not work together again, so it may be worth noting how Lord's boss perceived him in those years from 1923-1927.

'I found all the qualities which go to make the ideal executive: an analytical mind coupled with a lively inventive capacity and an ability to present a case with all the implications fully considered' said Woollard. *'One of my most cooperative and congenial colleagues'*.

'Decisive' and of *'prompt action'*; *'having the ability to pick the right men and to inspire and maintain their enthusiasm because of his own faith and belief in the work he is doing; more apt to smile than to frown'* with *'a realisation that business is not static but dynamic'* are other descriptions Woollard coins.

Many would disagree of course, some violently so. And maybe the course from Gosford Street did not run true. Our task is to assess whether it did or not and never to allow trivia to detract from the greatness of the subject. A good example of the ludicrous injustice heaped on Lord by authors and commentators comes in P W S Andrews's and Elizabeth Brunner's 1955 book *The Life of Lord Nuffield. A study in Enterprise and Benevolence* (Basil Blackwell Oxford).

This is undiluted William Morris hagiography. The only thing that can be said in defence of which is that it was penned in Morris's lifetime and with his 'cooperation' and, at that time, most writing on popular public figures was not known for fearless objectivity.

But in the section that deals with Morris Engines and, specifically, the transfer machines, Lord does not receive a mention; not even *en passant*. That is unforgivable. But let the facts speak for themselves. Peter Seymour in *Wolseley Radial Aero Engines* says, with justifiable pride:

'*the Gosford Street factory became a model for all British industry*' (presumably as regards flow line production, my assumption). That was not the work of William Morris, or, in reality, of Taylor or Woollard, but of Leonard Lord.

In addition, when the factory was visited in 1923 by Ford's chief production engineer from Detroit, he described the transfer machine as 20 years ahead of its time. In fairness, he was probably alluding to Taylor's original design rather than the Lord revision that actually made it work! But it is praise indeed, from the arch exponents of 'flow line'.

In this chapter, as in earlier ones, we have needed to digress to paint a picture of the background against which Leonard Lord was living and operating. Thus, in this section we have taken a glimpse at Hotchkiss and its reaction to the 1914-18 war in France, at the early positioning of William Morris, and we have considered the stance of the Continental Motor Manufacturing Company in Detroit.

In the cause of continuity, completeness and general interest we now need to examine a number of other characters and elements.

As we have already seen, when Leonard Lord was looking for fresh fields to conquer and Morris pressing Hotchkiss for more and more engines, Austin was going bankrupt.

The millions made from munitions and further cash raised in 1919 had been spent on a massive refurbishment and revitalization of the Longbridge Works to turn it into a plant that could make 150 cars a week. But Austin only had one model on the stocks (the Twenty), with no hope of selling it in anything like those numbers. Five hundred *a year* would have been optimistic. Furthermore there was a slump looming. By 1920 Austin had an overdraft of one million pounds and owed his creditors as much again.

On April 26, 1921, an emergency board meeting resolved to write to the London Joint City And Midland Bank Ltd and the Eagle Star and Dominions Insurance Company inviting them to appoint a Receiver and manager. The very same day Sir Arthur Whinney was given the job and chose an accountant, E L Payton, and a production engineer, Carl Engelbach of Vickers and 'Coventry Ordnance' repute, to help him.

Although Herbert Austin came to like and respect Engelbach there were initial resentments for obvious reasons. However, what is not so obvious, and has only been revealed by recent research, is the extent to which Carl Engelbach needed the job at Austin and would have been anxious to please and make an impact. Letters held at Birmingham Library describe how he had been acting as a consultant to various companies but not been paid. Thus, among the reasons he would have been vigorous in his role at Longbridge were its financial benefits and stability. His early difficulties with Sir Herbert may have stemmed, in part, from that enthusiasm.

Indeed, Engelbach almost got control of the entire works but Austin managed to retain for himself, most importantly, a design role. From the summer of 1921 the company had had a Twelve horsepower model to supplement the Twenty but Austin believed they needed a third, much smaller, car. He put this to the board on August 30 claiming potential sales of 500 a week.

A decision was deferred until September 9 when again the board prevaricated. However, for the meeting of September 20, continuing on the 21st, it is minuted: '*the board cannot discuss it (a small car:* my insertion*) with any usefulness at the present time*'.

Austin lived at Lickey Grange, just outside Birmingham and some 35 miles from Coventry. He went home that day having decided to design, privately, a light car of about seven horsepower. In October, he took an 18-year-old trainee draughtsman, Stanley Francis Edge, from the drawing office and into his own pay to ensure that whatever materialized would remain Sir Herbert's private property. Work on the Austin Seven began.

If we could have floated, ghost-like, across the elegant lawns of Lickey Grange late on those autumn nights, and looked beyond the warm-butter-glow of the library windows, we might have found Davidge and Hancock, who had been with Sir Herbert almost from the start; Depper and Yeal, two more from the inner sanctum of confidence and the 55-year-old Austin, of course. All with their backs to the wall—quite literally. We might even have found Edge; and if not him personally, his drawings spread out on the billiard table.

Stanley Edge does not, at face value, even have a walk-on part in the story of Leonard Lord. However, much later, he will make a shadowy appearance in the story, so it is worth placing his relevance in context. In recent years, certain historians and journalists have attributed to Edge a creative role in the 'design' of the Austin Seven. This is not credible. An engineer of the experience and calibre of Herbert Austin did not need an 18-year-old to help him design an extremely simple motor car. Edge was the draughtsman, little, and probably no, more.

On March 16, 1922, the Receiver's final scheme of arrangement for the Austin Motor Company was approved by the Courts. It agreed that from April the firm could be returned to the control of its directors. At a board meeting on April 5 it was resolved that three 'six horsepower' (Austin's Seven) cars would be funded, the company would have exclusive world rights to make them, and Austin himself would be paid a two guinea (£2.10) royalty on each. In effect, Herbert Austin was licensing *his* design to *his* company. On July 21 the model was shown to the distributors, four days later it received favourable publicity in *Light Car and Cycle* magazine and the next day the board signed off on full scale production.

Again for neatness, and although it is of no particular relevance to the life of Leonard Lord, it may be of interest to know that Hotchkiss continued in France as one of the nation's most admired motor manufacturers, the radiator badge of crossed cannon barrels always evoking their earliest history. The cars won the Monte Carlo Rally in 1932, 1933, 1934, 1939, 1949 and 1950. The company was nationalized in 1936 by the *Front Populaire* and took over French car maker Amilcar in 1937. Ainsworth was still there, but, very wisely, got out of Paris before the German Occupation. Peugeot took control in 1942. Ainsworth returned after the Liberation and once again produced cars of pre-War design, a light lorry and a tractor. He retired in 1950 at the same time as Peugeot pulled out.

Ainsworth's greatest legacy, and maybe the thing for which Hotchkiss is best remembered, is large numbers of Willys MB Jeeps built in France. As a military vehicle as well as private car expert he liaised with Willys Overland from London during WWII and, after the conflict, opened negotiations that eventually led to the production of some 27,000 'French Jeeps'.

Although Hotchkiss had merged with that other luxury French marque, Delahaye, in 1954, private car production ceased in 1955 and in 1956 the whole enterprise was acquired by Brandt of household appliance fame. Military vehicle activity continued in one form or another into the 1970s but eventually Hotchkiss ended up helping to make washing machines!

CHAPTER FOUR

SURFING THE BOARD

It was Frederick York Wolseley who realized that the best way to shear the 35 million sheep in New South Wales in 1880, was not with a hand clippers. Wolseley was an Irishman from County Dublin. He had emigrated to Australia in 1854, aged seventeen, his prosperous father having died some years before leaving a large family in dire straits.

Wolseley became the manager of a sheep station near Denliquin, and over a period started to develop mechanical sheep shearing machines. Eventually, in 1887, with patents in hand, he was able to found the Sydney-based Wolseley Sheep Shearing Machine Company Limited and that is how his career impacts, although peripherally, on that of Leonard Lord.

Herbert Austin was born in 1866 at Little Missenden in Buckinghamshire. The son of a farmer, the family moved to Yorkshire in 1870 and it was there the youngster grew up. After a couple of failed career attempts, an uncle visited from Australia and, lured by tales of sun, sand and adventure, Herbert, aged 18, emigrated to Melbourne. There a career in engineering did take off and after a series of jobs he ended up managing a small company.

The trouble with Frederick York Wolseley's sheep shearing machine was it did not work very well, although he was using a number of parts made in the works where Austin was employed. However, the young Herbert made suggestions for improvements and modifications that were so beneficial that Wolseley himself took him on. Soon afterwards the sheep shearing company was sold. The new owners established a branch in Birmingham and, in 1893, Austin was asked to return to the UK and run the outlet. He was now steered towards the business strategy that was directly opposite to that of William Morris.

Just as in Australia, the British-made shearing machines were plagued by poor quality, bought-in, components. So much so that, although the business was in financial difficulty, Austin scrapped the parts in stock and the work in progress, and even bought back faulty machines already in customers' hands. He resolved to make practically everything in-house. While this was being organized, and before the improved product could be re-launched, there was a hiatus and, to keep the Alma Street factory busy, machine tools, equipment for the cotton industry, cycle parts and even complete bicycles were made.

Austin, though, was growing increasingly interested in the embryonic motor car. Around 1895 he visited Paris to acquaint himself with Continental automobile practice. He was impressed by the Léon Bollée tri-car and its twin cylinder horizontally opposed engine and when he returned to Birmingham he persuaded Wolseley to allow him to build two similar cars. Shortly afterwards he experimented, fairly unsuccessfully, with a design largely of his own. The consensus now is this tri-car post-dates the Wolseleys whereas previously it was thought to pre-date them.

In 1901 The Wolseley Sheep Shearing Machine Company decided to divest itself of the car manufacturing business that had developed and it passed to arms maker Vickers Sons and Maxim Ltd as the Wolseley Tool and Motor Car Company, with Austin as general manager and works in Adderley Park, Birmingham. Despite healthy sales of the horizontal engined cars the financial performance was chequered. In 1902 J D Siddeley (who became Lord Kenilworth) and Lionel de Rothschild approached Vickers for support in building a car that followed more closely the trends of the day—a vertical engine and torque tube, instead of chain, final drive.

The Siddeley Autocar Company was established in Crayford, Kent, on a Vickers site. The car appeared in January 1903, was an instant success and as a result the parent company told Wolseley to take over the operation with Siddeley as their sales manager. Not surprisingly, this was not to Herbert Austin's liking. He still seemed tethered to the horizontal engine—or pretended to be. In truth he was performing some behind-the-scenes manoeuvring that involved Wolseley luminaries, A V Davidge and A J Hancock, who, many years later, we spotted in the library at Lickey Grange. He persuaded them to leave Wolseley and they moved into a spare room at Austin's home in the Birmingham suburb of Eardington and there began to work on an Austin design for a vertically engined car. Soon after Austin himself left Wolseley and joined them.

Austin and his wife, Helen, picnic in basket, found, one Saturday afternoon in the village of Longbridge, eight miles west of Birmingham, the vacant, fire damaged, works of White and Pike, who had specialized in printing on sheet metal. Austin acquired the property and some adjoining land. There they could manufacture his car. Thus, at the very end of 1905, The Austin Motor Company was founded. In April the following year 'number one' roared from the old 'printing' works.

Meanwhile, Wolseley motored on. The name Siddeley was left off the cars from about 1910. During WWI they built a variety of aero engines including the fine V8 Hispano-Suiza and it is probable this experience led to the development of a range of excellent post-War automobiles ranging from 10 to 20 horsepower. Some had overhead camshaft engines and a rear transaxle (gearbox and differential combined).

As with many others, the company's downfall came in the financially desperate years of the mid-'20s.

Wolseley had entered the period with their machinery worn out by war work. Yet they were optimistic. The plan was to exploit the luxury car market and also take a share at the bottom end with a subsidiary, the Stellite company, making a ten horsepower car branded with that name.

To this end Adderley Park, considerably extended anyway during WWI, was refurbished, as was a factory owned by Vickers on Drews Lane in the Ward End area of Birmingham. It had been used in the war by the Electric and Ordnance Accessories Company Limited to make fuses and shell cases. The 'icing on the cake' was extravagant new showrooms on London's fashionable Piccadilly. The debt and borrowing was already enormous and the underlying truth was that Wolseley was bankrupting itself, especially as a result of establishing 'Ward End'.

Then they went racing at Brooklands while their keynote six cylinder model, the 16/45, or 'Silent Six', stalled on the marketing grid as potential customers felt duped when they found it wasn't actually 'silent'. The crunch would finally come on November 1, 1926, when Wolseley Motors Limited was declared insolvent with liabilities of £2,000,000. But prior to that the failing company had its attractions, not least for all that impressively equipped work space. Herbert Austin, who, having worked at Adderley Park knew it well, realised this and in May 1924 proposed he, Morris and Wolseley merged.

Morris did not like the idea. He felt he would lose command and, with chilling prescience, said: '*the organization would be so great that it would be difficult to control and might tend to strangle itself*'. William Morris preferred to take Wolseley on his own terms. It was worth having for the plant, as Austin had appreciated; for its reputation, for the six cylinder engine, for its extensive dealer network, and because it might provide an entrée into a higher class market. Not to mention, he felt its presence would create a competitive edge within his own organization. Lord has been vilified for what is, perhaps, similar thinking 30 years later!

Morris bided his time until the declaration of bankruptcy, then bid £600,000. He felt sufficiently confident to pay a 10% deposit but Austin was back in the ring, along with a mysterious outsider named Julius Turner. On February 10, 1927, the senior Official Receiver, H E Burgess, was forced to conduct an inelegant 'auction' in the bankruptcy courts on staid Carey Street in the City of London.

Turner dropped out early on. It has been suggested he was the representative of the American giant, General Motors. Later thinking is that he was probably a nefarious speculator hoping to acquire a business to sell on at a large profit. But that is not to say he may not have had GM in mind as the customer.

Austin and Morris slogged it out. At one point Morris's 'people' told Austin's 'people' that Morris was prepared to go, '*just a bit further than you*'. He did. It was, William Morris said, '*the most thrilling hour of his life*'. Wolseley had been acquired for £730,000. Herbert Austin had, no doubt, been humiliated. It was, after all, the company he had placed on the motoring map. Yet, retribution would come.

It was into Wolseley Motors (1927) Limited that Leonard Lord walked in the year of its birth.

Graham Turner in *The Leyland Papers* (Eyre and Spottiswoode 1971) describes Lord as '*both crude in speech and manner*'. Yet at this stage, we have no substantive evidence—indeed no evidence at all—to suggest that Leonard Lord was foul-mouthed *or* ill-mannered. It is true the schools' inspectors had once criticized the English teaching at Bablake for leaving boys uncouth. But that is an unspecific term. It could just as likely allude to their knowledge of literature or grammar as to their general deportment.

At Courtaulds, with its predominantly female staff, it is reasonable to assume that a 17-year-old male would have been more 'victim' than 'aggressor' in shop floor banter. Although, undoubtedly, an incumbent's vocabulary of sexually orientated expletives would have expanded. The daily exchanges to which Lord would have been exposed at 'Coventry Ordnance', 'Daimler', 'Jig and Tool' and 'Holbrooks' have no reason to be any more 'colourful' than the norm for those particular environments.

While at 'Hotchkiss' and then 'Morris Engines', Lord was in a position of authority, almost certainly not dealing with anyone below the level of foreman, and with no need to demonstrate that verbally he could 'give as good as he got'. This is born out by Frank Woollard who said in that *Motor* article: '*He* (Lord) *is frank and direct in all his dealings and is able to give clear directions to his executives*'. Here we need to take on board that this was written in Austin's jubilee year (1955) when accounts of Lord's demeanour and *modus operandi* would have been at their height. So, in that sense, Woollard may be an apologist for Lord's style, and language.

Even if Woollard was an ameliorator we should ask whether Lord's 'foulness of mouth' has either been exaggerated out of all proportion or, conversely, writers and commentators over the last four decades have sanitized it for increasingly 'politically correct' consumption.

To take the first scenario—there are far more offensive swear words than 'bloody' and 'bugger'. And while it does not come within our remit to examine the semantics of the English language, in Midlands usage, the word 'bugger' is milder again. It is used as a noun, rather than the verb associated with sexual deviance, and usually alludes to what is merely an upsetting or unfortunate situation. For example: 'that's a bugger'. Thus the case against Lord for swearing may pale into insignificance.

It is worth noting that Bill Davis, who started at Longbridge as an apprentice and rose to become a main board director of BMC, is adamant that in all that time he only heard Lord swear twice. The few members of Lord's family who actually remember the man have scant recollection of his swearing. For my own part, with knowledge of the newspaper industry, the 'c' and 'f' words were common parlance; and that amongst national newspaper executives. Maybe we are being prissy over a minor failing, or, at the other extreme, perhaps we are trying to protect Lord from himself.

William Morris recognized the brilliance of the work Lord had done at Morris Engines. He also appreciated that to return Wolseley, with its 1,200 strong workforce, to profitability and capitalize on its prestigious reputation, it needed major reorganization.

The men Lord joined at this new acquisition were the incumbent works manager, Oliver Boden, and a new managing director, Leslie Cannell. Joining Lord at home was his and Ethel's first child, a baby daughter—Joan Marguerite.

Boden was a production engineer and had worked on munitions with Vickers before moving to Wolseley. He was hard working and well respected. Cannell came from Morris Commercial Cars Limited, the van and lorry arm of Morris, where he had also been 'MD'. He now started to style himself 'governing director'. Before joining the Morris fold he had worked for the London firm of Gwynne who made light cars, aeroplane engines and centrifugal pumps.

To start the process of revitalization the Adderley Park works was vacated and handed over to 'Morris Commercial' who moved from the former Wrigleys factory on Foundry Lane in the Soho district of Birmingham. E G Wrigley, who we encountered making parts for the first Morrises and was an early employer of Woollard, went bankrupt after hoping to mass produce the Angus Sanderson car. True to form it was subsequently bought from the Receiver by William Morris in 1924 to become Morris Commercial Cars Limited.

Wolseley then concentrated its operations on Ward End.

Lord and Boden set about the overhaul together. Although the overall result was incredibly successful it should have been obvious the relationship between the two was not going to work. We have a pair of production engineers. One a long serving, dyed in the wool, Wolseley man, the other a 'thirty something' newcomer from the organization that had bought Boden's long-term employer.

There is no question that what Lord was doing to rearrange the machinery and the production methods showed all his ability, flare and dynamism. But at 31, his age when he went to Wolseley, he did not have the personal maturity or adeptness to have a successful partnership with Boden, then 40, and no doubt still ambitious himself. Neither did Lord have the subtlety to deal with the rest of the management team.

Traditional techniques of 'last in, first out' and simple logistics made trimming the shopfloor workforce easy. Axing managers, the majority of whom Lord would not have known, was much more difficult. The solution came on what Morris aficionados know as 'black Friday'. Lord invited the team to his office for an 'ice-breaking' tea and biscuits session. As the atmosphere grew more convivial and the assembled company took to the chairs set around the room, their new boss could observe whether they had swarf embedded in the soles of their shoes—some say, lodged in their trouser turn-ups. Those who did—the managers who 'walked the job'—stayed, those who did not, went. It is an unlikely story. Purely, we must suspect, of Lord's own cavalier invention and masking a much more incisive and informed assessment.

Yet, Lord did what he has often been criticized for in later years; created warring sectors. As Miles Thomas said: '*It was evident that the Wolseley company was becoming split into two rival factions, those who supported Boden and those who supported Len Lord*'. To solve the situation, a troubled Morris, but now doubly impressed with Lord, put Boden in overall control of Wolseley Motors and Morris Commercial Cars (Cannell remained as 'MD' of Wolseley) and in April 1933 invited his new discovery to Cowley as 'governing director' of Morris Motors Limited. Lord was just 36.

Perhaps the most impressive of Lord's achievements before leaving Ward End, and the deciding one for William Morris, had been the speed with which he brought a new, eight horsepower, side valve engine into production.

Morris had entered the '30s with a small car called the Minor. This was the predictable bid, in 1928, to challenge the Austin Seven. The latter was still riding high in the miniature car market, the fastest growing sector, and one that had received a further boost in Chancellor Winston Churchill's budget of that year when he raised the price of petrol from 1s 2d a gallon (about 6p) to 1s 6d but left 'horsepower tax'* untouched.

A crèche full of manufacturers tried to snatch a slice of the Baby Austin's cake—Clyno, Gwynne, Humber, Singer and Standard—while William Morris was prompted to say: '*Some people think that my idea is to try to crush the Austin Seven off the market, which is absurd. But I can say this, my price will not be higher than that of the Austin Seven*'. Sir Herbert responded thus, perhaps rather unconvincingly: '*Personally, and as firms, we are on the best of terms with the Morris Company. The public will decide whose car they like best. Mr Morris's decision (to enter this sector) is no surprise to me*' . . . . And then added rather churlishly: '*I knew what was going on weeks ago*'.

The Morris Minor was a more advanced car than the Austin Seven. It came onto the market at £135 for the saloon and £125 for a tourer, the same as the equivalent models from Longbridge.

Ironically the Minor was not, in the main, designed at Cowley. Perhaps this was the 'competitive edge' that Morris had alluded to. Or maybe he was too pre-occupied with the appalling quality of the steel bodies for other models being made by Pressed Steel and delivered to the main works. Decades later the body builder would be acquired by BMC, now their performance rendered Morris: '*like a bear with a sore head*', said Miles Thomas.

The chassis for the Minor was made in the Wrigley works now vacated by Morris Commercial. The lively 847 cc engine was one of those said to have been born of Wolseley's experience of Hispano-Suiza aero engines in WWI. It had the dual phenomenon of an overhead camshaft with the drive taken off the back of the dynamo's armature shaft. The first feature was certainly to the Franco-Spanish** company's layout and probably the second owed something to their method of reduction gearing for an aeroplane propeller.

---

* At this time cars were taxed on the basis of a formula that provided an artificial 'horsepower' rating. Based on a calculation involving the cylinder diameter it led to highly unsatisfactory engineering—power units of small bore with very long piston strokes.

** It was only chief engineer, Marc Birkigt, who was Swiss hence 'Suiza'. The factories were in Spain and then France.

Sadly, Wolseley's interpretation made for a fragile and troublesome unit, particularly as regards the principle of the camshaft drive. It was compounded by the fact that the fabric covered body used so much wadding to ease its angularity it became extremely popular with birds who liked to peck through the outer skin to source felt for their nests.

As Miles Thomas has it: '*The first Morris Minor was a troublesome baby*'.

The realization of a solution—although not the origination—was down to Leonard Lord. In 1931 a new, simpler, tougher, engine came off the drawing board of Percy Rose at Morris Commercial Cars. He had served an apprenticeship with none other than Royce, as far back as the great man's days in Cook Street, Manchester. Rose joined Morris in 1922, initially at Cowley, then transferred to Birmingham and 'Morris Commercial'. There he penned, among other designs, the original running gear for the Minor. It was his 8 hp side valve engine Lord raced into production at Ward End.

In his book *Out On A Wing* (Michael Joseph 1964), Miles Thomas suggests that the side-valve Minor was the result of Lord being inspired by a Ford of similar capacity. This is misleading as it alludes to a train of events that came later. When Wolseley were finding a solution to the troublesome overhead camshaft engine the small Ford did not exist in any form.

The Minor was marketed from 1931 until 1932 with the choice of the ohc or sv engine. With the side valve as the only option, it lasted until 1933. A total of just over 86,000 Minors were built between the launch in 1928 and 1934.

When Leonard Lord arrived at Cowley, be-spectacled, with firey ginger hair, he was on the threshold of becoming a captain of British industry. Now married 12 years, a second daughter, Patricia Anne, had joined Joan in 1929 and a third, Pauline Ruth, in 1931. Thus he was also a heavily committed family man.

It has been said that Lord was proud of his new authority almost to the point of arrogance. Even before this description of his manner at Cowley was uttered, he had displayed extraordinary arrogance in his dealings with no less a figure than Morris. When offered the job at the Oxfordshire plant he said he would only accept if he had full managerial control, otherwise he preferred to stay at Wolseley. His experiences with Boden would have illustrated to him that there could be only one supremo, but his declaration was complicated by Cowley already having a managing director in Edgar Blake.

Blake had been brought in around 1925 from the Dunlop Rubber Company where he had been general sales manager. He was hired for his 'commercial' outlook and was one of the first 'outsiders' to join top Morris management. However, he did not have a happy liaison with his more technically minded colleagues and he was persuaded to retire in June 1933. Lord had had his way.

Yet it is a measure of the importance William Morris attached to Leonard Lord taking over at Cowley that he acceded to this manoeuvring. In truth, he realized, Lord was the only man who could reverse the trend in what was by now a declining organization. Morris Motors' profits for 1931 had been little more than half those of the previous year—£662,916 as opposed to £1,166,689. There was a slight climb in 1932 to £755,000 but '33 was disastrous with the figure standing at just £343,000. The reasons are varied and complicated.

By the 1930s the bulk of British motor industry output was in the hands of a small number of volume producers. This was partially attributable to Morris's own declared policy of absorbing the entire output of component manufacturers and/or buying them out. Because of this, both the availability and, more importantly, affordability of parts to small manufacturers was limited and the majority was forced out of business.

Also, overall, there was no clear understanding of what size car the public really wanted, or would be able to afford. For example, Austin had a spread of more than 30 models in their 1932 catalogue. In the 8 hp or under category, home sales soared from 18% in 1928 to 25% in 1929 and continued to rise until 1938 (30%) with just two minor blips in 1932 and '34 (24 and 23% respectively).

But as we have already seen, at the turn of the decade Morris, unlike Austin, were in the very early stages of developing a car to penetrate this promising market.

Meanwhile, from 1932 onwards, the 9-10 hp sector was extremely strong rising from 24% market share that year to 33% in 1938 and steadily outstripping the demand for the smallest cars. All the time an increasingly fickle and fashion-conscious customer was making the designer's job more difficult and the production department's more costly.

The export scene was fraught, either by virtue of local tariffs, or the unsuitability of British cars for nearly all markets, brought about by the engineering philosophy—narrow bore, long stroke—fostered at home by the horsepower tax. Conversely, there was competition *from* overseas. Both Ford and Vauxhall (the latter owned by America's General Motors since 1925) had a United Kingdom presence. Indeed, by 1934 the Ford Eight, flooding out of a new Dagenham plant, seized more than 50% of its sector with some 27,000 sales.

Morris's specific problems were that they had misjudged the market. From the late '20s onwards there was a general need to broaden the coverage—Austin added first a six cylinder Twenty and then a Sixteen to supplement the Seven, Twelve and four cylinder Twenty of the vintage (1920-30*) years. Soon there would be a dreadful six cylinder 'Light' Twelve, a splendid Ten horsepower 'four' and an unimaginative, ubiquitous and indestructible four cylinder 'Light' Twelve.

Morris could have jumped either way from his staple and much loved 11.9 horsepower cars of the early years. He chose upwards—first to 13.9 and, by the end of the decade, higher. It was a bad move. *But*, he believed he could not, profitably, oust the Austin Seven, particularly as others were trying to board the miniature car band wagon and would be taking varying proportions of sales. He was also attracted to the export market where the bigger cars might hold sway. In addition, he thought the British public could be wooed to these larger models.

In fairness, there had been a rush to 16 horsepower types through 1930 and 31 when they snatched 25% and 21% respectively of the home market. (Austin shifted no fewer than 5,560!). But the demand collapsed almost totally in 1932 (just 12% of all sales) as yet another economic recession bit.

Back at Morris, even in the late '20s, much depended financially on the archaic Cowley. Updated in appearance though it was, it was increasingly difficult for it to hold its own against better equipped Morrises in an ever-more fashion conscious market place. The company weathered the opening stages of the new economic depression satisfactorily as it was not dependent on high profit margins from its new small car and sales in this category held up reasonably well.

However by 1931 purchases of Morris Twelves—the Cowley's class—crashed from 26,000 to 17,000 while at the same time there was little market for the bigger models. Nor were 'business' cars selling. This sector had been a happy hunting ground for Morris, but now cash-starved

---

*   This is the very realistic definition formulated by the UK's prestigious Vintage Sports Car Club. It reflects a period of quality engineering and construction prior to the 'post-vintage era' when the motor car became much more a utilitarian commodity of inferior design and workmanship.

companies were holding on to their fleets. Morris was in deep trouble. Market share fell from 51% per cent in 1929 to 27% in 1933.

There were personal issues also.

William Morris, who had no heir, a situation he described as his '*personal tragedy*', failed to install a plan of succession or inject 'new blood' into the organization. While he may have been able to pick lieutenants who were capable of delivering what he wanted, he made one of the gravest managerial errors of all in not being able to delegate, then leave a competent subordinate to execute the instructions.

This was compounded by the fact that in the crucial years of the late '20s he appeared to have lost interest in the business, ceasing to attend the weekly executive meetings and taking long voyages to Australia, a country for which he had a passion. Ironically, it was Herbert Austin's old 'stamping ground'! Morris would stay for months on end, remaining on one occasion for seven.

In *The Leyland Papers* Graham Turner writes: '*While he frequently vowed to leave the management of the business to other people, he was furious if important decisions were taken while he was away; and if anyone displayed signs of real power, his days were numbered . . . . He was a proprietor who did not want to manage, only to intervene when he felt like it*'.

An example features Frank Woollard, still at 'Engines Branch' in Coventry, and Blake, towards the end of his tenure at Cowley. The latter authorized the 'secret' design of a 'Light' six cylinder while Morris was away on one of his cruises. Woollard produced what was a very innovative, but very poor engine. Extremely good, though, at boiling the oil in its sump and pumping it over the clutch. To get the project completed before 'the master' returned, a quickly made fabric body was slipped on. As soon as Morris was on hand, and with eager anticipation, the dust sheets were thrown back. Predictably, Morris instinctively hated the design that lay before him and in which he had had no hand or say. It didn't help that the Morris Fifteen was a commercial disaster. As Turner suggests in the broader context—Edgar Blake's days were numbered.

Yet, one occasion when Morris did get the formula right was with Leonard Lord. He chose someone who was young, gifted and the only man who could save a company that was so big even its founding father couldn't understand or control it. Lord was given what would be known in today's business world as 'personal objectives'. He had to modernize and overhaul the product range. That meant slashing a catalogue that had seen a rise from two basic models and 10 body styles for most of the vintage years to nine core cars and 26 coachwork types after 1928, all placed there in an ill-starred bid to comprehensively cover the market. It also meant doing something about the huge inroads into the 8 hp category being made by Ford.

He needed to modernize and fine tune the production facilities on the 200 acre Cowley site and elsewhere. To that end, at the Oxford factory, £300,000 in 1934, which had swelled to £500,000 by 1936, was invested in plant and accommodation. This included four mechanized assembly lines of the latest type and the expansion of the north factory to cover more than 40 acres. Brand new structures appeared to the south. All engine manufacture was focused on Morris Motors Engines Branch at Coventry except for power units for the heavier lorries. That remained with Morris Commercial Cars Ltd. in Birmingham. Administration was largely centralized on Cowley.

Spin-off objectives for Lord, which he probably regarded with little relish, were to minimize William Morris's estate duties and to merge his personally owned companies. This was a tedious affair in part brought about by what is euphemistically referred to by commentators, as 'the super tax case(s)'.

From 1922 individuals whose annual income was above £2,000 (Morris would have been earning that *a day* in 1933) were eligible to pay, in addition to income tax at a fixed rate, super tax on a sliding scale. Companies simply paid income tax at the fixed percentage. It was clearly advantageous for an individual to allow the money an enterprise was earning to remain within the business. But this was complicated in William Morris's case because he owned much of the organization personally.

The Inland Revenue made two bids to extract super tax from William Morris, the first in November 1926, and then in December 1929, for the years 1922/3 and 1927/8 respectively. They failed on both occasions because Morris managed to demonstrate his profits had been used for essential maintenance and development, which was permissible. But forewarned, Morris first turned Morris Motors into a public company (Morris Motors (1926) Limited). This absorbed the radiator, engine and body manufacturers he had owned privately. He also set up, in 1927, Morris Industries Limited, a holding concern that would enable him to move money around the firms without attracting tax.

Still unable to sleep at night for money worries after the 1929 claim, he decided to merge some of the remaining privately owned companies and place the shares on the stock market, thus further reducing his own tax liabilities. In simple terms, as far as such matters ever can be, Morris Motors issued, in 1935, ordinary shares to Morris Industries (the holding company) to buy itself back. Morris himself, i.e. Morris Industries, obtained 1,999,995 of them. Leonard Lord, Miles Thomas, Cecil Kimber (head of MG), Reginald Thornton (the auditor) and Andrew Walsh (the solicitor) received one each.

Morris Motors now raised £269,000 from more ordinary shares to buy Wolseley Motors Limited for £250,000 and the MG Car Co Ltd for £19,000. In October 1936, Morris Motors raised a further £381,000 in a similar way to buy Morris Commercial Cars Ltd and Morris Industries Exports Ltd for £300,053, plus the SU Carburetter Co Ltd at £50,000. The amalgamated businesses were named The Nuffield Organisation and the only companies Morris continued to own personally were The Morris Garages Ltd and Wolseley Aero Engines Ltd.

What Leonard Lord made of all these machinations is hard to judge. But they would certainly have given him a sharper insight than ever before into the financial administration of a major undertaking and the ploys that can be implemented for a variety of purposes. His final objective, and perhaps the most important of all, was to improve the profit from what, at this stage, was still Morris Motors Ltd.

The profitability of Morris's combined interests had soared, year on year, from 1920 to 1928—£50,000 to £1,595,000. There had been a blip in 1926 when the figure dropped from £1,556,000 in 1925 to £1,042,000, but this has been attributed to developing, then tooling for, 'Flatnosed' as opposed to 'Bullnosed' models and to Britain's General Strike. The latter didn't affect Morris directly as only three brave souls amongst the 3,000 strong workforce participated, but there was general turmoil in the land.

However, in 1929, for reasons already discussed, Morris's affairs took a downturn. Slowly at first—profits of £1,571,000 that year, just some £25,000 down; then £527,000 the next, 751,000 the next (up, but not significantly); until, when Lord arrived, they stood at £844,000, again, slightly improved, but only because of a modest upturn in the national economy.

Lord's prescribed objectives—modernization, profitability, tax efficiency and so on—were all to be realized. But undoubtedly his most spectacular single achievement in those years was the creation of the Morris Eight. The car was a direct response to a British Ford of the same power category that was making the devastating impact in that market sector that we have already seen—more than a 50% share by 1934.

The Ford Eight, or model Y, was produced at the American company's new British plant in Dagenham, on the Essex marshes. The factory had opened in 1931 and struggled for viability with Model A cars and light trucks derived from them. The former, particularly, were in the American mode and as unsuited to the British scene as the domestic product was to overseas use. The balance sheet looked so grim that Ford of Britain's chairman, Percival Perry, told his bosses in Michigan that unless they could provide a small car his arm of the company was 'finished'.

They heeded the message. In the parent drawing office, in under six months and aided by delegates from England, a stylish little saloon was created around a simple but smooth running and workmanlike 933 cc engine. The chassis was in the Ford tradition with transverse leaf springs front and rear and torque tube transmission. About 14 prototypes were constructed in the Rouge River works at Dearborn and shown to potential customers in London's Albert Hall in May 1931. Some 50,000 people paid 1s 3d (about 6p) to see.

The model, which was made in two—and four—door form (unlike the Austin Seven, for instance), was revised after its unveiling and went on sale three months later at £120. In its first short 'year' 8,260 were sold but in 1933 sales rocketed to over 37,000 and turned Ford's loss of £726,000 the previous year into a profit almost as large.

In 1935 the price of the 'Eight' was reduced to £100, allowing Ford to claim it was the first fully equipped, closed, car in the world at that price[*].

To suggest, as many have, that the Morris Eight was 'a Ford with frills' is disingenuous both to Lord and the men who actually designed it. It is true that Lord had a Ford brought to Cowley and assistant chief designer, Claude Bailey, based an engine very closely on that of Dearborn's. However, the Morris was a far superior car in every way. Superior also to the out-dated Austin Seven.

It was an attractive, well made, modern car with a quality feel. The 918 cc engine used the excellent in-house SU carburetter with an electric fuel pump of the same make and had enough power to mitigate a three speed gearbox. The chassis was fitted with semi-elliptic springs at each corner damped by hydraulic shock-absorbers. Brakes were also hydraulic, from Lockheed, and steering was of the Bishop cam design for lightness.

Prices began at £118 for a two-seat tourer with the basic four-door saloon retailing for £132 10s. De luxe models had best quality hide upholstery, a sunshine roof and extra chrome. When the car was launched, in 1934, it was a sensation. The planned production had to be doubled to cope with demand. Around 250,000 were produced in four years (it took the Austin Seven seventeen to reach 290,000), speeding Morris to its first total of one million vehicles built by 1939.

Ford sales were considerably reduced, Morris's profits reached record levels, sales revenue rose from £11.4m in 1933 to £21.1m in 1936 and market share from 27% to 33% over the same period. But it would be a bitter-sweet success for Leonard Lord.

---

[*]   Miles Thomas claims 'the first £100 car' for Morris with a Minor of 1931. But it was neither closed nor fully equipped.

CHAPTER FIVE

THE AGE OF AQUARIUS

If Lord's development and launch of the Morris Eight was spectacular, it was nothing in comparison with his decline within the company. There are complex issues which surround the circumstances and we need to review them all extremely carefully as they are pivotal to his story.

Not everything Lord did at Morris Motors was on a grand or dramatic scale. He shaped the future of MG, yet his impact on that company occurred almost by accident. However, the circumstances help give a further insight into the calibre of the man and his personality. Consequently we need to look in some detail at the story of MG.

As most devout sports car enthusiasts agree, MG probably stands for 'Morris Garages' although this is not proven. The 'garages' were a wing of William Morris's business that went back to the earliest days and formally received its title in 1910—The Morris Garages (W R Morris Proprietor)—when he began erecting new accommodation and generally expanding, what was, quite simply, a motor repair business and dealership for a range of car makes.

When Morris started to build his Oxford, fortuitously for MG devotees, The Morris Garages was allowed to remain a separate company and a new firm was formed to take on manufacturing. It was registered in 1912 as W R M Motors Ltd.

From 1921, a young man of 33 named Cecil Kimber was the sales manager of Morris Garages. Kimber was from a distinguished, but not affluent, English family. Richard Kimber had served with Oliver Cromwell. His grandson, Isaac Kimber, wrote a biography of the great Puritan republican. Other members of the clan included a Fellow of the Royal Geographical Society and a free spirited female artist. Later generations, however, were more mechanically minded and moved into the manufacture of printing and reprographic equipment.

Kimber was destined for this world too, even though the fortunes of his father's Lancashire ink business had taken a downturn, and despite his passion for motor cycles. Yet, fate took a hand. A stockbroker knocked Cecil off a borrowed Rex machine on the road from Grappenhall to Lymm, in Cheshire, and seriously injured him. The medical procedures of the day did not serve the young man well and after a series of excruciatingly painful operations it was decided to amputate his right leg altogether. When all seemed lost, the shattered thigh began to heal to the satisfaction of his surgeons. The amputation was abandoned, and Cecil Kimber spent the rest of his life with one leg two inches shorter than the other and a consequent limp.

Some of the sizeable amount of compensation received from the stockbroker put Kimber on four wheels with a 1913 Singer Ten. But nothing could compensate for the loss of his mother from cancer just a few years before. As his only sister left home to get married, his only brother

36

went to war, and the ink business went to the wall, Cecil Kimber suffered an irreparable rift with his father over the remains of the accident damages.

They never spoke again and Kimber committed himself to the motor industry. There was initially a vague link with a local Manchester firm, Crossley, before he joined Sheffield-Simplex. While there, he married Irene (or Rene)* Hunt from Ladybarn in Manchester and promptly quit, or lost, his job at Sheffield-Simplex. One theory is he could not tolerate being subservient and walked out when his employer was less than enthusiastic about an innovation he had suggested.

By 1916 he was working as a buyer for AC in Thames Ditton, Surrey, with Rene as his secretary. Then, two years later, with possibly a brief interval at Martinsyde Aircraft in nearby Woking, he headed north again and to our familiar E G Wrigley of Birmingham. This very firmly establishes the link with Morris, of course. But Kimber, who had bought shares in the company, was there as works organizer for the débâcle with the Angus Sanderson car, and there seems little doubt he lost most of his money as a consequence. Kimber got out in 1921 and secured the job of sales manager with Morris Garages.

Fate again took a hand. His boss at Morris was the 'Garages' general manager Edward Armstead. He had taken over Morris's bicycle business in 1908 and had clearly gone on to higher things. Not long after Kimber joined, Armstead mysteriously resigned and a few weeks later gassed himself to death, a suicide for which no explanation has ever been found.

Kimber was offered Armstead's post and began running The Morris Garages from March 1922. His enthusiasm for fast motor cycles and cars again came to the fore. Helped considerably by his wife, he started designing rakish coachwork at the couple's home in Banbury Road, Oxford, that could simply be 'bolted on' to the standard chassis from Morris Motors (this title had been adopted in 1919 and the name W R M Motors Limited dropped). The bottom line was that so treated, the cars could be sold for a third more than the standard models.

According to the young Hubert Charles, who was a production 'trouble shooter' working for Morris Motors at the time, and who used to visit the Kimbers at a new address on Woodstock Road, Rene was '*a most cultured, charming and wonderful person*'. Incidentally, Charles, a brilliant engineer, had cut his teeth as engineering officer during WWl to the squadron in which the legendary aces James McCudden and Albert Ball served. He worked, appropriately, on Wolseley Viper (aka V8 Hispano-Suiza) engines and later joined Kimber at MG as chief draughtsman.

Harold Connolly, who was the talented freelance artist who illustrated all the MG catalogues and brochures from 1929 onwards, also remembers Rene, and that she used to like to pose for publicity photographs with the new models. This is probably just as well because Kimber liked pretty girls to be seen in his cars and, by his own admission, Connolly couldn't draw them as well as he, the artist, would have liked.

Gradually Kimber developed the tuned, 'sports', Morris but output was very much on a peripatetic basis. The first cars were built in Longwall (the area of Oxford that accommodated the Morris Works on Holywell Street), then Queen Street, then another 'Garages' address in Pusey Street and finally in part of Morris's equally mobile radiator factory, which, by 1926, had new premises, built on the site of an old brick works, on Woodstock Road. In 1927 Kimber's enterprise got its own purpose-built plant in Edmund Road, Cowley and was registered as the MG Car Company Ltd on July 21, 1930, although 'MG' had been used as the name actually on the cars from 1928.

---

*　This is sometimes rendered Renée, probably incorrectly.

It was at Edmund Road that the elegant, Kimber-styled, MG radiator was first fitted, initially on the 18/80 launched in August 1928 using a tuned version of the six cylinder Morris Isis engine, and then on the Midgets, in which the Minor's overhead camshaft engine was to find a welcoming home.

In 1929 MG moved yet again, this time to a site in Abingdon, about 10 miles to the south west of Cowley, and, coincidentally, the ancestral home of the Kimbers.

The move was necessitated by growing demand for the Midget (altogether 3,235 were built in its four year life) and occurred at a stage when Kimber was becoming increasingly interested in racing. This is an important point.

We cannot be sure how committed he was to the sport for its commercial value. His talent for salesmanship and publicity was probably sufficient for his marketing needs without the competitive activity. For instance, he told Connolly: '*If the car's good let's make the literature good*', admittedly, somewhat regardless of print costs. He was also of the view that '*the catalogue is the salesman that goes home with you*'.

Other of his sayings included '*a sports car should look fast even when it's standing still.*' Connolly recalled how he could make the staid Bullnose Morris look quick. No tricks were applied by the artist to make them appear faster. '*He was after something beautiful, attractive; efficient in so far as it performed what he wanted it to do. He had a lovely idea of what the young lad of the village wanted and that's what he built*', explained Connolly. Thus the racing may have simply indulged a private passion.

All that accepted, there is no question racing and record breaking made MGs famous in no small measure. It also made them desirable. Kimber had seen the same effect at Crossley, where the famous pioneer racer, Charles Jarrott, was a director, and to an even greater extent at AC. Whatever the scenario it did not augur well. Although William Morris had been a robust racing cyclist in his youth, and, supposedly, one of his proudest possessions was the numerous awards for the sport contained in a glass case in his office, and even though he had driven his first cars in hillclimbs and reliability trials, Morris had a schizophrenic relationship with motor sport.

On the debit side, one of the first articles Miles Thomas wrote for *The Morris Owner*, the customer journal he had been charged with producing, decried the benefit of racing. '*For anyone to suggest that a concern that builds a successful racing car must* ipso facto *produce a good touring model is sheer rubbish*'. While Morris himself was wont to say: '*there isn't a motor firm that has supported racing that hasn't had the Receiver in*'.

On a more positive note, Morris provided the whole £3,100 prize money for the 1933 Ulster Tourist Trophy road race. Also, when Bentley were competing in the famous Le Mans 24 Hour *Grand Prix d'Endurance*, he loaned them the former Léon Bollée works in the city for each of the years from 1925-30. Morris had bought 'Bollée' in 1924.

But clearly there were reservations about racing and it is all the more impressive Kimber kept a full scale Works racing programme running for around five years—1929-1934. The anti-racing ethos was compounded by two unhappy events in 1934—one a tragedy in real terms, the other only as regards ego.

In the first instance, the well-known racing driver Kaye Don crashed an MG, killing his racing mechanic, Frank Tayler, who was an employee of the company. The accident happened on May 28, in the run up to the Isle of Man TT. Don was testing a K3 Magnette, outside the official practice period, at 10.30 pm, in virtual darkness, driving untaxed, uninsured, with neither lights nor horn. Having lost control of the MG on a bend he hit a 'civilian' saloon, killing Tayler and fracturing his own skull.

The inquest decided Tayler's death was '*due to the culpably negligent driving of Mr Kaye Don*'. The latter was charged with manslaughter, convicted, and sentenced to four months in prison, which he served after an unsuccessful appeal. The circumstances of 27-year-old Tayler's death were horrible enough but the ensuing bad publicity in the national and motoring press was considerably exacerbated by crass insensitivity from a number of quarters.

James Wentworth-Day, a prolific writer on a wide variety of subjects, was about to publish his biography of Don, supposedly a man with the common touch. He managed to include an account of the events in his book, which conveyed little remorse and scant regard for the grief of Tayler's family.

Meanwhile another voluminous scribe and himself a famous racing driver, S C H (Sammy) Davis of *The Autocar,* held forth on the injustice of Don being brought to trial and does not even acknowledge the victim by name in an October 26th article. This so repelled the readership that on November 23, the magazine was forced to devote a whole page to correspondents whose '*views differ from those of Mr. Davis*'.

Morris was unquestionably deeply upset by the death of a young man who had originally joined The Morris Garages in 1923, been at Abingdon since 1929, and developed into a first class mechanic. And we can be sure Lord was equally disgusted by the events and especially some of the attitudes.

On the second occasion, trivial by comparison, Morris, recently elevated to the peerage as Lord Nuffield and on one of his numerous trips to Australia, was to address a crowded public function. The introduction as '*the man who makes Morris cars*' was met by a sea of blank faces. Almost as an aside, it was added that he was also responsible for MG and while there may not quite have been uproarious applause, there was instantaneous and enthusiastic recognition. To repeat again Graham Turner in *The Leyland Papers*: the days (*Kimber's in this instance*) were numbered!

To recap briefly. Morris Motors Ltd bought the MG Car Company Ltd in 1935 using money raised by an offer of ordinary shares. This followed the deal to free Morris Motors from Morris Industries Ltd, in effect free it from Morris the man. As Leonard Lord was already managing director of Morris Motors he also became head of MG with Kimber, to all intents and purposes, demoted to general manager but with a directorship.

F Wilson McComb puts it thus in his book *The Story of the MG Sports Car: 'Things could never be quite the same again. Kimber's personality flourished only when he had freedom of action, when he was in a position to make quick decisions. He was anything but a committee man; still less a company man. MG owed their success to his personal control and direction, under which the Abingdon factory had become a close-knit unit owing loyalty to him, the personification of MG'.*

There is no evidence that Leonard Lord had any enthusiasm for motor sport on two, four or any other number of wheels—especially now. It is true that his youngest daughter, Pauline, had modest rallying success in the mid-1950s, but that, of course, is two decades later.

The surplus money that would have enabled Lord to take part in any form of competitive motoring when he was young would simply not have been available to the household, and we can reasonably assume that in the 1920s and '30s he would have viewed it as a pointless waste of time for the affluent classes and over-indulged rich kids. On an early visit to Abingdon, having toured the racing department, he is reported as saying: '*Well that bloody lot can go for a start*'.

Naturally, this has been seized upon ever since by those who think they can demonstrate the managing director's arrogance, short sightedness, his ruthless inflexibility and insensitivity, plus, no doubt, a simple lack of *joie de vivre*. Unfortunately, without having actually heard the comment and being able to judge Lord's demeanour, it is impossible to accurately interpret his words. It may have been a half-joking throwaway line, or, a declaration of what he intended to do, and did, but without malice.

Lord is now in a very difficult position. His boss has become unsupportive of the racing programme and he himself is committed to practical and economic objectives in a competitive commercial environment. And MG's figures are disastrous. Between 1930 and 1934 they had shown a total trading surplus of just £419. By September 1935 they had broken all their records by losing an incredible £28,156 with sales at a five year low. All this the work of a man described by Connolly as someone who could add up a column of figures three times and end up with four different answers. Lord must have asked himself, with another débâcle in view, what really was the point of continuing to run an expensive competitions department at Abingdon? He was absolutely right to do so.

In 1930 racing had cost just over £1,000, in 1931 it had consumed nearly five, was back to £2,700 in 1932 but at the all time high of £5,863 in 1933 while at the time of MG's acquisition by Morris Motors on July 1, 1935, it was already racing again towards £5,000. In addition the development costs for the R Type single-seater racing car were being concealed in the everyday accounting.

Furthermore, it was increasingly apparent that the Austin Seven, the MG's principal rival in the small sports car category, was out-dated and outclassed and there were sufficient customers possessing the excellent Midget and J Series MGs to race them privately. By so doing the prestige of the car as a thoroughbred could be maintained at minimal cost and new devotees wooed along the way.

To revert to a point expounded earlier. This was not a game. It was not a frivolous pursuit for amateurs acted out on the grassy slopes beside Brooklands, Donington or Shelsley Walsh race tracks, whilst lying on picnic blankets, listening to '78s' on a wind-up gramophone. This was hard-nosed commercial life and Leonard Lord was there to deliver.

Meanwhile, the incident in Australia, where Nuffield was upstaged, probably hadn't helped Kimber's reputation, particularly as we have another shadowy figure moving through the 'wings'—Lady Nuffield. A former seamstress and member of the sales team in a large Oxford draper, Elizabeth Maud Anstey had married Morris in 1904. Graham Turner says of her: '*(she) was an assiduous guardian of her husband's supreme status*'.

Miles Thomas, after describing the extremely tight rein she kept on domestic expenditure, adds: '*Lady Nuffield managed to retain her lines of communication with people in the works. Up to the time of his early death her brother, Bill Anstey, was transport manager to the company* (Morris). *Lilian, as Lady Nuffield was always called*', *kept an ear very close to the ground and any member of the staff who was guilty of a social misdemeanour at a dance, dinner or other public occasion in Oxford soon found he had registered a black mark for bad manners*'.

Later he reveals, and I paraphrase: At the inevitable works dinners and dances during the winter season the party never really began to go until 'the boss' (*William Morris*) and his wife had gone. On the rare occasions when she did not accompany him to a 'mixed' party things got under way much earlier in the evening. The significance of this cameo will take on more, possibly momentous, status later.

Also moving furtively about the 'set' was Wilfred Hobbs to whom Miles Thomas applies that 'accolade' that offends most people: '*he had a good war*'. Hobbs was the son of a golfing

---

* This is one diminutive of Elizabeth.

acquaintance of Morris who was a miller from Goring-on-Thames. The son was the accountant who Morris brought in to handle financial matters at Wrigleys when he acquired it. Further described by Thomas as '*the perfect bachelor*' he became the industrialist's *de facto* personal assistant from the mid-'20s until 1945. A man we learn, in the ambiguous statement from Thomas, who told Morris '*all that it was necessary for him to hear*'.

I would suggest that Lord dealt sensitively with Kimber. Rather than the villain he is portrayed as by some MG protagonists, he was the hero of the hour. McComb tells us (*The Story of the MG Sports Car*) that at a personal level the two men were '*quite friendly*', although Jonathan Wood, writing for *The Automobile* in October 2007, claims that Lord '*amongst his many prejudices disliked Kimber*' and had '*the perfect excuse to close down the racing department and drawing office*'—presumably the catastrophic finances.

I can find no evidence that there was any antipathy between Lord and Kimber and furthermore, let's be clear, Lord didn't need an excuse to close anything at MG. What he did was the obvious, intelligent and business-like course of action.

But to return to the personal level. Lord would almost certainly have known many of Kimber's circumstances. Of his mother's tragic death, if not his alienation from the father, and he must have had an empathy with that general situation. He probably also knew that Kimber's wife, Rene, had been diagnosed with a debilitating illness that increasingly prevented this once vivacious beauty taking any part in a family life that previously had been filled with activity and conviviality. He may also have known that Kimber had begun a relationship with another lady. Some sources suggest the liaison did not start until as late as 1936/7, others place the first sparks about three years earlier, but both these estimates are questionable.

Finally, Lord could well have been aware, as a father of girls himself, of the difficulties Kimber was experiencing with his own young family of two daughters. Their father could be severe and draconian domestically. He separated from Rene as her condition worsened, and the younger child, Jean, was sent to boarding school.

Betty, who later liked to call herself 'Lisa', turned into what was almost certainly nothing more problematic than a rebellious teenager. Naturally she quarrelled with her parent about make-up, clothes, music, politics. Lord may have feared all that would come his way too!

At a semi-professional level Lord and Kimber would have had much in common. The former was a superb draughtsman and liked to sketch and outline the details of cars. Kimber was the man who could make a sports car look fast even when it was standing still. In any event, Lord was perfectly placed to shield Kimber and let MG continue. And maybe he bought Cecil Kimber the time to save himself and MG.

The range of models was simplified to about five from an absurd 15, the annual sales of some of which were not reaching double figures. Output and sales rose, Kimber was reinstated as managing director and by 1938 his salary had more than doubled, although by the time all this happened Lord had already departed the Nuffield Organization.

Ostensibly, it was Miles Thomas who ended the career Kimber had loved.

When the outbreak of war brought motor car production to an end at Abingdon, Kimber, with commendable initiative one might have thought, secured a contract to build the front section of the Albemarle bomber. Those familiar with aircraft will recall this was a twin-engined, Armstrong Whitworth-designed medium bomber. It featured an extremely large nose that accommodated not only two pilots but also the navigator and radio operator. Six hundred were eventually built, all by A W Hawkesley of Gloucester, who placed contracts with a large number of suppliers for the components.

A weight issue arising from the use of steel rather than aluminium over the wooden frame meant the Albemarle only ever served as general and paratroop transports and on military glider towing duties. However, they did see action in such distinguished battles as those for the beaches of Normandy and at Arnhem.

Kimber's contract though was not to the liking of Cowley management and seen as the pursuit of 'non-conformity' when the 'party line' was unification. This is of enormous significance, as we shall explore later. It was Miles Thomas who was sent to deal with Kimber and leave him 'thunderstruck' after being told: *'he had better look for another outlet for his energies because he did not fit into the wartime pattern of the Nuffield Organization.'* Brutal and insensitive though that may seem we can probably take comfort from the accent being polished and that there was no swearing. In his autobiography, *Out on a Wing*, Thomas then launches into what most would find a repellant diatribe on his technique for firing high-level executives.

To what extent the 'Albemarle contract' caused Kimber's dismissal is uncertain. Rene had died in April 1938 and three months later, with the approval of his daughters, their father secretly married his lover.

Jean said afterwards: *'Gillie (her stepmother) had all the* joie de vivre *that poor Rene had lost. He (Kimber) used to be so grim, so stern. I can remember him sitting there for ages, not saying a word. He changed so much after he married my stepmother. I loved Gillie on sight. She was very good for him. Liberated him. He was more relaxed, happier'.*

This, of course, would not have met with the approval of Lord and Lady Nuffield, especially the latter. What had happened was more than 'bad manners' to coin Thomas's earlier phrase; or even bad form.

It is also reported (by Jonathan Wood in *The Automobile* article) that Kimber had transgressed further by refusing to fire a conscientious, unmarried, female employee because he knew of the dependency of her widowed mother. But the precise circumstances are unclear.

The moralistic comment should be, perhaps, not to make an assessment at face value; something Leonard Lord has been subjected to, so many times. We should not judge Lady Nuffield too harshly either, even if she *did* have a hand in Kimber's dismissal. She was a Victorian and unquestionably held the values of that age. Kimber is said to have flaunted his extra-marital relationship at a time when he had not only left the wife who had been his rock when he was struggling to get MG underway, but also departed when she was dying. The words of the Christian marriage vows probably passed through Lady Nuffield's mind.

After his departure from Morris, Kimber went to coachbuilder Charlesworth who were reorganizing for wartime aircraft production in Gloucester and then, his health breaking, to a job with the Specialloid Piston Company that he didn't particularly relish. *'Cabbage isn't good boiled twice, Gillie,'* he was prone to say. Or, to paraphrase, *'the motor industry is not as palatable second time round'*.

But by 1944, fitness and happiness were returning. There was talk of work from Harry Ferguson, of tractor fame, and at Triumph to build sports cars, and even of retirement. But on the Sunday evening of February 4, 1945, that malevolent hand of fate he had sidestepped before to find reward, caught Kimber.

The train taking him to a Monday morning meeting with diesel engine maker Perkins at Peterborough, on behalf of Specialloid, stalled in the steam drenched darkness of the notorious tunnels above London's Kings Cross station. Mishandling allowed it to run gently backwards. A signalman shifted his points to divert it from the main line, but a second too late. The last carriage derailed against a signal gantry. Cecil Kimber was one of the two passengers who died.

As Leonard Lord left MG in what would then have been the rustic Oxfordshire town of Abingdon after those visits of 1935 and '36 and returned to Cowley, there were philosophies developing that would have a profound influence on his own career.

William Morris was of the view that the privately owned light aeroplane could become as popular as the privately owned light car. He was not alone in this. Herbert Austin, who had vastly more experience of aeroplanes, dating back to a somewhat eccentric interest in pre-Wright days, and maturing in the development and large-scale production of aircraft in WWI, was of a similar opinion.

Austin, though, was more realistic, but even so, ahead of his time. He had experimented with a machine called the Whippet in 1919. With no bracing wires, no wood and a 16-foot fuselage made of steel tube, it was aimed at simplifying flying for the lay person. Furthermore, because of folding wings it could be accommodated in a shed 18 feet long by eight high and eight wide. Landing speed was just 30 mph and the plan was the fortunate (*sic*) owners would put it down on about 150 yards of grass near their home, collapse the wings that spanned 21 feet, then taxi along the highway to the shed-cum-garage-cum-hangar.

It was claimed by an experienced RAF instructor that he could teach anyone to fly a Whippet in 10 minutes, whereupon the newly qualified flyer could reach 95 mph, soar to 10,000 feet in 18 minutes and cover about 180 miles on two hours worth of fuel for the six cylinder Anzani rotary engine. To be fair, the machine proved stable, comfortable, reliable and simple to service.

Just what Morris envisaged? No. The Whippet flopped. To quote Bob Wyatt in his seminal work on Austin history (*The Austin 1905-1952* David and Charles 1981) ' . . . *not because the machine was in any way unsatisfactory or because of heavy competition, but because amateur flying did not catch on and people with money to spend in the immediate post-war period, even though they all seem to have disposed of it by the time of the slump which followed, certainly did not spend it on Austin aircraft.*'

Austin had one last attempt. The Kestrel was a Beardmore powered, steel tube fuselage aeroplane that could cruise at 80 mph at 3,000 feet for four-and-a-half hours consuming a gallon of fuel every 32 miles. But it landed fast (for this market) at 45 mph and needed 220 yards to stop. It didn't take off in the marketplace either. Yet it did not suffer the final indignity of the Whippet whose left over parts ended up as a pergola in Austin's son-in-law's garden.

Typically, Morris had a different approach. He wanted to build only the engines for aeroplanes. In 1933 he is quoted as saying, and I summarize: '*As the aeroplane improves and becomes safer, so it will be more popular as a means of transport, and the more aeroplanes that are sold, the more reasonable their prices will become. This also applies to the cost of the engines. I have no wish to build aeroplanes myself. I am just out to sell engines. There is no big demand for engines at the moment, but it was because we realized that the sale of aircraft would gradually climb—as did the sale of motor cars—that we decided it was time we set out to design engines for manufacturers. It might be true to say that the aeroplane is today where the motor car was in 1914. Where aeroplanes are sold in sufficient quantities, there is no reason why they should not be as cheap as the light car today*'.

A few statistics might be helpful. In early 1925 a de Havilland Moth biplane could be bought for £885 and was advertised as being for '*the school, the flying club and the private owner*'. The public imagination was first captured when a pilot called Alan Cobham took the prototype from Croydon aerodrome to Zurich, Switzerland, and back in a day during which he spent a total of 14 hours in the air.

Matters were helped considerably when around the same time the government, not for entirely altruistic reasons one suspects, decided to subsidise five light aeroplane clubs. They each got two Moths, a spare engine, £2,000 to spend, a guarantee that half the cost of replacing a crashed aeroplane would be met, plus a £1,000 grant for the first year to cover general expenses and a £10 bonus for every pilot who learned to fly using all this equipment. Over the next 11 years the scheme was developed and expanded.

By late 1927 de Havilland had 43 per cent of the light aircraft market and economies of scale had allowed the Gipsy Moth, now described as *'the motor car of the air'* to be reduced in price by £150. A year later the tag nose-dived by a further £80.

To capitalize on all this airborne activity, Morris instructed Wolseley in 1929, to develop a range of air-cooled radial engines suitable for light aircraft. Engineer Edward Luyks, who had been taken over with the company when Morris acquired it, was in overall charge of the 60-strong department. James Woodcock who had served his apprenticeship with the firm, and also been absorbed in the take over, was placed in charge of production.

Lord, who, of course, was works manager, reputedly told Woodcock when he pointed out he had never been near an aero engine that *'it's about time you bloody well were!'* We might wonder when *Lord* had been *'near an aeroplane engine'*! Almost certainly 'Coventry Ordnance'.

Barely a year later, a further boost to private flying came when a 27-year-old from the north of England, Amy Johnson, flew in a second-hand Gipsy Moth from Croydon to Darwin, Australia. Morris presented her with an MG 18/80, which she used to go to Buckingham Palace to receive a medal. Then she waxed incredibly lyrically about flight: *'You who fly; do tell your friends of the joys you experience in the air, of the exhilaration of knowing yourself free and alone in the glorious freedom of the skies, of the wonders to be seen. Show them by your example as a fine, careful pilot, how safe it is to fly a machine so shining clean and well cared for as your own'*.

Then she came down to earth with a bump, but in terms that would have pleased Morris. *'Flying is still pretty expensive because it is as yet a luxury for the minority instead of the pleasure of the majority. Think aviation, talk aviation, read aviation and if you're determined enough your chance will come'*.

By the early summer of 1931 the first Wolseley aero engine was ready. It was a seven-cylinder radial and made its maiden flight from Brooklands in July installed in a Hawker Tomtit. A nine-cylinder version was also developed and flew in the same Tomtit (G-ABOD) on the first day of September, 1932. Teams of three such aircraft then competed with moderate success in the 1933 and '34 King's Cup Air Race and by 1936 the company had a range of four radials on offer. They were all named after signs of the zodiac—Aquarius, Aries, Scorpio and Libra and spanned power outputs from 168 bhp for the seven-cylinder Aquarius (the only model to this configuration, the other three had nine cylinders) up to 505 bhp for the Libra.

Although the engines are interesting in themselves, proved reliable and were backed by a committed customer care, service and spares operation, what is most significant to our story is a quote from Nuffield where he says: *'I put up the aero engine factory because I realized that, in time of national emergency, firms with experience of building internal combustion engines might be called on for national defence, and I wished to play my part'*.

This leads us to the thorny area of Morris's involvement, or rather lack of, with the Shadow Factory Scheme. Later, we will need to look more closely at this concept because it is pertinent to the story of Leonard Lord. But for the moment it is sufficient to understand that this was a British government plan, devised in the mid-'30s and in anticipation of a war with Germany, to, firstly, facilitate the urgent expansion of the RAF, and then, if and when hostilities began, to guarantee an adequate supply of aeroplanes.

The idea was to rely on approved types of aircraft and engine from established suppliers, for example the Bristol Aeroplane Company and Rolls-Royce, but also to boost output by using firms outside the industry. They would work from new, dedicated factories to supplement, or 'shadow', the production of the established 'names'. Examples of the 'shadows' were Austin, Daimler and Rover and, at first and perhaps the exception, Wolseley Aero Engines Ltd.

However, there was controversy as to whether the best way forward was for the 'shadowing' firms to make the complete, ministry approved, engines that had previously been the staple business and exclusive domain of the core organizations, or if it was preferable for the 'shadows' to make sets of components—crankshafts from one, superchargers and pumps from another, etcetera.

From as early as 1933, Wolseley's managing director, Leslie Cannell, on behalf of William Morris, had been trying to interest the air ministry in the company's engines and had been fairly firmly rebuffed: *'I think it improbable we will be in a position to utilize either of the types of engine you describe in your letter,'* wrote an unnamed civil servant.

Cannell and Morris persisted and the correspondence grew chillier and more displeasing to the latter. I paraphrase a rebuttal that is typical: *'It is a matter of the greatest difficulty to provide the four engine firms already under contract, except for one which also relies on civil work, with enough to keep them employed. It is unlikely, therefore, that anything can be done to consider any engine of your design for Royal Air Force purposes.'* The reaction seems to slam the door unnecessarily on a valuable manufacturing resource!

Having, in July, 1935, asked for a meeting with the newly appointed air minister, Lord Swinton and been snubbed, Morris and Cannell did actually meet Swinton, and his adviser, Lord Weir, and Air Marshall Sir Hugh Dowding, air member (at the ministry) for research and development, towards the end of that year. However, matters were no more harmonious.

The point that Wolseley engines, with the possible exception of one under development (the 600 hp Gemini), were considered broadly unsuitable was driven home and Morris's suggestion that he make American Pratt and Witney engines for them under licence was not at all to the men from the ministry's liking. Thus it ended with Morris walking out with the words: *'God help you in case of war'*, and going off in a huff to Australia for four months.

While he was away, discussions on the shadow factory scheme gathered momentum. The policy of component rather than whole engine manufacture was broadly agreed and a committee, chaired by Herbert Austin (Now Lord Austin), appointed to liaise with the air ministry. Included on this panel was Leonard Lord.

It is not easy to understand how Lord now views himself . . . is he the diplomat, is he duplicitous, or is what follows an example of irrepressible ambition?

As soon as Morris arrived home in early May, 1936, he made it plain he disapproved of the shadow factory scheme—something his senior executive, Lord, had 'signed up' for—clear that he wanted to supply the ministry with finished engines and obvious that he believed any other production policy was beset with practical problems.

Almost immediately he revealed to the ministry, and Lord Austin's aero engine committee, just how out of touch he was. Morris, via a letter from Cannell, offered to build large quantities of Bristol engines at Ward End for the same price the ministry were paying the originator. He seems oblivious to Bristol having insisted that no company should have sufficient access to their designs to enable them to become a rival. Indeed, this dictate was probably the most important catalyst in establishing the 'components only' strategy in the first place.

Cannell, that is to say, William Morris, was rebuffed yet again and in a desperate bid to introduce some order to the situation Weir met Morris on June 16 and expressed concern that the latter did not seem to grasp how the ministry envisaged utilizing his production capacity. It was suggested that Leonard Lord show Lt Col H A P Disney, director of aeronautical production, what was available at both Morris and Wolseley. Lord, in the supposedly uncharacteristic role of diplomat, is now 'on the back foot'.

However, he tactfully points out, we suspect with no authority from William Morris, that while Wolseley is prepared to take part in the shadow factory scheme on the terms agreed by the aero engine committee, they would prefer to build complete engines.

This observation prompted Swinton to call a meeting with the committee on June 29, 24 hours in advance of their visiting the Bristol Aeroplane Company to view the components of a Mercury engine and be assigned the parts their companies would make. Swinton sought an assurance everyone was in agreement that: '*the only safe and practical scheme is for each firm to manufacture one section of the aero engines only*' and warns, perhaps pointedly, '*it would be a most serious matter if a mistake was made and an unsuitable plan adopted*'.

We next hear the gruff voice of committee chairman Lord Austin, 66-years-old, tired physically if not mentally. He affirms that although there was room for difference of opinion between the selected 'shadows' and that some, including the Austin Motor Company, would have preferred to make complete engines, he recognized such a course '*would not have secured the objects in view*'.

Leonard Lord then weighed in, and if he'd been on the back foot a few days earlier, he was now about to shoot himself through it. He said he thought the output required was most likely to be secured by specialization—the simplest and most direct strategy. He added that he had little doubt Wolseley would participate, but just for the moment this agreement was provisional as he needed to consult Morris. But back in diplomatic mode and taking a position that was not career limiting, he suggested the air ministry cover its options by obtaining engines '*from another source as well*'. One presumes that means, completely assembled and from Wolseley.

Lord did not linger in London to set out for Bristol and the factory visit the next day, but hurried back to Cowley to consult Morris, as he had promised.

The next morning he phoned Swinton with the news that would embarrass all: '*Lord Nuffield has decided Wolseley Motors will not co-operate in the shadow scheme*'.

Thus Swinton was forced to put a dampener on the day out at Filton when he sent a message to the Bristol Aeroplane Company and their guests from the aero engine committee telling them to '*proceed on the basis that Wolseley Motors would not co-operate*'.

Lord had compromised Morris and compromised himself. It was June 30, 1936. Before the summer was out he would do so twice, maybe three times, more. There is no question Lord's behaviour is puzzling and we see him next in a role that could very obviously lead to career suicide at Morris.

As soon after the Filton bombshell as July 7, he attended a meeting with Lords Austin and Weir where he advised the assembly that Morris had apparently changed his mind. The deal Lord tried to strike was for the air ministry to buy from Morris Motors a factory in Coventry and set it up as a shadow plant, whereupon they could again count Wolseley 'in'.

It is not known for certain which was the works in question, but it seems likely to have been the old Hotchkiss factory in Gosford Street that had subsequently become the home of Morris Motors Ltd Engines Branch. At the relevant time the latter were vacating for new premises on the city's Courthouse Green. Neither are we aware if Lord, who would have known Gosford

Street intimately, was the sole brain behind this piece of fast footwork or whether Morris was also privy to the proposal.

The next day Weir discussed the idea further, not only with Lord, but Morris himself; then rejected it. Predictably, if not petulantly, Morris responded that he did not want to take part in the shadow factory scheme. He did however, and for what it was worth, give it his blessing.

That was not quite the end of the matter. Not long after Weir's rebuttal the aero engine committee suggested Wolseley made some of the required parts at Ward End and also erected and tested engines.

Lord bided his time. We cannot countenance the idea he was consulting Morris. Then, on August 7, he phoned Disney (the air ministry's director of aeronautical production, you will remember). Wolseley Motors Ltd are definitely coming into the shadow factory scheme, he said, and went on to again suggest the ministry took over the Coventry works. When that was turned down a second time he agreed to establish instead, a similar facility in Birmingham. It was further agreed one of Disney's team would come to Ward End to make the detailed arrangements and on August 14 Lord submitted his plans for the building and equipping of a factory.

All of this must have been without the approval of Morris. Surely it was a policy Lord could not hope to survive. But why was he so determined to involve Morris, or perhaps himself, in the shadow factory scheme?

We must wait and see.

CHAPTER SIX

WHO, WHO, WHO'S YOUR LADY FRIEND?

Long before the days when scandal, sexual tittle-tattle and voyeurism became the stock in trade of the popular media, anyone who was interested enough to read anything at all about Leonard Lord, and there were few enough, learned, rather prosaically, that he left Cowley because of a financial dispute with William Morris.

We of that first post-War generation, if we fell into the 'interested' category, believed it. It was plausible.

Lord had restored Morris's market share and by virtue of the 'Eight' made the company Britain's best selling car manufacturer. The value of sales rose from £11,380,000 when he arrived in 1933, to over £21,000,000 in 1936, with the firm well on the way to being the first motor maker in the country to produce the magic million vehicles (achieved on May 22, 1939, with a Morris Fourteen). All the objectives on that 'mission statement'—revitalize the model range, modernize the plant, help resolve the tax liabilities and streamline the structure, and improve profitability—had been realized. Into the bargain, Lord had pledged to stay to witness one year of both peak profits and output. Already Cowley was the largest and most advanced automobile works in Europe with a production capacity of 2000 vehicles a week. Profits for the Nuffield Organization as a whole stood at £2,000,000.

There was still more. Even though some fell by the wayside when Lord strode into Cowley, he infused much-needed new blood. Robert Boyle, who had been a colleague at 'Engines Branch', became chief engineer. Boyle signed a young man from Humber, named Alec Issigonis, to work in the drawing office. Shortly afterwards, the brilliant draughtsman William (Jack) Daniels, at a loose end after the closure of MG's in-house drawing office, joined the same team. And it is worth re-emphasizing that Lord's centralization of design at Cowley, and insisting MGs be essentially derivatives of Morris models, led to the recovery and long-term survival of the sports car maker. The same rules applied to Wolseleys.

Whether you prefer to call it financial acquisitiveness or simply greed, in the realms of capitalist industrialists, it 'goes with the job'. Although Lord was not yet a captain of industry, he was heading in that direction. No surprise then, that he would ask William Morris for a rise and, as has been suggested in some quarters, a royalty on the Morris Eight. Herbert Austin had applied a similar strategy with the Seven. It is not inconceivable this was how Lord came by the idea.

There is an account in Peter King's *The Motor Men—Pioneers of the British Car Industry* (Quiller Press 1989) of the supposed financial aspects of Lord's departure. However, the sources are not disclosed and the version is not entirely factually correct.

'*Each year, when Morris had to set Lord's salary, the latter would embarrass his boss by asking for whatever Morris thought he was worth, rather than stating an actual figure*', suggests King. He adds: '*each time, he thought that the figure Morris settled on was an under-estimate. The crisis came in 1936 when Morris wanted Lord to take over* (running) *the entire Nuffield empire including Wolseley, MG and "Morris Commercial". This time Lord asked for a share in the business and Morris would not agree*'.

As we know, this could not have been precisely the situation, because by 1936, as managing director, Lord had already 'taken over' MG and Wolseley. Although, of course, he may now have been asking for a cut of the profits.

Morris Commercial Cars Ltd was transferred in October 1936 along with Morris Industries Exports Limited and the SU Carburetter Co Ltd. Therefore, if King is right, the cataclysmic rupture was over profit sharing and the management of 'Morris Commercial' and two relatively small fry; and Morris and Lord were both sufficiently foolish to quarrel on that basis. But '*Morris treated him* (Lord) *like a son*', King reports. I don't think so. What is beyond any doubt is that on August 24,1936, Leonard Lord left Cowley.

It does not seem to have been before about 1984 that another story started to be circulated. At first 'rumour', then 'an open secret' (at Cowley) and finally, and where my analogy at the start of this chapter is relevant, becomes '*in all probability, the real reason for his departure*'.

If it was Helen of Troy whose face was said to have launched a thousand ships, whatever a young female tracer[*] in the Morris Motors drawing office lowered, raised, or removed for Leonard Lord—*if she did*—changed the course of British motoring history and perhaps much else besides. There are those who are prepared to name the lady concerned and others to vouch for her physical charms. Because, at the time of writing, it is just possible she is still alive, I will refer to her only as Miss W. The story that seems to have emanated first from an Aberdeen Morris dealer, named Shinnie, is that late one evening, Morris returned to the Works and Lord's office, complete, no doubt, with the flickering coal fire the latter cherished, to discover him in a highly compromising situation with Miss W—his 'secretary' in the Shinnie version. An 'almighty row' is said to have ensued and Lord did not 'resign' but was dismissed.

Other peripheral circumstances that are reputed to have contributed to Lord's departure are relations with senior colleagues that were far less intimate than those he allegedly enjoyed with Miss W.

Miles Thomas was supposedly told: '*big as Cowley is, it isn't big enough for both of us*' and he transferred to 'Morris Commercial' as general manager. In reality the remark may not have the significance in terms of arrogance that some commentators read into it. Boden, still at Wolseley, had already solicited Thomas: '*are you still happy at Cowley?*' To which the response had been, words to the effect: '*it isn't the same as before LPL* (Lord) *took over*'. Just as well, we may muse. And were we to add a simple interjection or expletive, like '*eh?*', at the end of Lord's alleged

---

[*] For those not familiar with engineering, tracers copied the drawings of components onto translucent paper and sometimes dimensioned the parts. The translucent sheets were then placed on a machine to create what was, quite literally, a blueprint. These were then passed to the process workers who would make the individual items. Middle-aged spinsters were common in the tracing department but also young women, often from middle class backgrounds. The craft died out in the 1950s.

remark, possibly after having been told about the approach from Boden we have a kindlier, less high-handed tone altogether: '*big as Cowley is, it isn't big enough for both of us, eh Tommy*'?'.

Arthur Rowse went at this time. He had been the 'war only' Midlands superintending engineer for the ministry of munitions at the time of the mine sinker, way back in 1916, and was then recruited by Morris. Yet there is no evidence to suggest that his departure was anything particularly to do with Lord. More likely, it was William Morris's propensity to quarrel with those who had served, and could serve, him, best. But it probably didn't help that Rowse, like Lord, was a brilliant production engineer and Whitworth Scholar** to boot.

And we should not forget that Rowse, an ideal internal candidate to become Morris's deputy, was passed over in 1924, when the incumbent, Lancelot Pratt, died of cancer on April 19 that year, aged just 44. The unhappy alternative choice was Edgar Blake from Dunlop. That would not have endeared Rowse to Morris. Perhaps removing Blake to install Lord *was* the final straw, but the situation was not directly of Leonard Lord's making.

Incidentally, Frank Woollard had gone in 1931. He was an avid admirer of Lord and still running 'Engines Branch'. Incredible though it may seem, he was another victim of Lord and Lady Nuffield's impeccable morals. Ousted, it would appear, by an illicit love affair.

A 'Lord dissenter' we can be sure of is Harry Seaward. He had been a director of Morris Motors since 1927 and took over the sales function when Thomas left for Adderley Park and 'Morris Commercial'. Seaward was asked his views on the line of succession by Wilfred Hobbs—he who: '*told "the boss" everything it was necessary for him to hear*'. Hobbs then wrote to Walsh, the company solicitor: '*Mr Seaward is rather worried because he knows he is not* persona grata *with the managing director* (Lord) *and supposes, correctly I think, (my emphasis) that if such an occurrence did arise* (someone having to take over from Morris—my insertion) *he would be speedily invited to pass in his checks. I have mentioned the matter to Lord Nuffield who is sympathetic but, like me, is a bit hazy as to how to arrange protection . . .* '

These peripherals apart, it is time we reviewed the circumstances, actual or supposed, surrounding Leonard Lord's departure. There are several possible triggers.

Firstly, Lord was clearly at variance with Morris over the overall concept of the shadow factory scheme (covered only in this context in the last chapter) and wanted to be involved with it, irrespective of differing views among the participants. Yet, he had a well-paid, highly influential and extremely prestigious job that must have equated, at 38 years of age, with even his enormous ambition. On first impression, it seems inconceivable that he would want to be placed in a position where he might have to resign, or even be dismissed.

A supplementary point, however, thickens the plot. Lord must have known, taking into consideration Morris's petulant and frequently stated views on 'shadow' policy, he could not possibly survive his on-going offer to the Air Ministry of a Morris factory in Coventry for use in the scheme; even less so, his agreement to run an alternative site in Birmingham.

So we must suspect he may himself, have been honing the sword on which he would fall.

The second flash point, of course, is that of remuneration. William Morris was a renowned cost analyst. '*His best asset was his nice appreciation of price and costs. Basically, he was a buyer and*

---

*   A nickname for Miles Thomas.

**   Sir Joseph Whitworth was the British engineer who, in 1841, proposed the Whitworth thread system. Perhaps even more importantly, he introduced more accurate measurement in engineering (to 0.0001" instead of one sixteenth!). In 1868 he funded scholarships that are still available to further the advancement of talented apprentices.

a very acute buyer indeed'. Dealers paid cash for their cars and suppliers worked on credit. Morris estimated it took about six days to assemble an early Oxford or Cowley and he could obtain 60 days 'grace' from the component manufacturers. The original business was, in the main, on a sound financial footing.

Similar philosophies must have gone through Morris's mind at the time of the 'Eight'. What Lord was proposing may have thrown the sums out of kilter, not only for the small car, but perhaps other parts of the business. Furthermore, Morris was an extremely good payer. Lord's salary has never been disclosed, but research by Peter Seymour (*Morris Light Vans 1924-1934* and *Wolseley Radial Aero Engines* P & B Publishing (1999) and Tempus Publishing (2006) respectively) to whom I am extremely grateful for much of the information in this and the previous chapter, cites Carl Skinner's salary by way of comparison.

Skinner was part of the 'S' in SU (Skinners' Union). Thomas Carlyle Skinner and his older brother, George Herbert, of the Lilley & Skinner shoe shop empire, established their carburetter company in 1910. It was taken over by Morris on December 1, 1926, after George had pulled out. Carl ran the business from then on and in the Morris reorganization of 1935/36 became managing director. At that point he was paid £6,067 per annum in salary and bonuses. (Roughly £250,000 at today's values).

Lord held a much more senior position than Skinner so we can conclude his payments were enormous.

By way of a final example of Morris's generosity over salaries, the presence of the works in Cowley actually created a micro-economy in the wider Oxford area, not popular in some quarters. In the first instance, wages in the car factory were sufficiently high to inflate the accepted rate, not only in other local industries, but also across the board, including for unskilled labour. Secondly, because the Works' catchment area was so wide (as far afield as Reading, about 30 miles away), the high spending power of the Cowley workforce was dissipated.

Already we have a number of possibilities. Either Lord was being influenced by forces outside the Nuffield Organization or he was being extremely greedy, although there is no evidence that avarice was one of his vices. He demonstrates this years later when he is quite prepared to forego a generous gift of Austin shares.

If money *was* the dominant factor he could have been seeking, at one level, to compensate himself for being thwarted over the shadow factory scheme and, at another, for something more personal, which we will examine in due course. So, with this in mind, did he go for the 'jackpot and to hell with it'? Heed the word 'jackpot', because he actually uses it later, although the phrase I use here, is my invention.

A third possibility is, quite simply, he *wanted* to leave. Rid himself of the promise he had made to stay for a year of peak profits and output; change direction—as Andrews and Brunner (*The Life of Lord Nuffield*) have it: '*he had begun to think of a break from active management*'—although we may have our suspicions that the wind of change was blowing from a different direction. It is even conceivable he wanted to get out because of the personal reasons I alluded to a moment ago and to which we will return.

In reality though, what he asked of Morris, if anything, during those financial negotiations, was more likely to have been driven by a desire for power, and especially status rather than money. We cannot discount either that, in today's vernacular, William Morris was a control freak. That was largely the reason he quarrelled with almost all his lieutenants, however loyal or valuable they were, and there can be little doubt, the most valuable of all was Leonard Lord.

Consider the evidence; Morris was fortunate enough to secure an apprenticeship, in 1892, at a bicycle shop in St Giles, Oxford. He fell out with the proprietor, ironically over his pay, and, rather dishonourably, left to establish a rival business. After an enterprising period on his own in the cycle trade, he began building motorized versions and took his friend, Joseph Cooper, as a partner. They soon disagreed over financial policy and Morris bought his associate out. On this occasion, it does genuinely seem to be the case that they remained on good terms. Cooper eventually had a career at Morris Motors, albeit on the shopfloor.

A further alliance in what, to all intents and purposes was a garage business, followed, this time with a wealthy undergraduate and a local businessman in tow. That relationship failed too.

Matters were no better when Morris started building his own car. One of the largest investors was the Earl of Macclesfield, who was a motoring enthusiast and supported the company to the tune of at least £17,500. Unfortunately, Macclesfield was interested in how his money was being spent and a situation soon developed that parallels what may or may not have happened to Lord. The Earl liked to visit the works and chat with the workforce. On a single occasion he criticized an action of Morris, and, predictably, within a few days was bought out. Others who fell foul of the Morrises were Kimber, and, of course, Rowse and Woollard.

Supporters of Morris will, by way of contradiction, cite Lancelot Pratt as an example of someone with whom Morris certainly did not quarrel. Pratt was the co-owner of Hollick & Pratt, a Coventry body builder founded by his father-in-law in 1876. The firm made the coachwork for the Cowley (Charles Raworth & Son Ltd of Oxford only made the bodies for the costlier Oxford and the more exotic styles). From 1919 Pratt managed an independent, supplementary, body works for Morris. After a fire at Hollick and Pratt in 1922 Morris bought the company and Pratt became, effectively, his deputy. As we know, Pratt died two years later, but probably represented the closest Morris ever came to having a close business friend; perhaps the closest to a true friend of any description. It is worth thinking back though to the revelation in chapter one that it was Pratt who rented Riley their Coventry premises. Apart from anything else, by virtue of his wealth as a landowner, he presented no financial threat to Morris. That said and, given the latter's record, it is reasonable to speculate that had Pratt lived, Morris, or his wife, would have disagreed with him also.

People apart, Morris's desire to control businesses verged on the obsessive, although he was wont to say: '*I only buy a concern when they tell me they cannot produce enough of an article for our programme*'.

In addition to Hollick and Pratt (bought in1923), the Coventry branch of Hotchkiss (also acquired in 1923), E G Wrigley & Co Ltd (1924), SU (1926) and Wolseley (1927) all fell into Morris's hands. He also took full ownership of Osberton Radiators Ltd in 1923. This last was a company Morris had invested in in 1919, but bought, when, in truth in this case, it could not '*produce enough for his programme*'. His desire to control personalities and organizations may also manifest itself in the enormous amount of money Morris gave away—at the values of the day about £30,000,000 during his lifetime.

Of course, it does not matter one iota what the motive for his benefaction really was. Millions of people's lives have been enhanced as a consequence and society is still enjoying the fruits of this generosity. However, there would seem to be a controlling element if, for example, we take one of his biggest donations—£2,000,000 in 1936 to establish the Oxford University Medical School Trust.

Morris was of the opinion there should be an anaesthetics faculty, which was not the view of the medical professionals involved. However, the man with his hand on the purse strings pointed out that there would be no school of any description unless he got his way. Oxford immediately became one of the first universities in the world to boast a chair in that speciality.

Against this backdrop, it is not the least surprising Morris quarrelled with Lord. Confronted with such a dynamic genius, it was inevitable. He simply did not have the perspicacity to recognize a natural successor who could have developed and sustained the business his own talents had created.

Of course, all the time, we have Lady Nuffield scheming in the shadows. To reiterate Graham Turner in *The Leyland Papers*: '*Sometimes they* (the subordinates, this author's insertion) *stole the limelight which he or his wife (and Lady Nuffield was an assiduous guardian of her husband's supreme status) thought belonged to him alone*'. Yet, to be fair to Lady Nuffield, she had witnessed, in the very first year of her marriage (1904), the difficulties that had arisen through close association with others and the humiliation her husband suffered—he had to bid at auction for his own tools—when the first garage business failed.

Finally we come back to Miss W.

It would be remiss of us to ignore what sociologists and psychologists have maintained for generations. Presented with a sexual opportunity, however constraining the external circumstances may appear, the naturally aggressive male animal will take advantage of the situation.

It manifests itself, to the misery of millions, in every kind of extra-marital relationship. Therefore, we cannot discount that Lord was simply indulging in male sexual opportunism.

As we have seen, the story of Lord's mistress seems first to have surfaced via the Scottish agent, Shinnie. Lord was no particular friend of dealers. He was the man who said: '*make decent bloody products and you don't need salesman*', so he was likely to have detractors in that quarter. And the Works would have been rife with lewd gossip. To quote Miles Thomas writing a little earlier about a scene we will need to look at more closely in a moment: '*In a rapidly expanding full-bloodedly masculine industry, as the motor trade was in the early 1920s, there was admittedly a good deal of earthy vulgarity. As in any other form of movement to which the human frame is subjected, whether by horse-riding, self induced muscular exercise or the motion of a car, there is a sensory exhilaration in motoring. Good fellowship abounded*'.

The last phrase abounds with innuendo and if Lord was 'involved' at all with Miss W, as well as straightforward libido, there may have been the more complex dimension of sexual power politics. But we inevitably return to shopfloor vulgarity pure and simple, and whether Lord and Miss W were its victim.

To quote from a rather later source than Thomas that refers to Longbridge in WWII, '*a group of ladies from somewhere in London were temporarily employed until improved manufacturing facilities* (for anti-aircraft rocket boxes, my insertion) *could be installed. These ladies were described as rough and ready, not frightened of hard work and had friendly, kind natures . . . They provided a welcome boost to rocket box production and some "professional services" to the local men folk whether at work or during socializing hours*'.

Something similar is perpetuated by Barney Sharratt in *Men and Motors of the Austin* (Haynes, 2000). '*They were made in two halves* (Lancaster bomber fuel tanks, again, my insertion) *and if one started rocking you could guess what was going on inside. Some of the lovebirds found them ideal—much safer than in a cinema in those days*'. I suggest our tongue should be firmly in our cheek when we read these anecdotes.

To add weight to our scepticism with regard to Lord, we need to recognize that as far as all the available evidence indicates, he would have been acting totally out of character. He was 38-years-old with an excellent job, first class career prospects, a growing family and his only marriage stood firm until his death more than 30 years later. And although he was charming to women he was not a womanizer.

From April 1933, when he first moved to Cowley, Leonard Lord had been ensconced in a world of 'mummy's boys'—Thomas, Morris himself according to Thomas, Hobbs and Issigonis. Although in the case of the last, who only arrived in 1935, it would be unlikely, at this stage, that Lord had any real awareness of his existence. And let us not forget. Lord was a 'mummy's boy' himself. Many readers, I am sure, will take exception to my choice of that description. But I use it deliberately for its suggestion of effeminacy and, very faintly, of homosexuality.

If we study Miles Thomas's autobiography, *Out on a Wing*, we discover a level of sexual reference that is, arguably, in excess of what one might expect in a book that is essentially about a captain of industry and his progress and influence on the industrial and commercial scene. Although it was published in 1964, 30 years after the events we are considering, these issues seem very much on his mind.

'*I can conjure up the scene of a fat, rather stupid girl of about nine years old making some cheeky and unnecessarily provocative remark to some kids of her own age who were teasing her. One of the gang darted forward, tripped her up, in a flash there was a flurry of arms and legs, and her clothes were literally torn from her body. Stark naked, she was twirled over and over in the mud until her tormentors saw a teacher approaching, whereupon they all fled like a pack of jackals . . . That was the first time I saw a female form in the nude and realized it was much more tidy and smooth in shape than the male equivalent*'.

There are other accounts, of a sexually provocative schoolgirl, pubescent female bather and a verbal encounter with a prostitute, but the one quoted is apposite. Set in rural Wales around 1906 it is utterly unconvincing and likely never to have happened. But it is unmitigated, heterosexual male fantasy. Of course, I am not suggesting for one moment Miles Thomas was of any other persuasion. But what *is* interesting is all this material is the stuff of male titillation; in the example cited, that experienced by males when observing, for instance, female mud wrestling.

Thus, I would suggest, Thomas, who was born in 1897 and lost his father when he was just a year old and was deeply attached to an extremely indulgent mother, is making, and probably always felt the need to make, a very explicit statement of his heterosexuality. That would have never been more necessary than when he worked at Cowley. Remember his observation: '*a rapidly expanding full-bloodedly masculine industry . . . (where) there was admittedly a good deal of earthy vulgarity*'.

Thomas also makes the rather tenuous comparison between his own life, 'dominated' by his mother, and similar circumstances in that of Morris where '*he had to be the main source of support for his mother*'. While this is broadly true, William Morris's father, Frederick, was a self-taught bookkeeper and actually worked, until he died in 1916, alongside his son as chief clerk-cum-accountant.

Andrews and Brunner say of Morris's mother, Emily (*née* Pether): '*while giving him all the encouragement he required* (she) *left him free to follow his bent. There is no evidence of the dominating mother who is so often supposed to be behind a successful man. Having chosen what he would do, her son could even take over one of her front rooms for his showroom.*' So, in reality, there was marked parental support and involvement and, with more than one front room, a degree of comfort!

Thomas also links himself to Lord via the influence of their mothers. '*He had been another lad with a strong mother fixation*'.

The nature of these relationships seems to be constantly on Thomas's mind. Wilfred Hobbs is described as being '*tremendously attached to his mother*'. So much so that he disliked being out of the country for the length of time his role as Morris's personal assistant demanded. Although his position in the company would have always kept him away from the hurly-burly of that '*full-blooded masculine industry*' with its '*earthy vulgarity*'.

Alec Issigonis's relationship with his mother was almost certainly much more powerful than that of any of the people I have mentioned in this context. This subject and his sexuality are dealt with at some length by Gillian Bardsley in *Issigonis—The Official Biography* (Icon Books 2005). It is of no real relevance to the story of Lord at this point, or indeed later, but some of Bardsley's observations are of value to us.

She points out that, '*It is easy to make the assumption that a single man who has a strong attachment to his mother must be homosexual*' and goes on to say, '*By the beginnings of the 21st century, homosexuality is thankfully no longer regarded by the majority as some kind of perversion, but more than this it has become unimaginable that any person could or would wish to override their sexual urges for any reason. The atmosphere that prevailed during the first half of the 20th century was very different. Homosexuality was illegal until 1967 and the motor industry was a particularly male orientated and intolerant world*'.

It is the last part of the final sentence that is of most importance. If we totally discount any supposition of homosexuality on the part of Thomas, and I most adamantly do so, we find Miles Thomas promoting his *heterosexuality* in one way and Leonard Lord doing something very similar in another.

In essence, I suggest it was at Cowley that Lord's swearing and his abruptness of manner, the macho approach, the manners that were not admired, the hands thrust into his trouser pockets, the cigarette permanently on the lips as the ash was discarded with a puff of his breath, first manifested themselves to any appreciable degree. Purely and simply, they were the defence mechanism of a sensitive man who was deeply attached to his mother, who had worked to provide those 'little luxuries' for her and now sought to make himself as emotionally inviolate as possible in what Bardsley describes as that '*particularly male orientated and intolerant world*' and Miles Thomas knew as full bloodedly masculine, earthy and vulgar. Thomas himself acknowledges this, though not in specific terms. '*His* (Lord's) *apparent rudeness was a protective mechanism*'.

But let us return again to the latter's book because there is material that is, perhaps, even more important.

'*By now Hylda* (his wife, Morris's former secretary*) *and I had entered into the social life of Oxford. As befitted a rising and admittedly ambitious young executive, we had moved to a very pleasant house half-way up to Boar's Hill*'.

'. . . *Largely we younger executives and our spouses had a wonderful time. I would not say that we were patrons of the arts, but we were certainly patrons of the Oxford theatre and had permanent bookings for Saturday nights. We found that we were more popular if we did not arrive until during the interval, instead of lingering over coffee and liqueurs, getting in late and then squeezing past people into our seats*'.

---

* It is of passing interest that Hylda Church was engaged to a wealthy young businessman in the motor trade when she met Thomas and jilted her fiancé for him. I make no judgement on the romantic element, however, it seems surprising neither of the Morrises seem to have had any problem at all with this.

. . . '*In Oxford life seemed rosy*'.

. . . '*We circulated rather like goldfish in a crystal bowl, at weekends dining in each other's houses, playing golf with each other, even in a number of cases going on holiday together. Our wives took tea and had baby talk with each other. As executives of a highly successful business we had to develop a defence mechanism against gatecrashers*'.

And finally, apropos shooting game on farmland and in the woods near Pusey and water meadows alongside the Thames at Kingston Bagpuize: . . . '*Good, safe gunmanship is a latch-lifter to many a coveted social or business circle*'.

Clearly, I am being highly selective in my quotes which are from a nine-page-long passage. The point is, the section oozes smugness, privilege and self indulgence which is reflected also in details from Thomas's earlier life.

Such attitudes would not seem to sit comfortably with the boy from Coventry's Whitefriars Lane and then the Foleshill Road. The partying, pretentious theatre-going, tea sipping, shotgun toting clique do not seem to accord with the mind set of a man who had his school fees paid by the local authority, taught at night school to help fund the household and fought his way from one tool room and drawing office to the next.

Lord was a sensitive being. Although he was almost the top man, those young executives—and the not so young—exclusory, circulating each others homes with their prissy middle class wives, could have hurt him deeply. There would almost certainly have been snide comment about his background, his education and maybe even his lack of a war record*.

And there was undoubtedly considerable jealousy.

Certainly, Taylor and Woollard at 'Morris Engines' had been the brains behind the transfer machines; but it was a young 'Len' Lord who made them work. It was Lord who stormed into Wolseley and in a remarkably short time got a side valve engine into production that was to set the small Morris on the road to success. And it was Lord, aged 36, who hauled Morris Motors back from the brink of financial ruin and saved many of his peers' jobs.

The sorrow is he never completely seemed to rise above the elements in his life we have just examined, or perhaps those we looked at earlier. The *greater* sorrow is the abruptness and irascibility could always emerge and he never seemed to fully set it all aside, and take pride in his enormous achievements.

Lord's departure, quite remarkably, went virtually unnoticed. *Motor* in its column *You'll Be Interested To Know*, told any reader who *was* sufficiently 'interested': '*Quite the biggest sensation in the motor industry for some years is the sudden resignation of Mr L P Lord*'. That was where the 'sensation' ended.

*

Miles Thomas, however, could well have manipulated this. The 'old pal's act' had earned him a post as '*Thomas of The Motor*' just after WWI. He remained with Temple Press as a journalist until Morris wooed him away in 1924. However, he very sensibly maintained his contacts in that sphere, and, with what was, in those days, a suppliant motoring press, might easily have stepped in on Morris's behalf to deflect any embarrassing reportage.

Lord himself is said to have commented on the situation to 'newsmen': '*I was pig headed and Nuffield had his opinions. There wasn't enough room in the boardroom for two lords*'. The timing and

---

* Thomas, for example had driven Lawrence of Arabia-style Rolls-Royce armoured cars in Mesopatamia and later been a stunt instructor in the Royal Flying Corps. His good friend 'Drew' Organ, also on the sales side of Morris, served briefly as a foot soldier and then in the RFC before being taken prisoner-of-war.

context are questionable. Lord hardly, if ever, spoke to 'newsmen', although he occasionally gave private briefings. This comment may have been made later, apropos his renewed involvement with the shadow factory scheme and when he was joining Austin. Ironically though, part of the statement is probably more apposite if transposed—'*Nuffield was pig-headed and I had my opinions*'!

It would have seemed to most, if not to the man himself, that Leonard Lord had passed out of Morris Motors history. As he might have said, in one of his more gnomic utterances: '*the higher you are, the nearer you are to your hat*'.*

---

*   *To Cecil Kimber.*

CHAPTER SEVEN
'BRICK BY BLOODY BRICK'

That Leonard Lord had a passionate dislike of 'Morris' is so vague a generalization as to be valueless to those seriously interested in the man. That he had a passionate dislike of *William* Morris makes no sense at all. That he maintained a vehement dislike of Morris *Motors* and all that Cowley stood for is much more believable.

At the root of any discussion must be, what is probably Lord's most famous (or infamous) remark, and the most frequently quoted, albeit often quite loosely. *'I'm going to take that place* (Cowley) *apart brick by bloody brick'.*

Most of what Leonard Lord is reputed to have uttered was in the hearing of other people. *'If a door isn't open, kick it open'. 'Make decent products and you don't need salesmen'*, etcetera.

But the scene for his most publicized comment is Miles Thomas's office and Thomas is the sole member of the audience. The actual remark he reportedly made is: *'Tommy, I'm going to take that business at Cowley apart brick by bloody brick'.*

So we have to ask, did Lord say it, and, much more importantly, did he mean it?

To dispute that he *said it* is to question the truthfulness of Thomas on a crucial point, and we have no reason to do that. Furthermore, it is hardly a pledge anyone is likely to have invented.

But did he mean it? In the heat of the moment he may have. We all say such things in the immediacy of significant events, but to harbour such sentiments over nearly two decades (1936 to the formation of the British Motor Corporation in 1952) borders on the paranoid.

The 1930s equivalent of 'political correctness' dictates that William Morris and Leonard Lord parted friends and remained so; at least for a long time.

This is Andrews and Brunner in *The Life of Lord Nuffield* talking about what their subject looked for in a manager: *'He said that he thought the chief characteristic was "loyalty". The importance of this feeling of loyalty explains, we think, some difficulties which individual managers have experienced. It accounts for some of the apparent paradoxes: why, for instance, one manager may have felt himself harried at a time when the business might be doing very well, and another may be struck by the fact that he was given complete freedom and not worried at all at a time when much was at stake.*

'Whilst all his managers, of course, have in fact been loyal, he needs a feeling of rapport with them, and the feeling of "loyalty" carries this assurance that they will work with him. That this feeling has often been mutual is shown by the surprising number of executives who have told us that they joined his business without any salary being fixed in advance but knowing that they would be treated quite fairly.

'His most successful managers were those who could divine the way his mind was going in a discussion without his having to spell it out. He often disliked dotting his "i's" and crossing his "t's", but expected his managers to act as though he had'.

Apart from the obsequiousness of the writing, and that we may wish to question the veracity of much of what is being said, we cannot help wonder whether veiled allusions to Lord are included.

Later the same authors assure us: *'The parting* (with Morris) *was due to Lord's personal decision . . . He and Nuffield retained their respect for each other'*. To paraphrase a much earlier writer from the same region: *'Methinks they may protest too much'*!

Peter Seymour tells us (*Wolseley Radial Aero Engines*), from the mouth of Lord: *'There was no row between us. A few minutes after we had decided to break our business relations we had a gin and french* together, and we laughed over the fact we could sit drinking, although we had taken a step that grieved us both'*.

Other sources provide palliatives such as: *'Mr Lord stuck to his resolution of retiring at forty'* or, *'in 1936 Leonard Lord took a very courageous step; he resigned from what was regarded by everyone as a key position in British industry** . . .'* or, *'Lord retired with his family to the Isle of Wight'* but *'remained on good terms with Morris who much admired him'*.

Miles Thomas probably comes closer to the mark in *Out on a Wing* when he reveals: *'His rupture with Nuffield in 1936 hurt him deeply'*. Thomas places the 'brick by brick' quote at a time when, *'the strain and anger of the split were still heavy on him* (Lord)'.

While Graham Turner (*The Leyland Papers*) attributes to an undisclosed Austin source from some years later, the statement that, Lord *'was determined to screw Nuffield into the ground'*. We don't, of course, know whether that is Nuffield the man or Nuffield the organization, although, at face value, it reads like the former.

The Thomas and Turner quotes invalidate some of the smoke screening and obfuscation, call it what you will, but it raises the question—deeply hurt over what? Money; loss of status; his treatment and the attitudes towards him at Cowley? This last issue we have, of course, already attempted to examine.

Even 'deeply hurt' over Miss W.

Peter Seymour goes on to mention that: *'soon after they had agreed to part company'* Morris sent for Lord and said: *'Now that you're leaving me Len, I want you to take this with you'*. He apparently then handed him a cheque for £50,000—a huge sum.

Lord at first turned it down saying: *'I can't take it. I'll take the usual compensation if you like but I can't take £50,000 from you'*.

Morris is then supposed to have retorted: *'Len, if you don't take it, I'll never speak to you again. Our friendship will be over'*.

What the motives are here is extremely hard to gauge. Guilt on Morris's part; or perhaps he is attempting to re-open the door? There is evidence that suggests the latter.

Lord's time, immediately post-Morris, has been portrayed (again, Andrews and Brunner) as: *'what may be described as a sabbatical trip around the world'*. The dictionary definition of sabbatical is: *'a period of leave granted to university staff, teachers etc'*. Thus there is an implication that the links had not been severed and Lord could have returned.

---

*   For those who never lived in style in the thirties 'french' is French Vermouth!

**   It may be of significance that the writer here (Woollard) views Lord as key to 'British industry' not simply the *motor* industry. A theme that ultimately will be developed here.

Unfortunately, the most likely explanation for the use of the word 'sabbatical' is imprecise use of language by the writers. As an example, my earlier quote regarding executive's remuneration has them saying: *'knowing that they would be treated quite fairly'*. The use of 'quite' is clearly ambiguous, although here, the meaning is fairly apparent! Not so with 'sabbatical'. *If* they are applying the term correctly—and I doubt it—we have to ask, did Morris and Lord have a pact about which we will now never know?

What *is* known is that Leonard Lord and his family—wife Ethel, and growing daughters Joan, Patricia and Pauline—all went to live temporarily on the Isle of Wight. Here we witness a strange turn of events that seems to lend further credence to a 'reinstatement' theory.

The *MV Medina* was the first diesel engined ferry of the Red Funnel Line. Periodically, as she beat through the Solent between Southampton and Cowes, her big oil engine chattering and yammering in the background, we would have found Wilfred Hobbs huddled in the saloon.

Later, as the propeller thrashed astern and she came onto her berth, the man who told Morris *'all that it was necessary for him to know'*, but who apparently *'liked Lord'* would head for his former managing director's residence. His mission, to effect a reconciliation between Morris and Leonard Lord.

Not a born driver—*'he hated the long drives up and down* (from his home in Goring-on-Thames) *to the Midlands late on Friday nights and early on Monday mornings'**—the *'wretched'* Hobbs must have veritably loathed these tortuous trips from Oxford to Hampshire and onwards on the *Medina.*

In any event it was to no avail. But what is interesting, if it happened at all, is that it does rather negate the claims of both an illicit affair and a sabbatical. In the first instance, Morris was unlikely to have persuaded his prudish wife to overlook such a transgression and thus be able to open negotiations, and if the second situation was the case, discussion would have been irrelevant. By the same token it validates, to an extent, that the explanation for the departure, expounded over several decades, was money.

As an aside there is an alternative 'take' on the reconciliation talks from Turner (*'Leyland Papers'*). That the man with the messages from Morris was a former colleague of Lord, *'whom he met on holiday in the Isle of Wight'*. The sentence, again, is so fuddled as to leave us wondering whether it was Lord, the other party or both who were on vacation, but I think we can safely discount the whole episode.

As no compromise was possible and we dismiss the 'sabbatical' allusion, we might suppose the relationship between these two powerful men was at an end.

The 'Isle of Wight period' has proved extremely difficult to research. When Lord left Morris Motors the family home was Baron's Brow, Rutlins Lane, Headington, Oxford. This was probably their personal property and not owned by the Nuffield Organization.

The consensus among those who are familiar with executive accommodation for Cowley and Longbridge at the time is that that situation continued until Lord actually moved to Austin.

It seems likely, therefore, the residence on the Solent would have been rented and was somewhere Lord, for whatever reason, could spend a period out of the industry limelight. The address though is not now known but there were certainly donkey rides along the beaches for the girls paid for by an ever, if not over-indulgent father.

Lord himself spent part of the next six months visiting various motor plants. As Woollard puts it in the 1955 *Motor* article: *'seeing—studying—learning'.*

---

* The quotes are Miles Thomas's the insertion, for clarity, mine.

Again, there is no information as to whom he actually saw, but Lord could have pulled strings with virtually any car manufacturer or engineering company in the world and a reasonably safe guess would be, in America, Ford and Continental.

His links with Ford dated back to the early '20s when one of their engineering chiefs had been so complimentary about Taylor's transfer machine. In addition, the engine of the Morris Eight owed much to the rival Ford.

The relationship between Morris and Continental also went back to the immediate post-WWI years and there would have been much of interest to see and study in the Michigan plant.

Other possible hosts, closer to home, may have been Citroën and Renault. The former were using the latest production line techniques at their plant on the banks of the Seine and, of course, producing the ground-breaking, front wheel drive, independently sprung, monocoque *traction avant*. While Renault, at Boulogne-Billancourt, on their liner-shaped island just downstream from Citroën, could have been another attractive port of call as they were beginning to introduce transfer machines that were, eventually, to become very interesting indeed.

It may even be that Lord's choice of accommodation on the Isle of Wight was no more significant than its proximity to the port of Southampton.

All that is certain is that Leonard and Ethel Lord made one, month long, trip to America. They left for New York on the *Berengaria* on September 23 and returned to Southampton on the nearly new *Queen Mary* on October 26.

The 1930s were hard and difficult times for the British working class.

Global economic recession had decimated the shipbuilding industry, once the pride of the nation. The same *Queen Mary* that had brought the Lords from New York, had lain for years, abandoned and rusting, on the ways at John Brown's yard on the River Clyde. It was no better in the coal and steel industries. In some areas unemployment was at least 15 per cent.

It was the uncrowned king, Edward VIII, who, on a visit to Merthyr Tydfil, in South Wales, in 1936, saw the plight of the miners and said: '*something must be done*'.

Very little *was* done.

When, the same year as the king's comment, 200 unemployed marched the 300 miles from the Tyneside town of Jarrow to Downing Street, with an 11,000-signature protest petition contained in an oak chest, Conservative prime minister, Stanley Baldwin, was '*too busy*' to meet their representatives. Meanwhile, the Labour Party was disapproving of the crusade and the Trades Union Congress advised its regional councils to offer no assistance.

What *had* been done, in 1934, on this bleak and uncharitable scene, was the creation of Special Areas designated for relief. South West Scotland, South Wales, the North East Coast and West Cumberland were covered. They alone contained 250,000 unemployed.

The basic problem had been identified as an exodus of young, socially mobile, workers to more prosperous areas; for example, the motor manufacturers in the Midlands. This left an ageing, less able, residue behind who needed a high level of support. That in turn led to soaring local authority charges that still only provided low grade amenities in a desolate environment that discouraged the business investment needed.

The Special Areas (Development and Improvement) Act was administered by commissioners. In England the nominee was Sir Percy Malcolm Stewart. He was an industrialist-cum-philanthropist who had been responsible for establishing, in 1926, the Bedfordshire model village of Wootton Pillinge (renamed, more attractively, Stewartby in 1937) to house workers from his London Brick Company site. This was a later variation on developments like Port Sunlight, Bournville and, indeed, the Austin village at Longbridge.

Stewart's management of the special areas scheme was haphazard. In the North East, Newcastle was included while the county of Northumberland, with much higher unemployment, was not. Elsewhere things were as bad. In Wales the coal ports of Newport, Cardiff and Barry were excluded; so was, from the Scottish zone, Glasgow, while most of the total £2,000,000 funding went on public works, especially sewers.

In April 1936 the Special Areas Reconstruction Association (SARA) was formed. This provided loans of up to £10,000 to actually revitalize businesses or start new ones.

For reasons of which we can never be certain, Morris decided to get involved in all this. He was, of course, prone to meddle in government affairs. His League of Industry of 1930-35 that sought to provide tariff protection for British and empire industries and his stance on the shadow factory strategy are two instances.

His Special Areas Trust grew out of the success of a much more modest enterprise called the Subsistence Production Scheme. This helped the unemployed in the coal mining valleys of Monmouthshire in South Wales to establish cottage industries and to feed themselves from their own gardens. Morris had contributed £30,000 in 1933.

A flaw that Morris himself could see in the special areas policy was the constraints placed on the flow of government money. What Stewart described as '*limitations necessarily involved in the expenditure of public money authorized by parliament*'.

Morris bridged the gap with another £2,000,000 that could be drawn on to supplement government funding. The small print called for the aid to be paid back if a business made sufficient money. For the seven-year life specified for the trust the refunds were to be reallocated, but once it was wound up such monies would pass to the King Edward's Hospital Fund for London—one of Morris's beneficiaries.

The appointments Morris made as trustees included Sir Nigel Campbell, who was already a member of the Treasury advisory committee on special areas, and Viscount Portal of Laverstoke whose reports had been instrumental in the government scheme being launched. He was now chairman of SARA and was soon to join the aforementioned Treasury committee and also become chief industrial adviser to the commissioners.

As the Trust's manager on the ground Morris appointed . . . Leonard Lord.

There is absolutely no doubt Lord was the perfect choice. The need was for perception and swift decisive action, and few, if any, in the land could have done better. We might recall the words of Winston Churchill in the House of Commons, around the same time, berating prime minister Baldwin, and the Establishment generally, for being: '*decided only to be undecided, resolved to be irresolute, adamant for drift, solid for fluidity, all powerful to be impotent*'.

But for all Lord's conspicuous talents, it was a strange selection. Even stranger Lord should accept.

Morris had a tendency to seek reconciliation with those with whom he had quarrelled and we suspect these sentiments had already been at work over Lord. Childless and increasingly isolated from his executives, he clearly wanted to be liked if not loved. This gives us a further insight into his benefaction.

However, there is no reason to believe Leonard Lord sought popularity. One might even say it was of no consequence to him! As *Scope* magazine observed in 1947, '*He doesn't give a damn for any man.*' Thus, even if Morris was remorseful over the split with his managing director of just six months before, wanted to compensate and/or silence him still further, and may, even now, have hoped for a return to the fold, there is no reason to think Lord had similar pangs.

Morris paid Lord to manage his Trust out of his own pocket. The sum was £416 13s 6d a month which works out at almost exactly £5000 per annum. By 1937 standards, another huge sum. Lord, though, would not have needed the money. So, if he was not pining for a renewal of the relationship with Morris, what was his motivation? If we consider again his colleagues in managing the trust we might come to the conclusion that he was anxious to raise his profile in government circles. Something that would be of value, as we shall see.

Lord began work for the special areas in January 1937. His job was not only to assess the bids on the grounds of feasibility but also to offer practical and detailed advice on how the business plans could be implemented. In a way, he was the Sir John Harvey-Jones of his age—the ex-chairman of ICI who became a television celebrity in the 1990s through doing, on screen, what Lord now did behind closed doors!

That he was extremely successful is evidenced by the fact that in the first nine months of Lord's management £1,346,000 had been allocated for 43 proposals. One of the strengths of his period in office was boldness and imagination in backing some extrovert plans, and his insistence that the dynamism of the applicants was taken into consideration along with the cold practicalities. Money could also be provided for training, one-off expenses incurred by businesses and for public works.

Among the larger undertakings that got underway were the Weston Biscuits Factory at Llantarnam in South Wales. It received support of £33,000 from the Trust and was opened in 1938 in the presence of Morris, driving an Edwardian Oxford. The factory went on to give the nation the chocolate 'Wagon Wheel' and, as a factory, still exists.

Whitehaven Collieries in West Cumberland had been closed since October 1935 with the loss of 2,500 jobs. It was reopened thanks to the Trust. The Coltness Iron Company were persuaded to take on the abandoned mines in 1937 with an immediate return to work for 400 men carrying out repairs, then 1,000 on coal extraction, and subsequently the full complement of colliers.

The negotiations illustrate Lord's versatility and also the incredible speed with which he could operate. Minister for Labour, Ernest Brown, confirmed the colliery reopening in The House of Commons on March 2, 1937. It is clear from the ensuing debate that it was the Trust's intervention that expedited matters as George Garro-Jones, MP for Aberdeen North, declares, rather churlishly: '*While appreciating aid from any source, may I ask what element of enterprise has been brought in by the Nuffield trustees which could not have been brought in by the government at an earlier stage?*' This clearly implies it was the Trust that tipped the scales.

The value of the exercise was acknowledged by the Minister who said: '*I anticipate that in large measure the problem of unemployment in Whitehaven will have been solved and the hope of prosperity restored to the town and district*'.

This project earned Morris the Freedom of the Borough of Whitehaven, albeit in 1953! Nonetheless, he was, delighted to see the groups of unemployed men disappear from the street corners along with adolescents who had never had a job, and business premises open and thriving.

Other enterprises supported were involved in making clothes, socks, cable and many other commodities new to their respective regions.

The scheme itself underwent a number of detailed changes in 1937. The Special Areas Amendment Act removed the £10,000 limit on loans, provided money for rent and taxes and allowed firms outside the designated sectors to obtain backing.

Yet at the end of the day, the feature of the special areas legislation for which it will be popularly remembered is the creation of trading estates. One of the largest was in the Team Valley, near Gateshead. By 1939 it accommodated 110 factories employing 3,700 people.

By then Leonard Lord had long since moved on.

To briefly re-cap. One of the differences of opinion between Morris and Lord had been over the shadow factory proposals. After much dithering Morris eventually opted out. But just seven weeks before Lord's departure on August 24, 1936, he, and Morris, had offered to the scheme what we believe to be the old Hotchkiss/Morris Engines factory in Gosford Street, Coventry. When the offer was refused Lord continued to negotiate, without the authority of Morris, to the point where, on August 7, he had agreed to run a shadow factory in Birmingham and on August 14 submitted detailed plans for its configuration.

The idea for shadow factories first entered the industrial rather than the domain of formal government at a meeting in September 1935 between Roy Fedden, engine designer at the Bristol Aeroplane Company and Air Marshal Sir Hugh Dowding, the government's representative on aircraft research and development.

Dowding told Fedden that Bristol, because of the relative simplicity of its engines and thus their ease of manufacture, had been chosen as the company whose output would be shadowed, i.e. replicated, by other engineering companies.

The ultimate objective was to expand the RAF in readiness for a war with Germany at an unspecified point in the future. Originally the plan had been to set up a manufacturing infrastructure then hold it in readiness for when the war actually started. But in March, 1936, the Directorate of Aeronautical Production was established under Lieutenant Colonel H A P Disney to begin the production of both engines and airframes.

The shadow factory scheme was to operate on two fronts. The first involved enlarging the factories of those companies already supplying engines to the air ministry—Rolls-Royce, Armstrong Siddeley, Napier and Bristol themselves.

The second initiative would provide seven motor manufacturers with new factories to mass produce 4,000 Bristol Mercury and Pegasus aero-engines in parallel with the Filton firm's own output. Once the anticipated conflict began the premises would provide the nation with useful additional manufacturing capacity.

Even before Disney's department got involved, Lord Swinton, the air minister, had entered discussions with the seven.

The minister had had a varied career personally and politically. Born Philip Lloyd-Greame he changed his surname to Cunliffe-Lister in 1924. This was a family name of his wife's and instilled continuity when she inherited substantial estates from her grandfather. Throughout the '20s Swinton held government posts primarily associated with trade. A change of direction came when Stanley Baldwin took over from Ramsey MacDonald as prime minister in 1935. Baldwin made Cunliffe-Lister, as he now was, secretary of state for air. He held the post for three years, but acted from the House of Lords having surrendered his parliamentary seat for Hendon at the 1935 general election, whereupon he was enobled as Viscount Swinton.

On February 28, 1936 he visited Herbert Austin to explain the shadowing strategy and on March 13 he and Lord Weir met Sir Stanley White, head of the Bristol Aeroplane Company, and his board.

Weir was a Scottish industrialist who had been president of the air commission in 1918 and then, in 1919, minister of munitions. He subsequently came up with the idea of the national grid for electricity supply but was now an adviser on air force expansion and defence policy and requirements.

It was on that February day in 1936 the fly that was to cause William Morris so much grief and irritation first alighted in the ointment.

Swinton uttered some silver-tongued words to Bristol along the lines that they were not undertaking a commercial proposition, but being asked to participate in a national service. He then urged them to co-operate '*frankly and wholeheartedly*' in helping him and Weir accomplish '*their heavy task*'.

White affirmed that he was prepared to support the shadow factory scheme but not to allow other companies to have sufficient information to enable them to compete with Bristol at a later date. Furthermore, past experience had shown that training others to build complete engines was not time effective. If they were organised to produce only parts, disruption to the peacetime output of the shadow firms would be minimized and ultimately the overall policy would have a better chance of success.

This was not the view of Swinton and Weir, or Morris, or indeed, Austin.

Swinton feared that when war came the bombing of a factory making an essential component would hold up production as a whole and Weir felt White's plan was too complex to implement.

The motor manufacturers selected were Austin, Daimler, the Rootes Group's Humber company, Singer, Standard, Rover and Wolseley's aero-engine arm.

Clearly the civil servants and then Swinton had been misleading Morris when they told him in the series of interchanges that began in 1933 that his input was not required. ('*It is unlikely, therefore, that anything can be done to consider any engine of your design for Royal Air Force purposes.*'). If not for whole engines, he could have made a contribution and was 'pencilled in' to do so (via Wolseley), although, ultimately, it never happened.

The motor industry representatives met Swinton and Weir on April 7, 1936. Lord Austin, was of course, already privy to the scheme and, it would seem, already the intended chairman of an Aero Engine Committee formed at the meeting. Also present were Douglas Burton from Daimler, the Rootes brothers, William and Reginald, John Black of Standard, Spencer Wilks on behalf of Rover and Cannell for Wolseley.

At this time distance it is uncertain who attended from Singer, but the most likely candidates are either the chairman, William Edward Bullock, who was about to retire, or his heir apparent Charles Latham. Sir Arthur Robinson and Major George Purvis Bulman were additional members of the government team.

After the plan had been explained the financial arrangements were outlined. The government would build and equip a factory, or factories, for everyone. The companies would provide the staff and management for which they would receive a fee of £24,000 in the first year plus £75 per engine. Once the expansion of the RAF had been achieved the factories would be closed and not start work again unless a war was declared. Extremely flatteringly, only Austin and Wolseley were to be allowed to finally assemble and bench test the engines.

Shortly after the committee was formed, Leonard Lord, who of course was in overall charge at Wolseley, joined, and became embroiled in, the mysterious negotiating we witnessed in Chapter Five. Lord's involvement at this point was short lived because he departed the Nuffield world in August, 1936.

What he left behind in the shadow factory scheme was, initially, six players. Wolseley, as we saw dropped out. Then so did Singer, who were in such a parlous financial state that they could not proceed. That provided five motor manufacturers plus the Bristol Aeroplane Company.

At Morris, Oliver Boden took over from Lord. We might feel there was some ill-judged lack of urgency in the letter he sent to Disney, director of aeronautical production, on August 26, rescinding both his predecessor's offers of a Morris factory to participate in the shadow scheme or his management talents to run an alternative.

Disney sent for Boden to explain himself and the latter suggested an appointment 10 days later. Disney's request was reiterated, we suspect in rather more explicit terms, and the new managing director found himself at the Air Ministry that same afternoon! The outcome was Bristol themselves, and Longbridge, now had to share between them all the final assembly and testing of shadow factory engine output.

While Lord was on his 'fact-finding' tour in America, the factories, basically to a standard design, were being built. Major Bulman described the work as showing magnificent collaboration and goodwill between the firms, *'spiced with healthy rivalry'*.

Daimler received a plant on Coventry's Brown's Lane, Standard's covered a golf course next to their existing site on the city's Banner Lane, Rootes (aka Humber) was out of town at Ryton-on-Dunsmore to the south east of Coventry and Rover at Acocks Green, on the former market garden of the Westwood family, south of Birmingham.

Sheds, sometimes as long as 2,000 ft, were provided as the working space and there was brick built office accommodation positioned, as far as possible, facing a main road. They were either 'north-lit' or had a glass panelled ridge-and-furrow roof. It is interesting that the layout was extremely adaptable and many such buildings remained part of the British industrial scene well into the 1990s.

Austin got what was known as the Cofton Hackett shadow factory or, more commonly, East Works. As at Standard, in Coventry, the plant was adjacent to the existing Longbridge facility. The 23 acres were acquired from farmers in Groveley Lane. They were to the south of the company's WW1 airfield, bordered by the Birmingham-Worcester railway to the east, and the green expanse of Cofton Park in the west.

One of the largest 'shadows' in the country, planning permission was granted by Bromsgrove Rural District Council—they were hardly likely to refuse—as early as April 1936, suggesting that Herbert Austin had been privy to the government plan longer than the other participants.

The budget was £300,000 and some 5,000 workers were drafted in from August of that year to erect the building within six months. It was 1,530 ft long and 410 wide, the structure itself covering 20 acres of the acquired land.

Later there would be an airframe factory covering a further 15 acres. This had a 500 x 190 ft flight shed attached where completed aeroplanes would be housed before test flying.

After their trials the smaller machines began their delivery flights from the Works airfield. Transporters would take larger aircraft to Elmdon airport in Birmingham for final assembly and their maiden flight.

Under the agreed scheme, Austin manufactured crankshafts and reduction gear for the Bristol engines as well as undertaking final assembly and testing. The Mercury VIII, which was the staple (the Pegasus is a long stroke variant), was a nine-cylinder single row air-cooled radial, developing 825 brake horsepower at 13,000 ft altitude.

The engines were assembled on trolleys that could be wheeled along rails to the test cells east of the factory. They were 'run up' by an electric motor for a compression and oil pressure check then, if all was well, sent to another bay for power testing, and to establish if cooling was satisfactory.

Thorough though this may have been, the early days of shadow production were not without their headaches for aero engine committee chairman, Herbert Austin. William Rootes, making superchargers and petrol pumps at Humber, took it upon himself to ignore both Bristol and Bulman and supplement the specified Swiss-made Maag grinders with British Orcutt machines for making the blower gears. The Orcutt machined components started breaking up after about 40 hours of their hundred-hour approval test, wrecking the engines.

As the supply of superchargers dwindled, the output of 75 Mercuries a week required until October 1938 (increased from the 50 specified in March) could not be met and Austin faced an incandescent Bulman who declared no 'shadow' gears could be trusted beyond 10 hours.

Austin was more gung-ho some months later, however, when he was able to tell Swinton, and I paraphrase: '*A test was made by the Bristol Aeroplane Company of two engines, viz, one built entirely by them* (not in their shadow factory*) *and an engine which was assembled out of parts manufactured by members of the Shadow Group. The two engines were totally dismantled, the parts mixed up together and re-assembled and put on test. The test was entirely satisfactory, proving that the work done by the Shadow Group was quite equal to the work being done by the Bristol Aeroplane Company in their normal manufacture. In other words, the parts were interchangeable, justifying the shadow scheme "100 per cent".*'

Much of this—policies, plant, production and problems—Leonard Lord was to inherit.

---

* This would seem to be on or near their main site. There was a Bristol Aeroplane Company shadow factory at Weston-super-Mare but it was not opened until 1940.

CHAPTER EIGHT
OF SONS AND DAUGHTERS

In 1915, a war, futile and far more terrible than the one that was about to start, was raging its bloody path across most of Europe. We must now return to those horrific scenes.

The vicious battle line from Armentières to La Bassée, in the far north of France, became known as the 'forgotten frontier'. It was there on the morning of January 26, 1915, at about 11.30, that Herbert and Helen Austin's only son, Vernon James, took a sniper's bullet through his right breast. He was almost exactly two months past his 21st birthday.

Vernon was about six or seven-years-old when he left the Austin's home—St Anne's, number 31, Sutton Road in the Erdington district of Birmingham*—to board at St Cuthbert's School on Worcester Road, Malvern.

As to why Malvern and why St Cuthbert's we can only speculate. The town, nestling in Elgar's Malvern Hills, would have been comfortably close to home, appealingly gentile perhaps, and then, as now, offered a wide selection of schools.

However attractive, St Cuthbert's has long since disappeared along with its records. It had come to prominence in the late 19th century and overlooked the placid Malvern Links common, which further embellishes that elegant spa with a blanket of green. The school closed sometime in the first half of the 20th century.

As to whether, at the St Cuthbert's stage in Vernon's life, Herbert Austin seriously aspired to eventually handing over the company to him is hard to ascertain. Though this would be the natural dream of any father with an only son—especially in the 1900s. And it would have been practical and logical.

We have some confirmation that this was the case. Ironically, it is in Vernon's obituary, published in the *Birmingham Post* newspaper of May 24, 1915. It quotes remarks by Austin, that, when he reached the age of fifty, he intended to cede power. The intention is also born out by the March 1915 issue of Vernon's senior school magazine, *Canturian,* announcing his death. He is credited with having spent his time *'preparing to take his place in his father's motor works'*

How enthusiastic Vernon himself had been about all this is uncertain, but there is some evidence that for a short time he was working at Longbridge, or was closely associated with it.

The picture becomes clearer as he begins to grow up and take the entrance exam for the King's School, Canterbury. To pass he would have needed to be gifted, but not brilliant. There is no obvious connection between 'King's' and St Cuthbert's. Vernon started at Canterbury in September 1907, for the Michelmas term, but inexplicably left on July 1, 1909.

---

*   The Austins later moved to Bearwood Grove in the same district, then to Lickey Grange in 1910. Vernon would have left home about 1900.

Unfortunately, we know little about his time within those cloistered walls other than that he bore a striking resemblance to his father—there is at least one school photograph to prove this. Also, that '*he was keenly intelligent, of amiable disposition*' and ' . . . *always quiet, reserved and with grit, of which his contemporaries seemed largely unaware.*'

In those days the ethos of the school was 'service and the empire'. Of the 26 students who entered with Vernon no fewer than 23 enlisted for the First World War. One was awarded a Victoria Cross, two the Military Cross and eight went on to become either colonial civil servants or career soldiers.

While the highest academic standards were set, few King's scholars—for the period—entered the Church and we have the distinct impression that the adoption of a business career or in 'trade', as it would have been disparagingly termed, was also discouraged.

Prowess on the games field and participation in the social life of the school was highly acclaimed. The VC, Arthur Fleming-Sandes, was a sports all-rounder and a monitor by the time he left in 1913. Ralph Juckes, one of the MCs, could hardly ever have been out of his sports kit such was his superiority on the rugby and 'fives' fields, at rowing and in the boxing ring. The school captain, Kidson, who, like Vernon, perished in the War, edited the magazine and ran the debating society.

Vernon was none of these things. But he joined the Cadet Corps almost as soon as he'd unpacked and some authorities describe him as a keen golfer. We know he loved horses.

His classmate, Robert Lang, gets the curt reference in the school records: 'Left July 1, 1912. Advertising and Publicity Specialist. Club: Publicity Club of London.

Vernon, but for his military distinction, might have featured even less prominently, as his entry begins: '*Went into business*'.

Even if *Canturian* had not helped us by pointing out in his obituary Vernon's commercial background, and that he was '*becoming an experienced motorist*', the type of enterprise would have been obvious. The mystery, and the relevance, for us, is what direction Vernon's ultimate career was to take.

We know he was interested in motors. Some suggest that a serious looking youngster in a cap, caught in the background of photographs of Austin steering number one car out of the workshop is actually the boy.

Proof positive of his involvement with cars—and the company—comes as late as June 1914 and the Austrian Alpine Trial. The event started in Vienna and involved storming 25 mountain passes along an 1,800-mile route. It is now largely remembered for the performance of the Rolls-Royce of James Radley, which swept all before it including the newly introduced *Turracherhöhe,* or 'terror pass', to take top honours. But there were other participants—78 in all—including five British cars and Vernon Austin.

The latter was *co-driver* in a '20' (OA 4133) entered for Works tester Harold Kendall, who had a distinguished career with Austins in Continental events*. On this occasion they were one of only 14 finishers, covered 7,000 miles without breakdown and registered over 60 mph in the speed test.

---

* Winner in 1910 of the St Petersburg Automobile Club Trophy over a course considered to be the toughest in the world and a further outstanding performance from the same city to Riga in 1912.

Further proof of Vernon's involvement with automobiles, though less specific, comes just two months later, when we discover, again from *Canturian*, '*he was due to sail for Russia to take part in an important motor race* on the very day war was declared'. (August 4).

He is also reported as having spent time continuing his studies overseas in Leipzig and Sweden. This is hazy. Herbert Austin was a Francophile and a lot of his engineering influences came from just across the Channel. Whereas many would argue Germany has joint claim with France for the development of the automobile, it seems likely that if Austin had wanted his son to experience practices in another country he would have chosen France. And there seems to be no revealing information about Sweden unless the sojourn was market driven. Almost from the beginning Austin had courted Russian sales and may have perceived opportunities in another northern European country and sent Vernon to explore the openings in Sweden. Yet this is purely supposition.

At the King's school, as well as his core subjects, Vernon spent time in the army and engineering class. This is interesting because the two fields are not automatically synonymous and we might draw the conclusion he was studying the technical side of soldiering, born out later, to some extent, when he joined an artillery brigade.

We also know that he was one of the first Old King's Scholars to sign for the Special Reserve** and '*devoted a good deal of his time to his military duties*'. More, perhaps, than he did to his motoring. And was it in the army rather than the machine shops and drawing offices of Longbridge that Vernon felt his destiny lay?

He became a reservist around 1911, just two years after he left school. Aged 18 he was given the rank of second lieutenant in the regular army's Royal Field Artillery, gazetted in January 1912. Subsequently he was attached to the 22nd Battery of 34 Brigade.

*

The latter was one of the first units to go to France and by his 21st birthday, on November 21, 1914, Vernon had already seen action at Mons, the Marne and the Aisne and was about to take part in the push to the north—'the race to the sea'.

Around Bassée, losses to mines and snipers were heavy. On that fateful Tuesday, Vernon and his commanding officer, Lt Col Sandilands, coincidentally another Old King's Scholar, had gone forward alone to reconnoitre. It was on the way back, on an open piece of road, that Vernon was shot.

Sandilands held him while he died. The gloom among the 200 men of the battery that the Lt Col described to the Austins was nothing to the despair at Lickey Grange. Herbert Austin's heart was broken.

That Vernon's body was brought back to England indicates perhaps the depth of his grief. The War Office allowed this, providing relatives paid for transport back to the land fit for heroes. However, it was unusual. Mostly the fallen lie with, or near, their comrades.

Herbert and Helen Austin chose St Martin's Church, Canterbury, for Vernon's interment, near his old school. This is not to imply he was particularly happy there or even a distinguished pupil. One view though, is that King's has a claim to being the earliest school in the country and

---

*   This would seem to be a rally organized by the Automobile Club of Russia in conjunction with the Imperial Automobile Club of Moscow and due to finish in that city on August 19. It is reasonable to assume the event never took place.

**   Set up along with the Territorial Army and Officer Training Corps by Lord Richard Haldane while war minister in the governments of both Bannerman and Asquith.

St Martin's the oldest functioning church. As these credentials were under public debate when Vernon was a pupil, Austin may have felt that although his son's future had proved illusory he would be safe forever in the permanence of the past.

Years later, similar motives moved another Old King's Scholar, the author Somerset Maugham, to request that he be buried there too.

As soon after the war as 1919, there were preliminary talks about a union between Austin and Humber and although, of course, it never happened, it might have given Austin the opportunity to play a less pro-active role in a motor company.

A year later there were discussions with General Motors, one permutation of which was buying out Sir (as he now was) Herbert for something in the region of £700,000. Again nothing came of the negotiations and shortly afterwards Austin implied to a journalist that he was unhappy at missing the opportunity for comfortable retirement.

Everything points to a man wishing to be rid of the motor industry, his part of which was bankrupt anyway. Then came a flurry of activity in 1921 when he designed the Seven as a cure for his company's financial ills. The pain of having the precocious teenager, Stanley Edge, as his draughtsman in a room where Vernon had once 'talked cars' must have been intense. Any reluctance to engage in discussion with Edge is one explanation as to why the youngster, without ill intent, but nonsensically nonetheless, thought he was expected to, or being left to, contribute to the actual design.

Later again, in May 1924, Austin proposed a merger between his company, that of William Morris, and Wolseley Motors. Ostensibly it was to rationalize British car output and give the home producer a natural dominance in the face of foreign competition, given the protectionist McKenna Duties were about to be lifted*. That said, it is clear such an amalgamation would be another opportunity for Herbert Austin, personally, to play a less prominent role in the industry. In fact, Austin states at one point in the relevant correspondence: '*Mr Morris would have control of all the share capital and would virtually be in control of a concern capable of meeting any competition likely to be met in the near future*'.

Yet again Austin's plan was thwarted. For a variety of reasons, Morris refused to co-operate. Not least of these was his unwillingness to relinquish total control. It suited him better to seize Wolseley for himself a little later.

At some point in this period Sir Herbert Austin fathered an illegitimate child by his mistress. Who precisely Austin's lover was and when the relationship was first formed is not clear. There are a number of possible candidates.

When the Austins lived in Sutton Road they had a 22-year-old French governess and she must be a strong contender. Also, it may not be entirely coincidental that Helen Austin's health was poor. Her husband alluded to this several times—in a letter to a former Wolseley colleague as early as 1894: '*Mrs A has been ailing for some time, doesn't seem to get strong. She sends her love to Mrs H** and children. She would be pleased to get a line now and then from her so ask her to write soon. It will help to liven her up*'. In May 1895 to a landlady in Bournemouth, with whom the Austins were intending to spend a fortnight's holiday:

'*My wife is not very strong and may not be well enough to leave here on Saturday*'. And in September 1900 to Frank Kayser, friend, and later an Austin Motor Company financier: '*Mrs Austin has a rather unpleasant attack of neuralgia, owing I suppose to the changeable weather*'.

---

* They were lifted by the Labour government in the August but reimposed by a new Conservative administration the following summer.

** Probably Hancock

Another option is Marguerite Vaurigaud, who may well be the same person as the governess. She was originally from the linguistically ambivalent French region of Alsace-Lorraine, and served as Austin's interpreter on his frequent visits to the Continent. These dated back to the Wolseley days. But they increased markedly after 1911 when *Automobiles Anglaise Austin*, with showrooms in Paris, was formed.

Then in 1919 Austin established his tractor factory, at Liancourt, to the north of the capital and around the same time opened a service depot in Belgium. He was also involved in other Belgian enterprises but the details are unclear.

A third permutation is that Marguerite Vaurigaud was in some way connected to the du Cros family. They were heavily involved in the Dunlop company. Harvey du Cros, who became another of Austin's backers, had varied business interests including a Mercedes agency in London and widespread automotive involvements in France. It is highly likely Austin visited him regularly on the French side of the Channel and not improbable that he became romantically involved with a young lady he met as a result.

At exactly what point Marguerite's child was born is also unclear because the birth was almost certainly registered somewhere in France or even Germany[*]. But simple arithmetic and subsequent events suggest it was well before that other 'baby', the Seven, was conceived. In the years prior to that Herbert Austin would, firstly, have been heavily ensconced in war work, and then pre-occupied with the dire financial straits in which he found himself, not to mention designing a revolutionary motor car.

None of this, you may feel, is relevant to the story of Leonard Lord. Only in one respect. The baby was a girl.

I will not name her for the reasons I have adhered to elsewhere. Yet, there is another parallel with Miss W in the momentousness stakes. Had Sir Herbert Austin's illegitimate child been male the whole course of motoring history may easily have been changed and Lord himself faded into motoring oblivion soon after he left Morris.

In the interests of continuity it should be recorded that Marguerite's child grew into a beautiful and elegant teenager in the community where she lived and was referred to by its less discreet members as '*Sir Herbert's little baby Austin*'!

The locale was the Iver/Burnham area of South Buckinghamshire where the mother moved around the mid-'20s. Austin seems to have been the dutiful father, regularly sending his chauffeur to the county with money, having Marguerite, who was now known by an anglophone surname, visit him at the Works—the special mascot fitted to the car sent to collect her, so she could spot the vehicle, still exists—and sometimes visiting her by train. This is from whence the silly story of Austin model types emanating from the places where Sir Herbert had *mistresses* emanates—Burnham, Chalfont, Eton, Harrow, Iver, Windsor! In reality they are the names of stations or places on or around the rail route from Birmingham New Street to the home of his only known lover. Although we must not ignore the fact that the area was from where Austin originated so there may have been an element of nostalgia.

Herbert Austin and Marguerite's daughter married in London in the spring of 1937, the bride's father providing a monthly allowance paid into her husband's bank account.

The mother's love for Austin would appear to have continued to the end of her life. In the 1970s an 'admirer' who we can only conclude was Marguerite, approached the vicar of the 1,000-year-old parish church in Little Missenden and asked if a memorial could be erected.

---

[*]   Alsace was a province of Germany until after the Treaty of Versailles in 1919.

Sadly, the lady died before anything could be done but the money she donated went towards a new vestry and parish meeting room.

Leonard Lord would probably have been highly amused to find himself the 'adopted son' of two of Europe's leading industrialists! It is Peter King (*The Motor Men, Pioneers of the British Car Industry*) who has William Morris '*treating him like a son*'.

Clearly we cannot know whether in his heart of hearts Herbert Austin viewed Lord as a second son. But perhaps it is not without significance that when he strode into Longbridge in 1938 the latter was 41-years-old. Vernon would have been 45. Whether or not Austin saw Lord as a son, we can be fairly sure Lord did not regard Austin as a surrogate father.

It was not until February 1938, after his 'sabbatical' and the end of his involvement with the special aid programme, that Lord rejoined the shadow factory scheme.

Swinton is on the record as saying: '*I very much wanted Lord in the aircraft picture but we came to the conclusion that if he were agreeable we could use him elsewhere*', and we arranged that *he should join Austins to take charge both of the airframe production and of the engine and assembly work which that firm was to undertake*'.

This would seem to exclude Austin himself from the plan. But Barney Sharratt in *Men and Motors of 'The Austin'* cites an alternative version.

'*When Austin heard that Lord might be available he instructed Engelbach* (the same Carl Engelbach that we met at Vickers and 'Coventry Ordnance' and now works director at Longbridge) *to invite him to lunch, in order to discuss the possibility of him coming to Longbridge but with strict instructions to inspect his table manners!*' This was presumably at Lickey Grange.

From wherever the anecdote emanates it is deeply insulting to Lord. Here we have a well-educated man, who by his own considerable skill and presence had risen to be one of the most important figures in the British motor industry. A man who, not a year before, had sat at table with government ministers and peers of the realm and crossed the Atlantic on one of the most prestigious liners in the world in the company of the *crème de la crème*, and the implication is *that he didn't know how to hold a knife and fork*.

This is typical of the ill-judged assessments and observations that have, for decades, been made of Lord.

Whether or not such a lunch ever took place is impossible to establish, and irrelevant, as is whether Lord was wooed by what he termed '*the seductive smell of oil*' after being taken on a tour of the Works. What is clear is that as a consequence of his chairmanship of the Aero-Engine Committee, Lord Austin would have been well aware of Swinton's intent.

At the Austin board meeting of Friday, February 4, 1938, Engelbach announced that he would be prepared to step down if Lord took over. The contract was to be for three years, formally commencing on Thursday, March 1—St David's Day.

Lord did, in fact, start work on February 9 and attended his first board meeting, probably more as an observer than participant, on the 23rd of that month.

Herbert Austin was of the view that, as the newcomer was to perform a parallel role to his own, he should be paid the same. Thus the salary was £7,000 per annum plus a package that included a 2.5 per cent commission on the company's pre-tax profits in excess of £250,000. In return, Lord took charge of virtually everything except sales and service. Naturally he was precluded from taking part in any activity that might conflict with Austin's interests and, as the

---

* That is away from the Nuffield Organization and not running the new factory he had proposed when the Ministry had rejected the offer of, what was probably Gosford Street—see Chapter Seven.

small print said, was, '*to the utmost of his abilities, devote the whole of his time and attention, using his best endeavours to well and faithfully serve, promote and advance the interests of the company*'.

Or as Lord would put it, rather more succinctly: '*Austin with the whole jackpot*'. The arrangements seem much fairer and sensible than those at Morris. Lord, reputedly, could not resist informing his old chief about the new appointment. The former supposedly replied: '*Go ahead. I don't see why we shouldn't have a lot of fun cutting each other's throats*'.

As we have just observed Leonard Lord was now 41. If we take a very simplistic view he was an amazingly successful, young executive in the motor industry. His achievements must have been well up to his own expectations and wildly in excess of those of his adored and proud, mother.

His home, now at Greenhill House in quintessentially English Banbury, comfortable and imposing; the family members the epitome of upper middle class British society. He had had the money to take an extended 'holiday' on the Isle of Wight and visit America for a month. And he was about to order a 4¼ Litre Bentley Park Ward saloon (chassis B 186 MR registration FUW 3), one of the most acclaimed and expensive cars available.

Yet there are intriguing undertones. Austin was 72-years-old, tired and demotivated, yet with one of the largest shadow aircraft factories being established at his Works. We cannot help but wonder whether the machinations at Morris over the shadow factory scheme were being orchestrated from outside the industry—that is, by government—and to what extent, and from when, Lord was privy to the plan. For example, had Lord been told by Swinton and/or others to get definitive, executive control of the Nuffield Organisation or get out of that company?

Setting aside for a moment what Leonard Lord was to bring to the wartime aircraft scene we need to consider what he was getting in terms of a motor works. At the level of personal ambition, Austin's age and that of Ernest Payton, his Lordship's deputy and financial director, must have been attractive. So to, was access, for the first time, to a self-contained vehicle making 'machine'. This, as you will remember, was Austin's core philosophy—quite distinct from the Morris approach—buy in everything (and everybody) and assemble.

As regards the rank and file workforce Lord must have come as a striking revelation.

Sharratt quotes Stanley Edge, the draughtsman for the Austin Seven, as saying: '*it was as if a whirlwind had hit the place. Talk about a new broom. He was seen as a tyrant, a man who started turning the place upside down before he'd been there five minutes. He immediately tangled with Payton . . . and upset Haefeli, a senior designer, who found Lord giving orders to the men before he even knew who Lord was*'. This, of course, is pure hearsay. Edge left Longbridge, never to return, more than a decade before the period he is commenting upon. How could he possibly know?

Nonetheless, we have to acknowledge that Lord's arrival at Longbridge had a dramatic impact; just as it had at Hotchkiss, Wolseley and Morris itself. This was entirely necessary. The only imponderable was whether the actions were solely Lord's, to '*promote and advance the interests of the company*' and ensure its long-term survival and success, or whether, as just suggested, there were external influences.

To appreciate what Lord encountered at Austin we must understand something of the patriarchal environment within the company in the 1920s and '30s, of the ethos, and of the products themselves.

Herbert Austin had a capability, on a par with that of Henry Royce, to inspire a loyalty and affection in almost everyone with whom he came into contact. It manifested itself in some of his workers being prepared to forego their wages when the company faced bankruptcy after

WWI—they were rewarded with a job for life. Also in the wreath at Vernon's funeral that bore the inscription: '*Six Austin boys at the Front*'.

Much of this respect and regard stemmed from that priceless quality in any employer—the ability to do the job oneself, as well as, if not better than, the hireling. A virtue, incidentally, also possessed by Lord.

But creditworthy though the atmosphere at Longbridge may have been there were elements that were badly amiss. The vintage* years—1920-30—had been covered by a neatly configured range of wonderful, quality built, motor cars—in chronological order the four cylinder Twenty, 'Heavy' Twelve, Seven, six cylinder Twenty and Sixteen.

The Ten that followed in 1932 was another fine car in terms of fitness for purpose. So were the rest of the new models, which appeared in the '30s, as well as being, in the main, charming, sound, and well made. But they were extremely out-dated. This was largely due to what had become the 'dead hand' of Herbert Austin. The 10 and 12 horsepower four cylinders were sweet and enduring but had absolutely nothing in engineering terms to commend them. After the débâcle of a 'Light Twelve Six', produced in response to a marketplace fad**, all the traditional 'sixes' were as worthy as the 'fours'.

Styling from the end of the vintage era, through the '30s, was undertaken by Ricardo, ('Dick, sometimes rendered Dicki'), Burzi. Many unkind things have been written about Burzi, particularly regarding his work in the post-War era, even to the extent of likening him to the 'coffee boy' and a 'one-week'—whatever that means—'Italian designer'.***

Burzi was Argentinean by birth but had established his reputation with Vincenzo Lancia in Italy, the land of such design icons as Flaminio Bertoni, Guiseppe Figoni#, Guiseppe Farina and Ugo Zagato. Lancia was one of the most innovative automotive engineers of all time and it seems likely Austin saw Burzi's coachwork for the Italian make at the 1929 Paris motor show and recruited him.

An alternative story is, talented artist as he was, some unflattering caricatures by Burzi of the Italian dictator, Benito Mussolini, appeared in the local press and Vincenzo Lancia, who knew Austin, asked the latter to grant his stylist 'asylum'.

Whatever the circumstances of Burzi's arrival at Longbridge the ultra staid appearance of Austins prior to the mid-'30s cannot be laid at his door. It was Austin who believed that a rake on the windscreen of more than seven degrees from the vertical gave a driver eyestrain. Who said '*a car is to ride in not to look at*' and that '*the fancy day is brief and spasmodic. The utility day is with us always. We have innumerable fads and fancies in matters of shape, size, colour and trimmings, but when we get down to our bedrock need, then we find that what we are looking for is transport*'. He then raged that his company would make '*a bold stand against the fetish of change for change's sake*'.

---

*   Again Britain's *Vintage Sports Car Club* demarcation.

**   Fad, because six cylinders had become popular, especially in America and many manufacturers elsewhere tried to apply the format to small capacity engines. The Austin Light Twelve Six Harley was of 1493 cc capacity—less than that of the company's slightly later Light Twelve *Four*. It was intrinsically an unrefined, ill-geared disaster, although pretty in appearance.

*** Sharratt quoting Chris Kingham and Joe Edwards respectively *Men and Motors of The Austin*.

\#   Figoni actually practised in Paris, latterly with fellow Italian, Ovidio Falaschi.

Once Burzi was given a reasonably free hand he gave the Lichfield Ten and its larger sisters the cowled radiator, more flowing lines and removed the protuberances. When he was left totally unfettered he created, in the Cambridge series, some of the most elegant volume produced cars of the late 1930s, far superior to most of the opposition.

All this Leonard Lord needed to deal with. It did not bode well that he was seen in some quarters as '*a bloke from Morris*' but Herbert Austin gave him *carte blanche* and as befits any first class manager, for the first six months of his tenure, his secretary, Dorothy Palmer, worked alone in his office as Lord 'walked the job'.

What he carried back from those perambulations to Ethel, at Greenhill House, soon to be replaced by a company property—Moorcroft, in Cherry Hill Road, Barnt Green—we cannot know. But the scenario must have seemed Kafkaesque. Engelbach's sight was now so bad that the ailing Works director had to be led around the factory, and a useful proportion of production capacity was being devoted to a car whose roots went back to the immediate post-WW1 era and beyond and was an engineering abortion compared with his own 'baby' delivered for Morris.

Austin though seemed unconcerned when Lord quipped at his first ex-apprentices' dinner, a few months later, that by the time he had finished they would need a couple of coaches to take away redundant managers.

And Austin, a confirmed non-smoker, had nothing to say regarding Lord's lifting of the no-smoking ban for male employees in all but fire prone areas. The installation of cigarette dispensers soon followed. This, of course, legitimized Lord's career-long custom of permanently having a Kensitas affixed to his lip, even when speaking. It also eliminated the regular 10 minute long departures of workmen to the toilets for a smoke. The ploy though was not entirely successful in removing all but anatomical activity from the lavatories as someone still found time to scrawl '*Oh Lord give us Engel back*' on the toilet wall!

Detail organizational changes were trivial beside the real tasks in hand and Lord attacked these with awe-inspiring competence and almost super-human energy.

The issues as he perceived them were to re-vitalize the car range and to re-introduce an Austin lorry in the light commercial class. Both moves were visionary, prescient and impacted not only on the Austin Motor Company but on the British car industry for decades to come.

Vigorous and energized though he must have been in these early months, in the midst of it all, Leonard Lord was dealt the most painful of blows. On May 9, 1938, a cerebral haemorrhage took his mother. She died in Luton's Bute Nursing Home with her daughter Annie Blundstone, who now lived on the town's Claremont Road, at her side. Emma Lord was 74. She and Leonard had seen and experienced much together and had come a very long way.

CHAPTER NINE
HERCULES WITH A HOOVER

To appreciate what Lord did with the immediate pre-War range of Austin vehicles we need to look a little more closely at what was already in the catalogue.

The core styling was at the centre of a story—probably apocryphal—about Burzi wanting to re-work the series for the 1937 season. He grasped the rare opportunity of Austin taking a fortnight's holiday to meticulously revamp the format. When his boss returned, he called on the stylist and himself suggested an up-date might be warranted. Later the same day Burzi was able to 'produce' finished drawings. Austin would not have been deceived, but he was obviously impressed by what he saw and the go-ahead was given.

These cars consisted of the Ten in Cambridge saloon and Conway cabriolet form, New Ascot Twelve, Goodwood Fourteen, both also available as cabriolets not individually named, and a closed Eighteen that had three titles—Norfolk, Iver and Windsor—depending on the chassis length or configuration of the interior. A Twenty-Eight called Ranelagh would top the line-up a little later.

The 1125 cc Cambridge moved Austin dramatically forward. For the first time there was enclosed luggage space and, all in all, they were well appointed and finished, with excellent performance for cars in their price bracket (about £175). In addition Girling's splendid wedge and roller braking system represented a tremendous improvement over Austin's inefficient, in-house, rope and cam system.

The New Ascot was even nicer, its slightly greater bulk filling out the form to perfection with such added refinements as fitted suitcases in the boot and magazine nets for the rear compartment.

The Goodwood used basically the same body as the Twelve but its 1711 cc engine was a revised version of what had previously been defined as the 'Twelve Six' and gave the model impressive acceleration and top speed.

The Eighteen was not to every taste with its 2,500 cc engine housed beneath a stumpy bonnet, while the Ranelagh, when it arrived in October 1938, was an utterly magnificent marketing disaster.

At the bottom end of the scale, when Lord arrived, was the Seven, more or less in the final incarnation of the 'Jewel' series. It still sold in surprising numbers but largely on the basis of its long-standing reputation and public affection.

Slotted in, just above, was the *Big* Seven. An appealing and solid little car that had some Baby Austin technology, a much better 900 cc engine, excellent performance and appointments, but did look old fashioned and cost too much to produce for its £130 listing.

Extremely worthy as all this was, it was never going to set the marketplace ablaze and within less than a year Leonard Lord had swept it virtually all away.

At a special board meeting on March 9, 1938, he outlined a new range of cars the introduction of which would include three brilliant elements.

Firstly, the models matched the customer profiles perfectly and were on a par with the Seven, Twelve, Sixteen, Twenty spread of the 1920s. Secondly, they facilitated rationalized production; and third, the chassis design was modern and advanced. In addition, Lord inspired Burzi to pen another basic form that looked fantastic.

There were six cars proposed. An Eight* to replace both the Seven and Big Seven, then straight substitutes for the Ten and Twelve. Afterwards comes an anomaly. Speaking at the board meeting, Lord specified a Sixteen as the first of the 'large' cars, then an Eighteen and Twenty-Five all using an overhead valve engine—Austin's first in production vehicles. However, in a memorandum issued by his office the day before the board, no Sixteen appeared. But there was a *Fourteen* described in such detail as to specify the capacity (1812 cc) and the dimensions of the six cylinders—61.5 x 101.6 mm.

We need not attach too much importance to this as Austin 'horsepower' classifications are notoriously misleading. For example, not even those 'in the trade' ever seemed quite sure whether the 1711 cc Goodwood was a Fourteen, Light Twelve Six or a Sixteen!

This particular Fourteen never materialized. A Sixteen did, but later; maybe by accident or maybe not, as we shall see. Precisely what Lord had in mind in March 1938 is unclear. Suffice to say, none of the large cars went into production before the war.

The proposed engine though would seem to be a six cylinder lorry unit, or a variation of it, that Austin were already planning and which we will discuss in a moment.

Like the 'Fourteen', the overhead valve Eighteen never appeared at all although on paper it was to be exactly the same capacity and cylinder dimensions as the side valve model, and the 'Twenty Five' when it came, in 1947, was called Sheerline and did, indeed, adopt a form of the lorry engine.

As an aside, it is worth noting that for the first time names were largely dispensed with, the models being identified by horsepower rating.

Thus the cars Lord raced into the showrooms were all side valve and shared what became popularly known as the 'Lord-look'. It was typified by the Austin Eight. That came in two and four door saloon, tourer and van form. The closed cars differed from their larger sisters in having a single pane rear window. At the front there was a modern 'alligator' bonnet resting on side panels that could be detached for major engine work and an attractive, rounded, grille composed of horizontal bars, centrally divided by a vertical upright. The latter was emblazoned with a tasteful enamel badge in Austin's 'Aston Villa' colours of deep maroon and sky blue and stating the horsepower.

The body was attached, not to a conventional cross-braced girder frame, but to a pressed steel platform. It had box section side members, open on the outward side so that when the body, which could still be detached, was fitted, the 'boxes' were closed.

There were also transverse, boxed, cross members—at the front, a little further back to support the rear of the engine, then two others, one integral with the floor pan beneath the front seat runners and finally at the rear of the platform.

---

*   It is often stated, quite erroneously, that the Austin Eight used the Big Seven engine. They are of the same capacity, and similar, but there are numerous detail differences and the interchangeability of parts is limited.

In addition, ahead of the interior platform, the side members formed arms, or 'pontoons', on either side of the car that attached to a front crosspiece and added further rigidity to the structure. It was a dramatic step towards unitary construction.

The Ten came only as a four-door in saloon form and, as well as being visibly larger than the Eight, was distinguished by a divided back window. There was also a stunningly attractive Ten tourer and a smart van. The build process was the same as for the Eight—a platform 'chassis' with extensions at the front to accommodate the main mechanical parts.

The Twelve was the only one of these models to use a conventional frame—basically that of the New Ascot. The enlarged scale made the model extraordinarily handsome and there were some up-market additions like a spare wheel compartment beneath the boot, accessed via a neat, drop-down, panel that contained the registration mark, protected by glass, and flanked by the rear light assemblies.

Burzi's styling drew heavily on American practice, as it always had. That is no grounds for criticism. On the contrary, toning down the flamboyance of the contemporary Buick or Cadillac created cars that were neat and modern in appearance but suited the home market. There was no room in Britain for Italian and French extravagance or eccentricity.

Whether Lord's own sojourn Stateside influenced the thinking and thus, what Burzi drew, we cannot know, but it is very likely it did. Although to claim he foresaw that one day he would need to sell cars in the United States is probably to over-estimate even Lord's genius!

It is certainly worth mentioning though that at this time Lord's chauffeur-driven* company car was a mid-30s Buick that embodied some of the features incorporated in the 'Lord look'.

For him to have spurned the Longbridge range seems inexplicable. Admittedly there was no large Austin of the new generation and an Eighteen, or even the Twenty Eight when it was unveiled in July, 1938, would have linked Lord to the concepts from which he was trying to free the company.

A plausible justification is that he had been impressed by the Buick on his trip to America and was using it to illustrate to Burzi, particularly, but also others, the type of designs he had in mind.**

Mechanically the Lord-look Eight, Ten and Twelve were basically the same as the cars they replaced. The Eight though was rid of all the quirkiness of the Seven, receiving the full Girling treatment for the brakes instead of what Austin euphemistically termed 'semi-Girling', meaning it negated most of the advantages of the genuine article!

There was also a much sweeter clutch than on either the Ruby or Big Seven, a 'banjo' type rear axle to replace the three-piece, and later two-part D-shaped, design of the predecessors and conventional semi-elliptic leaf spring suspension and hydraulic (as opposed to friction) shock absorbers all round.

Both the Eight and the Ten had their valve timing re-worked, in a departure from that of the Big Seven and previous Tens, and the larger cars got an aluminium, instead of a cast iron, cylinder head. The two innovations were flawed.

The first, almost certainly, contributed to a propensity for burning exhaust valves. As one long-standing, and long-suffering, dealer put it to the author recently, perhaps a *little* harshly: '*If you wanted an engine to lose the war, this was it!*' The second 'novelty', caused excessive

---

*   Leonard Lord's chauffeur was Dennis Bush who remained until the chairman retired from BMC in 1961.

**   There is a parallel here with Herbert Austin who had experience of an American Hudson around the time of WWl and incorporated some of its features in his 'Twenty'.

condensation in the combustion chambers of cold engines, making starting extremely difficult, and, of course, the aluminium reacted with the iron of the block and created problems over cylinder head removal.

The 1535 cc Twelve's mechanics were left largely untouched and for all its good looks it was a pusillanimous animal.

Lord announced to the board at that March 9 meeting that the Eight could be available in February 1939, the new Ten in March, and the larger cars 'after Easter' which fell on April 17 that year. The Ten was late, materializing in May, as was the Twelve, which did not appear until August, just days before WWII was declared.

At a board meeting on July 31, 1939, Lord proposed an additional model—a Ten with the Twelve's engine as an option and priced at around £210. But just as time almost ran out for the 'proper' Twelve it actually did expire for this hybrid and it was never heard of again.

Lord may have been a few months askew in his timing for two of the model launches and he may not have been particularly well served by the engineering department, but the fact remains, he revitalized the Austin range spectacularly within virtually a year of coming on board. That is an incredible achievement and an enormous tribute to his vision, dynamism and sheer energy.

Furthermore, even Lord's detractors acknowledge his brilliance as a production engineer. However, even this short period at Austin, and that, a few years earlier, at Morris, when he was developing their own 'Eight', illustrate to perfection what an astute marketeer he was and his understanding of the business as a whole.

There is one mysterious sub chapter to the private car story at this time. Why did Leonard Lord stay his hand and not axe the Twenty Eight Ranelagh as soon as he arrived? Apocryphally, we would have expected him to say: 'That bloody thing can go for a start'.

Herbert Austin had always had delusions of grandeur regarding the luxury car market. It is true that pre-WWI the Austin had been an expensive, prestige automobile. It is equally the case that in the 1920s there were those who believed the four cylinder Austin Twenty comparable with, if not superior to, the Rolls-Royce of similar size. Astonishingly, if the coachwork was light enough, the big Austin could also give a Three Litre Bentley a run for its money. Although to quote one wag, your money would have been safer on the Bentley!

By the 1930s, Austin was primarily identified with the Seven and Ten and to a lesser extent the Light Twelve Four. The make had largely lost its aristocratic caché and making 20 horsepower limousines and landaulettes was an unprofitable waste of time.

The Twenty Eight was the final flowering of Longbridge's pre-War luxury car programme. An enormous, extremely elegant, fast and powerful vehicle it used a four litre (4016 cc) *side valve* engine. It suffered the ignominy of needing a price reduction within five months of launch (from £700 to £595) in a bid to stimulate interest. When it was withdrawn in early 1940 only 300 had been sold.

Why Lord permitted this car to consume resources when he was already planning a 25 horsepower, top of the range model, and had an overhead valve six cylinder power unit to hand, is difficult to understand. Even more so because, during this period, two prototype cars using the ohv engine were up and running. They would have been marketed in 1940, had not war intervened, as a model called—intriguingly—the Colonial.

It may be that he had too much on his mind and needed to prioritize. Or, he may have been demonstrating his sensitivity, in this case, towards Lord Austin. As we have seen, the latter was committed to a presence in the luxury sector and to simple, side valve engines for all his cars. At the top end of the market, these had the ability to run in almost total silence. Perhaps Lord was prepared to overlook the Twenty Eight and not hurt or disagree with the patriarch.

In parallel with his work on private cars Lord found time to put his weight behind a range of commercial vehicles.

The genesis of the post-WW1* Austin lorry is often set much later than the records actually show.

As early as the June 26 board meeting of 1934, Herbert Austin had expressed his wish to re-enter the light commercial field, although financial director, Ernest Payton, warned that those manufacturers already with a presence in the sector were not achieving an adequate return on their investment.

Austin though persisted, and told his board at the meeting of January 22, 1936, that a two ton lorry was being designed. By June 9 he was able to report that two such vehicles were actually in service with the transport department.

What is by no means clear is what engine was used. Most of the competition (for example, Morris Commercial, Commer, Dodge) adopted six cylinder side valve units. Austin had the 20 horsepower car's 3.4 litre 'six' that could have done the job. Indeed, it was used in Garner-Sentinel** lorries circa 1935 and there is some circumstantial evidence it may have been in the two vehicles of which Austin spoke.

That there was an overhead valve Austin in the offing at this time and it was being used—or soon would be—in the lorries that were running in the summer of 1936, also seems possible. Some credence to the belief that there was an early ohv is given by three board meeting references between October 1936 and April 1937.

The first, on October 28, alludes to continuing experiments with the 'new combustion head'. This seems more likely to be a cylinder head for an existing ohv engine rather than a conversion, or improvement, for a side-valve. But we can't be sure. Remember, the lowly Austin Seven could be converted to overhead valve. Austin Seven licensee, BMW, did this with both proprietary 'heads' and also when they launched their '320' model around 1932. The procedures are perfectly viable.

It is not until January 27, 1937, that the board learns: *'the engine had been tested and drawings were being prepared'*. This suggests that either a new cylinder head for an overhead valve engine, or the whole unit, if we accept that the first scenario above, was being adopted.

Finally, on April 30, it is revealed that two lorries had been *'brought up to date'* and were now *'running satisfactorily in the Service*** Department'*. We can presume that the up-date alludes to the new 'head'/engine. By the early autumn, three more prototypes had been built and handed to transport while experiments with two diesel versions were running in parallel, from very early in 1937.

---

*   Austin introduced an extremely advanced two/three ton lorry in 1913 that had some success both in military and civilian circles.

**   Henry Garner Ltd were a Birmingham firm that in 1909 were, quite coincidentally, appointed Austin agents for the Midlands. By 1914 they were the largest of the company's dealers in the country. Post-WW1 they began manufacturing lorries and in 1933, when Sentinel of Shrewsbury felt their steam wagon business was under threat from impending legislation, were absorbed by that concern. All non-steam Sentinel vehicles were subsequently badged accordingly and offered with a variety of engine options including the Austin 20.

*** Probably a slip of the tongue/pen for 'transport'.

Austin had brought in two German oil engine specialists, Dr Lehmann and Dr Collel, from Daimler-Benz and MAN respectively. They were responsible for one lorry with a Dorman engine and another with what is thought to have been an in-house four cylinder design of about three litres. They were run satisfactorily, for at least a year, and on a daily basis, between Longbridge and the service depot in Holland Park, London.

One of the petrol engined lorries was placed with Birmingham building firm, Trentham, and also received good reports for robust reliability.

Lord Austin was now becoming typically impatient with the board. At the meeting of November 24, 1937, he said that he thought '*a decision should be made with regard to the manufacture of this lorry as it was useless continuing expenditure on experimental work if they did not wish to proceed further*'.

He revisited the subject two months later to reveal that another lorry was nearly finished. It was then that some members expressed the view that '*it was not the right time to consider a big proposition of this sort*'. This was just a month before Leonard Lord arrived.

The dissenting members of the board would have formed their conclusions from publicly available statistics. Sixty seven per cent of the market was shared between Ford, Morris and Bedford. Fourteen went to the heavyweights like, AEC, Albion, Leyland, Maudslay, Thornycroft and so on, leaving under 20% for the smaller fry like Rootes, and potentially Austin, to fight for. Furthermore, commercial vehicle sales were in decline—105,000 in 1938, down from 118,000 the previous year. Exports also fell over the same period—from 20,000 to 14,000.

By an astonishing coincidence a memorandum emerged from works director Engelbach's office on February 28, just over a fortnight *after* Lord had arrived but before he had officially taken up his post, that stated it had been 'unanimously decided that the manufacture of three (*models of*) trucks *be investigated* (my insertion and my italics) on the lines suggested'.

The range, to be called the 'Austin Trader', was then set out. It was to comprise a 30 cwt and two and three tonners. All were to be launched on January 1, 1939, and each to use the same engine. This was briefly described as a 3,179 cc 26 horsepower 'six' with a bore and stroke of 84.14 x 95.25 mm which equates to no Austin engine ever put into production, overhead or side valve.

Each entry in the prospectus has the addendum: 'Same as "Bedford"'. This is highly ambiguous. It could mean any one, or all, of three things. That the payloads were the same as some of Bedford's, which they were; that the engine was the same as an Austin motor fitted to a lorry, known to exist at Longbridge around 1937, and disguised with a Bedford cab, bonnet and radiator surround. This would account for the use of quotes around the word 'Bedford'. Or, and probably most likely, the engine was actually 'the same' as Bedford's. It was dimensionally; and rated at the same 26 horsepower. Shortly this will become a major issue and one we will need to examine.

As we know, when Lord spoke at the board meeting of March 9, he mentioned this engine as being intended for the top of the range (25 horsepower) car and the trucks. I think we can assume him saying '25' rather than using Engelbach's '26' is merely semantics and 'marketing-speak'.

As with so much else, it was left to Leonard Lord to kick the project into action.

By March 28 he had convinced Austin, correctly for those days, that the way forward in the light commercial field was with a petrol engine. Work on the diesels ceased.

It also seems likely that he scrapped the 3.1 litre engine (*3,179 cc see above*) or had it substantially modified, because the unit which went into the Austin commercials was of 3,460 cc (85 x 101.6 mm).

While this was taking place Lord pushed through approval for 168,000 square feet of new workshops and 25,000 for a service department facing the Bristol Road at Longbridge. Seventy thousand pounds was invested in press tools and jigs and between £300,000 and £350,000 set aside as working capital.

The total outlay was at least half a million pounds and immediately raises the question as to why a board, that had been so recalcitrant a few months before, would now back this level of commitment. Lord's charisma and dynamism, of course. But was there much more to it than that, a question prompted in part by the fact that the dimensions and capacity of the engine were revised.

We need to remember that it was around 1936 that the national panic over German rearmament began to gather momentum. It was at this point Austin was co-opted as chairman of the government's aero engine committee where he was soon joined by Leonard Lord.

We have already seen how Swinton, undoubtedly with Austin's acquiescence, manipulated the situation to give Lord a controlling hand at Longbridge. '*I always wanted him in the aeroplane picture etc*'.

By the same token it seems entirely feasible Lord had an unminuted government brief to implement a lorry production programme. It may even be that Austin was privy to the strategy, but the 71-year-old no longer had the energy or drive to expedite matters. This may account for his irascibility at the board meeting of November 24, 1937.

Whether or not any of this was actually the case, Lord was pushing the project ahead. He reported on December 14, 1938, that trucks were being completed at the rate of one a week and set the dealer launch for the last day of January, 1939, at the Works. In advance of this a two ton model was sent to London's Holland Park service depot while the city's motor show was in progress—presumably so any interested parties could make the short trip across the west of the capital to see it. In addition a 30 cwt version was available at the factory for the board to inspect.

Around this time a story was given voice that the Austin engine plagiarized that of the Bedford and legal action was in the offing. This has become a long standing controversy that is still not fully resolved.

The upshot was the Austins would become popularly known as 'Birmingham Bedfords'. This would not have escaped Lord's vitriol; and a law suit with General Motors, the Luton firm's parent, most certainly not.

The facts are that the Bedford's power unit was an improved version of a 1929 Chevrolet overhead valve six cylinder known officially as the AC/LQ and colloquially as the 'Stovebolt Six' or 'Cast Iron Wonder'. Suffice to say it was strong, reliable, sweet running and cheap to make.

It went into Bedford W Series trucks in 1931 and for aspirants to the light commercial market, this became the lorry to beat. Not surprisingly, Austin would have studied it closely and it may not be coincidence that the engine Lord abandoned early in 1938 was of almost identical capacity and cylinder dimensions.

Bedford enlarged the unit to 3,519 cc (85.72 x 101.6 mm) in the summer of 1938 and around the same time the cab was re-styled. This was the O Series—one of the most attractive commercial vehicles on the road, if not of all time.

In reality, the Austin engine Lord adopted was substantially different from the Bedford's, not least, in that the camshaft and valve gear are on the opposite side—the left, as with side valve Austins. There are also many other departures.

Predictably, passing time has seen many embellishments to the plagiarism story. One appears to emanate from the Victoria Morris Minor Club in Australia* (they would know!). It suggests Lord hastily ordered the camshaft moved to avoid legal action. This makes little sense. It would compromise a layout the unknown designer(s), but probably Hancock and/or his deputy Jules Haefeli, had thought most appropriate and ignores the fact that the position of the camshaft as manufactured was in accord with basic Longbridge practice.

If any legal action was mooted it is much more likely to have been over the cab and its appendages. Although the Austin lorry is not *quite* as handsome as Luton's it *is* very similar.

There is no documentary evidence I can find to support lawyers being involved or even an out of court settlement. Furthermore, the Bedford fraternity have not been able to provide me with the name of any designer or stylist who may have been involved,** thus I am inclined to believe the Luton shape simply evolved and Longbridge's was a close, perhaps embarrassingly close, copy. Like so much else associated with Leonard Lord, the stories would seem to be hearsay. However, if he *was* embarrassed by the mechanical or external design he is unlikely to have taken it well. There may be scores to settle in the future.

A much more believable scenario for the similarity between the Bedford and Austin, which extended to the transmission line as well as the engine and bodywork, is that by the mid-to-late 1930s the Ministry of Defence had set parameters for military lorries of this size. Therefore, if they were looking for 70 brake horsepower and about 150/160 ft/lbs of torque using low grade fuel, 3.5 litres would have been around the only appropriate capacity. Both Luton and Longbridge could have accepted the brief and the rest is, perhaps, commercial shadow boxing for effect in the civilian marketplace.

It may be of interest to record that from 1942 onwards 400,000 trucks *a year* would be needed by the British armed forces. Despite any preparation for such an output by Bedford, Austin and others in the late '30s, there would be a considerable shortfall from the home producers. Consequently there was a top-up from across the Atlantic by the likes of Canadian Ford, Chevrolet, Dodge, and GMC, that peaked, in 1943, with 252,470 vehicles imported.

It was mentioned in the last chapter that it did not bode well in some quarters at Longbridge that Lord was a former Morris man. By the same token it could not have augured favourably that Swinton was his 'sponsor' on the aeroplane front.

As Big Ben was about to strike 4.00 pm on the afternoon of May 12, 1938, one of the most damning debates in the history of the Air Ministry began in the House of Commons. As we are aware, Lord Swinton, the air minister, chose not to contest his parliamentary seat for Hendon in the 1935 General Election. Instead he managed to secure a baronetcy. This placed him firmly in the House of Lords but, at this critical time, no longer directly answerable to Parliament.

The debate, that would lead to calls for a Ministry of Supply, was opened by Sir Hugh Seely, Labour member for Berwick-on-Tweed, directing his remarks at the absent air minister. He began by outlining the strength of the German air force—3,500 front line machines, production running at an extendable 4-500 a month to provide between 6-8,000 fighters and bombers within the year.

Exposing a litany of prevarification and misinformation Sir Hugh said: '*we had been asking about the Hawker Hurricane and when production should be ordered and when would they be completed? Of course, we never could get the information.*

---

*   I have failed to substantiate this is the case.

**   Or even motivated to reply to my enquiries.

'*On 3rd June, 1936, we were told that an order had been given for 340 and more. That is some two years ago. We see the news in the newspapers now. Can the minister deny that there are only 28 in service? Yet we are told that everything is alright*'.

He then set his sights on the Spitfire. '*Here again we expected something. In March, 1936, we asked: "Is it going into production?" We have been put off. But can the Rt Hon Gentleman deny that there is only one machine, that is all.*"

Sir Hugh continued: '*there is the question of guns. The modern gun in the Royal Air Force at the present time is the 1914 Vickers. The Noble Lord may say that we have the new Browning gun now and what a wonderful gun it is. But if you are to make it satisfactorily you have to arrange to make 10,000 belt links a week. In America they are making 35,000 a day.*

'*That is the position one finds throughout the Royal Air Force. At every station one finds that the demand is about four times the supply. I do not believe that that position can be met without creating a ministry of supply*'.

After an hour on his feet, he drove home the attack by declaring: '*You are pretending there is a real defence, but it is a camouflage and a farce, and you are trying to make people believe that there is security when it has not been developed in the way it should have been*'.

It fell to the Irish peer, Earl Winterton, designated the Air Ministry spokesman in the House of Commons, to respond. He had only held the post for two months and although described by one participant as being called upon to perform the work of 'Hercules with a Hoover', Winterton's performance was feeble, inept, sometimes inarticulate and woefully inadequate.

'*I must say that it seems an inappropriate time to wish to court martial the captain and the officers on the bridge*'. . . and . . . '*in regard to gun turrets the situation is far more satisfactory than it was in the past, and the production at the present time is satisfactory*' are typical of the tautological waffle Winterton uttered in a desperate bid to defend the government position.

At one point he alluded directly to Longbridge and the shadow factory scheme, saying: '*With regard to Austin the first machines are nearing completion and deliveries should commence almost immediately*'. He added: '*as regards engine shadows, all the factories are complete and in production. The numbers are rising progressively month by month and peak production is not very far distant*'.

The determination of the attack though was overwhelming. Clement Attlee, Labour MP for Limehouse, in East London, and a future prime minister, by way of highlighting the government's failure to simplify and standardize aircraft, quoted chapter and verse: '*I have details of a simple type of fighter aeroplane. There are 151 different sizes of bar, 147 different sizes of tube, 50 gauges of sheet, 105 sizes of rivets and scores of different screws, nuts and bolts. There are different sorts of steel and every kind of variation and specification. That is only one type. It is the same in regard to other types made by different firms.*'

It was the shadow factory scheme that was Winterton's only plank in a raging sea of gentlemanly and lordly opprobrium in which he seemed likely to perish at any moment.

'*Shadow factories are in step, that is to say, the production of frames and the production of engines are synchronized,*' he bleated as the debate grew to a close. '*And in regard to the other items, they are synchronized with production elsewhere. The shadow scheme is going forward well and the production from it will be on a large scale indeed within the present financial year*', said the earl.

His closing of the discussion had the ultimate ring of desperation. '*If the Archangel Gabriel stood at this* (dispatch*) box and produced an expansion scheme on behalf of the present government, I do not think it would satisfy some*'. (In that particular case Winston Chuchill, MP for Epping and another future prime minister).* The session had lasted more than seven hours and some forty members had spoken.

Prime minister, Neville Chamberlain, could not fire Swinton on the spot, because, naturally, the Air Minister wasn't there. But he did so almost immediately. Sir Howard Kingsley Wood took over.

I have given a fairly lengthy account of this extremely long debate because it points up very effectively the plight of the nation's defences, the ineptitude in high places and, of most relevance to us, what Lord was dealing with. Very soon we will see what he was to achieve and none should fail to appreciate what foresight, wherewithal, energy, sheer determination and commitment it must have called for.

During his contribution to the parliamentary debate, Clement Attlee had complained the pronouncements that: '*all was going smoothly*' were almost always followed '*by some drastic change, either of programme or of personnel*'.

It may be noteworthy that this did not occur in the case of Leonard Lord.

---

*   This is obviously a summary, and in some cases paraphrasing, of the debate but taken from *Hansard*, the parliamentary reporting service.

CHAPTER TEN

SUNDAY, BLOODY SUNDAY

It is doubtful whether the 500 agency representatives had a swell party when they lunched at the Works that January Tuesday the lorries were launched. The motor dealer and the industry are often uneasy bedfellows and the visitors were reluctant to take on trucks. They regarded the field as a highly competitive free-for-all, ridden by order snatching, price under-cutting and the need for inducements, sometimes of a quite avant-garde nature. It was thought that Austin coming on the scene would only exacerbate these conditions.

Miles Thomas had encountered a similar reaction when he took over Morris Commercial not long before: '*I discovered another rather disconcerting facet of human relations. When I was sales director at Cowley, and Morris cars were in great demand, the distributors and agents all metaphorically genuflected when we met because the Morris car franchise was a very valuable property. When I became general manager of Morris Commercial Cars many of those same agents—because they had to be persuaded to stock Morris Commercial trucks and to put more sales drive behind them—quite obviously cooled off*'.

Nonetheless, at Austin, Lord's dynamism had brought the commercial vehicle programme to fruition and the first examples rolled off the production line barely a month after the first 'Lord-look' cars.

Apart from the lorry launch, another party, of sorts, took place when HRH King George VI and Queen Elizabeth visited the Works. Whether or not the claims that Lord was not particularly comfortable in the company of those perceived to be the great and the good are true, in the photographs of this uplifting event, Lord's face suggests he is enjoying the limelight and it is Lord Austin who is discomfited! Maybe Austin was simply extremely anxious everyone got back to their desks and on with the job. There was certainly a vast amount to be done.

Among the less momentous tasks Lord must have contemplated would have been ending the expensive and unnecessary racing programme, as he had done at MG. As it happened, an extremely momentous world event—the start of a war—would do the job for him. But his unenthusiastic attitude towards the competition department has, yet again, left him unpopular in some circles and given rise to comments and opinions, that, when examined are not only inappropriately derogatory, but quite sinister.

Competition Austins date back to the very beginning of the company. We have already seen how Vernon was involved just prior to The Great War. Well before that, the marque was a significant force on the European racing scene.

The first foray had been for the French Grand Prix of 1908, run that year on a circuit around Dieppe. Longbridge fielded a team of three cars plus a spare. All had six cylinder side valve engines of approaching 10 litres, but two used shaft and two chain transmission.

To drive the cars three luminaries of the day were chosen. Dario Resta was to become famous for his exploits in Sunbeams and was eventually killed in one. Warwick Wright was a well known aviator and balloonist as well as racing motorist, and J T C Moore-Brabazon (Lord Brabazon of Tara), another flying pioneer, will appear in our story in a different context very much later.

So seriously did Austin take the challenge that he booked the entire *Hotel du Cygne,* in the town of Eu at the course's northernmost point, to accommodate no fewer than 60 Works personnel.

The preamble to the event did not bode particularly well with Resta proving something of a liability. In practice, which was conducted over public roads that remained in use, he managed to collide with not one, but two, horse drawn farm carts. Only the ire of the *agriculteurs,* not the damage to the wagons, is recorded, but we do know that the wreck of his Austin had to be rebuilt using the spare car and parts shipped from the factory.

However, on the day of the race, Tuesday, July 7, things went more smoothly. Although Warwick Wright was eliminated by a seized engine, Moore-Brabazon finished 18th in eight hours, forty three minutes, for the 10 laps and 478 miles. Resta took just three minutes more. Their average speed was in the mid 50s, considerably below that of the winning Mercedes's 69 mph, but the Austins had proved themselves fast and reliable.

The company took no further part in grand prix racing before WWl but a number of private owners competed at Brooklands and elsewhere. The most famous example on the Weybridge track was a 1907 '40' campaigned by Oscar Thompson as a tourer, and then two-seater, and called, for part of the time, *Pobble,* after the toeless creature of fiction. This mildly modified production car with its 90 mph performance became one of the prime attractions at the circuit in these Edwardian years.

The racing driver Percy Lambert ran a much more heavily modified car, named *Pearly III,* in 1911. A 15 horsepower, rebuilt as a slim single seater with cowled radiator and disc wheels, it was capable of around 70 mph.

After the war the deceptively potent four cylinder Twenty horsepower model found fame at Brooklands both in private hands and with Works drivers Lou Kings, the company tester, and Capt Arthur Waite, who, of course, was Austin's son in law and competitions manager.

The private entrant was Felix Scriven, a Bradford businessman, who, from 1921 to around 1925, developed what was basically a standard car into a 100 mph racer. He called it *Felix the Cat* after the cartoon character, and subsequently *Sergeant Murphy,* in honour of the 1923 Grand National steeplechase winner.

Around the same time, the works relied on two more Twenties. The less colourfully named *Black Maria* and a car with tandem seats and disc wheels originally created for the sand, or beach racing, extremely popular in that era. Both could achieve 90 mph plus.

From the mid-1920s, the full weight of Austin's racing effort was thrown almost exclusively behind the Seven. The baby car had made its competition début at the Midland Automobile Club's Shelsley Walsh hillclimb on July 29, 1922. From then on, innumerable racing engagements were fulfilled. At Brooklands, at Monza in Italy, at the Boulogne Speed Week in France, on the Ards circuit in Ireland, in Australia—to win, in 1928, that country's very first Grand Prix. Practically everywhere a motor race was held the Seven was a contender and the term 'Austin Ulster'* has become as evocative as any in the sports car world.

---

* The model name 'Ulster' has become universally adopted for the premier Seven sports but the proper designation, although a lot less glamorous, is Type EA Sports.

But, by the turn of the decade, the Longbridge product was becoming less and less a match for the MG Midget with its overhead camshaft engine and better designed chassis. Waite had already been frustrated in his desire to claim the accolade of '*first 750 cc car to 100 mph*'. George Eyston, in the Abingdon make, had taken that honour at Montlhèry, near Paris, in a spree that saw various records fall at between 101 and 103 mph.

For racing silverware Austin was forced to look more and more towards sprints and hillclimbs. To try to redress the balance the company head-hunted Thomas Murray Jamieson from the Brooklands premises of Amherst Villiers where he was engaged on supercharger design. Jamieson—Jamie, to his close friends—was of Anglo-Scottish descent and the brief at Longbridge was to build the fastest side valve car he could. In other words, a machine to beat MGs.

His first attempt, in 1933, was a wind-tunnel-tested aluminium bodied streamliner with sponsons between the front and rear wheels, and later, an aerofoil at the front. The heavily reworked engine used aluminium and magnesium alloys, had dry sump lubrication and a 24 pounds per square inch supercharger that could force out about 70 brake horsepower at between 6000 and 8000 rpm.

Driving it himself, the designer took mile and kilometre records at just below 120 mph on the Montlhèry 'bowl'. But a few days later Eyston snatched them all back at 125. This convinced Jamieson there was no more competition mileage in side valves. But he reworked the car again as a sprint machine for the Works 'regular' Pat Driscoll and produced another version for German driver, Walter Baumer, to use in Continental events.

At the end of 1934 Jamieson started to lay out a racing car that would not have seemed alien to today's world champions. There was to be a 1500 cc V8 engine amidships, a semi-inclined driving position in a monocoque chassis, plus adjustable front and rear aerofoils. There are those who believe that had Jamieson's brilliance come to full flower it would have advanced grand prix racing car development by at least a decade.

Not surprisingly, Herbert Austin was not impressed by what he saw on the page. After all, he liked to say that '*the same side valve engine as in your reliable Baby Austin*' powered the racers. We can reasonably assume it was a disgruntled and disenchanted Jamieson who returned to the drawing board.

Nevertheless, what he produced was his masterwork, and although any resemblance to '*that engine in your reliable Baby Austin*' was purely coincidental, the car was exquisite. One example, meticulously restored in recent times, displays handling and performance that is impressive by the standards of any age.

This is the famous twin overhead camshaft car of 1936. It bristled with innovation in practically every department while managing to look like a handsome, conventional monoposto. A trio was constructed plus enough spares for, possibly, three more.

Austin, personally, launched the design at Birmingham's Grand Hotel on March 18 by displaying one completed car and a polished chassis. He told guests that since 1922 the Seven had won 3,000 events and he hoped the new cars would continue the tradition; or, again, 'beat MGs'.

Predictably, the engine, which developed 116 bhp at 9000 rpm in sprint form and had the potential to reach 12,000 revs, did not run perfectly at first. This added to Austin's disillusionment with the car at the same time as Murray Jamieson was, reputedly, becoming weighed down by the internal politics and constraints at Longbridge. Very early in 1937 he left to join racing car manufacturer ERA.

By then the 'twin cam' was proving its potency. Among many successes, Baumer set new 1100 and 1500 cc class records at the Freiburg Hillclimb in Germany finishing third overall behind Rudolph Caracciola in a 5.6 litre Mercedes and Bernard Rosemeyer in his V16 Auto Union.

The little Austins swept the board at the Coronation Day meeting at Donington Park on May 12 and were now capable of average lap speeds of about 118 mph round Brooklands with maxima of 130.

If we believe journalist Jonathan Wood, writing in *The Automobile* magazine of October 2008, Lord '*loathed the talented young Murray Jamieson*'. Yet why should this be? Unless he knew him socially, which is extremely unlikely, Lord, who had little or no interest in motor racing, would never have met the Anglo-Scot.

At the first Brooklands race meeting of May, 1938, on the seventh of the month, Joseph Paul's huge V12 Delage caught fire as it started the Junior Car Club's International Trophy race. As Paul battled to steer it off the track he clipped another competitor and both crossed a safety barrier and hit spectators at a point where Jamieson was an official. A young woman, Peggy Williams, was killed on the spot and Jamieson died of his injuries in Weybridge Cottage Hospital three days later. As well as a young widow he left a five-week-old son.

Murray Jamieson had departed Austin about a year before Lord arrived and was dead by the time the latter was three months into the job. Maybe Lord was jealous of his conspicuous brilliance. Yet Lord had no aspirations himself to be either an engine or chassis designer. So what was this 'loathing' about? An aversion, seemingly so spite-ridden, that during WWII Lord ordered the parts for the twin cam engines scrapped '*so Jamieson's twin cam Austin racers would never run again*', says Wood.

When Jamieson left, Herbert—always known as Bert—Hadley became the engineering lynch pin in the competition department. He had joined the company as an apprentice in the mid-20s and spent most of his years displaying a considerable mechanical aptitude with the competition cars. He was also a talented driver and was number one *pilote* when the twin cams were at their peak.

His most notable achievements were worrying away at the 40 second barrier on Shelsley Walsh, not far behind Raymond Mays in the unlimited capacity class on an ERA. He also recorded a spectacular win at the Imperial Trophy Meeting on London's Crystal Palace circuit on August 26, 1939, just days before the outbreak of war. In the premier event he finished a full half-mile ahead of the nearest contender. It was an MG. The Murray Jamieson twin cam Austin Seven was firmly established as the finest 750 cc racer that has ever been.

Jamieson left Hadley a number of partly developed performance enhancers in the workshop at Longbridge—some merely blueprints but some part machined. These included a twin spark cylinder head, two stage supercharger and a limited slip differential. The latter imposes a mechanical constraint on a car's axle shafts that restricts wheel spin and would provide maximum traction for racing starts. The technology was coming tentatively into vogue in the mid and late '30s.

At the same time Hadley was experimenting with different forms of rear wheel and tyre configurations for broadly the same purpose. He said of Jamieson's innovations: '*The tragedy was that at this time it had been quite impossible to obtain the finances necessary to make use of these modifications*'.

His view of Lord, soon after the appointment, was that his new boss was unsupportive. He said of him: '*The new appointee* (Lord as works director) *seemed to work on the premise that if racing wasn't part of his remit then clearly it was of no importance*'.

Hadley believed Lord Austin was more amenable, talking of the need to win races to provide him '*with the ammunition to* defeat (my emphasis) *those members of the board who always pointed out gloomily the cost of going motor racing*' and reminiscing that '*Lord Austin had always maintained personal control of the racing department*'.

Leaving aside these observations for the moment, which are somewhat fanciful, we need to acknowledge that Austin did have his usual patriarchal interest in the competition section and particularly in the drivers. For example, his protectiveness extended to not allowing Kay Petre, arguably the finest female racing driver ever, to race the twin cams, confining her to the similar looking, but slower, side valve predecessor.

What he could not protect her from was the recklessness of others. Practising at Brooklands for the British Racing Drivers' Club 500, to be held on September 19, 1937, Reg Parnell in an MG made an ill-conceived attempt to overtake Petre's Austin that involved passing above her on the banking.

With insufficient speed the MG veered off course and touched the back of the Austin which somersaulted and threw Petre out. She suffered severe head injuries and a minute's silence was held for her on race day. Happily such homage was premature. Although she lay in Weybridge Hospital for some weeks, partially paralysed and in need of plastic surgery to her famously alluring face, her incredible determination overcame. We will meet her again.

Understandably, the accident upset Herbert Austin greatly. It was the second racing trauma he had had to bear in under two months. Leonard Patrick Driscoll was a fine driver of Irish descent. He had in-depth mechanical know-how of both motor cycles and cars and transferred from two to four wheels in 1930. And he was a master in the rain.

Pat Driscoll was talent spotted by Waite at the 1931 Brooklands Easter meeting while driving a Lea-Francis and offered a place in the Austin team. He soon rose to be their number one (prior to Hadley) and for the 1936 season had an example of the new twin cam cars.

On July 18, at that year's Madresfield Court speed trials in Worcestershire, Driscoll ran for the first time with twin rear wheels and had the differential locked—an expedient that has basically the same effect as in built 'limited slip'. The torrential rain that day should have been no great problem for the Austin star but he commented that his car had been '*dangerously out of control*'.

No one will ever know precisely what happened at Backwell Hill House hillclimb exactly a week and a day later. Driscoll was to attempt to take the record for the ascent. It had been a good Sunday's sport in the Somerset sun but just before Driscoll took off in the twin-tyred twin cam there was a scud of rain.

Beatrice Canning Brown, author of the definitive history of the racing Seven (*Austin Seven Competition History 1922-1939* Twincam Ltd 2006), takes up the story: '*Tension rose as the scream from the Austin's engine reached those at the top of the hill. As the little car came into view it seemed as though Driscoll had made it. The car was reaching 90 mph and going extremely well. Suddenly it seemed to flick and control was lost. A great gasp went up as he left the track and rammed into the adjacent woodland where it overturned and hit a tree*'.

Driscoll was thrown out of the car. He was not wearing a crash helmet, only his familiar thin, white linen, flying bonnet. When he hit the road he fractured his skull. He did recover, but never raced again and suffered partial blindness that persisted for two years.

Bert Hadley did not see the crash but opined that it was caused by a combination of the twin rear wheels that destabilized the car, and too low tyre pressures. There are other theories. That Driscoll simply 'lost it'—highly unlikely. That a ball joint in the steering gear failed—there is no evidence of this.

What we must ask is—was the differential locked? It had been the previous Saturday, when the car was '*dangerously out of control*'. Or, was there some other modification to the rear axle? The transmission was dismantled during that week between Madresfield and Backwell to change the gearing. So it *is* conceivable. And there is only one person who could have authorized that.

You may feel that I have spent far too much time discussing racing and, in particular, fairly minor incidents that occurred two years before Leonard Lord joined the Austin Motor Company.

Bear with me. This is about the claim that Lord '*loathed the talented young Murray Jamieson*', whom he'd almost certainly never met; and that he wanted to ensure the '*twin cam Austin racers would never run again*'.

This casts Lord as fractious, irrational and spiteful—a popular image. To refer to Wood again. He describes Lord as, a man of '*many prejudices*'. This time—*The Automobile* (October 2007)—where he's writing about our subject's 'dislike' for Kimber. Yet, as we have already seen, there is no substantive evidence of that either—on the contrary.

What we can be sure of is that Herbert Austin would have been deeply upset about Driscoll's accident, just as he would be about Kay Petre's, to the extent that he did not allow the wreck of the former's car to be rebuilt.

Although the racing programme was to blossom spectacularly, to quote Canning Brown: Lord Austin was already '*cost conscious and sceptical*'. Herbert Austin had been a fine engineer; advanced in thought if not always practice. It is possible he had his suspicions about what happened on Backwell Hill.

Racing was not only expensive, it had soured. And it was now pointless, as it had been in Lord's eyes at MG. The latter car had conclusively proved itself to be a more technically advanced small sports than the Austin Seven, and was faster on the road and in circuit racing. While the twin cams were Sevens in name only.

It may be significant that Jamieson left about six months after the Driscoll accident and only about three after Petre's, although there is no possible link between the female driver's crash and her car.

Herbert Austin and Leonard Lord were not 'soul mates'; they were certainly not 'like father and son'. But they were basically in accord. If Austin was uneasy about 'Backwell', however unjustly, and further disconcerted by Petre's misfortunes so soon after, he would almost certainly have mentioned it to his 'running mate', Leonard Lord.

As far as any typically Victorian-bred industrialist can be, Lord Austin was an honourable and warm-hearted gentleman. Many who actually knew Lord—including family and a number of close colleagues—comment, unprompted, on his great kindness. So it is interesting that when Jamieson was so tragically killed in May, 1938, leaving a young window and infant son in difficult financial circumstances, and notwithstanding he had left the organization, the Austin Motor Company did nothing to help; not even covertly.

If Lord loathed Murray Jamieson it was not personally. But he could have 'loathed' what he was *perceived* to have done. That may be unfair. It may be prejudiced. But it is understandable, and it is neither irrational nor spiteful. And remember, Lord had visited that realm before. He had seen a young working man's life unnecessarily sacrificed on the altar of motor sport as a consequence of the Kaye Don episode, and been a close witness of the subsequent and fairly reprehensible machinations within the racing community.

Contrary to popular expectation the civilian lorry sold impressively well between February 1939 and the outbreak of war. Some sources have suggested that only around 1,600 were built. However, recently discovered figures reveal output was at least 4,200, possibly as high as 4,600.

Car production was equally promising. The new Eight, which had the longest run—from February 1939—sold around 16,000. The Ten, which got away in May reached about 10,000 but the Twelve that followed in August, and had no chance at all, found a negligible number of customers.

Worthwhile as these sales were, Lord's master-stroke was to have vehicles in production—probably, in the case of the trucks, to a Ministry of Defence specification—that could be immediately adapted for various military uses.

Of course, adaptation was the order of the day. A workforce that had been declining, gradually began to grow. One hundred and twenty acres of roof glass at the Works were blacked out in three days. Men and women, more used to penning the elegant motor designs of the late '30s, joined art students, architects and graphic artists to produce a camouflage pattern for the 220 acre site. It would become the national standard.

Civil engineers who had, since 1936, been burrowing beneath the landscape to construct enough air raid shelters for 15,000 individuals, now did so with renewed vigour to provide huge underground manufacturing capacity. While something Lord would have excelled at—changing the tooling and production plan—progressed at an incredible rate.

The dynamic new managing director controlled all this with cigarette on lips, rhythmic Midlands accent in full song, displaying his incredible levels of energy. However, there was much more taking place behind the scenes.

The subterranean capacity at Longbridge was mysteriously large. It has been suggested that some of the accommodation was intended to house the War Office had the Germans invaded London by approaching from the south east. In the same way the RAF headquarters was destined for Worcester, the Navy, Malvern and the Army, Droitwich—all within a 45 minute radius of the Austin Works with a degree of air access via the Longbridge airfield.

If Lord was privy to such a plan, and if it existed at all he must have been, it adds further credence to the idea that he was, among many other things, the *de facto* 'man from the ministry'!

In any event, what Lord got out of it was his own, underground, emergency HQ. It was sunk not far from the south Bristol Road, at the north end of the site, just to the west of the trim shop and machine area number five in the South Works. It comprised three storeys. On the 'top' floor was sleeping space, storage for ammunition, weapons and food, plus a fully fitted bar complete with padded leather, button-quilted counter and a range of optics. Seven feet below came a control and planning area, small telephone exchange and a section with fitted desks and filing cabinets. The basement contained pumping and air conditioning equipment.

Many of these facilities received little use. Longbridge remained remarkably unscathed throughout the war which presents another grey area, as Birmingham, and indeed the Midlands as a whole, suffered heavily in air raids.

General Erhard Milch was the brilliant chief administrator of the *Luftwaffe*. He had taken over in 1933 and by 1939 built his country's air strength to formidable proportions. As late as 1937 he was in England viewing British aeroplanes, airfields and the new shadow factories.

In the fall of that year he was back, touring RAF stations, examining production of the feeble Fairey Battle in Austin's own East Works (the shadow plant) and discussing with Dowding,

Harris and others in both the RAF and War Office, the possibility of supplying aero parts to Germany.

One theory is that Milch, and his masters in Berlin, hoped that either Britain would see 'the light', appreciate the attraction of fascism, and join the push for world domination or, the nation would be defeated. Either way, a facility such as Longbridge would be of considerable value and was worth preserving.

These are unpalatable ideas. In France, there was considerable ambivalence over the forthcoming war and in many quarters there, the hope Germany would win. It is a sense of discomfiture and embarrassment in that country to this day. Many in the United Kingdom held broadly similar views. William Morris had been a supporter of the British Nazi leader, Oswald Moseley. The Prince of Wales—he of 'something must be done' and the uncrowned Edward VIII—kept company, pre-War, with Adolph Hitler. His mistress was an enthusiastic supporter and his sister-in-law, later Queen Elizabeth, was a committed appeaser at this time.

These are ideas, associated with cataclysmic political and social change that no engineer, or managing director of a motor company, should ever be asked to deal with. But they illustrate what confronted Leonard Lord and give us an insight into the stature of the man. He was a giant among his ilk. Austin was too old, Morris was incapable and there was no one at Longbridge or, in the industry, who he could fall back upon or could have tackled the situation that faced him.

It is all very well to suggest that Miles Thomas *'was the best leader the British motor industry never had'*. When Thomas took over at Wolseley Motors in 1936 he introduced new colours for the factory walls and ceiling and had the machine tools painted battleship grey with red, green or yellow handles. Walkways were marked out in the workshops, racks provided for outdoor boots and the canteen made more comfortable with an improved menu.

This is classic, management shilly-shallying. It is the stuff of training courses at country house hotels. It does not put world class fighter and bomber aeroplanes into the sky or an exceptionally fine ambulance and a multiplicity of other trucks and hardware onto the battlefield. That is what Leonard Lord achieved.

The light vehicle line up, until 1942, included the Eight as a War Department tourer and Services' saloon. A total of around 30,000 were built. The Ten was also made as a saloon for the armed forces but more commonly appeared as a utility or pick-up truck, famously known as the 'Tilly'. In all about 33,000 were completed. Finally, in the early days of the war, a few Twelves were produced as 'middle ranking' staff cars—perhaps no more than 2,000. Between 1940 and '41 nearly all the military's cars were produced by Austin but the numbers declined dramatically afterwards as other production took precedence.

On the lorry scene there was the K2 series ambulance and conventional lorry chassis. These were produced throughout the war, the ambulance peaking at nearly 5,000 between August 1940 and July 1941 and totalling just over 13,000 for the duration. The lorry's best year was '41/'42 with more than 4,000 made on the way to a final figure of some 14,700.

From August 1940 there was a six wheeled truck—the K6—that, after a modest start at just under 1,000 in its first 12 months, wound up to a total production of 13,000 plus. In the following year—1941—a forward control, four wheel drive appeared.

Designated K5 they were known in service parlance as 'screamers' or 'moaning Minnies', no doubt from the whine of the transfer box and axles, the product, we suspect, of wartime workmanship! Finally, there was a strange-looking gun carrying version of the K5 called the 'portee'.

From 1942 production of K5s was consistently high at an annual average of nearly 4,000 but although a total of over 12,000 were built survival rate today is miniscule.

The most famous of the Austin trucks was the K2 ambulance. Affectionately known as 'Katies', they were immortalized in the 1958 John Mills/Sylvia Syms film *Ice Cold in Alex* and were the most prolific vehicle of this type in the field.

With wood and canvas coachwork, principally from Mann Egerton of Norwich, but, it is thought, also Marshall of Cambridge, the ambulance could carry four stretcher cases, double-decked, bunk style, on either side, or nine 'walking wounded'. There were many innovative features including a lead or galvanized steel drinking water tank and an on-board compressor to inflate the tyres, although the latter were of a bullet-proof design. Katies were powerful, fast, manoeuvrable and easy to drive with an excellent ride that resulted in them often being reserved for the most serious cases.

Almost as famous, and equally popular with their crews, was the ATV (*Auxiliary*—not Austin as some believe!—*Towing Vehicle*) supplied to the National Fire Service. They took over from taxis and commandeered cars in Britain's blitzed cities to tow trailer pumps—often Austin powered—and provide commodious accommodation for fire fighters and their kit. There was a more up-market version called the hose reel tender which, apart from the equipment that gave it its name, had a roof ladder, spot lamps and the badge of office of any self-respecting fire appliance, a bell.

For these vehicles, we have Leonard Lord's determination and foresight, in 1938, to thank. Some, like the K2 and K6, were so well designed and engineered they continued to be operated by the emergency services well into the post-War era. Many went on to serve in private capacities long after that. One inventive user even turned a K6 into a coach!

Apart from 'own-brand' trucks Longbridge found the capacity to build or adapt Morris Commercial C8s, most familiar as the 'Quad' field gun tractor. The ubiquitous Bedford QL was also a regular visitor to the Works. The C8s were constructed as chassis/cab units and fully bodied off the Austin site by, among others, Nuffield Metal Products. The Bedfords came to have their chassis lengthened, probably for use as wireless vans. Again, they were completed elsewhere.

The inclusion of these vehicles make it difficult to arrive at a definitive figure for Austin lorry output in WWII but it is at least 80,000, possibly as high as 100,000.

At its peak the Works was building 500 trucks a week, however, in reality this was only a contribution of some 10-12% to the national need. The major emphasis, as we shall see, was on aircraft, various forms of weaponry and ancillary items.

In 1940 Lord made a move on the personnel front that would have colossal long term consequences. He appointed George Harriman as machine tool superintendent. Harriman and Lord went back a long way. Right to the days of Morris Engines Branch in the old Hotchkiss factory.

The new Longbridge incumbent's father, another George, had been the works manager at Gosford Street. Wearing his bowler hat he strode the shops at a vast pace, talking almost as rapidly and with great enthusiasm, in a bid to extract maximum production from the plant Leonard Lord would soon redesign.

He also secured an apprenticeship for his son necessitating the sobriquet 'Old George' for the father and 'Young' for his son. Young George was 12 years Lord's junior and soon came to hang on every word the dynamic and charismatic reorganizer said.

It is difficult to assess how Lord viewed this. He would undoubtedly have been flattered. And he could not have helped realize Harriman was malleable. Years later a colleague of them both was to say: '*He* (Harriman) *did what he was told. That's why Len Lord liked him*'. The comment may go a step too far but Lord's background, general approach and attitude was such that he probably enjoyed having someone around who liked as well as respected him.

To that end, when Lord was rushed into Cowley in 1933 'Young George' soon found himself located there also. By 1938 he was assistant works superintendent. Therefore, at face value, his recruitment for Longbridge is logical and for the moment it was of no great significance.

On a drizzly November day in 1940 the pilot of a lone German raider spotted, from the cockpit of his Heinkel 111K, the reflection from the wet rails on the Birmingham-Worcester railway line alongside the Austin Works. He followed the tracks until he reached the point where a branch line entered the factory.

Turning across the site he released his bombs, which exploded in the vicinity of the foundry and forge. Three workers were killed and others injured.

At the time of the funerals the weather had not improved. Lord Austin naturally wanted to attend. At one interment, in the cold and rain, he caught a chill that developed into pneumonia. Although he recovered, his strength never returned and he died suddenly of a heart attack at Lickey Grange on May 23, 1941.

He was one of Britain's greatest automotive engineers. An innovator, entrepreneur, a person of courage and determination, a gifted and imaginative publicist, patriot and patriarch, bluff and a little gruff of voice, a committed Francophile, and, of course, the man whose Austin Seven had changed the motoring landscape for ever. Now, at 75, he was gone.

Chapter Eleven
REACH FOR THE SKY

On Austin's death, Ernest Payton, the former financial director, became company chairman and Lord technical director.

In an age when warfare is almost exclusively conducted against civilian populations, it is almost impossible for us to imagine the gargantuan amount of equipment that is required when millions of service men and women are locked in what may be termed long running, formalized, conflict.

Four million machine gun magazines, five million soldiers' helmets and two million more for fire watchers; 600,000 jerry cans, 14,000 railway wagon-loads of ammunition boxes and 20,000 stationary engines mean little, even when it is realized this is the output from just one factory. And, at face value, the figures, however enormous, reveal little about Leonard Lord.

Slightly more telling is the information that to achieve any of this output the plant had to be 'tooled, re-tooled and tooled again'; the workforce 'trained, and retrained, allocated, re-allocated and re-allocated all over again'. Furthermore, as orders, contracts and specifications changed at an ever increasing pace the specialist machine shops needed to be planned to provide their production counterparts with a vast range of implements, from precision cutters and jigs to heavy press dies weighing up to 26 tons.

This was Lord's métier. The shadow factory, free of shafting and belt drives with a full range of services laid on, provided with wide clear gangways, consistent lighting and a bright clear atmosphere were the model of efficient factory layout.

We have already seen that the output of Austin motor vehicles was relatively small despite the rather esoteric figure of 5,440,200 combined brake horsepower having been calculated for all the truck engines produced! But it was in aircraft construction and the manufacture of aero components that Longbridge excelled and we suspect it was to ensure that was so is the real reason Lord was there.

The Air Ministry had accepted Austin's first set of engine parts on September 15, 1937, and the motor—the first of nearly 56,500—ran on October 25. The first aeroplane proper they were to build was the Fairey Battle. The initial orders for these had been placed with Longbridge as early as May and June 1936 and amounted to a batch of 400 with parts for 100 more.

Production did not actually begin until September, 1938. The aircraft was a single-engined light bomber. The Belgian born chief designer, Marcel Lobelle, had designed it for the Fairey Aviation Company of Stockport, between 1932 and '33. Even Fairey believed that the Ministry specification, coded P27/32, was ill-conceived while the RAF were of the view that the machine, which carried a crew of three and 1,000 lbs of bombs disposed between a bomb bay and racks under the 54 foot wing span, was hopelessly outclassed by the German opposition.

Irrespective of that, the 'Battle', which first flew on March 10, 1936, was the only light to middle weight bomber to have type approval and much of its appeal to the ministry lay in the fact that it could be produced in large quantities, not only by its parent, but the Austin shadow factory. This would help address the vexed issue of parity with the enemy's strength that we have already examined in some detail.

As workshop space covering some 20 acres began to fill with aircraft, and with Lord firmly at the controls, there was an order for a further 386 Fairey Battles in the offing. For the moment, it failed to materialize, as the Air Ministry wanted Longbridge to switch to Wellington bomber production.

This much loved and versatile aeroplane was the sole British aircraft of its type to be produced for the duration of the war, but its manufacture did not come Austin's way either. It was decided that Longbridge, relatively untried as they would have been at that point, were not capable of building it and the entire output of 11,460 came from the factories of its designer, Vickers-Armstrong, in Weybridge, Chester and Blackpool.

In truth, and despite Lord's drive, aircraft production at the Birmingham shadow factory was not entirely on course. Sir Ernest Lemon, director general of aircraft production, reviewed the overall scheme towards the end of 1938. Lemon was a railroad man. He had been, very briefly and despite having little knowledge of steam locomotive technology, chief mechanical engineer at the London Midland and Scottish Railway (LMS), replacing the great Henry Fowler. He probably knew even less about aeroplanes, but reported that Austin were already lagging behind on Fairey Battle production and by the spring of 1940 were likely to have fallen seriously short of their delivery commitments.

What Lord was to recognize as: '*problems innumerable and immense*' and then add, '*but why dwell on them? They were solved, some decisively, most with sufficient success. If they could not always be forestalled, the personnel and technical problems of war, broad or specific, were dealt with as they came along*'. With typical flamboyance and bravado Lord responded to Lemon's criticism by asking for an order for another 670 of the single-engined bomber that would be supplied before March 31,1940!

Not surprisingly this was not forthcoming, but he was given a contract for 363 and another on June 27, 1939, for still more on condition the workforce was increased by five per cent over the next few months. The number of employees was now rising steadily towards a final total for the whole Works of 32,000.

In all, Austin built 1,229 Fairey Battles between September 1938 and December 1940—more than Fairey Aviation itself, whose output was 1,155. The total ordered from Longbridge was 1,263 but this was reduced to 929 in late 1940 as the factory geared up for Stirling bomber production. The final Austin figure is a consequence of part of the later batch being reinstated at the last moment.

It has to be said there is some confusion over the final figure and some authorities quote 1,029, but a number of company sources insist on 1,229. This could be the result of simple arithmetical errors, might be associated with those last adjustments, or with the fact that some tandem seat, dual control machines were also built.

The aeroplane itself had a number of distinctions. It was the first to enter service with the iconic Rolls-Royce Merlin engine, a few months ahead of the Hawker Hurricane. It scored the RAF's first 'kill' of the war when, on September 20, 1939, Gunner Sergeant F Letchard downed a Meschersmitt Bf 109 near Aachen in Germany. Furthermore, a Battle (P2204, identification code PH-K) was the aeroplane being flown by Flying Officer Donald Garland when he and his navigator/observer, Sergeant Thomas Gray, earned two of the RAF's first Victoria Crosses of the Second World War. Tragically, these were awarded posthumously. As it happens their 'Battle' was Fairey, rather than Austin, built.

Garland and Gray had found, like too many other brave young men, that the Fairey Battle was a useless fighting machine, pathetically under-armed and so slow it could be eliminated by a light anti-aircraft barrage, and in some cases, small arms fire. It suffered unacceptable losses. This was in no way the fault of Austin, nor indeed Fairey Aviation, who had submitted superior designs to the ministry. It had to be withdrawn from the front line in October 1940 although some fought against the German and Italian forces invading Greece in the spring of 1941.

After that the 'Battle' was confined to secondary roles like target towing, but particularly, by virtue of its excellent manners, training, with a variety of air forces including those of Australia, Canada and South Africa.

Austin moved on to the Stirling.

This was the first four-engined British bomber and given to Longbridge after Short Brothers' factory, at Rochester in Kent was heavily bombed on August 15, 1940, by low flying Dornier Do 17s. The Stirling was an entirely different proposition to the Fairey Battle. This was a big aeroplane, sharing its wing design with Short's S25 Sunderland flying boat. It was in the same class as the Avro Lancaster, Hadley Page Halifax and the American B-17 Flying Fortress and B-24 Liberator.

The brief facing designer, Arthur Gouge, when he saw ministry specification B12/36 was extremely stringent. He needed to provide for a bomb load of up to 14,000 pounds, a maximum range when more lightly loaded of 3,000 miles and, burdened with three gun turrets, a cruising speed of 230 mph at 15,000 feet. In addition, the machine was required to function as a troop carrier, capable of taking off from 175-yard runways, at outback airfields, then clear 50 foot high trees inconsiderately planted at the end. Yet another demand was that it could be disassembled and moved around by railway. The ingenious and bizarre plan was for the new aeroplane to transport soldiers to the far flung outposts of the British Empire, then be able to bomb the living daylights out of the enemy to clear a path for the infantry.

Gouge's design beat the 'spec' on most counts but it all amounted to a machine that was more than 87 foot long, had a wing span of nearly 100 foot, was not far short of 30 foot high and weighed in the region of 20 tons unladen.

The raid on Shorts could have delayed the introduction of the type by as long as a year but Austin intervention meant it went into service, named after a Scottish town, in January, 1941.

Of the 2,383 Stirlings built, the Austin contribution was 720 and although some sources put the total much lower this seems to be incorrect. The rate of production was an astonishing one-per-day.

Overshadowed as a bomber by its contemporaries the Halifax and Lancaster, it served until the end of the war in transport and glider tug roles. Its engagements are relatively unacclaimed although it took part in the Normandy Landings, in June, 1944, and Operation Market Garden that September—the successful prelude to the unsuccessful assault on Arnhem Bridge. Both campaigns were the biggest military operations of their kind in history.

The Stirling was relegated to secondary roles at the end of 1943. In May of that year Longbridge had taken up its successor, the Avro Lancaster, most famous British heavy bomber of all time. The total number of 7,377 Lancasters flew 156,000 sorties, twice as many as their closest comrade, the Halifax; dropped around 600,000 tons of bombs, saw more than half their number destroyed in the air or on the ground and endured the frightening statistic of just 35 of the total completing more than 100 missions each.

Designed by Roy Chadwick, the Lancaster evolved, in 1940, from the troublesome, twin Rolls-Royce Vulture-engined, Avro Manchester, and when fitted with four Merlins was capable of around 290 mph carrying a normal bomb load of about 18,000 pounds over a range of some 1,600 miles.

Austin received two contracts for the Mark VII version. The first was in May, 1943, for 180, and another in April, 1945, for 150. The Longbridge output is distinguishable from that of other wartime manufacturers (Avro themselves, Armstrong Whitworth and Metropolitan Vickers) by having the dorsal turret further forward and two 0.5 inch calibre guns at the rear instead of four 0.3 inch guns. Production was at the rate of about six a week.

'Longbridge Lancasters' were amongst the aircraft that took part in the 1954 film *The Dam Busters* that dealt with an attack on the Ruhr dams in 1943 by 19 of the type. However, the real raid was slightly too early for 'Austins'.

In addition to their 300-plus Lancasters, Longbridge built around the same number of Hawker Hurricane fighters for the North Africa campaign. Designed by Sydney Camm, the Hurricane was the hero of the Battle of Britain and, although overshadowed in popular myth by the more glamorous Spitfire, it accounted for nearly 60 per cent of the 'kills' claimed.

A New Zealand pilot wrote thus of flying the type: '*The coolant pipes are lagged and they give off an appropriate odour. When mixed with the various fumes from the engine it all becomes a very distinctive concoction. Very soon a slight haze appears — yes, I am definitely in a Hurricane.*

'*At cruise power, 2,000 rpm no boost and lean mixture, she gets along nicely at around 180 mph. Plus four boost gives a healthy 235 mph. The flight controls are lovely and light and reasonably well harmonised and it is surprisingly stable — a good gun platform! The elevators lack a bit of feel but it is a known problem with a new Hurricane and they will eventually free up. Power up to 2,650 and six pounds boost for some manoeuvring and it really comes alive.*

'*The large thick wings allow good sharp turns, good enough to out-turn all of its contemporaries, and there is a characteristic tuck in to watch and control as things tighten up. However, drag is relatively high and she runs out of steam a little quicker than other World War II fighters. The ailerons are light but rate of roll is relatively poor—behind the Spitfire. Loops and rolls are fine but acceleration is slow. As the nose is accelerated to around 250 mph for a loop, the cockpit becomes noticeably warmer and the haze increases. Through the inverted portion of the loop it gets cooler and clearer, and down the other side, warmer again*'.

While output of this fine machine was lamentable in the crucial years immediately before WWII, 14,000 were eventually produced, mostly by the parent company. It was, though, an ideal aeroplane to be farmed out to shadow factories. The structure of wood and fabric over a tubular steel skeleton was extremely simple and could be made with basic tools.

That is not to detract from the skill of the operatives at Longbridge because, as part of the Civilian Repair Organization, they also undertook the refurbishment of damaged or battle weary Spitfires, providing they could be flown onto the factory site. The work on this metal, welded construction, semi-monocoque machine of duralumin, was much more complex. Most of the examples treated at Longbridge returned to service with overseas air forces or as trainers.

Quite apart from the complete aircraft built by Austin the factory produced, respectively, 1,100 and 3,000 wing and fuselage centre sections for the Miles Master and Beaufighter.

The former, named after its designer, F G Miles, was completed entirely by Phillips and Powis Aircraft Limited of Reading. It was a fine aeroplane used primarily as an advanced trainer for pilots who would later handle Hurricanes and Spitfires.

The heavyweight Beaufighter was an extensively used fighter/bomber design of the Bristol company and as well as the sections made at Longbridge whole aeroplanes were constructed under the shadow scheme by Rootes. They built 260 of the 5,930 total, which makes an interesting statistical comparison with the overall volumes from their colleagues in Birmingham.

From 1941 onwards, Austin began production of the Horsa glider. These plywood craft were principally constructed in the former body shops and are the best known and most successful of their type. The intention was to concentrate troops at a battle site avoiding the dispersal associated with parachuting. The Horsa was 67 foot long with a wing span of 88. It normally carried 29 fully equipped soldiers plus, usually, a bicycle! It could also manage a jeep or a six-pounder anti-tank gun. They were towed by a variety of aircraft including the Stirling, Albemarle, Halifax, Whitley and Douglas DC3 'Dakota', the 'tug' being attached by a harness to each wing of the glider. Of the 3,800 that entered service Austin built 360. Horsas were active in many arenas but most famously the Normandy landings and Arnhem.

I have covered the different types of aircraft produced at Longbridge in some detail, not so much because of the breadth and extent of the output, which was a justifiable source of pride to the workforce, but because it helps us put in perspective the enormity of Leonard Lord's contribution to the war effort.

No other British industrialist could have implemented what was required of Lord. The fruits of his success sprang from the soil of a thorough background in mechanical engineering especially in terms of production. They blossomed in some quite astonishing early achievements and were nurtured by the Establishment to grow to maturity in the most challenging mechanized environment the world has ever seen. The ever-changing requirements of the ministries, not only as regards the spectacular large scale projects, but dozens of mundane items, called not only for amazing alacrity but incredible energy and drive.

One small example was the Oerlikon gun magazines made by Longbridge. The 20 millimetre cannon was of Swiss origin and relied on a precision made, 60 round, drum magazine. In 1941, to obtain the 110,000 output required, Lord revolutionized the production process. The craftsmanship was instantly dispensed with and he ordered the design of a drum that was a simple pressing, incredibly cheap to make and intended to be thrown away after being replenished with ammunition just a few times.

What became known as East Works, but in the '40s was generally referred to as 'the Aero', was configured on the vehicle assembly line principle with the addition of dedicated appendages, for example, the Beaufighter 'shop'. Here a male and female mix of 1,600 workers toiled.

Complete aeroplanes were built in the main part of the building, itself like a giant hanger, ablaze with floodlights under their hemispherical shades and overhung from a steel roof joist by a huge clock that would have done any railway station or town hall justice.

Later there would be an airframe factory covering a further 15 acres and a 500 x 190 ft flight shed for storing completed aeroplanes before test flying. The latter was across the road from East Works and the aircraft were towed across Groveley Lane and pulled up a ramp into the shed. At the time, this building was claimed to have the longest, unsupported roof span in the world*.

---

* The flight shed survived when most of Longbridge Works was demolished between 2006 and 2008. There has been a campaign, unlikely to be successful, to preserve it.

When the time for flying came the aircraft were moved to the airfield (always known at the Works as the 'flying ground') on a conveyor.

The smaller machines were winched onto the airfield, test flown, then ferry piloted directly to their units. The larger aircraft were taken in sections by lorry to Elmdon aerodrome—now Birmingham International Airport on the eastern flank of the city. Final assembly and testing was undertaken there.

As we know, Lord's influence on the aircraft industry extended far beyond the Austin shadow factory and one aspect of his involvement that is, predictably, controversial is worthy of mention. It is the subject of my next chapter.

CHAPTER TWELVE

THIS IS MY TRUTH, TELL ME YOURS

(Aneurin Bevan)

In 1940 Lord Beaverbrook, the Canadian-born newspaper baron, was appointed minister of aircraft production by his friend the prime minister, Winston Churchill.

Since June 1935 the government had been seeking a turret fighter that had considerable fire power from a single dorsal installation behind the cockpit. Designated F9/35, it was intended to shoot down unescorted enemy bombers. They eventually chose, in 1937, a design called the Defiant from the Wolverhampton firm of Boulton Paul Aircraft.

The original company dated back as a manufacturing concern to the Norwich of 1797 and the height of the English Industrial Revolution. By WWl they were sufficiently well established to approach the War Department for work. Rather than being contracted to make assorted equipment, they were surprised to be asked to build 50 Royal Aircraft Factory FE2b aeroplanes. Having successfully accomplished this, they moved on to additional machines and ended up having produced, not only the most FE2bs, but also more of the illustrious Sopwith Camel than anyone else.

Filled with confidence, Boulton and Paul decided to continue aircraft manufacture on a large scale and, by a strange coincidence, head-hunted John Dudley North from Austin's aeroplane section. North got Longbridge's commendable AFB1 fighter off the ground, it having been designed by Albert Ball, WWl air ace and son of an Austin director.

As we have seen elsewhere, the demand for war materials ceased abruptly with the Armistice. After struggling for 15 years the Aeronautical and Research Department of Boulton and Paul, that had been so optimistically formed in the closing stages of the war, was sold, in 1934, to a consortium that included North.

The new company was named Boulton Paul Aircraft Limited and in the year of its inception it moved to a new, purpose-built, factory at Pendeford in Wolverhampton, and triggered a chain of events that would eventually involve Leonard Lord.

By the mid-1930s, the Air Ministry realized that the increasing speed of warplanes had led to a decline in gunnery accuracy and they contracted two firms, one of whom was 'Boulton Paul'', to design a more effective turret. The latter's was originally destined for a twin-engined, medium bomber biplane they were developing called the Sidestrand IV that subsequently went into production as the equally out-dated Overstrand using, essentially, its predecessor's air frame.

---

*   The other was Parnall Aircraft who were to produce a turret for the Hawker Demon fighter.

North's concept was to replace the three open, defensive, gun positions with a pneumatically controlled, fully enclosed unit—the first of its type in the world. The design was so successful that it increased hits from 4% to 75% of rounds fired; such an incredible improvement, in fact, that the government took the patents for themselves. This meant Boulton Paul could not exploit their innovation and, worse still, the know-how could be shared with all their competitors.

The existence of the turret was soon an open secret and the French aircraft company, *Société d'Applications de Machines Motrices* (*SAMM*), approached North with a somewhat superior electro-hydraulic design from the engineer, J B A de Boysson. It could carry four machine guns of a type favoured by the French navy and from the celebrated gun maker, Darne of St Etienne. Alternatively, a single 20 mm cannon could be fitted. North entered a long-standing liaison with *SAMM*, which, in these early days, focused on the armament for an anti-bomber fighter to replace the Hawker Demon. It became Project 82 or, the Boulton Paul Defiant.

Affairs at the Wolverhampton factory now become extremely complex. In parallel with the Defiant, an aircraft carrier-based alternative was planned (Project 85). This was to be a companion machine for Blackburn Aircraft Limited's Skua dive bomber that would enter service with the Fleet Air Arm in 1938.

After lengthy prevarication by the Air Ministry, the P85 was rejected in favour of another Blackburn design, the Roc, named after a mythical bird. Its principal feature would be a turret behind the cockpit. We can conclude that this accounted, in no small measure, for Boulton Paul, with their gun installation expertise, being asked to make the armament.

Contracts for the Roc took a full three months to prepare but were ready by July 1937. However, no aeroplanes flew until December 1938 and none were delivered until the following April. The Defiant was ordered in April 1937. A 'turretless' prototype made its maiden flight that August but the type was not introduced until December 1939, although this was largely attributable to engine and undercarriage issues.

The delays were compounded by an extremely unimpressive ministerial scene. We have witnessed several times the department's tardiness, and by 1937 it was under pressure from the Admiralty over its generally *laisser faire* approach to machines for the Fleet Air Arm and, more specifically, the length of time it had taken to reach a decision over the Roc. Thus, Boulton Paul's contract for the latter contained a clause instructing them to give preference to the Blackburn machine and complete them on a one for one basis with the Defiant. This was difficult.

North's team needed to rework and re-stress the drawings for part of the Skua's fuselage to convert it into a Roc, but there were delays in obtaining the relevant information from Blackburn Aircraft, and also over reaching agreement on component sourcing.

By May, 1938, slow progress on the Roc was jeopardizing the start of Defiant production, the order for which had been considerably increased with a deadline of March, 1940, for full delivery. Extra shifts were introduced for the Navy's fighter and a parallel production line started for the Defiant.

But it was a forlorn hope that there would be a valuable interchange of construction techniques and the two tracks would advance in unison. Assembly procedures for the Blackburn-designed fuselage proved much less efficient than on Boulton Paul's own structure.

As 1939 wore on there were increasing difficulties. In June a Roc delivered to RAF Worthy Down, near Winchester, was found to be 'nose heavy'. Eight more already with their squadrons, and those still on the production line, had to be modified. In July, along with a continuing torrent of detail changes from the ministry, the wings were altered. Again a delay ensued in receiving the drawings from Yorkshire-based Blackburn.

The latter were subsequently asked to help Pendeford solve a shortage of this essential component by producing 50 pairs. They couldn't oblige. Therefore, to obtain the part quickly, Boulton Paul were forced to provide their workers with bonuses over and above the premium wage rates already being paid to attract and retain skilled labour. Not surprisingly, the company was in some turmoil.

By October 59 Rocs were in the air—88 by year's end. Then, in February, 1940, Boulton Paul refused to tender on an order for 33 of the type for the Finnish air force. Blackburn turned down the work as well and the required number of aircraft had to be sourced from the existing complement. Shortly afterwards, with the Roc and Defiant to produce and a new twin-engined escort fighter on the drawing board (P92), two further invitations to tender were refused.

By now the embryo Ministry of Aircraft Production (MAP) was flexing its wings in a way that was not to the liking of Boulton Paul. As Defiant deliveries fell behind, it revealed they would be expected to tool for Bristol Beaufighter production when the contract for the former was completed.

The Type 156 Beaufighter was a popular and versatile aeroplane developed from Bristol's Beaufort torpedo bomber. The name is an amalgam of 'Beau' and 'fighter'. The design appealed to the Air Ministry, especially as Bristol's proposal came at the moment the Westland Whirlwind was proving a disappointment. Eventually, some 6,000 'Beaus', as they were affectionately known, were built. They would take part with distinction in almost all arenas of WWll and the intention was that Boulton Paul would, along with Fairey Aviation, become part of a 'Beaufighter team'.

This was extremely unpalatable to a firm that wanted to go on designing and producing its own aeroplanes.

However, as early as the infamous 'Air Debate' of May 12, 1938, (See Chapter Nine) Sir Hugh Seely had said: '*Take next the question of types. This is a point about which I am certain and so is every person who has anything to do with industry—certain that the government will always fail if they try to produce too many types. We have said that if numbers are wanted the government have to narrow down the number of types. I believe that the number the ministry have at the present time, for which jigs have been set up and plans worked out is 93. I do not say that all these are being made, or even that it is contemplated they will be made. The Noble Lord (*Winterton, representing the ministry in the absence of Swinton*) may answer me by giving the figure of 40, or he may produce the figure of 27. If he does that, it will be another position, but the system of types will still be there, and even if only 27 are being manufactured, the figure is too large if we are to get production comparable with that of an enemy within striking distance*'. It is obvious, therefore, that when MAP was formed in 1940 it would be committed to heavy curtailment.

Boulton Paul also wanted to continue developing and manufacturing turrets, of which, circa 1940, it already had more than a dozen in the 'catalogue'. And to be fair, the ministry was encouraging it to build, on site, a dedicated factory to produce 80 a month. The requirement was soon to be *180*. Irritating although all this must have been, along with the administration's insistence on single shift working, relations were soon to become very much more acrimonious between the government, then MAP, and Boulton Paul.

The Establishment view was that a whole range of companies should take on the role of 'sub contractors', mass manufacturing to support core wartime industries. To this end, Boulton Paul were told, in February 1939, that Lucas, the electrical giant and a 'preferred supplier', should undertake a large proportion of their turret production.

Lucas, whose base was Birmingham, were in the process of establishing a ministry-sponsored shadow factory alongside Grange Road, in Cwmbran, South Wales. That it should receive turret work irked Boulton Paul and the relationship between the two was unhappy. The latter felt there was constant prevarication by the contractor who had received an immediate order for 400 bomber turrets. The *coup de grâce* was the apparent suggestion by Lucas that they should be given all Wolverhampton's production work and form a joint company in which they would be the lead player.

To be fair to Lucas, the dilly-dallying was probably attributable to considerable difficulties with their new factory. Bad weather, a shortage of construction materials, untrained local workers and a waterlogged site with buildings that had no doors, lighting or heating prevailed until spring, 1941. But by then Boulton Paul had broken off amicable relations with Lucas and complained to the ministry about their attitude. It was also around this time that Pendeford needed the loan of staff. Ironically, these came from Austin, who supplied some 500 workers between April 1940 and February, 1941.

When Winston Churchill took over from Neville Chamberlain as prime minister, on May 10, 1940, Boulton Paul's contract for the P92 (twin-engined fighter) prototypes was soon cancelled and a number of turret projects suspended.

It was into the mêlée that Leonard Lord stepped, or rather, was 'parachuted'.

Ironically, Lord's 'Boulton Paul period', which lasted less than a year—and some would say, in terms of positive activity, no more than three months—has spawned as much opprobrium towards him as was ever engendered in the motor industry!

Furthermore, the episode has been one of the most troublesome to research in the whole of this book. For my part, I have to admit, that my knowledge of the aeroplane world is extremely limited. On that basis the only advantage I have is that I came to the subject of Lord and Boulton Paul with total neutrality. Indeed, I had not heard of the company until my interest in Leonard Lord enlightened me. Along the way I have drawn my own conclusions about the company and Lord's relationship with it. It is for the reader to do the same.

Beaverbrook had the authority to appoint aircraft plant production managers with control over the regular staff. Lord was sent to Boulton Paul. He would have two assistants, named Wickwar and Smith. It is not clear who either of these individuals were but both are thought to have been Longbridge men.

Lord's appointment was announced in the June 6 issue of *Flight* magazine on the same page as a large illustration of a Boulton Paul Defiant, the caption for which heaps glowing praise on the aircraft. The entry for Lord, although accompanied by a formal portrait of him, is more restrained. It describes him as 'government manager' and assures readers that the 'arrangement' is with the approval of company chairman, Lord Gorrell, and his colleagues.

The new man's detractors claim that during his tenure Lord did virtually nothing to increase output. That he stalled turret production and took the manufacture of 20,000 of these components away from the company. This gave the knowledge, and thus potential sales, of electro-hydraulic aircraft systems to Lucas who were to be a post-War competitor of Boulton Paul.

The difficulty with this is we have no definitive information as to exactly what Lord's brief was from the Ministry of Aircraft Production (MAP *aka* Beaverbrook and Churchill) Boulton Paul's board minutes were deliberately destroyed in the early 1980s when the firm was Dowty Boulton Paul Ltd, which, as Dowty Aerospace, ceased to exist in 1992. But in any case, as with Austin and many other companies' minutes, they would only be clipped summaries of events and, more importantly, framed in such a way as to reflect an impression the organization, or even an individual, wished to give. In addition, Beaverbrook's style was often informal, instructions being given verbally or by telephone, rather than in any permanent form.

Lord's denigrators seem to cast him as little more than a MAP messenger-cum-overseer, tasked, at first, with conveying the decision that North, who had run in tandem with Herbert Strickland as managing director, was to be replaced by the latter as the sole incumbent; that North would be concentrating only on the development of new armament; that all turret production would be transferred to Lucas and Defiant output the responsibility of Boulton Paul's chief aircraft designer, H V Clarke. His critics are also of the view that few within the company had ever heard of Leonard Lord.

This last point suggests an unbelievable lack of awareness of the man who had recently turned Morris into the nation's leading car manufacturer, had served on the government's Aero-Engine Committee and was a cohort of two air ministers, first Swinton and now Kingsley Wood!

It maybe that Lord was not expected to, nor *did* make, any tangible contribution to increasing aircraft production. What figures exist are so obscure as to be virtually worthless. They are clouded by estimates, predictions, confusing terminology as to aircraft completed but not delivered, aeroplanes on test with the RAF but not officially 'delivered', plus those built but awaiting a few minor, or even significant, parts.

It has been suggested that Lord's very presence on site provided impetus to the production drive which would seem to contradict the contention that hardly anyone knew who he was and another that he was rarely there physically. Setting aside aircraft manufacture, it may help if we consider the elements we believe to be Leonard Lord's *raison d'etre* at Boulton Paul and one or two other factors.

As regards North being removed as joint managing director, it is easy to accept that this was a London decision and Lord was, indeed, 'the messenger'—the instrument not the instigator. However, North is reputed to have abhorred any government officer and to do all in his power to avoid them. Irrespective of the thinking in Whitehall we can be fairly sure Lord would not have been impressed with this approach. He would probably also have felt, in the light of his experience with Boden at Wolseley, that joint control arrangements were undesirable*.

Lord was acutely aware politically, even if he was not particularly sensitive to the political persuasions of others. He was also fiercely patriotic. Although it occurred two months before he was appointed, he would have known about the introduction of bonuses to secure Roc wings and, no doubt, viewed it philosophically. Yet, in addition, there had been a two-day strike by electricians to obtain still more cash. He could well have interpreted this as setting the tenor at Boulton Paul and, again, been unimpressed. After all, the propensity of certain sections of the workforce to agitate for more money when their comrades, paid a pittance by comparison, were dying at the Front had been a running sore since at least the First World War.

Undoubtedly the issue at the heart of Lord's tenure in Wolverhampton was the transfer of turret production to Lucas. It freed space in the new Pendeford factory for subsequent aircraft production. It was not his fault that Cwmbran were slow off the mark. When that facility did come fully on stream it had an impressive record for meeting its targets—'*100% became a matter of course*'—and the workforce were motivated and committed.

The contention that Boulton Paul were robbed of technology that would have ensured their future prosperity is hard to understand. Lucas also made Bristol, Daimler and Frazer-Nash

---

*   It is ironic that Lord was placed in that position a second time, in that he became 'joint managing director' with Payton at Longbridge after Austin's death.

turrets, at least one of which was an advanced electrically operated type (Bristol's), therefore they had a variety of formats at their disposal had they chosen to utilize them.

I think research undertaken by Lucas historian, Jackie Hill, and quoted above, confirms my belief that Lord's handling of Boulton Paul was both appropriate and an accurate interpretation of his ministry brief. And we must never lose sight of the fact that he was not imposing his own philosophies but those of the government.

It was clear, as early as the beginning of 1939, that Boulton Paul not only had serious difficulty keeping pace with detailed changes to turret design, but also in meeting demand. This is most likely to have precipitated the ministry's action in seeking an alternative supplier. Naturally, it was an unpopular development as one order alone—for the dorsal armament for the Lockheed Hudson aeroplane—was worth £208,000 to the Wolverhampton company.

The situation was exacerbated by Boulton Paul's failure to deliver Halifax turrets on time. Even with the new factory on the Pendeford site, output only reached 250 a month against Lucas's 400. The shortfall should also be viewed in the light of an ever increasing requirement—85 turrets a month for Defiants, an enlarged order for Halifax equipment and for 500 units for Albemarles, plus all the necessary spares. Admittedly, Boulton Paul were hamstrung by the need, at one point, to provide 18 variants of their designs and by having to sub-contract specialist machining to suppliers whom they found attached little priority to the work.

Overall, rightly or wrongly, it was a picture that would have been anathema to Leonard Lord. Don't forget, this is the man who, if the machining capability was not available would, and could, provide it himself (milling machines for Morris Engines and later, and even more impressively, transfer machines for Longbridge)). He was also capable of achieving the most dramatic increases in output along with savings in manpower (Morris again). Which is why I find it so astonishing that the finest production engineer in the country, possibly in Europe, could, apparently, bring so little that is positive to this relatively small company. The moreso when we have a radiant example of his talents at the Longbridge plant 20 miles down the road.

Eventually, Lucas in Birmingham and Cwmbran made 20,000 Boulton Paul turrets and at its peak production stood at 1,410 a month.

Another area of contention seems to be what we may loosely describe as Lord's profligate spending, or that of his assistants, or even of Boulton Paul personnel coerced into doing so by 'the men from the ministry'. This hinges on a follow-up order for 500 Defiants.

The board were told of the requirement on July 5, 1940, and apparently complained that the government managers had ordered, in anticipation, a considerable £1.5 million's worth of materials and parts without completing the formalities. This, of course, is classic Lord.

Some years later, during the country's life or death struggle for economic survival and his own drive for vehicle output, he was to say: '*Get the stuff in by hook or by crook—any way you like . . . just get it in*'. Even if he was not directly responsible for the procurement at Boulton Paul we can visualize him encouraging Wickwar and Smith.

The substantial order for Defiants may have been one of those verbal commitments that were part of Beaverbrook's *modus operandi* and this would have appealed to Lord (his decision, years later, to commit millions to the Mini would take about five minutes). When the paperwork materialized the order had been reduced to 300. Thus, the commitment, in the first instance, to what had almost certainly been an excessive amount of raw material was, now, even more alarming to Boulton Paul's board. However, there may have been an element of Lord 'getting as much as he could, while he could'.

But it is worth noting just how desperate the nation's plight was at this time. These events coincided almost exactly with the catastrophe of Dunkirk (May 24-June 4, 1940) and the quite devastating loss of equipment—around 60% of the nation's artillery and anti-tank capability and 50% of its tanks. Matters were complicated almost immediately by the surrender of France (June 14-17) and America's entry into the war was 18 months away. There seemed every likelihood Great Britain would be defeated and overrun.

Perhaps, upon reflection, we should commend Lord's decisiveness and dynamism and maybe even suspect that that was precisely what he was there to display.

Naturally, there are peripheral criticisms of the 'government manager'.

That Lord was divisive.

This is a familiar complaint. In this context it refers to antipathy between those who were working for Boulton Paul and those for MAP. I will do no more than quote Lord Swinton, speaking to Sir Stanley White of the Bristol Aeroplane Company, as early as February, 1936. He told White his company were '*not undertaking a commercial proposition but being asked to participate in the national interest*' (in this case the shadow factory scheme).

Another complaint against Lord is that in-house design projects were abandoned in favour of MAP approved types from elsewhere. Yet that was nothing to do with Lord, simply the 'party line' as government heeded the remonstrations of men like Seeley in the 'Air Debate'.

In February, 1941, Lord was asked to take-on, first the P-39 Airacobra, an American fighter by Bell Aircraft (later rejected by the RAF), and then either the Hawker Tornado or Typhoon when the designs became available. However, he 'resigned' the following month. By then Defiant production had stalled because of the non-availability of the Rolls-Royce Merlin XX engine that was required for the Mark II version.

Not wishing to become involved in pedantic semantics, I nonetheless place the word 'resigned' in quotes. Although there was certainly a letter of 'resignation' and whether or not Lord had been at Pendeford, personally, after the end of August, 1940, and it is maintained he had not, it seems more likely that he was 'recalled' by Beaverbrook because there was nothing more to achieve.

I question whether Lord would have been in a position to 'resign' in the accepted sense. I take as a parallel, from many years later, George Harriman saying of premier, Harold Wilson: '*When the prime minister asks, it's not a good thing to say "no"*.' Even Lord would not have contravened Churchill's wishes and I believe 'recalled' or 'relieved of his duties' are words that serve us better and give a more accurate impression. Managing director Herbert Strickland *did* resign, but two days before Lord went. Whether the two departures are connected is unknown. I suspect not.

North, who was on a Beaverbrook assignment in America, was placed back in command and immediately wrote to the minister saying Boulton Paul did not want to 'foster' the Bell Airacobra and would prefer to handle the Mustang which was better than the P-39 (Airacobra).

Business as usual?

I now reiterate what I said earlier in this section. The above is my value judgement on events that took place 70 years ago. No one who was present, and in a position to know, is still alive, and there is little, clear, reliable or unbiased information on record. Obviously, I am prejudiced in favour of Lord, but that said, I approached this issue with no preconceived view of Boulton Paul. There will be those who disagree with my interpretation. But, as this book is about 'LPL' and not 'BPA' I emphasize that the reader must judge for him or herself and, if sufficiently concerned, undertake further research.

Before leaving the topic altogether it may be of interest to look briefly at the Defiant fighter. In service it was soon found to be fatally flawed and it had an extremely short and chequered career. Although there was no forward armament the type had some initial successes from the Boulton Paul/SAMM turret with its four Browning guns against both German fighters and bombers and it took part in the Dunkirk evacuation. Possibly *Luftwaffe* pilots mistook them for Hurricanes and had not yet realized the frontal vulnerability. Once that ceased to be the case the Defiant was transferred to night fighter duties, proving quite successful during the 1940/41 London Blitz. However, it was rapidly relegated to secondary roles when more accomplished aircraft, like the Beaufighter, became available.

One final aircraft episode is worthy of mention, not so much because of its aeronautical significance, but for the foretaste it provides of future events. In 1941 Short Brothers Aviation opened a factory in White Cross Bay, on the shores of Lake Windermere, in the north of England, to build Sunderland flying boats.

When the Shorts' plant in Rochester, Kent, was attacked by German aircraft in 1940 the distant location in the Lake District was viewed as far less vulnerable. A disadvantage was the shortage of skilled labour and it was to Lord and Austin that the ministry turned to help provide the workers that were needed. Quite apart from being what we might term a 'centre of excellence', Longbridge was the obvious source because it was already building the four-engined Stirling bomber from the same design team and made using similar techniques.

Unfortunately, and in spite of the expertise they contributed, the Austin contingent emerged as a 'Trojan horse' within the Windermere camp.

Allan King, author of *Wings on Windermere. The History of the Lake District's Forgotten Flying Boat Factory* (Mushroom Model Publications 2009) says: '*The Austin men brought more than just their skill. They also brought their union membership cards and a knowledge of working practices which were a revelation to the young lads from Westmorland.*

'*Originally there had not been a proper scheme for paying bonuses on the main assembly work. Workers were on a low basic wage which could be topped up if a job was done ahead of the time allowed. The car workers arrived and demanded changes. They achieved their aim and a bonus scheme was created which enabled large amounts to be earned if extra time was put in. Of course, care had to be taken or the rate fixers would change the time on the job reducing the size of payments.*

'*Neither had the locals ever heard of double time but after the Austin people came they started getting it for a lot of things. We might have thought we were getting experts from Birmingham to help us build the aeroplanes but what they were expert at was extracting money from the bosses!*

'*Unfortunately, despite their success at setting up the bonus scheme, the Austin workers were still not satisfied and the factory buzzed with rumours of strikes. The real problem was that money for accommodation, mostly in hostels at the specially built Calgarth Village, was deducted from their pay. They had been well paid at Longbridge but having to maintain a home in Windermere and Birmingham was too much.*

'*A group did actually gather in the hangar for a sit down protest. It was just the Birmingham crowd, not all the workers. They went from the hangar up to the detail shop and formed a crowd outside but the trouble was quashed. However, the Austin workers kept up a limited form of industrial action with regular absenteeism for several months. Some were sacked and the rest never got the extra money they were claiming*'.

Altogether 35 new Sunderlands were built on Windermere, each taking about six months. Around another 25 were upgraded or refurbished.

If Winston Churchill had any view of Lord's performance in the aircraft industry it is not recorded but he said of his own protégé, Beaverbrook, that his innovation and dynamism, generally, had '*an enormous impact on production when it was desperately needed*' and added: '*His personal force and genius made this Aitken's* finest hour*'. He subsequently promoted him to minister of supply. What is of specific interest to us is that the instrument of that 'genius' and of the 'enormous impact' was, at least in part, Leonard Lord.

---

*   The family name.

CHAPTER THIRTEEN
DUPLICITY OR GENIUS?

Lord was now living, certainly for some of the time, in an imposing company house called Moorcroft in the rustic and select village of Barnt Green, to the south of Birmingham, and within a convenient drive of the Austin Works. In 1942 he became joint managing director alongside Payton, who was, of course, also chairman. It is probable that around the same time the company formally acknowledged Lord's enormous value to them and recognized that he was no longer adequately remunerated.

They were also concerned they may lose him to a competitor, although in reality there was not many places he could have moved with advantage and it is unlikely he would have wished to leave Austin anyway. Even so, on March 10, Payton, in association with R G Ash, Waite and Engelbach*, who were the only members of the board except for Lord himself, sought to address the situation and in the first instance contacted a London barrister, Charles Harman, at his Lincoln's Inn chambers.

They made the point that: '*His* (Lord's) *remuneration is, in view of the magnitude of the business and the responsibility involved very considerable, but owing to the incidence of taxation his net income is not commensurate with the labour involved. Indeed if he left the service of the company and acquired a much smaller business of his own or took a post with a smaller concern little difference would be made in his net earnings*'.

They went on to recognise that: '*Mr Lord's services are a valuable asset to the company*', and added, '*the Directors have been seeking some means of binding him more closely to the company by enabling him to acquire on favourable terms a substantial capital interest in its undertaking*'.

The question to Harman was simple. Whether, without seeking the approval of the shareholders, the board was entitled to give, or offer, Lord, on preferential terms, a non-taxable portfolio of shares. Harman's opinion was that the Austin directors could reward their new managing director in the way proposed.

By coincidence, Lord himself had taken professional advice on the subject, particularly with a view to discovering whether an acquisition of shares would increase his tax burden.

Precisely what Lord was given is not recorded but his position was consolidated. His desire, previously evident at Morris, to directly access the profits, had also been addressed and a precedent set for further allocations. For their part, the other directors must have felt reassured that he had been '*bound more closely*' to the firm.

---

*   Carl Engelbach retained his seat on the board when he retired in 1938.

In addition, they could also avoid the embarrassing circumstance that William Morris allowed to develop, whereby a key player in the industry could join a rival virtually as soon as he had left the Nuffield Organization and, if inclined, hand over all their secrets.

By now Lord's MX Series Bentley would have been nicely run in, not only by his commuting but also on the scores of other trips for the Air Ministry. Some commentators cite the car as an example of arrogance. This is invalid. Both during the war and after, Lord divided his time at the wheel between his own vehicle, various Austins and the Buick we encountered earlier. Perhaps we should take heed of the axiom that '*ownership of a Rolls-Royce* does not show the depth of anyone's pocket, merely their good taste'!

In Lord's case, when visiting ministries and works such as Boulton Paul, the Bentley would have given him gravitas; a superficial indicator of his engineering judgement, patriotism and overall standing. He was hardly going to arrive in an Austin Twelve!

Now is a convenient moment to deal with another piece of trivia sometimes used to denigrate Lord—the supposed 1940 instruction to George Harriman to scrap the parts from, or for, the Jamieson racers stored at the Works in surplus space within the underground production facilities.

This would seem to emanate from Peter King in the 1989 book, *The Motor Men*.

'. . . *a national drive to collect scrap for conversion into war material was in full swing. Lord seized on the opportunity to get rid permanently of the car*** *designed by a man he had hated, Tom Murray Jamieson, who had died in 1938. Two of his Exquisite* (sic) *1936 racing cars existed and Lord ordered Harriman to send their crankshafts, connecting rods, pistons and cylinder liners for scra*p'.

We have already looked in some detail at the alleged 'hatred' of Jamieson—a man not even on the payroll in Lord's time. But we should now go a little further. Two of the 'twin cam' cars survive intact to this day and although the third—the Driscoll example—was badly damaged in his accident, there is no suggestion it was scrapped; simply 'never rebuilt' and probably dismantled. It is also generally accepted there were enough parts to build a further three machines.

All in all there was a lot of valuable metal lying around—aluminium from the pistons, nitrided steel from the cylinder liners and crankshafts, RR50 manganese alloy from the crankcases and cylinder blocks, not to mention other alloys in wheels and fine metals in other components.

As we have seen, France had fallen in 1940, America's entry to the war was some way off and, as Britain stood alone, her survival hung very much in the balance. Salvage, or scrap drives, may have been of little practical value but they were great morale boosters and extremely useful in consolidating the population behind the war effort. Lord would have known all this. Also, even if there was to be a free world, he had no intention of taking Austin back into racing and would never have wanted to sell such a complicated and sophisticated car as the 'twin cam' to privateers.

It was, therefore, eminently sensible and utterly justifiable to scrap at least some of the remnants of the Jamieson era. Remember also, there was no National Motor Museum, no British Motor Industry Heritage Trust collection to which to donate, and no perception that there would ever be the passionate interest in historic racing cars there is today. At a time when production was all, it seems inconceivable, that Lord—or anyone else—would have diverted manpower to strip the racers and sort the material but he may have ordered the redundant spares to be scrapped.

---

*   Rolls-Royce had owned Bentley since 1931.

**   This in itself is misleading. If such an instruction *was* given it would seem to allude only to spare parts, not the cars themselves.

If the instruction to recycle was given, Harriman did not make a very good job of it! He took some of the parts home and they were returned to British Leyland after his death in 1973; and two complete cars survive!

We can rest rather less comfortably, though, with the story of the dismissal of Joe Hancock.

A J Hancock was one of the workers that went so far back as to have been recruited by Herbert Austin from Wolseley in 1905. He was soon chief designer, a post he held until one fateful day in October 1941. Hancock was probably one of those who reputedly worked without wages in the company's desperate financial plight immediately after WW1 to be rewarded with 'a job for life', and was the man who picked Stanley Edge as the draughtsman for the Seven. Other highlights would have been working on the excellent, top selling, Ten-Four, one of the archetypal Austins of the 1930s.

His demise is recounted by Barney Sharratt, from the lips of Edge, in *Men and Motors of the Austin*: '*When Lord had sent for Hancock one day Joe intimated that he would be up as quick as he could but at that very moment he'd got a traveller* with him. When Hancock went up Lord said, "When I send for anyone I want them right away. You don't seem to like that so we'd better part. Go home and don't come back. I'll send your salary".*'

Edge, of course, wasn't there. He'd left in 1925 and, again, must be relying on hearsay. Although he makes the judgement—Sharratt once more—'*It was shameful. Joe was a real gentleman and most courteous*'. Real gentleman and most courteous, he may have been, but you didn't mess with Leonard Lord. Hancock displayed remarkable lack of judgement in his response, particularly as he should have got the measure of his boss over a period of more than three years.

But there are a few further points worth making, one superficial, another, perhaps, of greater consequence, We have to ask why the *chief designer* thought it so worthwhile to spend time with, and be courteous to, a 'traveller' in preference to Lord at a time when the company was embroiled in the most onerous production schedule in its history. That would have annoyed Lord enormously.

It is possible the managing director was biding his time to dismiss Hancock. When he arrived the engineering design of the cars was moribund and there had been the machinations and prevarification over the lorries. It is hard to see that Hancock had any useful part to play in the future of the company. Certainly, Lord showed indecent haste in removing him so soon after the death of Lord Austin. And it was a harsh move that no doubt hurt a 'father of the firm' deeply. Yet times were harsh.

We have neglected for a while the serious business of military vehicle production. The Austin Ten car was the only type whose production was maintained throughout the war. Although most went to the Services the continuity is significant. All the truck models were manufactured continuously from around August 1941 onwards and it is at this stage that some crucial developments began to take place.

The 85 x 101.6 mm 3,460 cc lorry engine had its bore and stroke increased to 87.31 and 111.1 respectively giving a capacity of 3,993 cc. This unit became known as the 'Long Stroke' or 'Four Litre'. The change broadly coincided with the introduction of the K6 six wheeled, three tonner, in the latter half of 1940 or first six months of 1941, and the four wheel drive, forward control, K5 around mid-1941.

There is an opportunity here for us to dispel some further myths. It has been claimed that the six cylinder overhead valve Austin cylinder heads suffered from valve head failures and the

---

*   We are more familiar with the term 'sales "rep"'.

cylinder heads themselves were prone to crack when the vehicles were driven hard. This last fault arose, supposedly, because the castings were not allowed to weather and inbuilt stresses led to internal flaws. The story continues with the 'better-manufactured' Bedford component being in high demand by workshops servicing the Austin so simple substitution could provide an easy solution. This, of course, would be impossible as the two engines have their camshafts on different sides!

Horrendous 'running on'—up to four or five minutes—was also said, unjustly, to plague the engines. However, as has been explained recently, the stories do have an element of truth. At the time Bernard Johnson worked for Alf Depper, the head of the experimental department. He says: '*Normally Austin castings were "weathered", but the demand for engines and trucks during the war was so great the "heads" were used immediately. If there was a problem with stress cracks it was because of the pressure for output*'. While running on was a later affliction that Johnson will deal with in a moment.

In these days of deep conflict the Battle of the Atlantic was at its height. In the operations room at The Admiralty a graph covered the whole of one wall. Near the top was a thin red line. While the loss of ships stayed below that band Britain could survive. Rise above it, and all was lost.

The figures were not encouraging. The U-Boats of Admiral Karl Donitz were to sink 15 millions tons of Allied shipping, nearly 75 per cent of the total merchandise lost and contained in more than half the British cargo fleet. As well as the enemy, the brave men of the Royal Navy, merchant service and RAF Coastal Command fought over and on some of the most vicious waters on earth. Waves were so powerful they could buckle the fo'csle of a blunt bowed freighter every time they broke against it, sending shards of paint flying over the deck. So powerful that hardened sailors cringed when they started to look *up* at the sea from their destroyers, frigates, corvettes and sloops.

In these waters the British lost American lease lend trucks and tanks, oil and petrol, raw materials of many kinds, much of the million tons of additional food a week they needed to live; and Jeeps. Losses of the latter became so burdensome that the War Office resolved, in early 1943, to build a domestic alternative. With typical flamboyance Lord muscled in on this situation—'*kicked open the door*'—with an offer to supply the engine for this British 'Jeep'.

The wraps had come off what was to become the American Willys/Ford version, in virtually its mass-produced form, in the early summer of 1940. From then on, its overhead valve, four cylinder, 2.2 litre format was common knowledge.

Whether or not the six cylinder Austin lorry engine was to a government specification, Lord would have realized its suitability for a wide variety of civilian duties. Indeed, his proposals, in 1939, for the larger cars were based around this engine and eventually it would power larger lorries than the War Department types plus coaches, construction equipment, agricultural vehicles, railcars and a prestige automobile.

For the moment it was particularly fortuitous that by removing two cylinders from the earlier, 3.5 litre type, and reducing the bore to 79.4 mm, the resultant 'four' ended up at almost exactly the Jeep's specification. Over and above the basic criteria, 50 brake horsepower was required on 'pool' (67 octane) petrol. The relatively low output was to prevent over-taxing the American Jeep's well proven four-wheel-drive transmission.

This is where the issue of 'running on' arises. Bernard Johnson blames the compression ratio having been raised (6.8:1) above that of the truck, and on poor fuel. '*We tried an in-house solution from ex-MG man, Hubert Charles. It involved making an experimental "head" in bronze and revising the water spaces but it was unsuccessful and the well known expert in the field, Harry Weslake, had to be consulted. He re-shaped our "bath tub" combustion chambers to ones that were more of a "heart" form'.*

It was only a partial answer to the four cylinder's difficulties*. Nonetheless, it was sent to London for a ministry inspection. There is no evidence to suggest it was rejected but the scheme to build a British version of the Jeep did not proceed at this point.

As an aside it is interesting to note that the original idea for an American vehicle of this type came from the Bantam organization whose stock in trade was building a version of the Austin Seven inherited from the failed American Austin Car Company. Bantam eventually lost out to Willys and Ford because of production constraints and, ironically, lack of a suitable engine!

The Jeep motor was the first of a series of jobs Weslake undertook for Austin including applying similar techniques to the overhead valve six cylinder to turn it into a powerful car engine.

The real significance of Leonard Lord's involvement with the Jeep is that it legitimized the development of a brand new power unit that would be perfect for a private car once war ended. Seizing that opportunity, undoubtedly to the disadvantage of other manufacturers, would place Austin in an extremely strong position. It is for the reader to decide whether Lord was demonstrating duplicity or genius.

Some time after Bernard Johnson and his colleagues were battling with the overhead valve 'four's' combustion chamber problems and six weeks before the D-Day (June 6, 1944) landings, the six-cylinder unit caused its own serious concerns. As preparations for the Normandy offensive were taking place, K5s began to suffer potentially catastrophic engine seizures while undergoing wading tests.

The trucks were being warmed up then driven into deep water, just as they would be when leaving a landing craft. The sudden violent cooling contracted the block to such an extent the cast iron pistons 'picked up' (seized). Lord implemented a crash revision programme that involved round-the-clock working, seven days a week for several weeks, as hundreds of the lorries were returned to have their standard pistons changed for an under-sized version.

It was not an elegant solution, but the fundamental need was for the vehicles to simply get out of the water and off the beach with their essential loads. As Lord himself might have said: '*Why dwell on it? The problem was solved, with sufficient success!*'

Bernard Johnson has his own bitter-sweet memories of the K5. With a wry smile he recalls tackling the remedial work to the incredible pace set by Lord. '*I used to pull off the "heads" which was no problem in itself as there was plenty of room in the cab. But I had to beg for a few hours off on a Sunday afternoon to continue my engineering studies,*' he says. He also remembers lapping the cylinder bores. '*I used an old piston coated with grinding compound to take out the rougher patches on the castings. Every batch was a different consistency.*'

Lord installed the four cylinder 'Jeep' engine in at least one 1939, HR1 series Twelve to create the prototype 'Sixteen' registered FOG 717. He used it himself in the latter stages of the war and it was loaned to the press in the early autumn of 1944. It was not until *eight months later* that hostilities in Europe ended.

---

*   The author can confirm this as he has a letter from The Austin Motor Company dated June 28, 1948, that addresses the problem of persistent running on in a 1946 Austin Sixteen (BSI 2541), a model that used this engine.

But Austin were now positioned as the only British mass motor producer able to enter the post-War market with a new car, albeit one that wore, like all the others, pre-War clothes with a nip and tuck in the hem. Leonard Lord, emulating Churchill, was to write of the period: '*for us too, it will rank as our finest hour*'.

On Victory in Europe (VE) Day there was dancing and bonfires, parties in the streets, pubs were drunk dry and complete strangers hugged and kissed each other. Some weeks before that eighth day of May, Lord had announced not only civilian lorries but the BS1 coded Austin Sixteen car. The future, though, was not to reflect the joy or the confidence.

The issue of consultants and external solutions to internal problems, described a moment ago by Bernard Johnson, provides us, albeit indirectly, with an illustration of Lord's integrity and fairness. We must begin by looking as far back as 1919, to the work of Harry Ricardo. He was to become one of the world's most talented and versatile mechanical engineers.

Apart from being the man who gave us petrol octane ratings, among his many claims to fame were the design of the most effective tank engine of WWI and the development of the high-speed diesel. On the automobile front, he not only helped produce Vauxhall's racers for the 1922 Tourist Trophy, but an overhead inlet, side exhaust valve cylinder head (F Head*) for a commendable engine** for the Four Litre Bentley. It was required, in 1930, by the ailing company's management after W O Bentley himself had run out of steam having created his Eight Litre overhead camshaft dinosaur.

By then Ricardo had established a consultancy in Shoreham-by-Sea, Sussex, and in the desperate financial times of the day was trying to survive on royalties from a design of combustion chamber called the 'turbulent head', or, more colourfully, 'Comet'.

The engineer had long realised that, in a combustion chamber, swirl increased flame speed and thus, overall, engine performance. Also, providing the chamber was as compact as possible, it reduced the absolute distance the flame travelled and the risk of detonation ('pinking'), an engine 'killer', was reduced. To achieve these results Ricardo off-set the combustion chamber from directly above the piston and gave the former a hemispherical, or domed, 'roof'.

By the late 1920s and throughout the '30s motorists appreciated how much the layout improved the performance of staid side valve engines and either bought a 'Comet head' from an accessory shop or started to demand car manufacturers adopted its principles.

In Britain and continental Europe royalty payments to Ricardo Consulting Engineers were largely, but not entirely, honoured. In America the situation was different. Ford, General Motors and Chrysler all flouted the patent to the extent of telling their representatives on the other side of the Atlantic: '*how to bust it wide open*'. Ricardo's US licensee, Harry Horning of the Waukesha company, was unwilling to take on the giant's so the designer resigned himself to the *status quo*.

Matters came to an unsavoury head when Ricardo suspected the, now largely forgotten, Hillman Wizard of 1931, and other British models, were illicitly using his invention. A friend from Vauxhall days, Percy Kidner, had entered the motor trade and agreed to take plaster casts of the suspects' cylinder heads and especially that of the Wizard.

Ricardo's fears were confirmed and he approached the Rootes brothers, owners of Hillman and the worst offender, asking them to desist or pay up. A terse and dismissive response ensued. The court case opened in October 1933.

---

*   In F Head engines the overhead inlet valves are usually operated by pushrods and the side exhaust valves by tappet blocks bearing directly on the camshaft.

**   Interestingly, Weslake (and others) also worked on this motor.

Mr Justice Farwell presided over the nine day hearing in the High Court with Richard Stafford Cripps KC, MP* leading Ricardo's legal team. Judge Farwell found in the latter's favour, observing that the turbulent head was '*the result of long and painstaking research, the royalties were not excessive and it had been of great benefit to the automotive industry*'. However, he added that the wording of the patent was woolly and granted Rootes right of appeal.

As it happened, all this came to nought. After a few months ritual dancing by the defendants the parties reached an out-of-court settlement. It entailed the agents of the American companies who had infringed the patents, or incited firms like Hillman to do so, paying royalties in arrears. Ricardo also asked for a nominal £1,000 from all other transgressors.

It took at least 18 months to sort matters out and there was still one sour note to Ricardo's non-vindictive and generous scenario. Henry Ford, and Herbert Austin, refused to comply.

Rancorous litigation loomed. Kidner, now on the Ricardo board, was tasked with resolving the issue. He held office in at least one of the corporate bodies that represented the motor industry and had the ear, not of Austin, but his recently appointed Works director, Leonard Lord.

Discovering why, and how, Lord persuaded Austin to change his stance is problematical. That he did so, to considerable effect, is beyond doubt. The 'why' is easiest. We have already considered, although this author advances an alternative view, that Lord's rift with William Morris may have hinged on money and/or *royalties* for the Morris Eight. This possible 'bone of contention' would have been very recent at the time of Kidner's approach and Lord very susceptible to the argument that '*talent deserved its just reward*'.

The 'how' is harder, but may hint, among other things, at the fearlessness of Longbridge's new senior executive. Herbert Austin's financial bacon had been saved, in 1921, by claiming from the company a royalty on the Austin Seven he had designed. Lord may, indeed, have pointed this out! He might also have mentioned that Austin was extremely 'patent conscious' over everything he had invented or designed and would himself have expected royalties.

Whatever the detail, Lord's case was watertight. Austin became prepared to pay up, and, take up the cudgels with Ford on Ricardo's behalf. Austin and/or Lord, no doubt with Kidner in tow, prevailed on Percival Perry, the head of Ford in the UK, to approach his American supremo. Somehow, Perry persuaded a man, whose power and wealth had seemed to set him above civil law, agreed to settle the royalties owed by both the US and British Ford companies.

However indirectly, Leonard Lord had changed the policy of a man whose morals, to say the least, were ambivalent and contradictory. What it tells us about Lord is, he was a man of integrity who would listen, and act, on a fair argument.**

---

* This is the Stafford Cripps who later held a number of ministerial posts, including that of Chancellor of the Exchequer (1947-50). He was a lifelong Socialist and nephew of Beatrice Webb, a significant campaigner for, and architect of, major social reform in Britain. Ironically, it was Cripps who would deprive Lord, by taxation, of the bulk of his post-War gratuity from Austin.

** The author is endebted to Morris historian, Peter J Seymour, for relating the 'Ricardo anecdote' to him and providing much of the information.

CHAPTER FOURTEEN
EXPORT OR STARVE

By the time the Second World War ended the United Kingdom was bankrupt.

We began Chapter Eleven by trying to put into perspective the enormity of the demand for war material. It is even more difficult to come to grips with the dimensions of Britain's financial impoverishment. Quite obviously, once the conflict began, revenue from international trade ceased, not that the accounts had shown a particularly healthy picture throughout the 1930s. Whereas in 1913 exports had accounted for 23 per cent of the Gross National Income (GNI) the figure had slumped to 9.8 by 1938, the last full year of peace. The annual trade deficit for most of the decade averaged about £275 million but by the end of the period was nearer 400 million as markets for traditional British goods—coal, textiles, railway equipment, ironwork and ships—contracted and the nation became less competitive.

But by far the greatest contributor to a desperate plight was 'lease lend'. This was an American Act of Congress, passed on March 11, 1941, that allowed the president, Franklin D Roosevelt, to provide Britain, and subsequently other countries, with the tools of war.

Initially, one billion dollars was allocated but eventually the infusion would amount to more than fifty billion. Of that around 31.5 (about £440 billion at today's value) went to Britain, 11.3 to Russia, just over three to France and 1.6 to China, all of whom were fighting the Axis forces—Germany, Italy and Japan—before America itself entered the war on December 8, 1941. An important attraction was that there was to be no repayment. The goods, largely munitions, food, Jeeps, trucks, and transport aeroplanes, if not consumed or destroyed, were to be returned.

In a somewhat cumbersome quote Roosevelt described the plan thus: *'It is comparable to one neighbour's lending another a garden hose to put out a fire in his home. I don't say, "Neighbour, my garden hose cost me $15; you have to pay me $15 for it". I don't want $15—I want my garden hose back after the fire is over.'* A more elegant description of his portrayed the United States as *'the arsenal of democracy'*.

The president's magnanimity had placed him in a difficult situation. He had taken a long step from the isolationist policy to which America had adhered since the end of The Great War and the neutrality laws that required foreign administrations wanting arms to pay for them in cash or gold. He had also sought to redress the troubled issue of Britain's WWI loans being repayable. Now he needed to hold the line that supplying the Allies with material aid might facilitate their victory and prevent his own country becoming embroiled in any kind of conflict.

But there were clearly those who thought Roosevelt was 'out to lunch' and, unfortunately, 65 of his supporters were, quite literally, when the Republican senator for Illinois, Everett Dirksen, secured a majority in the Senate that amended the Lease Lend Act. What Dirksen actually achieved was the removal of the president's autonomy over lease lend policy and secured a means of altering the spirit of the agreement. No longer the *'repayment in kind rather than receiving an invoice for the dollar amount'* Roosevelt had wanted.

Nonetheless the vital material came through, sustained the Allies as America itself geared up for war and eventually helped ensure the upper hand was gained.

On the afternoon of April 12, 1945, Roosevelt was at home in Warm Springs, Georgia, sitting for a portrait by the artist, Elizabeth Shoumatoff. He complained to her of 'a terrific headache' and went to lie down. Later that day he died of cerebral haemorrhage. The American public were shocked that he had gone. Having striven so hard to end the war in Europe, when the finish came, he was not there.

The British were similarly shocked, on September 2, when Roosevelt's successor, Harry S Truman, suddenly ended lease lend. In addition, and something that no doubt satisfied Everett Dirksen, everything had to be paid for; in annual installments, over 55 years, at two per cent interest. Even goods in transit or ready for shipment were included, although Britain was allowed to pay for durable items it already had—trucks, for example—at a 90 per cent discount. This amounted to another £1075 million of borrowed money, while also on the slate was about $6.8 billion in rent for overseas bases.

The consequences of this phenomenal debt can only be appreciated when it is realised that it was not cleared until *2006* and repayment had to be deferred on six occasions. The WWI loan has never been fully repaid.

Leonard Lord though, with outstanding skill and perspicacity, had been manoeuvring the Austin Motor Company into a position where it was poised to dominate the British and Empire mass production motor industry. The model range was neatly spread across the customer base. It was attractive looking and recently, if not freshly, from the drawing board. The engines were in place—three reworked four cylinder side valves, an excellent overhead valve 'four' and a big six cylinder of the same configuration. All were also capable of sustaining a light to middle weight commercial vehicle range.

But the crippling financial position in which the country as a whole found itself put a different vista on the entire landscape and emphasizes the breadth of the problem with which Lord was dealing.

Politically, Conservative premier, Winston Churchill, was about to snatch defeat from the jaws of victory. There had not been a general election in Britain since 1935 and as the war drew to a close the Labour Party withdrew from the coalition, or national government, that is the norm in wartime, and precipitated a ballot. Voting took place on July 5 but the results were not announced until the 26th of the month because of the inevitable delay in collecting results from Service personnel operating overseas. Just a month before the polls Churchill's popularity rating was 83%. Nonetheless, he suffered a crushing defeat when the Labour Party leader, Clement Attlee, was elected with a majority of 145.

One fairly superficial explanation for the 'carnage' is that Churchill had opened a lack-lustre campaign with a speech that included the extremely ill-chosen observation that any Labour government would need a Gestapo-style body to implement its policies.

The reality was that Labour offered measures that were extremely attractive to both civilians and Servicemen and women who had witnessed the deprivations, and widespread poverty of the almost entirely Conservative-governed 1930s. Churchill might have been the national hero but his competence as a peacetime leader was viewed with scepticism.

The alternative was the promise of a full welfare state including a nationalised 'cradle to grave' health service, expanded state education, national insurance and a much-needed housing policy. The plan was actually the work of a Liberal economist and sociologist, William (later Lord) Beveridge and when published in 1942 had the rare distinction, for such a document, of becoming a best seller. The Labour Party adopted it eagerly.

Kind and compassionate though Leonard Lord often was, when he read Labour's manifesto he would have found aspects that were not particularly encouraging. It spoke of the 'great economic blizzards' of the pre-War age and of slumps that were *the sure and certain result of the concentration of too much economic power in the hands of too few men. Men who had only learned how to act in the interest of their own bureaucratically-run private monopolies which may be likened to totalitarian oligarchies within our democratic State*. Wisely, it warned against removing controls that would create a 'racketeers' and 'profiteers' paradise'.

The detailed plans would have caused Lord most concern. On the subject of social and industrial reform it said: *'The Labour Party is prepared to achieve it by drastic policies and keeping a firm constructive hand on our whole productive machinery; the Labour Party will put the community first and the sectional interests of private business after. Labour will plan from the ground up—giving an appropriate place to constructive enterprise and private endeavour in the national plan, but dealing decisively with those interests which would use high-sounding talk about economic freedom to cloak their determination to put themselves and their wishes above those of the whole nation.*

' . . . All parties are ready to promise to achieve that end by keeping up the national purchasing power and controlling changes in the national expenditure through Government action. Where agreement ceases is in the degree of control of private industry that is necessary to achieve the desired end.

'In hard fact, the success of a full employment programme will certainly turn upon the firmness and success with which the Government fits into that programme the investment and development policies of private as well as public industry'.

' . . . No more dole queues, in order to let the Czars of Big Business remain kings in their own castles. The price of so-called "economic freedom" for the few is too high if it is bought at the cost of idleness and misery for millions.

'The whole of the national resources, in land, material and labour must be fully employed. Production must be raised to the highest level and related to purchasing power. Over-production is not the cause of depression and unemployment; it is under-consumption that is responsible. It is doubtful whether we have ever, except in war, used the whole of our productive capacity.

'This must be corrected because, upon our ability to produce and organise a fair and generous distribution of the product, the standard of living of our people depends.

' . . . In suitable cases we would transfer the use of efficient Government factories from war production to meet the needs of peace. The location of new factories will be suitably controlled and where necessary the Government will itself build factories.

' . . . There are basic industries ripe and over-ripe for public ownership and management in the direct service of the nation.

' . . . There are big industries not yet ripe for public ownership which must nevertheless be required by constructive supervision to further the nation's needs and not to prejudice national interests by restrictive anti-social monopoly or cartel agreements—caring for their own capital structures and profits at the cost of a lower standard of living for all'.

And so the manifesto spoke of new heights of industrial efficiency; of craftsmen, designers and scientists being given full rein; of state help for exporters where 'the laggards and obstructionists' would be 'directed into better ways'; a society where there would be necessities for all before there were luxuries for the few.

The problem was—the nation was *totally 'bust'*.

Clement Attlee could not have fully appreciated this until he arrived in Downing Street. However, there was a financial lifebelt floating towards him in the shape of the Marshall Plan. This was an extremely complicated raft of, again, American legislation named after its most high profile architect, Senator George Marshall. In broad terms it sought to rebuild, physically and economically, Western Europe and repel Communist trends in countries where it was increasingly realized there was a dearth of post-war progress. On average, agricultural production stood at 83 per cent, industrial output at 88 and exports on 59 per cent of 1938 levels.

In a very long speech to Americans on March 5, 1946, Winston Churchill, now leader of the parliamentary Opposition in Britain, but back on oratory form, first coined the phrase 'Iron Curtain': *'From Stettin in the Baltic to Trieste in the Adriatic an iron curtain has descended across the Continent. The safety of the world requires a unity in Europe'*.

The severe winter of 1946-1947 saw Germany in especially dire straits with people starving or freezing to death in their homes. Britain was obviously not as badly hit, but industry came to a standstill as domestic consumption of limited fuel supplies soared.

Just three months after the 'Iron Curtain' speech, on June 5, Marshall himself gave a deliberately low profile address* from the steps of the Memorial Church at Harvard University. Without quoting figures or parameters, he offered to fund an aid programme for Europe that participants could organize themselves.

In July 1947 he persuaded Congress to rescind a directive ordering the forces occupying Germany to 'take no steps towards economic rehabilitation', and replace it with one that declared: *'An orderly, prosperous Europe requires the economic contributions of a stable and productive Germany.'*

In effect, his plan had been launched; although it was not signed-off by Truman until April 3, 1948, when the Economic Cooperation Administration (ECA) was set up to administer it.

Thirteen billion dollars was allocated to 17 countries. It was spent initially on basic commodities like food and fuel but soon embraced reconstruction materials of every kind, as was the intention. Ironically, towards the end of the scheme the money was being used by Britain to re-arm for the Korean War, which began in 1950.

It is a myth that the United Kingdom was hard done by under the Marshall Plan. It received more funding (about 3,300 million dollars) than any participating country—nearly 2,000 million more than Germany and 1000 more than France. The lifebelt did support Attlee, both politically and economically, but he wore it very uncomfortably.

Much of what the Labour manifesto promised in 1945 would otherwise have 'gone out of the window'; probably, the government would have gone with it. Thus, when Marshall aid was subsequently accepted, it was spent largely on the welfare programme and not the intended reconstruction that would make the rest of Europe economically potent.

In fairness to Attlee and his cabinet, and although the philosophies emanated from visionary Conservatives and Liberals (Rab Butler and Beveridge and John Maynard Keynes respectively), it has to be said, the social reforms of the 1945-51 Labour administration were the most significant in 20th century Britain.

---

* The speech was actually written by Charles Eustos Bohlen, who was a key adviser to Marshall and an expert on the USSR.

Meanwhile, and elsewhere, America was richer than it had ever been in its history. Germany was being rebuilt into an industrial powerhouse. The aid it received, and the guidance of Britons, even got the legendary Volkswagen into production. France, predominantly a peasant culture, rebuilt its shattered cities and landscape and got one technically astonishing Citroën back on the roads, launched another and restored its reputation as, arguably, the most beautiful country in the world. While Japan was reorganized and reconstructed by America in the guise of the Supreme Command of Allied Powers (SCAP), under General Douglas MacArthur, and became one of the globe's major trading nations.

This was the almost inconceivable environment in which Leonard Lord had to work. Driven relentlessly at one level by the desperate need for dollars. Constrained at another by allocations of none too high quality steel. And soon to be beset by a myriad of labour relations difficulties.

During the war, British industry had consumed 72 million tons of home produced steel. But even by 1939 much of the smelting plant had been worn out, and in an industry cushioned by protectionist government policies, the practices and technology were outdated.

In 1945 provision of steel was geared to an organization's ability to export. The government set great store by the motor industry's contribution. President of the Board of Trade, Sir Stafford Cripps, despite being once mis-announced by the BBC as 'Sir Stifford Crapps', was an intelligent, cultured man of integrity. He was also the person who would control that very fibre of the car makers' existence—steel.

He told guests at a Society of Motor Manufacturers and Traders' dinner in November of that year: '*We must provide a cheap, tough, good looking car of decent size. Not the sort of car we have hitherto produced for smooth roads and short journeys in this country and we must produce them in sufficient quantities to get the benefits of mass production*'.

His audience was uniquely placed to respond. As the trestles and clamps, the gun tools and stamping machines, the spot welders and saw benches were moved out of the shadow factories the motor magnates took over a heaven-sent resource.

Yet, with blinkered and myopic vision, all the majority wanted was a return to pre-war conditions, when, in 1938, an astounding 97% of new British cars could only find homes in controlled markets—i.e. via domestic showrooms, those in tariff protected zones or in the Empire.

'No!' and 'Tripe!' was the barrage from the floor that Cripps was subjected to on the night of his enlightened speech, prompting the robust riposte: '*I have often wondered whether you thought that Britain was here to support the motor industry, or the industry was here to support Great Britain. I gather from your cries that you think it is the former*'.

He was only reiterating what had been voiced earlier by a prominent Ministry of Supply civil servant: '*The motor industry is of central importance. But it is a wild horse. Every time we get on the saddle it throws us off*'.

The hard fact was, that when, for instance, the industry was offered Volkswagen on a plate, no one was interested. Even the Board of Trade took the view that the design did not have '*a long term civilian application for British producers*' and the manufacturers' only enthusiasm was for stripping the Wolfsburg factory of its machine tools for their own use and to obviate future competition. As it happened the Volkswagen was precisely the kind of car Cripps was describing when he spoke to the SMMT.

Perhaps not *the* only person who was singing off the government's 'hymn sheet', but one of the very few, was Leonard Lord. Although we do have to concede he may have had fore knowledge of the tunes and politically would not have stood within the main body of the choir.

Nonetheless, he hit the ground running. As early as November 1944 Lord, with extraordinary shrewdness, was preparing Longbridge for civilian production.

He had managed to steal a march on other manufacturers, whose wartime car output was virtually nil, by continuing to make Austin Ten cars; as many as 6,880 from August 1943 to July '44 and another 3,550 between that August and June 1945. The justification, of course, was that they were for the Services and approved essential users. But the activity would not have been entirely altruistic. Lord wanted to be first off the mark in the coming peacetime market—what was thought might be a boom—and naturally, to place Austin in pole position.

The boom never came.

Sometime after the First World War the phrase, 'winning the war, losing the peace', was coined. Attlee readily adopted it for his 1945 manifesto as a situation Labour policies would avoid. But there was little food in the shops, no smart clothes, no new cars on the road, the trains ran late and railway sandwiches were the butt of many a joke. Britain was again in the process of losing the peace. For the motor industry its policies were, as Peter Hennessy puts it (*Never Again*, Jonathan Cape 1992), '*ultimately ruinous*'.

In April, 1945, Lord had £100,000 in his pocket, agreed by the board, to spend on new tooling and machinery. He also had targets. He met every one in volume if not quite by date. The civilian Tens started rolling off their military counterpart's track in June. That was relatively easy. Carry on as before. To hit July 16 for the Eight involved repositioning some 5,000 items of existing heavy equipment. On August 4, the Sixteen, with its brand new engine, came on stream followed by a revised* Twelve on October 9.

There were also lorries, including a new five-tonner and a coach chassis, although it is extremely unlikely any of the latter appeared much before 1947.

As regards volumes Lord's projections were exceeded though not in quite the intended proportions. Over the six months he wanted 2,000 of each model of car. The hope was for 2,000 'commercials' and although this was considerably exceeded it was by virtue of 4,000 car-derived (Eight and Ten only) vans.

In November, as Longbridge approached Lord's targets, the ailing Ernest Payton, retired as chairman. He was only to live for a few months more. Lord took over. It now really was '*Austin and the whole jackpot*'.

However, if Miles Thomas, now the disgruntled head of the Nuffield Organisation, is to be believed, it could all have been very different. In what has to be described as an underhand move, Payton personally approached Thomas in 1946 and over a lunch at Longbridge invited the Morris executive, as the '*best commercial man in the business*' to '*run in double harness*' with Lord—'*the best production man*'.

Firstly, such a conversation could not have taken place in 1946 as Payton had already retired, would soon be dead and Lord was supremo at Austin. It is possible Thomas has muddled the date. Yet, supposing the offer was made in 1945, it seems inconceivable Lord would have agreed to such an arrangement so Payton must have been acting independently. Furthermore, it seems highly unlikely someone of Thomas's high profile in the industry could have been at the Works

---

*   To all but the extremely observant the post-War HS1 coded Twelve was the same as its pre-War HR1 sister. But some of the panels were contoured slightly differently because the 1939 dies had been destroyed or lost and the interior was different most visibly at the instrument panel. The pre-War car used the speedometer and circular gauge cluster in front of the driver like most of the late '30s Austins while the HS1 had an entirely different, central panel, almost identical to that of the Sixteen.

without Lord knowing. It is feasible, of course, that Payton arranged the meeting for a time when he knew Lord would be away. However, he would have had to have been very distant indeed not to have got wind of the encounter and he was not out of the country during 1945, or indeed 1946.

All that said, Thomas turned down the offer, larded as it supposedly was with share options, out of loyalty to William Morris and because he knew his wife would be 'revolted'. Whether that was revolted at having a husband who worked at 'the Austin' or revolted at the prospect of a renewed association with Leonard Lord we don't know!

To jump ahead somewhat, but in the interests of dealing at a stroke with what could well be Thomas's alter ego, he tells another, very similar, story in his autobiography, *Out on a Wing*. This time Austin and Morris have merged and Thomas is ensconced in a new job as chairman of the British Overseas Airways Corporation (BOAC) but still dabbling in the motor industry and in contact with Lord Nuffield.

In this scenario Morris himself is the matchmaker and puts a proposal very similar to Payton's to Lord. This time discussions apparently took place between the latter and Thomas. Later, as Thomas tweely puts it, Lord came to tea at BOAC headquarters. But we gather the fare was a trifle acerbic and the two men parted for good.

To get one of the 1945 Austins a customer had to justify need to the Ministry of War Transport and obtain a purchasing certificate. There were only four-door models available, the 1939 Eight and Ten tourers and the two-door Eight saloon having been deleted. The post-War Eight cost £225 – 38% more than pre-War. The Ten was £310, 40% up, while the Twelve leapt 45% to £415. There was no Sixteen immediately before the war but that type now cost £445.

And it was almost '*any colour as long as it's black*'. Not quite; as there were about two other options. However, the models were what we might term de luxe, meaning trimmings like sunshine roofs and full width bumpers to add value in overseas markets.

If the less salubrious end of the motor trade was not a '*profiteer and racketeers' paradise*' it was not far short. Vehicles of any description, let alone any new ones that found their way onto the home market, commanded huge premiums. The waiting lists for new cars were as long as three years and it was not unusual for customers to order four or five different makes and take the one that arrived first.

This, of course, made nonsense of manufacturers' calculations of both demand and production.

Petrol, naturally, was rationed; to seven gallons a month, which would give in the region of 175 miles motoring in an Austin Sixteen and about 280 in an Eight. The quality of the spirit though was poor, the octane rating being around 76-80. This brought, as we have seen, technical problems with the more sophisticated engines.

Leonard Lord would have been in his element reorganizing the Works to ensure Austin were the first motor manufacturer back into this mayhem of civilian production. But the skills he possessed were much broader than that. The need to earn dollars was desperate and although the line up of models Lord had connived and manoeuvred to propagate from the 1938 Austin stable were perfectly suited for the domestic market, there were real issues about their appropriateness Stateside.

North Americans like big cars, have the environment to use them and until very recently, considered petrol consumption an irrelevance. Herbert Austin discovered this as early as 1929 when he promoted the American Austin Car Company of Delaware to manufacture a version of his Seven.

At face value, the Sixteen would appear to have been the best model with which to cross the Atlantic. It looked like a pre-War Buick, had some dandyish accoutrements, like a Bakelite instrument panel and trim, sumptuous 'armchair' seating in the front compartment that even Lord's Bentley could not boast, heating and demisting as standard and the novelty of in-built hydraulic jacks operated from under the bonnet.

The Sixteen at 2.2 litres was, of course, still small by American standards. If we take as our bench-mark Ford, the smallest 1945 car was a 3.6 litre six cylinder and the ubiquitous V8 was a 3.8. Buick were way above at 5.25 litres, Chevrolet a bit closer with, like Ford, the 'Master' models in the 3.5 bracket and Dodge were in that league too. Yet the Austin was a smooth, powerful car, with a good turn of speed, brisk acceleration, excellent Girling brakes and first class handling.

Lord though, went in an entirely different, and very imaginative and visionary direction. He chose the Ten as his US flagship in the hope that Americans would take to it as the ideal second car. It was a balanced judgement. America was more affluent than ever before. Many of its wives and daughters had adopted the motoring habit. Yet the Eight was just too small to have any appeal at all, the Twelve would have been a hopelessly underpowered sheep in wolf's clothing and the Sixteen too big, yet not big enough.

The first GS1 Ten arrived in New York on July 18, 1945, the very first British car to be exported post-War. It was joined that month by 21 more Austins of the same model priced at the equivalent of £400—about $1,600. The Fords and other American cars mentioned earlier were, very broadly, around $500 less.

Not surprising there was little interest. But this was more to do with the car itself than Lord's philosophy. Even a manufacturer at the opposite end of the spectrum—Rolls-Royce—experienced difficulties with the American market. Like Herbert Austin's bid to build Sevens there, their attempt, in the same decade, to make the 'Silver Ghost' and Phantom in Massachusetts had failed.

Now, in 1945, the Crewe company intended to sell a new model in America called the Silver Dawn. In what was almost certainly a fit of panic, the 'Dawn' was held back and a very similar Bentley sent 'over the top' first. The thinking seems to have been that if the latter, a marque that was relatively unknown in the United States, failed, it would be far less damaging than if a car bearing a universally prestigious name did so. As it happened, neither the Bentley nor Rolls-Royce did well. Crewe were to accept, as was Leonard Lord, that their models had to be much more closely tailored to American tastes if they were to succeed.

Accurate Austin production figures for 1945-46 are difficult to obtain and can be contradictory. But very broadly, 3,550 Tens were made in the ten months between August 1944 and June 1945, the majority of which would still have been for the Services. Approximately another 1,250 were produced between July, the month of the first exports, and December. Given the government were insisting that half the output was exported it is reasonable to assume that about 600 Tens went to America in 1945. A total of 1,400 of the three alternative models (Eight, Twelve, Sixteen) were exported in the same period, mainly to countries like Australia and New Zealand, although none was really suitable for the local conditions.

The government sanctioned production of 200,000 cars in 1946 and again stipulated that 50% should be exported. Steel and coal allocations were of paramount importance.

The late Geoffrey Rose, who became Austin works manager in 1953 and later served on BMC's subsidiary board, had been a long-serving Wolseley man before and after WWII, but also spent two years at the Ministry of Supply dealing with steel allocations. He suggests that attempts at bribery were not unknown. It was against this backdrop, beset with bureaucracy and laden with paperwork, that Leonard Lord became a formidable and ruthless campaigner for Austin's share of the materials.

Bill Davis, who went on to become another BMC director, tells this appealing story of Lord from the same period. With the immovable cigarette on lip and surrounded by allocation forms that demanded a reference number before they could be submitted, Lord arrives at a particularly innovative solution. '*Write in a chassis number*'.

By now, other manufacturers were appearing on the scene but only with mildly revamped 1938, and occasionally '39, models. Morris was probably the best of the bunch with their Series E Eight that did actually rival, for appearance, the 'Lord-look' Austin of the same engine capacity. But this apart, Nuffield only had a Ten. Standard had an Eight, a Twelve and a good-looking Fourteen. Hillman only the Minx.

Longbridge had a deservedly good year in 1946. In March alone they produced more than 4,000 cars and well over 1,200 commercials. In May prices were forced up by the rising cost of material and labour. The hike averaged about 8% and saw the Austin Eight rise to £270; the all-important Ten to £330; the inconsequential Twelve up £35 to £450 and the Sixteen on £495.

As a whole, the industry made just over 291,000 cars that year but exported barely 86,500. By Christmas Austin had exported 25,500 cars and van derivatives, and 5,450 trucks, a valuable percentage going to America.

1946 saw other landmarks for Longbridge. The most spectacular was making their millionth car. The publicity that surrounded the event gives us an insight into Lord's emerging promotional skills. Well in advance, at the board meeting of December 28, 1945, it had been agreed that in high summer the following year the company should be able to create an event around this manufacturing milestone. It was minuted as the 'Austin Progress Convention', but as far as can now be ascertained this was merely a rather grandiose term for three days at the Works themed to this one happening.

The 999,999th car was to be raffled among the workforce on the first day of the celebrations—Tuesday, June 25—and the 1,000,001st on the last—June 27.

Publicity manager, Jim Bramley, was given the job of identifying the correct cars. This was a difficult task in the light of what has been said earlier about the questionable nature of some of Austin's production figures.

With commendable good intent he calculated vehicles that ought to be produced in January 1947 would hold the honours. It's estimated he was about 35,000 out. But whether Lord's sums were more accurate is doubtful. Much more likely the chairman was demonstrating the instincts of the public relations professional, determined not to let facts get in the way of a good story; or rather, one that should 'break' when the weather was most likely to be bright and sunny and the media would be in the throes of their traditional 'silly season' when there is a dearth of news.

The cars taken from the line were a Ten as number 999,999, a Sixteen for the actual millionth, and a Twelve as the 1,000,001st. They were ingeniously registered GOF 99, GOF 100 and GOF 101 respectively. The Ten was won by a worker in Number Two machine shop and the Twelve by a die maker.

The Sixteen had a matt cream finish and was set aside for everyone who had contributed to its manufacture—including Leonard Lord—to write their signatures in the paintwork which was then re-treated in transparent cellulose to preserve the names for posterity. The car is now with the British Motor Industry Heritage Trust at Gaydon in Warwickshire.

Maybe the exercise did not quite have the panache of William Morris buying, in 1939, his company's millionth car, giving it to the Ladies' Association of Guy's Hospital and them raffling it to raise £1700. But it was a foretaste of Lord-backed stunts to come.

At a more prosaic level, April, 1946, saw the formation of the Austin Motor Export Corporation Limited. This had been agreed at the same board meeting as the 'Progress Convention' was conceived. The new undertaking was to be headed by Colonel Arthur Waite who, as we already know, was married to Austin's elder daughter, Irene, and had been one of the company's directors at the time of Lord's appointment.

Waite was born in Adelaide, Australia, in 1894, and served an engineering apprenticeship in his hometown before embarking on a distinguished WWI career in which he both won the Military Cross and attained the rank of Captain. He was later elevated to a full Colonel. He joined 'the family firm' on April 19, 1919—his 25th birthday and seven months after his marriage to Irene. In 1927, possibly because of sexual improprieties, his father-in-law packed him off to his homeland to work with Melbourne Austin distributors, Cheyney Pty. It was during this period that he did such great things for the Austin Seven's racing reputation by winning the very first Australian Grand Prix.

Waite returned to Britain in 1929 and, as a driver, promoted the sporting Seven still further until a life-threateningly severe accident in the 1930 Ards Tourist Trophy race, witnessed by Sir Herbert and Irene, ended his career at the wheel. However, he continued to manage the team until he joined senior management in the late 1930s.

In 1946 his brief was to oversee all the export business and increase sales, especially where they could earn dollars. On his appointment he declared, not with the style of a classic 'Lordism', but evocatively nonetheless: '*The world is our blueprint. Austin will become an even greater force in world trade than ever*'.

. . . But only if they could get the coal and the steel. That was down to Lord.

Also in 1946, Austin acquired Vanden Plas (England) 1923. This was a Kingsbury, north London-based, coachbuilder that until then had been most famous for building the majority of the four-seat tourer bodies on the 'Le Mans style' vintage Bentley, largely by virtue of its works being in the same area as that of Bentley. The company was of Belgian ancestry and had a complex lineage until the Kingsbury years. In the 1930s, after the original Bentley company had failed, Vanden Plas were one of the first builders to make batches of one body design for prestige manufacturers like Alvis, Rolls-Royce-owned Bentley and Daimler. During WWII they concentrated on aero work but immediately afterwards returned to their roots.

Under Austin's auspices they were one of the few famous British coachbuilders to survive into the latter half of the 20th century and gave Longbridge a presence in the luxury car market of which Herbert Austin would have been proud and was to Leonard Lord's liking.

Chapter Fifteen
THE SHIPS ARE WAITING

The winter of 1947 was the most brutal for 300 years. While the sun barely shone for weeks and temperatures approached minus twenty, the snow stood to the eaves. Railway locomotives froze on their tracks. In the Midlands the distinctive crimson buses were trapped or buried in the drifts. And that was before the thawing rains came. Surface water, unable to soak into the steel-hard soil, flooded into streets and homes and institutions across England.

Leonard Lord now lived at Halesend, in the tiny village of Storridge, just to the west of Malvern. Never would he have needed so much the great belted, double breasted overcoat he had taken to wear, or the trilby hat.

It would be a gross exaggeration to say there was a silver lining to the clouds over Britain, or those enveloping Lord that year. 1947 was to be, not only extremely active for Lord, but extraordinarily stressful and one of the most testing of his life. It is hard to arrive at the name of any British industrialist, in or outside the motor industry, who could have withstood the pressure.

In the industry itself, the mental stability of Standard's John Black was questionable. He was to be forced out of office by his own lieutenants. William Morris was a spent force, had been for years, and was about to have a difference of opinion with his one-time protégé, Miles Thomas, who left for pastures new. The Rolls-Royce motor management were minnows on the automotive scene. Daimler, Humber and Wolseley were virtually unheard of in the absolutely crucial American markets.

Although Austin had no high profile in that country, they had a foothold. The American Austin, and the Bantam car it subsequently hatched, were familiar names, although total sales never reached more than about 24,000. However, thanks to Lord, Austin had impressive resources in its home country and the means to attempt a re-entry into the North American market.

No silver lining; but there were a few faint streaks of lighter grey. Lord, for instance, had, in 1947, further new vehicles to release and an imaginative former-BBC journalist to help him do so. The cars were the progeny of the 'Colonial'—the replacement Lord had planned for the 28 horsepower Ranelagh before the War and that had been on test with the 3.4 litre, six cylinder, overhead valve, lorry engine. They were seen as the capital weapons in the arsenal of Waite's new export department and would be launched at the Geneva motor show opening on March 13—Europe's very first post-War salon.

The new models also gave the chairman the opportunity to revamp the company image. Taking the radiator cap from his Bentley with its handsome 'Winged B' mascot, designed by renowned artist Gordon Crosby, Lord asked Dick Burzi to rework it for Austin—a dangerous brief, given Rolls-Royce's propensity for defending their signature items in the courts.

Burzi, however, reshaped the 'B' and inclined it the opposite way to make an 'A'. Crosby's beautiful rendering of the pair of wings then metamorphed into a single, highly stylized version, attached to the trailing edge of the letter. Once it had been wrapped temporarily in silver foil Lord had what he wanted; all in the space of a day!

A new overseas-orientated insignia—'*Austin of England*'—complimented the bonnet ornament. The flamboyant and intricate script for the prototype of that took longer. About a fortnight of painstaking filing from brass, but ultimately the finished result looked well on bonnet sides and boot lids.

Along the way the 'house colours' were also changed. Harriman oversaw this project, which was concluded when sales manager, Chris Buckley, a director of local football club, Aston Villa, suggested the team's livery be adopted. Thus claret and a light blue were placed on a beige background. First to emerge with the paint pots was distributor George Startin, known in bygone times for building some of the earliest Austin Seven vans, and who were actually located in the Birmingham district of Aston.

The fresh models for Geneva were to be called Sheerline, for the big saloon, and Princess for a touring limousine. 'Princess' was the idea of publicity manager, Alan Jarvis, simply because the names of the British princesses, Elizabeth and Margaret, were appearing in the news almost daily. Lord liked the concept and shouted it to his secretary, now Ruth Bailey, in his outer office. She approved and the titles were 'rubber-stamped' in what could have been little more than a minute.

The cars were additionally designated A110 and A120 respectively—an entirely new nomenclature. It arose because, from January, 1947, the government, in a bid to encourage the purchase of smaller versions of what few new cars there were, abandoned the RAC horsepower rating for taxation purposes and charged £1 per 100 cc although the old formula remained for vehicles already in use.

Interestingly, Lord had advocated such a system for many years. Now, adopting the Treasury's lead, it was confirmed at the board meeting of July 10 that future Austin model descriptions would accord with the new structure. That is, reflect brake horsepower and not some contrived output. A flat rate of £10 was introduced in 1948, flying in the face of the five pounds with extra duty on petrol to promote economy, that the industry had asked for.

Only the first 12 Sheerlines and 32 Princesses received the 3.4 litre engine. The four litre was substituted almost immediately and the nomenclature changed accordingly—A125, A135.

Perhaps inevitably, on the basis of its appearance, the Sheerline, which was made at Longbridge, while the Princess was coach-built at newly acquired Vanden Plas, was dubbed a 'poor man's Bentley'—some say by Lord himself. The war had changed little in a classist, demimonde British society! It remains a mystery why the A125 looked so like the coarse relation of Crewe's timelessly elegant and perfectly balanced Mark VI model.

There is evidence to suggest[*], Burzi was active on what was to become the Sheerline, as early as 1943, but in secret, because he should have been employed on war work. At least one photograph exists that shows him, reputedly towards the end of the conflict, with a plasticine model of what is either the intended A110 (aka A125) or another large post 'Lord-look' saloon. Effectively, a model to follow the Sixteen. However the dating of the picture is suspect. Burzi is shaping a soft, curvaceous saloon, quite unlike the razor-edged Sheerline, or the Bentley, that was a gentler interpretation of the same genre.

---

[*]   Trainee draughtsman Barry Kelkin quoted by Sharratt.

The only person at Longbridge likely to have known what was being planned at Rolls-Royce was Leonard Lord. Bernard King, one of the definitive experts on early Crewe-built Bentleys, writing in his own book on the Bentley Mark VI says the first experimental chassis (1-B-V1) was finished in late November, 1945. To speed progress, and although all the standard*, i.e. non-coachbuilt, examples of Mark VIs had bodies by Pressed Steel, this prototype was sent to H J Mulliner for its body.

It was completed in February, 1946, but between then and November 1947 made frequent visits to the coachbuilder's Chiswick works for rectification, including one stay of seven weeks. The second experimental chassis (2-B-V1), finished in late 1945, was actually bodied by Pressed Steel and was at their factory until March 1946.

At an Austin board meeting on August 7, 1947, the bill for a new Bentley for Lord was signed off. It was Mark VI, chassis B 246 AK, London registered JGY 1, supplied through Car Mart but delivered to the chairman in July. The saloon coachwork was by H J Mulliner whose custom-built styles were closer to the 'off the shelf' Bentley—referred to as the Standard Steel Saloon—than those of any other specialist builder.

Clearly, the design for the Sheerline was completed well before Lord received his new Bentley, but it is feasible that he went to Mulliner to choose or finalize the specification of his car much earlier and spotted 1-B-V1. Even more likely, as Austin were a major and long-standing customer of Pressed Steel and about to place their own orders with the firm, is that he visited and saw the Bentley project. He could hardly have missed it, as they would have been preparing for, in Rolls-Royce terms, 'volume' production!

We will probably never know whether, as with the bonnet ornament, and probably his Buick, Lord thrust a scrap of paper or an illustration onto Burzi's drawing board, or called him to the window and said: '*That's what we need!*' But one senses that he may have had a far greater influence on both styling and engineering design than that for which he is credited.

If he *did* re-work the Sheerline from how it was originally planned, and as an accomplished draughtsman Lord was perfectly capable of doing so, we have to ask: was it misjudged? The answer is both yes and no. What has to be remembered is the pressure to export was enormous, no one had any in-depth experience of the all-important US market and even had there been time, the highly sophisticated customer research techniques that are familiar to us, did not exist amongst UK manufacturers.**

As we know from Lord's philosophy for the GS1 Ten, he, very wisely, did not attempt to beat the Americans at their own game, but looked to the second car market. Similarly with the Sheerline and Princess, he tried to offer something different, as did Rolls-Royce. A large, traditionally British, prestige car that exuded quality and, perhaps, even a touch of quaintness.

Lord certainly loved his Bentleys and I don't think there can be much doubt that he was inspired by the Mark VI. However, one authority suggests the Princess, at least, was influenced by Packards of 1939. Moreso, I would suggest, those of 1938. This is entirely possible and

---

*   Pre-War, all Rolls-Royces and Bentleys had their bodies built onto the chassis by independent coachbuilders to the customer's individual requirements. From 1945 onwards there were standard 'off-the-shelf' models.

**   It is true that market research was taking place in industry in the 1920s and the philosophies were appreciated long before this. However, the procedures were practiced, in the main, by American organizations. This is evidenced by the customer sampling we witnessed in an earlier chapter when discussing the eight horsepower Ford.

extremely logical. Trends from both the 110 and 160 series and the earlier Packard 'Six' are apparent, as, indeed, they are from Buicks and Cadillacs of around the same time.

The features are even more striking in the 'Lord-look' cars of 1939, of course, and we suspect we know why! Furthermore, the plasticine model Burzi is pictured working on and mentioned earlier, reflects all these shapes. Thus, for American customers, Lord may have also have built in an element of nostalgia for their pre-War styles.

If he can be blamed for misjudging the Sheerline market, it was at home. Whether or not he actually described the car as 'a poor man's Bentley' he would have been wrong. There is no such thing. Bentleys are bought for their ethos and the qualities they embody. There is no substitute however much it looks like the genuine article. Just as there could never be a 'cheap Bentley' there could not be a very expensive Austin, especially in those economic climes. Apart from the snub of 'proletarian Bentley', the Sheerline had to endure the snide observation that it was 'the best trimmed lorry in the world'. Yet what it lacked in looks and prestige it compensated for technically.

Austin went to considerable lengths to refine the engine for both the Sheerline and Princess. As well as being rubber mounted the unit had such ingenious innovations as a felt pad pressing against the timing cover to dampen resonance and an in-fill of similar material between the double walls of the rocker box for the same purpose. There was an anti-surge cam profile that had been designed for the Sixteen and, from the same source, oil-cushioned interfaces between pushrods and rockers, while the crankshaft got a bonded rubber Metalastik vibration damper bolted to the pulley.

The more populist road testers gave the engine credit for giving 'real power without fuss' and even the influential *Automobile Engineer* magazine described it as 'sweet and silent'. The rest of the running gear incorporated some important Austin production 'firsts'. They included independent front suspension, hydraulic brakes, and a column gear change.

The interior had a pleasingly airy and modern atmosphere with pale walnut veneers for the dashboard and capping rails, cream faced square instruments, a light coloured steering wheel rim circling a horn ring with the indicator switch placed on top of the boss. There was also the option of cream leather for the upholstery of a bench type front seat that inherited the fold-down armrests of the Sixteen. The rear compartment was fitted with a central rest then elbow pads on each side that extended upwards to provide head rests. (Shades of the Bentley!)

In the United Kingdom the models were priced at £1,000 for the Sheerline and £1,500 for a Princess but they attracted nearly £280 and £420 respectively in purchase tax.

The Works testers found the cars suffered from brake fade, overheating of the wheel bearings, heavy steering and vibration transmitted through the column on poor surfaces. These problems were largely unresolved on the examples sent to the Geneva show. On the one hand, that Lord allowed this is an example of his impetuosity and the commercial pressure upon him. On the other we see a man who is very much alone 'at the helm', who must continually take bold and dramatic decisions in troubled waters and take the full responsibility.

The scheme to implant Miles Thomas as his running mate had been ill-conceived. The deputy he *did* have, Harriman, was indecisive and largely ineffective. The fresh talent, like that of Hubert Charles in the experimental department, who, for example, had designed a viable but disregarded independent front suspension system for the Sixteen, was being stifled by members of the old guard, such as Jules Haefli, from the 'Hancock school'.

Lord could certainly be tactless and irascible—these were the inevitable consequences of his position. He also had charm, humour, generosity of spirit and a deep sense of morality.

Sometimes he needed colleagues who would apply the brakes. Sometimes ones who could join in his dynamism. No one had the courage. If they had, the cars, and possibly much else, may have been better.

The new man in the publicity department was Alan Hess. He smoked a big cigar and sat in a corner of the advertising department ruminating on stunts to promote Austin. Apart from his BBC credentials he had been active at Brooklands in the 1930s in MG circles and was undoubtedly well connected. In mid-November, 1946, he went directly to Lord with a plan to take three Austin Sixteens through seven European capitals in seven days and arrive in Geneva to coincide with the appearance of the Sheerline and Princess at the Swiss motor show.

'*I imagined that Leonard Lord would agree,*' Hess said afterwards. '*The scheme was* big *and anything in that category appealed to him*'. Lord agreed on the spot. It was not so much that the plan was ambitious but that the chairman was cultivating one of the best 'eyes' in the industry for publicity.

However, to emphasize the point made a moment ago about the 'dead wood' that existed in the organization at the very time when the models needed to be developed and kept in the spotlight as never before, Hess faced a barrage of discouragement. Waite, whose export department would need to release the cars for the expedition, his sales manager, Bert Hegarty, and their respective deputies, Alan Tookey and Joe Bache had no enthusiasm at all for the scheme. Tookey, though, was about to embark on a trip to Scandinavia, on Hess's itinerary, and did agree to 'test the water', or snow, as it was to turn out.

Further doom and gloom arrived in his half-hearted report of December 5.

'*To visit a certain number of capitals in an equal number of days will be virtually impossible. The roads are reasonably good but not very good and they are not signposted well enough for the uninitiated. It would be necessary for local guides to be appointed*'.

He went on to claim the dealers did not believe the adventure possible so could not '*focus their thoughts on it*' and concluded by recommending '*some more leisurely procedure*' although it would then be '*difficult to obtain a news story of worldwide value*'.

Hess, new to the job as he was, must have been devastated. To his credit he carried none of this to Lord with whom failure would have already ceased to be an option. Instead he made his own approaches. To the famous racing driver and motoring writer S C H Davis of *The Autocar*, the same individual we encountered pontificating about Kaye Don's MG accident. To Fox Photos, Reuters news agency and British Movietone News. They enthused about the adventure and it began to gain momentum.

What Hess, nor Lord, nor anyone else had bargained for was the winter of '47. The route would lead from Stavanger on the west coast of Norway, to the capital cities of Oslo, Stockholm and Copenhagen then on through the heart of western Europe by way of Amsterdam, Brussels and Paris before a final leg to Geneva.

The line-up was Hess himself, who carried no co-driver to make room for one of the leading cameramen of the day, Movietone's Dick Harris, and all his equipment. Dennis Buckley, a pre-War racing driver, was to have partnered George Coates who had been at Austin since 1919 and was one of their most respected testers. But, ironically, the Sheerline and Princess were presenting so many problems that he could not be spared and Arthur Rook from production was substituted. Their media man was Reuter's Bob Brown.

Davis had the racing accolade of having beaten a giant Bentley in an Austin Seven at a top Brooklands event in 1930. Another Longbridge man, Stan Yeal, accompanied him. It was Yeal who, while working in the pre-War competitions department, had originally talent-spotted

Murray Jamieson. He went on to take charge of the apprentice scheme. They carried E C (Shep) Shepherd from Fox Photos.

The cars themselves were left hand drive models—GOV 288 for Hess, GOV 289 for Buckley and GOV 287 for Davis. All were in standard trim but fitted with the optional radiator muff and what proved to be an ineffective windscreen defroster that looked like a stringless tennis racket placed on the inside of the glass.

A shake-down trial took place over the weekend of January 24, just as the arctic conditions took hold. With the weather worsening, wretched German prisoners of war, waiting to be repatriated, struggled to dig trains out of the snow drifts around Birmingham. It seemed the team would not get much beyond Longbridge let alone reach the debarkation port of Newcastle-upon-Tyne. However, superhuman efforts and company pride on the soon-to-be-nationalized railways got the cars a passage north and aboard the *RMS Jupiter*.

A vignette from Hess may be appropriate here to illustrate in microcosm the torpor and ineptitude that Lord faced, on a much broader scale, from the Establishment. The RAC had been asked in early December to provide paperwork for the cars but when they arrived at Stavanger, in March, nothing had arrived and the Sixteens were temporarily impounded. Also, while in London, Hess had sought to have the cars exempted from purchase tax as they were to be left in Geneva. After a whole day perambulating from one government building to the next he arrived in the office of a Mr Rees. Hess recalled: '*He is the only really helpful civil servant I have ever met. He shattered the organization's traditions by being prepared to make decisions involving initiative*'. Interestingly Rees also recognized that the trip could help British exports and Austin's prestige.

Out of the pound, the adventurers made good time over a combination of soft snow and glass-hard ice first to Kristiansand then Oslo and Stockholm. The dealers en route, who according to Tookey '*couldn't focus their thoughts on the scheme*' had each prepared postcard-sized versions of their national flags to be fitted in a bracket above the windscreens.

Crossing Denmark events took a downturn. Strategically placed between the seas of the Kattegat, off the west coast of Sweden, and that of the Kieler Bucht, north of Kiel, is a square of Danish water known as the Store Baalt or Great Belt. The crossing is by ferry from Korsor on the east side to Nyborg in the west. But as the team headed away from the Austin dealership in Copenhagen towards the shipping terminal, random reports that the passage had been closed by ice for weeks and was unlikely to open in the foreseeable future were confirmed. It seemed all the team would be able to do was resign themselves to failure amid the jam of stranded lorries at the seaport. So desperate was Hess that at one point he considered hiring an aeroplane to fly the cars, one by one, across the Store Baalt.

The fates had a simpler solution.

Firstly, the harbour master had a partiality to fine cigars and English cigarettes. The supply of both gave the adventurers a favourable audience at which they were told an ice-breaker had struggled across that very morning and a ferry sailing was imminent. Second, there was a newspaper strike in Copenhagen and there seemed no possibility of adverse publicity if the official allowed these foreigners to queue jump and escape a throng of drivers already hostile to their presence.

The campaigners and their cars were smuggled aboard the ferry from a side door in the ferry building and spent the afternoon watching with relief as the vessel inched its way through a beam's width tear in the ice.

But the good fortune that had smiled on the earlier part of the run now seemed to have wholly evaporated. Even before they had reached the German border at Krusaa for a night-long drive across that country, it was snowing again and the wind was rising. Stranded drivers warned that the nation's roads were 'officially closed'. It took five hours to cover the 120 kilometres (about 80 miles) from Odense to the frontier. At one point they tried to melt the snow with a flame thrower they had included in their gear, but in the end it was the stamina of the cars and the skill to inch them through the drifts that got the party to Flensburg just inside Germany.

The swirls of wind were now so strong that at one point Hess's Sixteen, whose laden weight would have been well over 30 cwt, was blown across the road and into a snowdrift. Eventually the trio rolled into Hamburg amid the frenzy of a freak electrical storm. Dazzling blue cloaks of light swept across the blackness that obscured the tortured and broken skeleton of one of Germany's most bomb-devastated cities.

Close to exhaustion, soaked and short-tempered the drivers battled on. But there was no respite. Taking the autobahn onward to Bremen called for seamanship rather than motoring skills as they encountered flood water deep enough to cover the door bottoms and head winds so strong they reduced progress to a crawl. The normal roads were no better, strewn, or closed altogether as they were, by broken boughs and fallen trees.

In Amsterdam the dealer was sufficiently 'focused' to give the cars a routine service but also make a seamless repair to the front doors. Hinged on the centre pillar ('B' post), they had been torn out of the crews' hands by autobahn gales. and creased. By now, crowds thronged the streets to see the Sixteens pass, and, as always, eager for bad news and inaccurate as ever, the British popular press were reporting the adventurers *'missing in Germany'*.

In reality, they could now speed on to Belgium to be greeted by the British ambassador in his own Sixteen, and in Mons, be presented with a replica of the city's emblem—a brass monkey—considered 'appropriate' by all . . .

. . . Speed on into France to be met at the Porte de Chapelle, just north of central Paris, by Monsieur de Vries, the agent for the whole of that large country, with the comment: *'I speak as many words of English as years I've represented Austin—twenty'*. Unlikely. He had fought on land and in the air during WWI, played hockey for France, been a Captain in the Free French Army in the more recent war and was a holder of the *Légion d'Honneur, Médaille Militaire* and *Croix de Guerre*. He was also, as we will discover later, a devoted admirer of Lord.

De Vries organized a sparkling evening at the French automobile club in the glittering Place de Concorde—dismissed by 'ambassador' Davis with the words: *'I don't care a damn what they think of us or what happens. I'm an old man (60 actually!) and I must go to bed'*!

Meanwhile, de Vries's mechanics, at his garage in the suburb of Neuilly, worked to service the Sixteens, completely overhaul the brakes, and, presumably in anticipation of sunnier times, fit four bladed export fans.

It was easier now. The team left Paris on March 19 and having made it to Berne, were met by yet another Sixteen bearing Hess's wife, Diana. They stayed in the provincial city overnight and cruised into the capital the following day to arrive at the salon on schedule, to the minute. Leonard Lord, of course, was there to meet them and to declare his patriotism, pride in the immense achievement, and to cock-a-snoot at the doubters. *'Naturally we are proud of our cars but we are no less proud of the eight Englishmen who won through on time under such appalling conditions'*.

It was the Sixteen's finest hour. Perhaps it was Hess's. Maybe even Austin's, in demonstrating to the world the stamina of its ordinary production cars.

The BSI Sixteen went on to become one of the company's best loved models, popular as police patrol cars, as executive transport and in many other quarters. Hess came up with more escapades, although none as spectacular or creditworthy as this. For Austin the difficult times continued, while in the country as a whole, for the Labour government, things could only get worse.

In the latter part of 1946 the National Union of Mineworkers, whose members were soon to be employed in a nationalized coal industry, had consistently over-estimated coal stocks to Attlee's Minister of Fuel and Power, Emanuel Shinwell. The reality was a four-week reserve, or 30% of the pre-War level. A situation that would be exacerbated by absenteeism in the new organization 2.5 times higher than when the mines were privately-owned.

Shinwell gambled on a mild winter to ensure he could avoid a confrontation with the NUM. The consequences were catastrophic. When the savage weather bit the diminished supplies either froze in the coal yards or on 750,000 wagons trapped in the ice and snow. One hundred thousand British troops, Polish comrades based in England and some of those German prisoners who had helped Alan Hess, worked by hand to open the roads and tracks. But to little avail. The population, anticipating the fuel shortages, bought electric fires and overwhelmed the output of power stations that could barely keep pace with normal demand.

The government reacted by cutting the domestic electricity supply between 9 am and noon and 2 pm and four (although it varied according to region) and they shut it off to industry completely. Austin was forced to close in February for three weeks. Not that it mattered on the home front as the petrol ration was cut by a third and soon disappeared totally. Meanwhile, MPs met by candlelight, in an unheated Westminster room, to discuss with a Russian and Icelandic trade delegation, the export of coal to those countries.

Then food started to run out. The weekly tea ration was set at two ounces, that for meat reduced from 1s 2d-worth (about 7p) to a shilling's (5p); bread supplies, never restricted through two world wars, were rationed, as were potatoes, a situation unheard of in the history of the nation. Even aspirins, to relieve the enormous public headache of deprivation, worse than during the hostilities, were in short supply being a coal by-product. Shinwell needed police protection.

Newspapers were considerably reduced in size, most magazines banned from publishing, radio broadcasts reduced and, perhaps symbolically, the mechanism of Big Ben, the great cracked bell that, as the signature of BBC new bulletins, had spoken for the nation in wartime, froze solid. American journalist Howard K Smith was to write: '*A country so small and weak as Portugal could have invaded and conquered England prostrated by cold. If ever a people deserved a happier fate it was the common people of Britain*'.

One of those 'common people'—an anonymous ex-serviceman interviewed by the social research organization, Mass Observation—commented: '*1.30 pm-3.30. I lie without lights, my bedroom is rather dark so this means I cannot read. I cannot listen to the radio. I cannot sit up in bed and do anything since the power is off and I cannot use my electric fire. The place is almost unlivable in from the point of view of heating, from early morning to six at night. I wish I were back in Egypt. I wish I were anywhere but in this goddamned country where there is nothing but queues and restrictions and forms and shortages and no food, just cold*'.

As recently as February 2009, *The Times* columnist, Paul Simon, wrote: '*The huge damage to the economy (in 1947) led to savage cuts in public spending, and contributed to the devaluation of sterling the following year; thousands of people simply gave up and emigrated. Many historians believe the winter of 1947 was a milestone in the decline of Britain as a world superpower*'.

Fiercely patriotic, and irrespective of how true are these statements, Leonard Lord would not have wanted to acknowledge their accuracy. However, the circumstances just described ought to illustrate very clearly what he was dealing with and as we progress we should come to appreciate what a pivotal figure he was within British industry.

As early as March, 1946, Lord had said: *'I cannot share in the spirit of easy optimism which can see unlimited markets ahead with continually shortening hours of work and greater rewards for less and less productive effort.'*

With a sense of theatre that makes his apocryphal maxims pale to insignificance Lord chose the days on either side of Christmas Wednesday to confront the government over coal allocations. He threatened to close Longbridge if he did not receive immediate supplies. His tonnage for the first quarter of 1947 had just been cut to the extent that a projected output of 3,000 cars was slashed to only 1,800. The story made headlines for three days in the national newspapers and was the lead on BBC news for three consecutive nights—reputedly, the only occasion up until that time, when an industrialist had achieved such coverage.

Whether it earned Lord extra fuel is an irrelevance. By early February lack of electricity had closed the Works anyway. But as Shinwell mouthed the idiotic riposte that Austin were using coal too quickly Lord acquired the reputation amongst the Left-wing press of having sought to embarrass government.

If Lord was that politically manipulative we cannot know. The National Coal Board's vesting day would fall on January 1, 1947, and the implication that it couldn't 'deliver', from one of the country's top businessmen was certainly harmful. And he is on the record as saying that he didn't care who *owned* the mines but was in despair as to who *controlled* them.

Not long after, an elaborate display panel was erected on Longbridge's West Works to indicate the coal stock and, very pointedly, what would be its impact on the following week's employment. An interesting, if somewhat heavy handed, example of Lord's employee communications! We have to accept that he had a ferocious antipathy towards the *political* socialist movement in general, and the Labour and Communist parties in particular.

In March of that very year he told the Midland branch of the National Union of Manufacturers: *'We are told that we must co-operate with the workers. With whom are we going to co-operate—the shop stewards? The shop stewards are Communists'.* Bob Wyatt, that most mild-mannered of commentators, puts a similar sentiment very squarely in *The Austin 1905-1952*. *'Lord disliked the Labour Government'*.

But we need to place this firmly in context. Particularly now, in the 21st century and if we live in Britain, where Communism, and indeed Socialism, have become pallid and inconsequential doctrines. This is no place to attempt a history of the Communist movement. But the reader does need to understand the paranoia, to which Lord would have been a subscriber, that existed towards that political outlook from the Twenties until the end of the 'Cold War' in the very early 1990s.

The Communist Party of Great Britain (CPGB) was founded in 1920 but reformed the following year. Initially it had been an amalgam of small Marxist organizations, socialist groups and clubs, shop stewards and workers' committees. It was bolstered first by the presence of the complex individual, Cecil L'Estrange Malone MP, and then both by the arrival of a communist group led by Sylvia Pankhurst, daughter of Emmeline, and also the Scottish Communist Labour Party, who pledged their joint support.

All this stemmed from a 1919 conference, headed by Lenin and Trotsky that followed the Russian Civil War and established what became known as the Third International or Comintern. One of its objectives was: *'to overthrow the international bourgeoisie by all available means, including armed force'.* This sentiment was endorsed in the British movement by Malone who had been everything from a naval, and then decorated army officer, to an advocate of enhanced memory tuition and a foreign correspondent.

Having secured a seat in Parliament during the wartime coalition he converted to Communism and delivered a speech in November, 1920, that asked, in the event of a workers' revolution, '*what are a few Churchills or a few Curzons**(*hanging*) on lamp posts*'.

In the light of this it is easy to see how the seeds of suspicion and fear were sown throughout the British middle classes, although Communist Party membership in the United Kingdom never actually exceeded 60,000 and the movement was, essentially, purely political. It lacked the committed militancy it exhibited in many other countries.

Nonetheless, the flames of distrust were considerably fuelled by the General Strike of 1926 which, interestingly, in the light of what we have been discussing, was, in reality, a struggle between a Conservative government and mine workers. Significantly also, it would almost certainly have been the first time Leonard Lord, aged 30 and at Morris Engines, had witnessed, albeit from the sidelines, an ugly, highly divisive, labour dispute and the harsh choice between different political positions.

In essence the decline of the British coal industry post-WWI resulted in the mine-owners, with the acquiescence of the government, reducing their labourers' wages and extending their hours. Much of manual working Britain rallied to the call: '*not a penny off the pay; not a second on the day*'. However, Prime Minister Baldwin, and his Chancellor of the Exchequer, Winston Churchill, persuaded the majority of the population that the Left's advocacy of a just cause was in fact, subversion.

The CPGB, travelling on a Leninist, pro-revolution, ticket found itself in the anomalous position of having to try to persuade the Trades Union Congress to lead its members in the steel, iron, railway, dock and print industries, as well as mining, in a revolutionary direction. Yet, on May 13, after just ten days, the whole affair was called off. But it was not affluent students driving railway locomotives and genteel ladies giving lifts in their motor cars that had broken the strike. The working man was betrayed by the TUC who conceded everything, and more, to the government.

The miners fought on through the summer, autumn and early winter before hunger and hardship forced the fortunate back to the pits. However, many colliers never worked again. The CPGB though supported the cause throughout and attracted a strong following.

As we saw earlier, only a handful of Morris workers joined the General Strike and that was the norm throughout the motor industry.

The fear of the Left intensified through the Thirties as the CPGB accepted a fresh strategy from the Comintern's new leader, Joseph Stalin, of 'class against class'. Part of this involved an unsuccessful bid to infiltrate TUC affiliated trade unions and establish 'red' or more militant organizations. Words like 'Labourite' passed into the middle class vocabulary and some industrial towns were dubbed 'little Moscows'; parlance that remained until the 1960s.

When Adolf Hitler came to power in Germany in 1933 the Communists repositioned once more. The party took the view that fascism was now the greatest threat to the worker and sought to align itself with the Labour Party to meet the challenge. We now see the CPGB fighting on two fronts. At home it opposed the Conservative government's appeasement policies towards Germany but resisted war on the basis that it was the product of imperialism and the working class should not take sides.

---

*   A British statesman best known as a viceroy of India.

What blurs the picture is that in Britain, as in France, especially up until the end of the 1930s, a sizeable proportion of the middle classes and *bourgeoisie* respectively, saw the Nazis as a beneficial influence in Europe. The French, who had around 600,000 Communist party members in their midst, believed the British could not win the war that seemed increasingly inevitable, that Hitler would rid France of Communism and a unified Europe would be led by their own country and Germany.

The British position was not so strongly defined. We cannot find an archetype. The titled Sir Oswald Mosley established his Union of British Fascists that brought repellant anti-semitic violence to English streets. But self-made William Morris, backed Mosley's movement to the tune of £50,000 and said he believed in benevolent dictatorship. Mosley also counted among a mixed base of fascist-leaning friends royalty, writers, intellectuals and parliamentarians.

Of all these trends Leonard Lord would have been acutely aware. He would have made strong personal judgements. He would also have arrived at managerial assessments, although these would not be as relevant as in later years.

Once the war started the CPGB ignored the '*national unity consensus*' and continued to disrupt industry. In the first few months of hostilities there were 900 strikes and a year on year increase in disruption. Although this did not change throughout the war there was a total Communist *volte face* in 1941 when Germany turned on Russia, its former ally. Harry Pollitt, CPGB general secretary, would eventually say, perhaps to music sweet in Lord's ears: '*Why do we need to increase production—to pay for what we are compelled to import. To retain our independence as a nation.*'

Even so, and to the extreme embarrassment of coalition Labour MPs and in spite of fines and imprisonment, there were over 2,000 stoppages in 1944 with a loss of 3,714,000 working days. Most of the disruption was in the coal and heavy engineering industries. Significantly trade union membership was rising; from 500,000 in 1938 to 7.5 million in 1946. Leonard Lord would have noted all this.

When the War ended, the Left, however pink of complexion, took its revenge. In the 1945 General Election the total number of votes available was 33,204,517, Attlee's Labour Party took 11,967, 476 compared with the Conservative poll of 9,101,000. The Communists score was just 102,780 or 0.4%.

Yet suspicion and apprehension of the working class remained at what ultimately became a debilitating level. Miles Thomas actually believed the decline in British fortunes was directly attributable to that 1945 Labour victory. He goes on to reveal his very typical prejudices with an anecdote in *Out On A Wing* about an intended celebration for a Conservative victory that turned into a wake. He hears a young technician employed at the hotel to operate the election leader board and whom he describes as '*in need of a haircut and possibly a good wash*' say—'*now we've got the bastards where we want them*'.

He adds: '*I realized then that militant trade unionism and the whole shop steward system was henceforth in control. These were the men who were going to determine the wage rates and thus the cost of civilian production and the whole industrial economy of the country from that moment on.*

'*Men who had been earning high wages from making munitions were determined that their weekly wage packets were going to stay at high levels irrespective of the true values of the peace-time goods they produced. They had, it is true, a sense of loyalty to each other. They said that the men coming out of the Forces back into civilian jobs were not going to be penalized for their wartime services and that their rates of pay were going to measure up to what the "munitioneers" on the shop floor had been receiving.*

'Thus came the start of runaway inflation. From that moment the pound began to decline in its international value and the conquered countries, Germany and Japan, were given a grand opportunity of coming into economic competition with their so-called conquerors. They had lost the war but could still win the peace.'

Leonard Lord was much more direct than Thomas in his assessment of the situation. In this immediate post-War era he claimed *'he liked the TUC'*. Why is not really clear. It may be disingenuous to suggest that it was because they castrated the General Strike 20 years before. More likely that, with his strong moral stances and sense of fairness, he believed the Congress offered a safe route across the landscape I have just described, particularly as he went on to say:

'The responsible TUC official secretly feels as I do. They are good and honest men, led by the nose by a small faction of Communists who talk themselves into office and get themselves elected as shop stewards all over the country. It isn't hard. The more extravagant your promises, the more trouble you can cause, the more you'll get your pictures in the paper. And then, of course, you're somebody.

'You can't do it any other way. You cannot do it by ability or honest hard work. You never hear of the honest hard worker. I don't know why. I've got thousands in my factory'.

Yet he was not totally convinced over how hard these men worked and, paraphrasing Churchill again, was inclined to say: *'Never in the field of human endeavour has so little been achieved by so many'*. David Kynaston, in a recent but not very accurate assessment of Austin at the time (*Smoke in the Valley*, Bloomsbury, Austerity Britain Series 1948-51, 2007) observes: *'Predictably, he (Lord) saw the unions as at best a more or less evil necessity, and in the post-war years his approach to them was almost unremittingly hostile'*. As we shall soon see, such comments are, if not a mis-interpretation certainly a vast over-simplification.

CHAPTER SIXTEEN
YES, WE HAVE NO BANANAS

Eventually Spring came.

As George Orwell, the 20th century's best chronicler of English culture, who had burnt his furniture and his child's toys to keep warm in the winter of '47, put it: '*Don't worry! Two days ago after a careful search in Hyde Park, I came upon a hawthorn bush that was definitely in bud, and some birds, though not actually singing, were making noises like an orchestra tuning up*'.

For Leonard Lord, on the automotive scene, much was coming on song. After the Geneva motor show Hess said: '*I was struck by the complete lack of originality displayed by the exhibition authorities, for, with the exception of the Austin exhibits and some of the Italian, and, of course, the French midget cars practically all the stands were filled with vehicles which were more or less the same as their pre-War counterparts*'.

This underlines once again Lord's achievement, but the reference to 'midget cars' is also interesting. Most notably this would have been the Renault 4CV, as Citroën's 2CV did not appear until the following year, although there were a number of other miniature French cars like the electric Faure in existence, if not at the show.

Lord himself had alluded to midget cars in January 1947, actually coining the term 'mini'. He told sharcholders that he was not ready to make an ultra small model, but maybe we gain a further insight as to the way his mind was working long term. Particularly as he had initiated experiments with a three cylinder, two stroke, six horsepower unit as early as 1941.

Immediate concerns though were with very much larger cars. In June, two Sheerlines, one bearing the Surrey registration LPL 888, pre-empting the latter day vogue for personalized plates, were taken back to Switzerland for further testing. Whether or not the shortcomings were ever fully resolved is open to question. When the press was reviewing the model as late as 1948 the directional stability was still criticized along with the convoluted column gear change, while the brakes only received a lukewarm reception.

Although Lord pinned much hope on the Sheerline and Princess in the American marketplace, his trump card would be a small car, a replacement for the AS1 Eight, GS1 Ten and HS1 Twelve, designated A40 and named Devon for the four-door and Dorset for the two. Their creation was, perhaps, even more significant in motoring history than that of Sir Herbert Austin's Seven. Only the prosperous future of a company turned on that little car. To a large extent, the fortunes of a nation and its entire motor industry hinged on this one.

The new models were built on a conventional 'girder' chassis, whereas the Eight and Ten had used an innovative platform design. This apparently retrogressive step needs some explanation, not least, because it illustrates Lord's shrewdness and his understanding of global marketing. In engineering terms the existing Eight/Ten type of platform would not have had the rigidity to support the independent front suspension that would be demanded by the intended customers, and there was insufficient time to re-work the floor pan.

Much more importantly, a separate chassis frame enables a vehicle to be sold in completely knocked down (ckd) or 'kit' form in economies where imported, ready assembled, vehicles might attract punitive taxes. It also permits customization—the métier, for example, of the Australians with their 'utes' (pick-ups) and convertibles.

The excellent, overhead valve, 1,200 cc engine was totally new. Originally the Dorset was to have received a 1,000 cc unit and been narrower (4' 9" as opposed to 5' 1") than the more powerful Devon. But either because it simply looked awful in slim line form, or offered no identifiable advantages, this model, which was to have been branded A35*, was deemed unsuitable for export markets and was never made, not even for home consumption. Above all, the motor, from the hand of engine designer Johnnie Rix, was tough, reliable and lively; able to deliver its 40 brake horsepower at 4,300 rpm with a maximum 59 lbs/ft of torque on tap at 2,000 revs.

Technically the engine was totally conventional. A notable improvement over the side valve models it ousted was a proper oil filtration system. It came from AC-Sphinx, who also made the fuel pump, and centred on a by-pass design with a disposable element, renewable every 6,000 miles. In addition, there was a coolant pump with thermostat control—neither the Eight nor Ten had these useful devices, relying on the ancient concept of thermo-syphon. It all added up to a commendable 33 bhp per litre compared with about 29 for the old Ten and Twelve.

But more interesting than the engine was the chassis. Here we have Austin's second attempt at a production independent front suspension system. (The Sheerline and Princess you will remember had the first). It used coil springs and wishbones mounted in Metalastik bushes then connected to Armstrong double acting shock dampers. The rear springs were conventional, reverse camber, semi elliptics, underslung and with zinc inter-leafing in the Austin mode. Again there were hydraulic dampers and an anti-roll torsion bar *à la* Twelve and Sixteen but not Eight or Ten.

The car steered by a fairly typical independent front suspension two rod system incorporating an idler box. Braking was Girling hydro-mechanical. The hydraulic section had twin leading shoes while at the rear well-tried wedge and roller devices activated by rods were used.

Thus Lord had a competent, well founded design, even before the entirely fresh body was added. Burzi's work here was much more pleasing than what most other popular car manufacturers were to produce as they strove to Americanize or recreate their styles into dollar earners. Lord described the A40 in what was not one of his best crafted quotes: '*Handsome yet honest, avoiding airy flamboyance on the one hand or sombre dignity on the other*'. It was probably the advertising department who wrote for him: '*the colour has come back into motoring*'. In actuality—ever popular 'sombre and dignified black', but also royal blue, burgundy, Portland grey and mist green.

The process for achieving these shades was new too. It used thermoplastic enamel that needed baking but was more flexible than the old celluloses, needed no abrasive finishing and was more durable. To paraphrase the literature: '*of higher lustre, more weather-proof and sparkling than buffed cellulose giving an air of modern elegance not hitherto achieved in a car of this class*'.

Lord would create the most advanced motor manufacturing plant outside America to build cars like this.

---

*   A different A35 did appear later, of course.

But we need be in no doubt that the shapes—the 'smiley Buick' grille, concealed hinges and full depth doors—the colours, and the '*en suite*' furnishings, were designed to appeal primarily to the North American market. Success elsewhere was largely incidental.

Be that as it may, the A40 was a genuinely, well appointed car. There was a mix of rectangular and square, cream faced, instruments in the Stateside mode of the day; similar to the Sheerline's, but now back in the pre-War Austin location directly in front of the driver. The rest of the metal dashboard, with its lidded glove box, was finished in body colour. Not quite so much leather featured as on the Twelve but there was a central armrest in the back of the Devon and for £6 and £30 respectively there could be a heater or up-market ECKO radio.

The models were trialled in Switzerland, Norway and Belgium as well as extensively between Longbridge and the Welsh coast. As Lord boasted: '*Test and re-test and you will never have tested enough*'—and, alluding to other manufacturers,—'*before introducing new models the Austin Motor Company believes in putting them through rigorous tests under actual conditions—even though the cost of doing so is infinitely greater than the cost of submitting them to less arduous tests at home*'. But handsome though they were, and despite all this testing, the reports from the Continent were a litany of disaster. The prototypes shook themselves to pieces and broke their chassis. As wings came lose and pushed the bonnets out of line the latter flew open. Brakes faded.

George Eyston, of MG record breaking and 'Thunderbolt' World Land Speed Record fame, was enlisted by Lord to try the cars over the Alps and was able to say, with honesty, that the engine and gearbox were good and the brakes worked. (At least for a while). Whether it was as truthful to claim the '*sure-footedness of a mountain goat*' is questionable.

After 7,000 miles back at home the steering gear was wearing unacceptably, the dampers becoming 'tired' and tyres were scrubbed of their tread in half the test distance. The shock absorber arms were modified to try to improve the suspension but fundamentally the problems were not concerned with engineering.

Time was the issue. When confronted with a component that was having to be modified, Lord would storm: '*Does what we have work? Yes? Then use it!*'

With only hindsight to help us, it is hard to appreciate the urgency. Yet, by way of example, there is a parallel between Lord's position and that, in 1934, of André Lefebvre, brilliant architect of Citroën's *Traction Avant*. By the time the last pencil stroke was placed on his Parisian drawing board Citroën were bankrupt. To save the company he had to gamble on releasing a potentially world beating new model although panels were ill-fitting and brake problems abounded. In Lord's case it was the very country that was bankrupt. He had already lost around 10% of annual production through the political duplicity that had surrounded the previous winter. The materials that would keep Longbridge afloat through the next, and beyond, depended on the dollars the A40 was intended to earn.

On Sunday, May 18, with many of the Devon's and Dorset's problems unresolved, Lord sailed from Southampton for New York on the 83,000 ton Cunarder, *RMS Queen Elizabeth*. He was accompanied by his eldest daughter, Joan, now 19, his trusted secretary, Ruth Bailey and Austin Burdon an engineer, and, at 51, a year Lord's senior. None of the usual sources can tell us who Burdon was. He is not a name from Rix or Haefli's teams or from the Works generally. What we *can* be certain of is that Lord was travelling to America to pave the way for the dealer launch of the Sheerline, Princess and the two A40s a few months later.

To promote the A40s Lord spoke to the British dealers on a gramophone record posted to them. This was not an entirely original idea at Longbridge. Herbert Austin eagerly used modern techniques such as sound 'movies' to urge a variety of audiences to buy his wares. Even as early as 1928 he had used an annotated silent film of himself to address, in absentia, a dealer's banquet.

Now, in a heavily scripted delivery, Lord's light Coventry brogue told of a new era in the business, the benefits of standardization, cars that were small but the right size, that looked right and were right.

On July 7, 1947, he came home from America, also on the *Queen Elizabeth* and to the same port, then onwards to Storridge. There the family would have enjoyed an affluent lifestyle.

There were ponies for the girls while Halesend itself was a large, square, Georgian style country house with an angular portico at the front. A neatly trimmed lawn rose gently along one side to a long narrow loggia set at right angles to the main building. There, a selection of reclining chairs was protected by glass-panelled doors giving onto the grass and the rest of the grounds.

Burdon had returned by the same sailing as Leonard Lord but his occupation was now described on the passenger list as 'director'. What precisely is this gentleman's connection has so far been impossible to establish.

Lord took the *Queen Elizabeth* back to New York on Wednesday, August 27, accompanied by export sales manager, Bert Hegarty, and examples of the cars for an unveiling. Ironically, but maybe appropriately, the Americans would be the first to see the only all-new post-War British family car.

Press comment Stateside was guarded. The celebrated motoring journalist, Tom McCahill, a descendant of the 17th century outlaw Rob Roy, as well as the writer who is credited with having 'invented' the '0-60' mph road test parameter and who was prone to such prose as: '*hairier than a Borneo gorilla in a raccoon suit*', was less colourful on the subject of Austin. In a somewhat ambiguous piece for *Mechanix Illustrated* he wrote that the A40s were '*not bad to look at*' but '*not up to the usual continental* (sic) *standard*', then went on to praise the workmanship and quality of materials and the economies that were in the offing.

At least it saved Lord the trouble of a McCahill-esque retort!

The dealer response was much more encouraging and prompted the chairman to establish, before he returned to his cabin aboard *'The Queen'* on September 23, the Austin Motor Company (England) Ltd with himself as president and local man Joe Dudley, as his deputy. The new firm's headquarters was in part of the celebrated, half million square foot, 26 storey, 1920s Fisk Building, at the junction of West 57th Street and Broadway. It overlooked Central Park. Later the company would take more floor space nearby and employ 50 people to run a nationwide sales and spares operation.

That Lord had again considered his attack on the American market very carefully is evidenced by the details of the campaign, although some elements do show a degree of naïvety. The four-door car was priced at $1,660 and the two at $1,595. If anyone could have got one in the UK, a Devon was tagged at £325—about £15 less than a Ten—but with purchase tax of 36%. The Dorset was £315. By mid-1948 only 1,000 A40s had reached the domestic showrooms.

In America, as with the Ten, Lord was aiming at the 'second car' market and also, some suggest, the more technically discerning customer who might revel in the small, neat, relatively powerful overhead valve engine. Ford of America, for example, still used large capacity side valve motors and would do so for some years. So did up-market Cadillac and many others.

That this was Lord's approach, at least as regards second cars, is confirmed by some double *entendre* advertising that showed a preppy adolescent proudly standing beside the Devon that his father has bought him as a reward for '*being head of his class*'.

The Austin campaign actually got underway with what would have been an ineffective ditty on commercial radio that alluded to fuel consumption and saving cents. Nothing learnt here from the abortive pre-War attempt to launch the Seven Stateside, where the anticipated appeal of miserly mpg came to nought.

Much more sensible and of more impact was a push to educate Americans on the driving technique for a small British car—copious use of the intermediate gears to maintain revolutions and achieve what the brochures claimed would be driving 'excitement'. To some extent the publicity was self generating when the locals found they could not get into a Devon or Dorset and sparked a lively discussion on how one should enter an A40, overturning the preferred and age-old traditions of either stepping, or even walking, into American cars.

Exposure, if that is not to make a rather *risqué* pun, was further enhanced when car washes started offering a 20% discount on Austins by virtue of their size.

Individuals also took up the banner on Longbridge's behalf. One proud owner of a Dorset, engineer Frank Hocevar from Gary, Indiana, drove from New York to San Francisco visiting all 48 state capitals. He later crossed the country west to east in 57 hours 27 minutes along the 3,000-mile Route 66. No mean achievement for a man of 58. Average speed was an impressive 53 mph and petrol consumption just over 30 mpg.

Alan Hess, of course, was always on hand to provide official publicity stunts. But rather like the man who air-dropped Christmas turkeys to starving Africans, only to discover the bird is flightless, Hess realized that it *can* rain on the famously parched Bonneville Salt Flats and it was very wet indeed at the time he had booked the venue for a 10,000 miles in 10,000 minutes run in a Devon.

A quick change of plan and location by Hess and co-driver Colonel 'Goldie' Gardner, another pre-War MG exponent, resulted in 36 stock car records being taken on the twisty perimeter road of the Suffolk County Airfield at Westhampton, Long Island. They included 1000 miles at an average 65 mph.

Did the initial publicity and what followed—the Long Island successes were in April, 1949, and the 10,000 miles/10,000 minutes was accomplished at Montlhèry, near Paris, over a year later—have Lord's desired effect?

In less than 12 months 8,000 cars had been shipped to the USA and there were some 25 other countries on the destination list; from China, which took 1,100, to Scandinavia with an impressive 5,000. The board minutes for December 17, 1947, suggest 600 cars a week of all models ready for shipment, almost all A40s.

By then Lord would have received that contentious figure—the steel allocation for 1948, with the less than conciliatory observation that it would be based on his performance in 1947. For the industry as a whole the government raised the target from 300,000 to 475,000 cars and sanctioned enough raw material for Austin to make 3,400 vehicles a week. Ironically, the company itself only counted on 2,000!

This was Longbridge's peak year for American exports with 11,740 heading that way.

In the first year of the A40, 1947, exports of luxury goods to Canada were banned, largely because of balance of payments issues. These hinged upon high, pent-up, consumer demand at a time when domestic manufacturers were struggling to revitalize peace time production. The Austin board expressed their concern over the situation at their January 1948 meeting but by February, as the Marshall Plan came on stream, and Europe had money to spend in North America, the restrictions were lifted.

By the end of the month Austin had export licences for Canada, valid until August, for up to 3,000 cars. The following year Hess proceeded from the record breaking at Long Island to Toronto. The journey was observed by the American Automobile Association who confirmed averages of 33 mpg at 31 mph. Lord exploited the Canadian outlet with its slightly more free-spending customers by hiking the price of the Devon by $80 and the Dorset by $90. This is an important point to note.

By June 1950, 800 A40s a week were being exported to Canada and by September Austins for North America had already earned $8,400,000 dollars. In November, A40 production was still 450 a day. Output figures were being broken, almost by the hour, and a bewildering array of statistics poured forth.

In February, 1948, 1,050 of the 1,200 cars Britain sent to America were Austins; in March a record 5,720 vehicles worth £2,000,000 were shipped from Longbridge. That month, one cargo of 420 A40s, aboard the Furness Line's *SS Pacific Stronghold,* was said to have been the biggest shipment of British cars ever. By June, 100,000 Austins had been exported since the Armistice. In both July and August, 7,000 cars were sent to the States. In May 1949, the 100,000th A40 was made and in November 1950, the 250,000[th], with the cars being produced at the rate of 2,250 a week.

The quarter millionth was a Devon for the important Australian market but, inevitably, had to get there via New York for display at the American motor show. Eighty per cent of that quarter million had gone to America and earned $70 million. By the end of 1950 Canada had taken a total of 23,000 A40s while Australia had imported 18,000 and their cousins in New Zealand 6,200.

Austin were now exporting 30% more cars than any other British manufacturer, typified by a statistic from South Africa which showed A40s and other Austins were the most popular British make. While in Australia, Longbridge was selling 5,000 more vehicles a year than all other importers.

At home, the A40 had been declared the branded product that had earned the most for Britain and had helped make the nation the world's biggest exporter of goods. The government acknowledged that the sale of a Devon in Canada bought Britain 163 tons of grain and, sold in Australia, 114 tons of wheat, 53 of meat or 14 of butter. Naturally, a proud Lord put it more prosaically with the interesting calculation: '*Austin is making £115 a minute from exports; enough to feed 187 average Britons for a week*'.

Not everything was so palatable.

As early as 1947, in the last months of Ten production, there was a dispute on the chassis line over piecework. For those not familiar with manufacturing industry it is important to understand the concept and ramifications of this system. It appeared in the British engineering industry at least as early as the mid-19th century and as well as piecework was known as 'piece wage'. Condemned by Karl Marx, the father of Communism, as '*in harmony with the capitalist mode of production*' and, at this stage, generally despised by workers, it nonetheless spawned the growth of workshop committees and shop stewards.

They would bargain for a fair wage for an employee based on a fixed sum for performing a given task over a set period. For example, if fitting a wagon wheel was valued at 6d (2.5p) and four identical wheels could be attached in an hour the labourer would receive a minimum rate of 2s (10p). Fit five and you were flying high; three, and as often as not, 'on the street'.

The approach is not necessarily conducive to either camaraderie or quality—as the Trade Union Congress's Vic Feather pointed out in the '30s: '*men are told that if someone is holding them* up, *"push him out". The atmosphere is so tense men are willing to strike* (sic) *their mates down'*. Yet piecework had operated tolerably well throughout WWI, especially in the munitions industry, where both sides were under pressure to produce. Even immediately post-Great War, it was possible for unions to negotiate a system where a worker could earn a minimum percentage above what he or she would receive from a flat hourly rate.

In the 1920s and '30s the system became the motor industry norm, except at Ford, where an hourly rate was applied. However, rising unemployment, the fear of long seasonal lay-offs and the consequent emaciation of the unions gave the employers the upper hand in any negotiation. With the outbreak of WWII this situation was dramatically reversed. There was full employment and/or a shortage of labour. Piecework flourished providing there was solidarity amongst the workforce.

Normally, these later arrangements provided a nationally negotiated award known as the supplement or so-called 'bonus', plus the rate itself. The latter was calculated on the performance of a relatively inexperienced worker to allow for an individual, as they became adept at the task, to increase their earnings.

Much more significant for motor management than these working practices was the appointment by Churchill, in 1940, of Ernest Bevin as Minister of Labour and National Service*. Huge of stature, the impact of his policies were similarly proportioned. As he said with amazing prescience: '*They say Gladstone was at the Treasury from 1860 until 1930. I'm going to be at the Ministry of Labour from 1940 until 1990*'. The most far reaching actions of Bevin were the 'Coventry tool room agreement' and the Conditions of Employment and Arbitration legislation.

The first aimed to create regional parity between toolroom (i.e. skilled) operatives and production line workers. The object was to stabilize the labour scene and draw men towards what had been less remunerative flat rate work. Its effect was to create an ever-increasing wage spiral.

The employment and arbitration measures then drastically reduced the power of the employers. It forbade lock-outs, but more importantly, bound management to agreements made within a trade or district whether or not they recognized the unions involved.

In essence the government message was motor manufacturing was too important to be left to the motor manufacturer. The implications were colossal and paved the way for the interventionist policies of future decades. Or, as Bevin had quipped, his influence lived, long after he was dead.

There are intrinsic flaws in piecework. Those who worked at Longbridge around the time of the 'Ten' stoppage say that such interruptions were fairly commonplace. It is a facet of the system that every time there is a specification, materials or styling change, however minor, the rate has to be 're-fixed' and this is an obvious area for dispute with much leverage on the side of the employee if output is crucial. Around the launch of a new model would be typical. Furthermore, in any major plant, there are jobs to which piecework is not applicable. For instance, electricians and general maintenance workers.

To maintain parity with their production colleagues these hourly workers have to be given bonuses, and as piecework rates change for any of the reasons stated, there are demands for the flat payment, with its additions, to be adjusted to preserve differentials. This is known as 'wage

---

* The term 'National Service' in this context should be taken literally and not confused with the later system of compulsory enrolment of young men into the armed forces that was also known as 'national service.

drift' and is a dangerous phenomenon for any company when there is strong competition and a need to raise output and keep costs down.

Dick Etheridge, who we will come to know extremely well in later chapters as Longbridge's trade union Works convenor, said of the system: '*The piecework system was implemented in different ways depending on the company but each had underlying flaws and, because human ingenuity is such, wage systems have always been open to abuse by the workforce, some of it blatantly fraudulent, of which I strongly disapprove.*'

A simple example from the Mini era has two operators making connecting rods for the A Series engine. One is working on items for the conventionally installed motor in the Farina A40, the other on that component for the transverse Mini engine. The latter is paid more, prompting the A40 worker to ask for an adjustment upwards for what is virtually the same work. When the imbalance is corrected the Mini operative immediately demands another change in the rate to restore differential so beginning a vicious circle that is almost impossible to resolve.

The above should illustrate the hazardous labour landscape that was emerging at Longbridge and some of the endemic problems that Lord would face. That is not to say there were no industrial relations issues at the Works pre-WWII. Immediately after the 1918 Armistice there was a major dispute over the alleged victimization and dismissal of the chairman of the works committee. Another serious confrontation followed in 1923 over—inevitably—piecework, and an even more acrimonious one in 1929 over Englebach's reorganization of the plant. It began as a 'stay in' and turned into a 'lock-out'. As was usually the case, Herbert Austin backed down.

The newspaper of the National Union of Vehicle Builders (NUVB) who already had a foothold in the factory, said, in 1923, somewhat tongue in cheek we suspect: '*Austin gracefully gave way and promised not to offend in future*'.

While biting his lip, by the end of the next decade, Sir Herbert had 'gracefully' agreed to mutuality—mutual agreement of rates between management and workers. Also, to recognize NUVB shop stewards, and even provide accommodation in which they could meet.

In general, though, the climate was much more moderate than that which Lord encountered. There were not large numbers of disillusioned Servicemen and women coming into industry who, when they looked at the country as a whole, must have wondered what they had been fighting for over the last six years. The new breed was not as supine as their forebears. In the main, they had not seen the hell of the Great War or been so scarred.

They could not be subjugated so readily and their new-found colleagues, whose wages had leapt from fifth among Britain's sixteen major industries in 1938 to second by 1940, had both a moral duty and a vested interest in ensuring the newcomers received the same levels post-War as themselves.

Leonard Lord sent Harriman, in unusually decisive and aggressive mode, to resolve the 1947 'Ten' chassis line dispute. Remarkably he got away with telling the protagonists: '*The pricing* (piecework rate) *stands. Anyone who wants a job, back to work. The rest can go to personnel and will be paid off immediately*'*.

Lord would have found the developing power of the factory floor and closed shop extremely alien. The 'Ten' dispute was minor and, given the custom and practice of negotiation, he could not have been expected to become directly involved or to have confronted the recalcitrants personally. Had he been prepared to do so, and we might suspect there are precedents—one

---

*   Sharratt quoting Bill Chance, a rate fixer.

of his mentors, Herbert Austin, almost certainly 'dealt direct'—he may not, ultimately, have become so adrift from the mood and political tenor of the workforce.

But, of course, he had already said, among much else: *I will not have certain ministers or known crypto Communists in the Works except on my terms. They can come and talk to the men. But they aren't going in a huddle with the shop stewards first. I want to vet their speeches and I want no rabble-rousing in my factory. The men get a square deal from Austin and Austin expects a square deal from them. And what's more Longbridge is an English factory worked by Englishmen. That is a proud enough title for any man in this island and no one will address them as "comrades".* Much as this gives a further slant on Lord's outlook, and though we must view it in the context of its time, it did not bode well.

One of the arguments surrounding the stoppage on the Ten had been that the men were being 'flogged to death'. Maybe they were. Lord's own energy was incredible; as was the pace he set. In wartime, more affectionately, he was known as a man who had no eyelids, so it was impossible for him to sleep.

By now he had a battery of telephonists pursuing, chivvying, sourcing essential materials. An enormous placard would soon be hung in the car assembly building bearing the words 'The Ships Are Waiting'. It was over-printed on a docks scene busy with freighters, lighters and barges. Around this time Lord uttered one of his most dramatic quotes: *Get the stuff in by hook or by crook—any way you like—wagons, trains, planes, just get it in*.

It has been suggested that this was also the period when it was not unusual to hear on the production lines: *If they want them bad, they can have them bad*.

Others indignantly dispute that such remarks were ever made. John Moore*, who circulated the plant on a bicycle, was the Works chief inspector, at the time. He had immense power being the only shopfloor worker with the authority to stop the lines and would have had no compunction about doing so if he identified sub-standard work.

Nonetheless warranty claims on the A40 are reputed to have cost £750,000. It is possible these were more related to design than workmanship, but it was not auspicious and after the peak year of 1948 sales in America declined significantly. Devoutly patriotic though Lord was, and for all the statistics, he was pained to point out that Austin was buying dollars for the rest of Britain at a loss to itself. Effectively each A40 earned about £205 worth of green backs while the materials alone cost £203. He estimated that between 1948 and '49 this trade had lost his company £150,000.

The cars may have made their mark—eventually one even secured a highly unlikely 'drive on' part on the Hollywood set of the 1951 film *An American in Paris*—but the reality was a lot less glamorous.

Lord visited America three times between June 1948 and the same month in 1949. On one occasion, in the September, Harriman accompanied him and the situation that confronted them at the Fisk Building could not have been particularly encouraging. So much so that he told a board meeting on June 22, 1949 that 500 cars from the American stock were being transferred to Canada and 1,200 saloons and vans brought back to England. The latter had been held for so long that they needed refurbishment and up-dating.

Financially, the situation was not much better in Canada. Although demand was strong, local taxes meant it cost more to produce cars at the Hamilton plant than it did to export them

---

* John Moore was married to Joy Dawson, who was Ruth Bailey's assistant in Lord's office.

complete from Longbridge. As a consequence plans to supply America from north of the border were abandoned and by mid-1949 Hamilton's main role was as a spares depot.

As we have seen, Australia, New Zealand and South Africa were strong markets. The kits for Australia were assembled, variously, by a new Austin subsidiary formed from the reconstituted Ruskin Motor Body Works of Melbourne, by the All-British Motor House in Adelaide, Brisbane's UK and Dominion Motors, Winterbottom in Perth, or Larke, Hoskins in Sydney.

In New Zealand individual distributors assembled the cars, while in South Africa Austin established a factory at Blackheath, outside Cape Town, supplemented by output from a plant operated by dealer, Stanley Motors, in Johannesburg. By 1949 there were also manufacturing facilities in Argentina, Brazil and Eire.

Lord had spent over a month in South America between March and April 1948 travelling from Southampton to Buenos Aires and back on the recently refitted Shaw Saville liner *Andes*. He described the trip as 'private' but we can assume that it had some relevance to manufacturing Austins in this region.

There was also an abortive plan to set up a plant in India to be operational by 1948 and based on a £2,500,000 investment. The idea dated from before WWII but was revived in 1947 when a delegation of major Indian dealers met Lord at Longbridge. However, 1947 was probably the most inauspicious point in history to enter the sub-continent. Centuries of resistance to British rule had culminated in, among other events, the ugly Royal Indian Navy mutiny of 1946. Political instability was rife. The left-leaning Jawaharlal Nehru was about to become the president of an independent state with every likelihood he would nationalize British interests. While at home, prime minister Clement Attlee was anxious to withdraw. Lord showed his political judgement and did not proceed.

In all, the A40 Devon was marketed in more than 20 countries. Before its demise in February 1952, around 344,000 had been made, 77% of which were exported and earned Britain £88,000,000.

The two-door Dorset was discontinued at home in September, 1948, and ceased everywhere in October, 1949, about 16,000 having been built. Most customers hadn't wanted a climb-in-the-back, bum-in-the-air, car and could afford a few pounds/dollars more for four doors.

Apart from the saloons there were 10 hundredweight vans and pick-ups.

In the tradition of pre-War 'Open Road' tourers, Austin considered an 'open' version of the A40 in the summer of 1948. It came to nothing. It was left to the Australians to develop this appealing concept. Larke, Hoskins had the Falcon, Dominion a model they called the Smart Set, as well as a nasty wooden floored, doorless, concoction called Rouseabout. Naturally, there was a selection of utilities (pick-ups in English and American parlance, 'utes' in the local vernacular) of varying attractiveness.

Globally, there was also an ultra basic A40. As standard it had a leathercloth upholstered bench front seat, if you were lucky, a driver's wiper mounted above the windscreen, and that reassuring standby, a spare wheel without a tyre. Even at £328 they didn't sell well.

Before we leave the immediate post-War era it is essential we consider an innovation by Lord that is quite unique. The idea of an Austin pedal car 'just like father's car' first came to him in 1946. It was loosely linked to the celebrations surrounding the millionth Austin; more importantly, to his plans to make Austin a world leader in all its chosen areas of production with the techniques tailored to the job in hand.

For this project he hand-picked a three-man team. It consisted of Jim Blaikie and Ron Phillips of the Post War Planning Office that Lord himself had created, plus Alf Ash from Body Assembly Planning.

Lord's brief was for a car that could carry a child aged between four and nine years with space for a smaller brother or sister. There was to be an opening boot and bonnet, lights, a dummy engine, a brake, moveable gear lever, registration plates and a host of other seductive embellishments.

However, the master stroke was arranging to have the miniatures built by former Welsh miners incapacitated by pneumoconiosis—over 5,000 in 1945—in a dedicated factory. Pneumoconiosis appears in one of its most severe forms in colliers and in their case is caused by the inhalation of coal dust. Known colloquially as dust disease or simply 'the dust', it leads to breathlessness, dizziness and ultimately heart failure. Attlee's government, working through health minister and South Walian, Aneurin Bevan, whose own father had died of pneumoconiosis, was anxious to aid sufferers.

We have no reason to doubt that Lord identified with these desires. He was a compassionate and sensitive individual and his success running Nuffield's trust for Special Areas in 1937 is unquestionable. However, it has been suggested, extremely cynically, that he saw an opportunity to increase Austin's steel allocation and that some material procured for pedal cars found its way onto the presses at Longbridge. We shall never know.

In the run up to the launch, Lord would sit in the old experimental shop that had been provided as a secret location for the planning, push his trilby onto the back of his head, and with the ever present cigarette clinging to his lower lip, sketch the shapes. What emerged was based on an open Eight and incorporated most of Lord's intended features except for a registration mark. 'JOY 1' for something that's a joy to own, was subsequently the chairman's personal—and perfect—selection.

Two prototypes were made followed by an alternative model based on Jamieson's 'Twin Cam' racer and called Pathfinder. As an aside, and to hark back to an earlier chapter, it is unlikely Lord would have approved this if he '*loathed Jamieson*'. This was a version he loved, roaring with rapturous delight when he first saw the strapped down bonnet removed to reveal the dummy engine.

The Austin Eight-style Joy Car never went into production. It was, very logically, revised by the experimental department into an equally superb A40 Devon/ Dorset inspired creation. The factory was established in the dismal Rhymney Valley town of Bargoed. Twenty four thousand square feet were provided by government funding and at a 50% reduction in rates on the basis it employed 100% disabled. More than half were in an advanced stage of their disease.

The conditions were astonishing. There was an on-site medical centre with an expert on rehabilitation on tap and another on coal miners' pneumoconiosis available part time. The impact on the local community was enormous. '*I'll tell you the factory is perfect. I and everybody here won't have a word said against it. I would just like everyone to know it is not just a convalescent home!*' was the observation of a shop steward.

Typically the men would say: '*Years ago a man like me would have been treated as a useless individual dependent on family or charity for his existence. Today I can become, once again, a skilled worker proud to earn his own living and be able to look his fellow men in the face on equal terms*' . . .

... or: '*This factory gives even the worst cases hope for the future*' and ... '*My greatest sense of achievement has come from knowing that I was making something that would give children pleasure and make them happy*'.

Production of Pathfinder, a simpler 'vehicle' to make than the Joy Car, began in the first half of 1949 using nine redundant presses from Longbridge while the

J (Junior) 40 did not come on stream until spring 1950.

Initially the Bargoed factory produced pedal cars exclusively, but as it was appreciated the work had a seasonal focus (Christmas) capacity was devoted, from around 1953, to activities for the main Birmingham plant. For example stamping tappet gallery and timing chain covers, rocker boxes and making lorry seats.

Between its introduction and withdrawal, in 1971, a core workforce of around 55 made some 32,000 J40s. To the '*customers of tomorrow*' the miniatures were a priceless advertisement. As well as appearing in films, on stage and at circuses, they spawned a generation of fairground roundabouts some of which are still in use. In addition, the cars were used extensively for road safety training by police forces and other organizations. They were introduced to New York dealers at their annual dinner in the Park Sheraton Hotel on October 19, 1949, and so became an invaluable teaching—and promotional—tool in America.

The joy the enterprise gave to tens of thousands of children is, of course, heart warming. Yet the greater benefit was its social contribution in a depressed community, blighted by a horrible medical condition. That was unique on the industrial scene and it was the concept of Leonard Lord alone.

In *The Leyland Papers*, Graham Turner writes of Lord: '*Nor was he even a believer in the simpler forms of training for industry. When, after he had moved to Austin, one of his senior executives tried to promote an apprentice scheme, Lord strenuously resisted the idea*'.

This is a remarkable statement and totally untrue. When Lord arrived at Austin in 1938 the existing apprentice scheme was the pride of the industry and the new incumbent not only continued a commitment to the structure but also seems to have had a particular rapport with, and respect for, this particular group.

Bernard Johnson remembers his indentures being signed personally by an affable Lord who presented him with a book token and commented on the brightness of his shirt. '*I'll remember you when I see you next*'.

Bill Davis, another ex-apprentice, who, as we have seen, eventually sat on the BMC board and became deputy-managing director, still reflects on the occasion when, in wartime, he was recalled to Longbridge. Still in uniform, he met Lord at some swing doors. Both men immediately stepped aside to give the other priority. But it was Lord who said: '*Come through you silly bugger*'. Incidentally, this was one of only two occasions Davis heard Lord swear!

Apart from the apprentice programme, a training scheme for young managers, identified by Lord or Harriman as having particular potential, was based on the pedal car factory at Bargoed. The nominees usually served two years running the out-station and gained invaluable experience in operating a self-contained plant.

That is not to say Lord could not be as irascible and impetuous with apprentices as he could with everyone else. There is the story of him firing a trainee draughtsman for having a cup of tea perched on his drawing board. Severe perhaps, but the youth's deed was both arrogant and bad practice, with the potential to destroy painstaking work, and, it had happened several times before.

But his humour and camaraderie with his future craftsmen were ever-present. For reasons that are almost certainly associated with his nephew's plans to become a doctor, Lord took a keen interest in medical matters and had a close allegiance with the profession. The Works hospital was an innovation by Lord in conjunction with Payton. One company doctor recalls Lord at an apprentices' annual dinner, which he always attended and addressed. He asked the young men if they knew the pressure in the human bladder. '*Sixty pounds, sir*' was the loud response from one individual in the dining hall. '*Bloody hell lad, if it was that you could piss over the Eiffel Tower*' said a laughing Lord.

CHAPTER SEVENTEEN
THE PACE QUICKENS

'*Britain has made it*' was the legend stencilled on the crates of A40s awaiting dispatch from Longbridge. It was a clever play on words. Lord, ever the visionary, appreciated the value of slick advertising and in 1948 had appointed Sam Haynes from 'Morris Commercial' to handle this side of the business. On Haynes's appointment, Lord told him: '*I want the job done properly. I don't want you telling me you've saved a couple of thousand quid by skimping on something*'.

By 1950 the annual publicity budget was already in excess of £2,000,000. And with that defining characteristic of an excellent manager, Lord would sign off the expenditure after just one explanatory meeting; not spend weeks prevaricating. Of course, what lay behind slick slogans and polished promotions was much less cut and dried.

Lord still had grave concerns about the state of the nation, the motor industry in particular and Austin within this context. In a 1947 interview with Olive Moore for the right wing industrial magazine *Scope* he covered most of the burning issues.

'*When I'm asked will America take our export markets, I say, "why not?" If America wants to, America will. Our "planners" will see to that. Nothing can stop American cars flooding any market they choose with their low prices and production costs. How can British cars compete against the iniquitous purchase tax, government interference and increased costs and shortages of raw materials?*'

Lord laid many of the ills of the motor industry firmly at the door of the Labour government. Although he was not entirely correct in doing so, many of the criticisms he expounded to Moore as he continued the interview were relevant to the future policies of administrations of both Left and Right persuasion. They even impacted on the motor industry after Lord had left it and, to an extent, after he was dead.

'*Speaking for myself* (Austin) *we have all the orders in the world if only we were free to make them. The question comes down to freedom. We want freedom from controls. We want freedom from interference by all those inexperienced academic planners. We want to apply the principles of adventure which have made this country what it is down the centuries and that goes for everyone in industry. For the motor industry, we want, first of all, lower taxation in every form—the initial taxation on the car and the heavy taxation on petrol. In other words we want motoring made cheaper and thus made available to a far greater number of people*'.

There are some extremely 'Ford*ian*' concepts here. It was the American pioneer who began to establish the motor car as a utility product. '*Our working class must also become our leisure class if our production is to be balanced by consumption*', said Henry Ford. An idea he linked to investment, pricing and profit. Maybe it is not coincidental that around the time Lord was expressing similar thoughts he was looking ahead to the major reorganization at Longbridge that would provide him with the most advanced motor works outside Ford's homeland.

It was also in this period that he was becoming ensconced in funding his nephew's medical training and as we have seen before, he enjoyed anatomical analogy. Not least when he was talking to Moore and warming to the theme of government meddling. '*I have got a lovely picture in my mind of British industry. It is like a sick person. You can imagine the poor chap in a darkened room surrounded by hundreds and hundreds of people. Some are trying to draw his life's blood out of him; others are trying to find a way through the crush to give him a few more injections. Others, again, are hovering on the outside to see if they can find another spot on which to place yet another leech. Others are just hanging around to see the fun and helping their pals to carry the leeches and injections. Others are grabbing any limb they can get near and applying a few more bandages. And now, in the last resort, while the poor chap is leeched and bled and bandaged, the surgeons—the real surgeons—are refused permission to dispense unless they take into consultation with them the men and women who sweep the wards, the bloke who drives the ambulance, the night watchman and the hall porter! All these, mark you, are to have an equal voice with the specialist in the diagnosis*'.

From this homily we can see to what extent Lord understood, as early as 1947, the predicament of the British motor industry.

He goes on to cut closer to the bone. '*British industry isn't sick! It is only tired. It is overdosed. It has taken too many prescriptions written by quacks, and too many injections given by inexperienced theorists, and too many bright ideas from the hall porter! Imagine a sick bloke who isn't even ill, told he's dying, when all that's the matter with him is he can't breathe because there are so many charlatans crowded round his bed. Let him stretch his muscles and get out in the air. Throw the window open and let in the sun. Sweep the quacks into the dustbins. The poor chap is only suffering from claustrophobia, brought on by the load of forms, documents and red tape suffocating him. And what are they doing? They are prescribing for the very disease they brought about themselves. But asking the hall porter's advice or the views of the man who sweeps the factory floor, isn't the way it's going to be cured*'.

Lord probably did believe '*British industry was not sick*'. That it needed a tonic not surgical intervention and that with a different 'medical team' all would be well. Yet he was mistaken. The growth that seemed benign and, at first, was not too troublesome was terminal cancer. Yet in these final years of a traumatic decade there was still much to do in the serious business of making and promoting motor cars.

There were frivolous distractions too.

On Saturday, July 17, 1948, Lord hosted a prestigious Veteran Car Club of Great Britain rally at Longbridge. It was a chance to show off the 100 horsepower racer of 1908 French Grand Prix fame and the very first 'Austin Seven' of 1909* as well as his own blossoming daughters.

They had moved on from the saddle-strewn days at Storridge when any tooth-brace, boarding school, 'waif' was given a billet for the long summer holidays by a soft-hearted Leonard Lord. Now, as the landmark Austins took their place alongside British motor industry icons like the contemporary tiller steered Lanchester landaulette, Lord's girls wore the full skirts so fashionable that year, hats that would have done any Easter parade justice, and slightly risqué sling back shoes.

Daddy, for his part, and when he was not sharing the driving of another pre-WW1 Seven with celebrated BBC broadcaster Richard Dimbleby, straight from the previous night's *Twenty Questions* radio programme, sat on a stool at the top of the road from the Works fire station to the flying ground. It had been co-opted on this occasion as a hillclimb course.

---

*   This was a fairly unsuccessful single cylinder car not related in any way to the famous 1922 'Motor for the Million'.

155

A cigarette hung on his fingers, and now, almost as familiar, a trilby sat on his head pushed slightly back to the crown as was customary when he was relaxed and enjoying himself.

The VCC event is a previously unexplored enigma, which is unfortunate, as it gives us a precious insight into Lord's personality. There is no evidence to suggest Austin's chairman had any particular interest in veteran* cars. He was barely old enough, at the dawn of the automotive age, to now remember, with nostalgia, the primitive, creaky, vehicles of those days. And in his formative years, he was not from a social class that would have had any involvement in motoring.

Yet it was solely at his behest that the club came to Longbridge for what was the largest gathering they had ever staged**. Eighty six cars turned out, one from as far afield as Land's End. Overall, a remarkable achievement, given stringent petrol rationing still applied.

The event was to have opened with a sprint match over the hillclimb course by Alan Hess in the 100 horsepower Austin and a 1904 Mercedes. But the German's magneto failed and Hess performed the honours alone. A burst of ribald humour was no doubt emitted by Lord when he learned that the VCC president's similar Mercedes was a non-starter as a result of its driving chains, despatched for repair, being lost on the recently nationalized railways!

The racing was divided, by age, into eight classes. Fastest time of the day went to the stripped 1910 Rolls-Royce of club luminary, Sandy Skinner. There was also a relay race composed of six teams of ten cars.

In between times Patricia and Pauline Lord passengered a 1906 Siddeley-Deasy. This decidedly appropriate car, in view of the make's connection with Herbert Austin, was reported by the *VCC Gazette* to have taken the hill with such gusto as to cause the Lord girls to almost lose those extravagant bonnets.

Father, by contrast, made an inevitably unspectacular ascent, partnering Dimbleby, who even in youth could never be described as svelte, in another of those diminutive pre-WW1 Austin Sevens. While a Lieutenant Atkinson forewent all hope of a trophy by 'strapping' a weighty public address system to his 1906 Adams-Hewitt to provide a description of his climb.

Sacrificing an award was not as inconsequential as it may sound. Lord had commissioned from an artisan called Edward Jones, for that very day, an exquisite, solid silver model of the VCC president's 1898 Benz. It is described in the *Gazette* as: *'the most beautiful thing amongst our club's many treasures'.* It exists to this day and is the club's premier award for a competitive event.

Lord was rewarded with a Perspex cigarette box. Appropriate, and not as unstylish as it sounds. The material was popular and totally acceptable for the production of a huge range of products from the 1930s until as late as the 1960s. Lord said of the case: *'I will treasure it greatly'.*

Nine thousand Austin workers bought tickets to attend 'Lord's VCC day' and it is estimated that 3,000 more—invited guests and hangers on—were present. Among the dignitaries were such automotive legends as Frank Lanchester. Yet we are left with the mystery as to why this extraordinary jamboree ever took place.

To begin to find an explanation we must step back two years to an issue of the *VCC Gazette* where James Allday, the year he became president, writes: *'I am convinced that dreams can be made into realities, always provided that one tries hard enough, and now at long last, we have reached*

---

* Classified by the Veteran Car Club as pre-1904. 'Edwardian' is pre-1919
** The larger annual London to Brighton Veteran Car Run is primarily a Royal Automobile Club event.

reality, and thanks to the personal generosity of a friend of mine, this particular dream is going to be realized.

'Yes, at long last we have our London headquarters! Mr L.P. Lord, chairman of the Austin Motor Company, has offered us, entirely free of charge, a really delightful home in his company's Oxford Street premises, within a stone's throw of Marble Arch.'

What was being provided was fairly lavish. '*. . . a beautiful large room, which will serve as a club room, office and committee room, and also he has included storage space for eight or ten veteran cars . . . We have a private entrance from North Row and really it would be impossible to improve upon the situation or the accommodation'.*

He continues in somewhat hagiographic vein: *'I have found it extremely difficult to express to Mr Lord and his company our deep sense of gratitude for this truly generous gesture . . . I have a shrewd idea that apart from his natural generosity and interest in our club, Mr Lord is inspired with that somewhat rare gift—appreciation of the historical value of the automobile, in the development of which his company and Lord Austin played such a great part.'*

Forty-six North Row remained the club's headquarters for more than a decade. In 1957, again as the result of overtures from Allday, the organization was provided with *'if not palatial, more commodious'* accommodation at 14, Fitzhardinghe Street, Portman Square, by the British Motor Trade Association.

I have already contended that Leonard Lord had no special interest in early motor cars, or, for that matter the VCC. A more likely explanation for his undeniable generosity is his personal relationship with Allday.

At this distance it is difficult to determine upon what that was based. Gilbert James (Jim) Allday was a Birmingham boy, born in 1891. Leaving school he received a fairly comprehensive engineering and commercial training before becoming a director of his own Birmingham cyclecar company PDA (Pickering, Derby and *Allday).* During WWI he served with the British Expeditionary Force and later in the Royal Flying Corps. In 1918 he joined Wolseley, probably as head of the service department, and remained until 1921. This, of course, is long before Lord had any connection with that company.

Allday then founded Weybridge Automobiles in the town he was to make his long term home, and later, Reading Automobiles, and Boats and Engines Limited. The experience stood him in good stead to be seconded, in the Second World War, to various committees dealing with vehicle repairs, but, perhaps more significantly radar equipment and as chairman of the Engineering Industries Association.

If Lord did not form his friendship in this period he may well have done so post-War as Allday became a prominent member of the Society of Motor Manufacturers and Traders (SMMT), the British Motor Trade Association and the Motor Agents Association.

On the other hand, the development of the relationship may have been for no more complex reason than both Allday and Lord had daughters; Lord three and Allday two. All were of approximately the same school-age, and possibly attending one school.

Thus the question remains, why, what we can only describe as excessive generosity, was advanced. Admittedly, the corruptly extravagant prices of central London property did not apply at the time, yet, even then, what was on offer had considerable commercial value.

As an explanation we must fall back upon, not only Lord's close friendship with Allday, but our subject's enormous patriotism. The war had just been won. One could take pride in Britain's extraordinary role in that victory and, as part of the same sentiment, the role of its motor industry—and to a large degree Austin—in vanquishing the aggressor. The masses, and many of the influential, including perhaps Lord, still believed Britain produced the best car(s) in the world, so why not underpin the efforts of an organization promoting such ideas?

Rather more cynically we might be inclined to say, Lord took the opportunity to display his power. Also, and if we are more generous, to illustrate his spontaneity—both a positive and negative aspect of his character—and his repeatedly proven generosity. Yet none of this really explains Lord's close involvement with the VCC from 1946 through more than a decade, or the spectacular rally of 1948.

It at first becomes clearer when Allday writes, retrospectively, in that year's **Gazette** : '*The conception of holding this meeting came out of a chat I had with Mr Lord about a year ago, for I was so anxious that we should show him in some very definite form how much we appreciated all that he had done for our club*'.

What comes next, from Allday, is particularly interesting. '*The suggestion that we should hold a rally at his company's works for the pleasure and entertainment of his company's many thousands of workpeople and their families, immediately appealed to him*'.

This post-dates the arbitrary dismissal (the norm in the industry at the time) of workers when Ten and Twelve horsepower car production ended in 1947 and pre-dates the violent conflict with the workforce that followed in the mid-1950s.

We are left with the questions; was Lord the ultimate benign despot? As, arguably, Lord Austin had been and also were the likes of Henry Royce. Did he genuinely, *naïvely*, wish to reward and acknowledge a workforce, the majority of whom had performed so superbly well in the recent war and whom he trusted to shape a victorious future? Or, was it self-aggrandizement—showing off to his friend of many years his personal achievement embodied in Longbridge?

I mentioned Lord's increasingly habitual trilby earlier. It is not recorded where, exactly, it was placed when he positioned himself in the design studio on a stool that had been specially made for him and told the stylists not to let Harriman in.

The conception of the A90 Atlantic was the first time Lord had involved himself directly in the design of an Austin since he detailed the pedal car's specification. Now, apart from a personal seat, he had a plane to whittle away at the wooden mock-up. The 'Atlantic' was an extension of Lord's desire, indeed his need, to penetrate the American market. The means was to be the first glamorous and sexy post-War Austin—arguably the *only* pure-bred, glamorous and sexy post-War Austin.

Lord's designs for this car have been derided as creating something akin to a 'pregnant hamster' or 'clockwork mouse'. This merely reflects the literary pretensions of some latter day motoring journalists. Yet, even at the time, when the press were either bland or euphemistic, the best *Motor* could do was '*striking*', while *Autocar* offered the somewhat back-handed compliment that the appearance would be '*apt to grow on one*'.

Maybe we should start from the premise that Lord was incapable of bad draughtsmanship. To realize this we need only remember he had studied the subject in depth and recall the beautiful three-dimensional drawings of factory layout that he produced for Taylor and Woollard in his Morris Engines days. We might go on to cite the first Morris Eight, which, although he would not have shaped it personally, and was certainly influenced by the rival Ford, was essentially Lord's creation—one of the smartest small cars on the market at the time and leagues ahead of the angular, outmoded Austin Ruby.

We ought also to acknowledge that in choosing three Bentleys as his personal transport he recognized what was, in all three coachwork designs—Park Ward, H J Mulliner and Rolls-Royce themselves—one of the most timeless and finely executed styles of the era. While finally, those who remember his home, vouch for its subdued good taste evocative of the quintessentially English gentleman.

Admittedly, even now, most people either love the A90 Atlantic, or they hate it. With panels as curvaceous as Hollywood star Jane Russell's thighs; embellished and bejeweled, it is seen as equally sensual; or, with its 'Cyclops' spotlamp, about as artistically accomplished as the worst monster movie.

Whatever an individual's stance, it is fair to say the 'Atlantic' was the most imaginative attempt by a British manufacturer to attract US sales. The approach was as intelligent as any that could have been mounted from British soil at that time. More fit for purpose, say, than the admittedly Americanized, but outdated, styling of the Riley RMC roadster or bizarre looking Alvis TB14. Both makes, by the way, would have been virtually unknown in the United States. All that apart, beneath the Austin's rather extravagant applications of 'face powder and lipstick' lay a sound, well engineered, car.

For all these reasons it is worth considering the A90 Atlantic in some detail.

It is said Lord's inspiration came from a Pinin Farina cabriolet mounted on a 1946 Alfa Romeo 6C 2500S chassis (number 915.169). This has some credibility. That car was owned, in 1947, by the wealthy Italian, Giuliana Tortoli and according to Barney Sharratt (*'Men and Motors'*), was seen by Lord in Geneva in 1946. The date would seem to be inaccurate. There is no evidence Lord visited Switzerland at all that year although the car itself was displayed in October at an exhibition of the *mode Italien*; but in Lausanne.

If we were to guess, it is possible Lord saw the car when he was visiting the 1947 Swiss motor show. But again, there is no evidence the 'Alfa' was present, either privately or formally. However, it was only a few days after the show closed that it won a *concours d'elegance* in Monte Carlo, having been paraded by Senor Tortoli's wife and an equally glamorous companion indicating it was circulating fashionable continental Europe at the time.

Farina now seems to have bought the car back and, soon afterwards, sold it to Lord. Wherever the latter first saw it, he must have been extremely impressed and very quick off the mark to replicate the design because an 'Atlantic' prototype was ready in early 1948 and available sources suggest the Alfa Romeo was not in Lord's hands until that very year.

Lord reputedly sketched his interpretation of Farina's design PF 448 on the back of an old brochure and handed it to Burzi to finesse. He then personally shaved away at wing and bonnet profiles to produce something that was infinitely better looking than the celebrated Italian's creation.

Lord's pronounced downward curve of the bonnet was embellished with chrome down the centre, a 'Flying A' was set on each catwalk and the whole ranged above that central spotlamp and an enormous bumper.

Where the idea for the former came from is hard to determine. Rover used it on the '75' around the same time. It also appeared on their headline hitting and phenomenally advanced turbine car. Lord's Mark VI Bentley—JGY 1—used a lamp in a similar position. Some even suggest it was an allusion to the single headlight carried by locomotives on the American railways!

At the rear, the bonnet centre decoration was repeated on the boot lid but divided by a prominent Austin winged wheel motif. There was a bumper as extravagant as that at the front placed below neat tail lamps faired back into the wings; plus the encumbrance of wheel spats, *à la* Farina, and indeed, again, most contemporary Bentleys!

Inside, the driver was confronted by an 18-inch diameter, wire spoked, sprung steering wheel that was praised by road testers for being perfectly raked. It also had telescopic adjustment that harked back to some pre-War Austins and allowed it to be positioned even more accurately.

Faddish modernities included a horn ring allowing an over-sized control for the indicators to be located on the column boss. Cars for America flashed their side and stop/tail lights to predict a change of direction but home market Atlantics had to persist with semaphore indicator arms. 'Winkers' were not legalized in the UK until 1954. There were also to have been treadles on the lower edges of the doors, instead of conventional handles, but these never materialized.

A pressed steel dashboard was covered in upholstery leather and fitted with a comprehensive instrument board incorporating a speedometer and rev counter with the supplementary dials set four square between them. Nick-nack boxes on either side of the panel had the commendably safe feature of upward opening lids. There was a column gear change as preferred by Americans and the driver's seat abutted the passenger's and amounted to a bench design.

A particularly attractive touch was pressing the thin leather door facings over a winged 'A' former so the emblem appeared in relief. The side windows were raised and lowered electrically from behind these panels.

The hood was operated by an under-bonnet hydro-electric pump, the switch located between oddment bins in the driver's door. Theoretically, and providing the top was not tucked up in its fabric bag, the cover could be raised or lowered without the *pilote* leaving his or her seat, but as might be expected, none of this was trouble free.

The canopy was to have rested on a windscreen that curved sharply into the pillars. However, glass maker Triplex did not have the technology to create this feature, so tightly radiused sidepieces were tried, the joins being concealed with Perspex strip. But the fillets broke if the screen had to be removed and in the end chromium plated brass end pieces were fitted.

The engine for the car was derived from the now familiar Austin Sixteen unit. Indeed, in its prototype form the Atlantic was called the 'Sixteen Sports'. The plan had been to enlarge the bore from 79.4 mm to 87.3 to give 2,660 cc but there was insufficient metal and a new cylinder block had to be cast.

The independent front suspension chassis was that of the Austin A70 Hampshire saloon, a car we will return to a little later. However, it is worth mentioning now, and as an illustration of the talent that Lord had at his disposal, particularly amongst the younger members of the design team, that when Atlantic prototypes suffered ferocious scuttle shake attributable to the chassis having lost the rigidity provided by a closed body, aircraft technology was adopted as a solution. It was the work of the brilliant Ken Garrett, who devised a transverse torsion box that was patented in both Britain and America.

With its 7.5:1 compression ratio, twin SU H4 carburetters and 88 brake horsepower at 4,000 rpm, the Atlantic was capable of nearly 100 mph. All in all, one would have thought it was destined for success in America. Lord rushed to announce it there a month in advance of its launch at the first post-War British motor show taking place at London's Earls Court from October 27-November 6, 1948.

By the late spring of 1949 it was becoming clear, for whatever reason—cost (initially around $4,000 but soon $1,000 less, the biggest price cut in motor history), size, styling—the Atlantic lacked appeal in the United States. It was a job for Hess. On April 12 he and a team of co-drivers, including Dennis Buckley of 'Seven Capitals' fame, started pounding a 'metallic seafoam green' A90 around the Indianapolis Speedway. The object, under the scrutiny of the American Automobile Association, was to break production car distance and endurance records.

After a false start on April 9 caused by a cylinder head carelessly damaged, the Atlantic ran continuously for seven days and nights clocking up 11,850 miles and shattering 63 records, many of which had been held by Studebaker since the late 1920s. It consumed 694 gallons of petrol. Or, as Hess laconically put it: '*The equivalent of 13 years basic petrol ration in Britain!*'

Lord was equally lugubrious. '*I doubt if the Indianapolis event generated a single extra sale.*' Neither did the introduction of a fixed head Atlantic at the 1949 London motor show help. Moreover, a lowered axle ratio spoiled the performance and made the engine fussy. The accommodation had also become more cramped, particularly to American eyes accustomed to acres of space within a car.

The brutal reality was this brave, imaginative, exciting and well-engineered car from the hand of Lord was a marketing disaster. He had the honesty, courage and confidence to admit his disappointment not only concerning the Atlantic but the American market as a whole.

The drophead A90 that had also been available with a manually operated hood was discontinued in November, 1950, but the closed car struggled on until December 1952. A total of just under 8,000 Atlantics were built. Only a dismal 350 of all versions found a home in America—100 less in Canada. In Australia sales totaled 820, in New Zealand 160 and in continental Europe about 750. Ironically, the balance of this flamboyant machine ended up in a still-dowdy Britain.

The Austin A70 Hampshire was announced at the same time as the Atlantic. A medium-sized saloon, styled, once more, on American lines, it was never sold in that country. There was an element of subterfuge in Lord's initial contention that the car would supplement the Sixteen. It was actually the logical replacement for this dated but much-loved model, production of which had ceased by March 1949. (The Countryman version was built until May).

The Hampshire used the Sixteen's engine in a reworked Devon/Dorset chassis and was lighter by 2.5 hundredweight than its predecessor and, with a top speed of 83 mph, about 8 mph faster. Ultimately there would be estate cars, a pick-up, other coachbuilt commercials and a convertible, although it is doubtful any of the latter were made.

It has been suggested Lord decided on the Hampshire saloon having been shown Standard's intended Vanguard. Although this may seem excessively precipitous it is feasible. The Coventry firm's chief, John Black, unveiled his post-War model in July 1947 long before he was able to make it.

At 2088 cc the Standard was broadly the same engine capacity as the old Austin Sixteen (2199) and the styling followed the same basics as Lord had adopted for the A40 Devon and Dorset he was about to reveal. Thus it was logical for him to move swiftly in the direction he did, particularly as he was considering a highly rationalized range of cars, based on one design but in different sizes. Also, he must already have had a market-embracing range of Austins in mind.

Predictably, given the pace and pressure of the times the A70 took its toll on careers. Jules Haefeli had joined Austin in July, 1914. A Swiss, he soon became Hancock's deputy, the position he held when Lord arrived in 1938. We suspect the new man was not impressed with the vacillation that surrounded the truck engine for which Hancock and Haefeli must have been responsible. Expediting this project was almost the first thing Lord was called upon to do.

When Lord dismissed Hancock it was, perhaps, surprising, if not generous, that he allowed Haefeli to take over as chief designer. Problems with the A40 and the Sheerline were to follow. Then in October 1947, in the very early stages of Hampshire development, having tried what was basically an up-rated Devon, Haefeli told Lord: '*I don't like this car at all. It is against all engineering principles*'. The second sentence was exceptionally ill-advised as Leonard Lord himself was the inspiration for the excellent engine*. It was a few days later Haefeli announced: *'I'm leaving. I shall not be back'.*

Almost everyone who worked at Longbridge in this period agrees about the speed with which events were moving.

There were the new cars themselves. Some ingeniously balanced by Lord and Burzi to combine British conservatism with transatlantic trends; others extravagant and groundbreaking; all struggling to meet the extraordinary needs of the time.

To varying degrees those we have already seen—Sheerline, Princess, Devon, Dorset, Hampshire and Atlantic—were disappointing. It is true, the Devon and Hampshire were more successful in export markets than their British contemporaries. A total of around 274,000 Devons were made, about 80% of which went overseas and very roughly a quarter of those to America. Hampshire output totalled 35,000 of all types, many of those that went abroad finding homes in Australia. But Lord, almost in despair, said in 1949: *'Our market in America has simply dried up. We are out if our prices do not come down'.* In the same vein he said of the Atlantic: *'We went to Indianapolis to prove what the British car could stand up to, and I think we proved it. Now the question is—what benefit have we got in sales in America? I am afraid the answer is none.'*

As regards the Sheerline and Princess we can do no better than cite Bob Wyatt (*The Austin 1905-1952*) writing about pre-War large Austins—*'they were hardly worth the trouble'.*

Viewed as a financial strategy for the Austin Motor Company, Lord's American 'adventures' had been a failure. Yet to regard them in this light is to overlook the real purpose, and *that* was an outstanding success. Furthermore, it reveals Leonard Lord's stature as an industrialist far beyond the realm of his own industry.

The A70 Hereford arrived at the 1950 London motor show to replace the Hampshire. It had a slightly extended wheelbase and was wider and a little longer overall than its predecessor. The engine and chassis were as before but some of the Atlantic's styling, like the front wing line and details from its grille, were subtly incorporated in a new body.

Of more significance was the introduction a year later of the A30. In the immediate post-War years, with such a huge emphasis on earning dollars from a market where small cars were *'persona non grata'*, it was of no great importance that Lord did not have an up-to-date model of this type. However, he must have been aware of his vulnerability when Morris launched the promising Minor in 1948, although this would have been ameliorated by continuing discussion about a merger between his own company and Morris.

The desirability of such a 'marriage' had, to an extent, been highlighted in 1947 by electrical giant Lucas, when they appealed to the industry to standardize and abandon policies that represented *'individualism gone mad'.* William Morris and Lord responded in 1948 with the Austin-Morris Agreement whereby there was to be a *'constant interchange of information on production methods, costs, purchases, design, research, patents and all the items which would be likely to result in manufacturing economies'.* Even on paper, given the personalities involved, it did not sound like having much likelihood of success and the pact collapsed in 1949.

Lord was now galvanized into action on a small car project to confront the Morris Minor. The model he produced was the revolutionary A30, that we will look at more closely in the next chapter. He delivered three more marketing coups at this time for which he is rarely given full credit.

---

*   The unit for the British substitute for the WWll Jeep.

Brothers Richard and Alan Jensen had started building motor cars on their parents' lawn in the late 1920s. At the time, Richard was an apprentice at Wolseley Motors, not that long before Leonard Lord arrived at the Birmingham company, while Alan was training at nearby radiator manufacturer, Serck.

The basis for the young men's first machines was the ubiquitous Austin Seven. The lines the brothers created were so pleasing they were invited by Standard to design a sports body for their Nine. The version subsequently went into production by coachbuilders Avon.

Soon the Jensens branched out on their own, building coachwork for small Morrises, MGs, Wolseleys and Singers. In 1934 they launched their own big sports car called the White Lady, using a Ford V8 engine. Later this became an even larger four litre model with an American Nash straight eight motor.

However, it was not until after WWII the company came to the notice of Leonard Lord. By now Jensen had on board the extremely talented and vastly experienced designer Eric Neale, who had not only worked on coachwork for Mulliners* of Birmingham and Daimler, but, in the late '30s, both Austin and Wolseley.

He arrived at Jensen in 1946 and was the architect of their return to civilian production with the famous and long-lived Interceptor. At first it used a six cylinder Meadows engine but before too long the brothers wanted a more mainstream unit and began to cultivate Lord to obtain both Sheerline engines and A70 frames.

Lord played 'hard to get' and would only release the components if Jensen designed him a sports car. The result was a beautifully scaled down version of the Interceptor that could utilize the A40 chassis. When Lord saw the sketches he displayed the decisiveness that was one of the hallmarks of his brilliance, and ordered a car built. An order for more than 3,000 followed an initial batch of prototypes.

The commitment from a firm the size of Jensen was enormous. A new factory was established in the Midlands village of Pensnett between Kingswinford and Dudley. The bare chassis, fitted with an uprated A40 engine, were driven there from Longbridge, the mainly aluminium bodies fitted and finished, then the completed cars returned to Austin for dispatch.

An even more significant initiative, in broadly similar circumstances, arose over the introduction of the Austin Healey 100. After being downed by 'friendly fire' in the First World War, Donald Healey was invalided out of the Royal Flying Corps aged just 18, took a correspondence course in automobile engineering, and opened a garage in his native Cornwall.

He subsequently became an accomplished rally driver and went on to manage Triumph at the time of the sporting Gloria, the first Dolomite, plagiarized from an Alfa Romeo, and the Coventry firm's Southern Cross model. After WWII he took over a former RAF hangar near Warwick and began building, under his own name, advanced, yet simple and effective, Riley-powered sports and saloon cars.

This evolved by way of a new, export-intended model that was powered first by Nash or Alvis six cylinder engines, into the Healey 100 for which the Austin A90 Atlantic's 'four' was chosen.

It is not entirely clear how Lord became intimately involved. At face value the most plausible explanation is that suggested by the late Bill Boddy (*The Sports Car Pocket Book,* Batsford 1961). He maintains that the Austin chairman was impressed by the performance of the prototype '100' in the 1952 Le Mans 24 Hour *Grand Prix d'Endurance* that took place over the weekend of June 14/15 and that this led to the birth of *Austin* Healey and the licensing links that followed.

---

* A separate company from H J Mulliner in London and Arthur Mulliner of Northampton.

This contention is an elaboration of what historian John Stanford claims in the 1957 book *Sports Car Development and Design* (Batsford again). However, Le Mans records indicate the two cars Donald Healey ran, without distinction, in 1952, were Nash engined models. It is true that Healeys had performed creditably in both 1950 and '51 and this would equate not only with Lord being 'impressed', but possibly renewing a conviction that, even though his own Atlantic was failing, there was export potential for a glamorous British sports car.

By the time the 1953 Le Mans came round the Healey 100 had become the A90-powered *Austin* Healey. They finished second and third in the three litre class and earned the pleasing accolade of being '*by far the least expensive car on the Sarthe*' circuit and essentially standard'.

A more straightforward explanation for Lord backing the Warwick firm emerges from the lips of Ivor Greening in Sharratt's '*Men and Motors*'. Greening worked in the publicity department at Longbridge and recalls that by the time of the 1952 London motor show Healey had received a handful of A90 engines and other components to facilitate the launch of his '100' and undertake speed trials with it.

Not surprisingly for a car that looked correct from every angle the model was a sensation and within a very short time its creator had American orders for around 500, with Austin's own dealers clamouring to sell examples at home.

With the deftness of which only he seemed capable, Lord undertook to make the car and within the space of 24 hours the name was changed, a bonnet badge created, the price cut from £850 to £750 and Healey's Earls Court show stand rebuilt in Austin mode.

The third entrepreneurial masterstroke was more prosaic and centred on the production of a limousine to replace the ungainly long wheelbase A125 Sheerline. As we have already seen the coachbuilder, Vanden Plas, was acquired by Austin in 1946 and was soon constructing bodies for the Princess touring limousine. In the 1930s the company, whose roots stretched back to the late 19th century, had been bought by the Fox brothers. It was Roland, son of one of the new guard, and a sensitive draughtsman who empathized with Lord, who was asked to give an opinion on the slow-selling A125 limousine.

The performance, staged in Lord's private underground garage at Longbridge, contained some histrionics. These involved the chairman feigning to walk off 'the set' when told the Sheerline's roof line was too low. Fox was told: '*make the damn thing yourself*'.

The result was another new Austin at the 1952 motor show. The British royal family ordered two of these DM4 series Princess limousines on the spot and three more pairs followed into the royal mews, at intervals, before the model was withdrawn in 1968. The Austin appellation was dropped in 1960 to recognize Vanden Plas now assembled the chassis as well as body.

Perhaps it is only from a distance we can fully acknowledge the merit and significance of these three projects.

Given the A40 Sports was never going to be high volume—the body dies were of short-lived light alloy used on a press with a rubber bed—it was a truly classic design. Eric Neale's hand was more experienced than Lord's when the latter styled the Atlantic. He was less vulnerable to the chairman's wrath and less introspective than Burzi. The result was subtler.

The all-important perception of the market, though, was still not right. For all Johnnie Rix's good works on the already excellent engine, the A40 'Sports' was still a Devon at heart and in spite of Neale's personal enthusiasm and protestations that the car was '*ideal and attracted a great*

---

*   The French *departement* in which the Le Mans circuit is located.

deal of interest whenever it stopped', it is hard to identify an economically viable sector where they would actually have sold.

Nonetheless, Lord was on an important learning curve. There would come a day when there *was* a worthwhile market, at home and abroad, for attractively priced, good-looking sports cars that offered a modest improvement in performance over more mundane models. BMC's MGA, MGB, MG Midget and Austin Healey Sprite are good examples. For instance more than 100,000 of the 'A' were built and well over 500,000 of the 'B'.

What the A40 achieved at the time and in that short life from the London motor show of 1950 to its demise, 4,000 examples later, in 1953, was to help provide Jensen with revenue to produce the models that earned it a place in the minor aristocracy of British sports cars.

If the Austin Healey 100 was a sensation at Earls Court in 1952 it was a stunner in the marketplace. Its simple elegance and perfectly balanced lines were again more sophisticated, more measured, than those of the 'Atlantic' whose mantle it adopted.

As soon as the exhibition doors closed Longbridge geared up to produce 100 cars a week by mid-1953. The Healey factory prepared examples to display at motor shows in New York, Los Angeles and Frankfurt. Donald Healey himself undertook a promotional tour of America.

The '100', named, it is said, for its speed potential, was declared '*international car of the show*' at the 1953 New York motor show. It also took a premier award at the Miami World Fair the same year. Speed records followed—in 1954 Healey drove a supercharged streamliner at 193 mph over a flying kilometre at Bonneville and US race ace Carroll Shelby took 16 international records at an average of 160 mph at the same venue.

An upgraded gearbox was introduced in 1955 and other modifications made. When the model was replaced by a six cylinder '100' in August 1956, 14,600 had been made, just 1,400 as right hand drive models and of those only about 500 for the British market.

The big Austin Healey has become an iconic sports car and competed head-on in the market place with other legends such as Jaguar's XK120. Yet, without the vision and dynamism of Leonard Lord, and on the evidence of its progenitor's inability to reproduce his beautiful baby, the Austin Healey would probably have been stillborn.

Jensen got the valuable contract to form the panels for Healey but Eric Neale had wanted to produce the replacement A40 Sports. He failed to have it ready in time for Earls Court where the deal with Healey was conceived and struck. Or, as Lord colourfully put it: '*It was born in the vestry that one. Just too late*'.

An interesting additional dimension to these scenarios is disclosed in David Thirlby's book *Frazer Nash* (Haynes Foulis 1977). The account is inaccurate and confusing but according to Thirlby, '*some months before the Motor Show* (1952) *Leonard Lord had told Aldington* (Frazer Nash's proprietor) *that the Nuffield* (sic) *Organization wanted to build a sports car. They would like the prototype to use Austin* (sic) *components from the Austin A135 and whatever Aldington required would be made available at cost price (the Austin A135 engine was a big four of 87 x 111, giving 2660 cc).*

'*The Works* (Frazer Nash) *built a car, the Roadster, similar to the Targa Florio* (Frazer Nash) *in body shape and into this was placed the Austin engine and gearbox together with the column mounted change; it was felt by many that the Works had not put their full enthusiasm into the project . . . . During the Show with Lord Nuffield and Leonard Lord present it was announced that Austins were to manufacture the Healey. Aldington said that Leonard Lord was apologetic that the Frazer-Nash had not been selected, but he agreed to take back the Austin components and refund Aldington's investment in the six or so engines he had bought. The Roadster was to have supplemented the Le Mans Replica*

Mark ll (Frazer-Nash), *the newly introduced Targa Florio in its two forms of Turismo and Grand Sport and the Millia Miglia.'*

Lord had chosen wisely in the Healey. But let us look at the detail. In 1952 he would not have been speaking for '*the Nuffield Organization*'. If he spoke in this context for anyone '*some months before the Motor Show'* it would have been either Austin or BMC.

The A135 engine was most definitely *not 'a big four etc'.* The A135 was the six cylinder four litre Sheerline engine derived from Austin's lorry motor. The 2,660 cc is the A90 unit as used in the Austin Atlantic and, of course, by Donald Healey in the Austin Healey 100. Reference to *Autocar* pictures of the '*Leonard Lord Frazer-Nash'* on the latter company's stand at Earls Court make it abundantly clear that the model could not have accommodated the A135 engine.

Finally, it is not clear from Thirlby's account how Leonard Lord's proposal would have given 'Nuffield' or indeed Austin or BMC a sports car in the sense that the brilliant deal with Donald Healey did and one with Jensen might have. If the Roadster was to have '*supplemented*' five Frazer-Nash models presumably it was to have been badged as an F-N. Even if it adopted the persona of some kind of BMC hybrid surely it would have had difficulty achieving the iconic and enduring status of the Austin Healey in its many forms.

As a further aside, it is interesting to note, Donald Healey became chairman of Jensen Motors when BMC was taken over by Leyland in 1968.

Of the Vanden Plas-built limousines all that need be said is the beautifully proportioned DM4, with its under-stated dignity, was the most popular and elegant formal carriage, arguably in the world, from 1952 until it was replaced in 1968 by the grotesque, Jaguar/Daimler inspired, Daimler DS420.

Apart from the mainstream vehicles there were the oddities and the specials.

Very much in the former category was a turbine driven Sheerline that was under development from 1949 until the mid-'50s. Although he was apprehensive about riding in it himself, it was born of Lord's desire to emulate and keep pace technically with Rover.

The Solihull company had been developing jet propulsion for motor cars since 1946. When they ran a very successful prototype in 1950, chief engineer Maurice Wilks, said publicly: '*It is obviously the Rover company's intention to produce a gas turbine engined car as a marketable proposition if and when that becomes practicable'.* He set the time scale at just three or four years hence and added: '*It will certainly be as good as, most probably better than, existing piston engine cars in respect of performance and weight. Probably though, it will not be quite so good in respect of fuel consumption, but to balance that the performance will be superb'.*

This was as strong an incitement to Lord as there could have been, pledged as he was to make products far more advanced than anything that had gone before. Indeed, a Longbridge team led by the highly qualified Dr John Weaving had their own 'turbo', registered TUR 1 (Rover's was JET 1), ready for road test in August 1954.

Weaving was Birmingham born and left the city's King Edward Vl Grammar School in 1936 to join Austin as an apprentice. He subsequently secured a Whitworth scholarship to Cambridge University where, having gained his BSc, further research produced a PhD. In 1946 he returned to Longbridge as a development engineer and by 1948 had become superintendent in charge of development in the South Works.

In truth, and although General Motors had considered turbines as early as the 1930s and had concept cars running in the '50s, and the French showed the SOCEMA-Gregoire at the Paris salon of 1952, Rover were the first manufacturer to produce sensible gas turbine cars. Chrysler went much further, much later, but both projects came to nought.

Maybe Austin did not take the enterprise sufficiently seriously and Lord was wise to stay clear of the machine. Its engine was being developed in a building rented to The Admiralty for the storage of live shells. It used compressors from scrap Rolls-Royce Merlin aero engines and on occasions it was started by poking a burning rag up the exhaust outlets. In service it placed machinery rotating at 23,000 rpm immediately in front of the driver and passenger's anatomy and was known to catch fire.

Ultimately the turbine-powered Sheerline succumbed to the faults that have beset most cars of the type—ravenous fuel consumption (an average of about 4.5 mpg of diesel for the Austin), high noise levels and a considerable delay in response to changes in power setting. The experiment though was not wasted. Longbridge used the technology in a range of stationary engines that were marketed successfully.

Much more outlandish than the turbine car was the agreement Lord entered in late 1946 with the long-established firm of Crompton Parkinson to form Austin-Crompton Parkinson Electric Vehicles Limited.

As early as 1878 Colonel Rookes Evelyn Bell Crompton had installed electric lighting at such prestigious properties as Windsor Castle and Holyrood House. Frank and Albert Parkinson's manufacture of electric motors went back to the early days of this technology and they formed an association with Crompton to make vehicles powered by this means and also a wide range of other electrical equipment. Crompton Parkinson had an interest in Morrison (no connection!) Electricars who made lightweight commercials for urban use such as, and particularly, milk floats, but also bread vans and even small coal delivery wagons.

From January 1948 Austin dealers were supposed to sell the 'Morrisons', a venture, we would surmise they regarded with little relish. In 1950 'Austin Crompton' obtained a controlling interest in the Midlands firm of ITD Stacatruc who manufactured electrically propelled industrial handling vehicles like forklift trucks. Little more is known.

If we were to speculate, and as all this took place at the time Rover were developing their turbine car and Lord was examining similar means of propulsion, it is just possible, with his fertile mind, immense energy and expansive view of the transport scene, Lord was also interested in the development of electric vehicles. Perhaps this was to have been the entrée.

One specialist vehicle that did find its way into the public domain was the world's best known and best loved purpose-built taxi. The FX3 was launched in 1948, funded by specialist dealer Mann Overton and Coventry coachbuilder Carbodies. Although it is unlikely, as some 'cabbies' claimed, fares would call them off a rank because the Austin was preferred to lesser marques, the model was extremely popular with both passengers and operators.

Based on the BS1 Sixteen, the FX3 was certainly a fast and mechanically refined machine. With an open luggage platform* next to the driver it was the last Austin cab to this traditional London design and preserved the company's domination of the hackney carriage market in the capital and other major cities.

The earlier examples used, exclusively, the 'Sixteen's' powerful, torquey, petrol engine, but in the early 1950s proprietary diesel engines became available and Longbridge itself had such a motor from 1954. The diesel detracted from the speed and smoothness, of course, but reduced the thirst of what was, essentially, a commercial vehicle. In the continuing drive for dollars, a small number of FX models were exported to America but, predictably, did not appeal.

_____

* There was a very similar hire car version—the FL1—that had a door on the front passenger side.

Meanwhile stunts and promotions continued. Some conceived by Hess, others private ventures.

In October 1949 two adventurous motorists set out from the White Cliffs Hotel in Dover to drive an A70 Hampshire to Cape Town. Ralph Sleigh was a 39-year-old former RAF squadron leader from Hitcham, near Ipswich, and his companion, Peter Jopling, an ex-army major, aged 29, from Merston, outside Chichester.

The two met after Sleigh had advertised in a daily newspaper for a partner to accompany him on such escapades. By 1948 they had already motored from Algiers to the Cape in record time. With the Hampshire they took a familiar route for the period, when such ventures were in vogue. Boulogne-sur-Mer, Marseilles, Algiers then to the southern lip of the Sahara. There, because of a complete absence of roads, the pair were forced to head for Nairobi on the east side of the continent before plunging south again to the Cape via Livingstone and Bulawayo.

They arrived at Shell House in Greenmarket Square, Cape Town, having covered some 11,000 miles in just over 24 days, knocking an incredible eight days off the previous record. The Algiers to Cape Town 'best' was also beaten by almost four days. On this occasion Lord would have been better throwing in his lot with Sleigh and Jopling than with Alan Hess.

By the time the Festival Of Britain opened on May 3, 1951, the latter had managed to get himself and Lord enrolled as 'goodwill ambassadors'. The festival was focused on the south bank of the Thames, not far from London's Waterloo station, but there were also satellite exhibitions in provincial centres around the country. In the words of one of its instigators, deputy Labour Party leader Herbert Morrison, it would be *'a tonic for the nation'* with its displays of architecture and industrial and scientific prowess, while the ambassadors were to *'take Britain to the peoples of the world who couldn't themselves visit'*.

To this end Hess proposed driving an A40 Sports around the world in 30 days and, in a piece of corny theatre, Lord bet him *'half a dollar'* it couldn't be done.

An opportunity to pander to America was never missed.

Hess then established some remarkable infrastructure to facilitate the stunt.

It involved a tie in with airline KLM who provided a Douglas DC-4 Skymaster aeroplane, named *Edam*, to 'shadow' the trip. Not only did it carry a press party and the off-duty drivers, one of whom, incidentally, was Ralph Sleigh, but transported the car over oceans and other untransversable areas.

The trip was completed in 21 days without significant problems. When the Skymaster subsequently landed at Prestwick, in Scotland, the Austin was driven, via Longbridge, to London airport from where it had departed on June 1. There a beaming Leonard Lord handed over his wager in front of the photographers before the car headed for the Thameside Festival of Britain.

Unfortunately, Harold Hastings, Midlands editor of *Motor* magazine, asked Lord, quite reasonably, why a car that had supposedly been around the world had only 8,500 miles recorded on the odometer.

Even Hess embarrassed Lord at his peril. It may have been remiss of the chairman not to have kept a closer watch on what his public relations officer was doing and the likely outcome. Yet there was a great deal happening at the time and Lord now felt his trust had been misplaced. Hess would soon become another casualty of the period.

It has been said that most people rode in a Daimler twice in their lives—to their wedding and to their funeral. The adage is intended to illustrate the stature and social significance of the marque. If we take a broader and more prosaic view, as we move into the 1950s, we see how Leonard Lord had shaped Austin to impact upon almost every aspect of daily life.

The majority of people would not have gone to their wedding in a Daimler, but an Austin, similarly to their funeral. There were now Austin coaches to take them on holiday, light commercials to buy ice cream from when they got there and J40 pedal cars to ride on when they went to the fun fair. Austins lined the frontages at most provincial railway stations and dominated the London taxi scene; they took the national newspapers to the railway termini for the midnight train*, brought the milk next morning and then the bread, they put out our fires for the fire brigades and served the police from Cornwall to Edinburgh.

All that apart, Lord had installed in Austin showrooms a cohesive, intelligent range of stylish, well-engineered cars that perfectly covered all mainstream market sectors and, in addition, took in the limited demand for a mildly tuned sports car and for an extremely potent one.

---

* The FX3 taxi chassis, bodied as a van, was extremely popular with Fleet Street newspaper proprietors for delivering their editions to the London rail termini.

CHAPTER EIGHTEEN

AUSTIN BASTARDS, MORRIS BASTARDS

Labour won the general election of February 1950. But a spirit of national disillusionment reduced their majority by 140 to just five—'*the light of great joy which shone in 1945 has faded*', said a delegate at that year's Party conference.

In the wider world, and astonishing as it may seem, considerable tracts of it were to be at war again, just four months after that February vote. The threat of a Third World War had never really disappeared after 1945, but the arena for this conflict would be Korea. To help fund British support for America's involvement on the side of the South Koreans in their bid to repel invading northern kinsman, but in reality, to conduct the Cold War by proxy, the new British Chancellor of the Exchequer, Hugh Gaitskell, introduced prescription charges for spectacles and dentures.

It wasn't, in truth, the end of the Socialist dream. But was sufficiently catastrophic to split the cabinet and also, for decades, the Party. The fiery Welsh health minister, Aneurin Bevan, who had introduced free 'cradle to grave' medical care, walked out. Harold Wilson joined him from the Board of Trade as did John Freeman from the Ministry of Supply. In October, 1951, in a bid to strengthen his position, prime minister, Clement Attlee, went to the country again. Although the Labour Party polled over a million more votes than the Conservatives, it was to bolster constituency majorities not win new seats. It was Winston Churchill who was returned to power.

If Leonard Lord had a dream it may have been this. The Labour government had not served him well, but neither, at root, would a Conservative administration. Bob Wyatt (*The Austin 1905-1952*) puts it with devastating simplicity. '*Lord disliked the Labour government*'. The reasons are expressed in graphic detail in that rare and outspoken interview with Olive Moore.

While Lord was the only British motor manufacturer to comply almost precisely with the exhortations of Stafford Cripps, when president of the Board of Trade, to: make a car that was '*cheap, tough, good-looking and of decent size, not the sort of car hitherto produced and in sufficient quantities to benefit from mass production*', he had endured much under Labour in his business life. The ineptitude of Shinwell that helped precipitate the power shortages of 1947; tax on company profits increased from 25 to 30% and there was a constant battle for steel allocations, yet relentless pressure for dollars. Bevin had empowered the workforce as never before and the possibility of nationalization, to which Lord was vehemently opposed, was ever present.

This last strategy had been strongly hinted at in Labour's 1945 manifesto. Coal and the railways had already followed that route and within the government there were some 150 advocates of a nationalized, volume production, motor industry. A vociferous example was backbench MP, Ian Mikardo, representing Reading. He published a Fabian Society pamphlet in 1948 entitled *The Second Five Years* in which he outlined a totally ill-conceived proposal that Britain's major car manufacturers should combine under government control to make a cheaply available '*people's car*'. Inexplicably, he missed the point that Ford and Vauxhall were American owned, and probably because of being, as Lord would have said, '*inexperienced and an academic planner*', was unaware that the last thing on earth the dollar spending market wanted, at that time, was a '*people's car*'!

It is easy to understand Lord's loathing of Labour. It may be that his decision to cut the Sheerline's price by £1 to £999 when, in January 1948, the government introduced double purchase tax (fractionally over 66%) on cars listed at £1,000 and over, was a small expression of his contempt. Perhaps: '*Quite how the Austin company manage to produce this machine at under a thousand pounds remains something of a mystery*', was plainer to see than the journalist* who wrote those words thought!

Lord was not left unscathed by Socialism in his private life either. At the board meeting of October 26, 1949, he was awarded a tax-free bonus of £225,000 plus 20,000 ordinary shares. However, it has to be said that the various sources for this information are contradictory. My figures are from the minute book but even that document is not infallible. For example, it even records incorrectly the registration mark of the Bentley bought for Lord in 1947! The package was conditional on Lord having no further involvement in the motor industry in the very unlikely event of him leaving Austin.

The TUC (Trades Union Congress) put pressure on the government to block such rewards or, at the very least, make them taxable. Lord, to coin the modern idiom, 'didn't need the money'. At Halesend he was increasingly living the life of the country gentleman he seemed to crave. As a consequence he was prepared to forego this financial acknowledgment of his immense contribution to the company. However, when the matter was put to the vote, the shareholders insisted he '*took the money*' by the sizeable majority of 608,000 to 100,000. The government changed the tax rules in April 1950—retrospectively—and Lord paid surtax at 95% on his reward for services, which, in no small measure, had been to them.

John Black** of Standard was knighted in 1943. Miles Thomas the same year. Even Harriman received an OBE that year and a CBE in 1951. Leonard Lord, who had done vastly more in the industry and for the war effort than any of them, had to wait until 1953 for his knighthood. Wyatt, perceptively we suspect, suggests enoblement would have come sooner had he been more amenable to the post-War Labour Government.

There have been suggestions Lord was offered, but refused, such honours. It is possible. He liked to give the impression at least, that he shunned ceremony, pomp and pretention. Perhaps it is all best left rest with his own words: '*Knighthoods? Peerages? What's the good of them to me? They don't cure your rheumatism! I was born a peer in my own right, and being a Lord, how could I be more honoured?*' But maybe he did smart at the injustice.

Three momentous events in the daily life of Leonard Lord took place between 1950 and '52. In order of importance they were the amalgamation of Austin and Morris to form, in 1952, the British Motor Corporation; the construction of Car Assembly Building One at Longbridge, commissioned in 1951; and the introduction of transfer machines from 1952 onwards.

---

*   SCH Davis.

**   Black was subsequently another 'victim' of the tax regulations having received from Standard a gratuity in shares.

As we have seen, the Austin-Morris Agreement on mutual corporation collapsed in 1949 and rumours of a merger became as vacuous as ever. However, Lord still aspired to what was effectively a take-over, rather than the formation of a combine, and he manoeuvred towards that end.

According to Graham Turner in *The Leyland Papers* the broker was Charles Kingerlee. Quite apart from regarding himself as a close friend of Lord, he was from an Oxford family who had long associations with Morris. He was also the jilted fiancé of Hylda Church, who Miles Thomas subsequently married. It had been Thomas, who, years later, engineered Wilfred Hobbs moving from the post of personal assistant to William Morris, to that of company secretary, and Kingerlee's appointment as Hobbs's replacement. A piece of juxtapositioning, incidentally, that so upset Morris that it contributed to the subsequent rift between himself and Thomas.

It was Kingerlee who, on October 10, 1950, Morris's 73rd birthday, picked up the ringing telephone in his modestly furnished outer office and listened to the mild brogue of Leonard Lord. Ostensibly, the latter wished to extend his good wishes to his one time chief. We will never know whether that was the real reason for the call or whether Kingerlee was manipulating the situation.

According to Turner, the latter had pointed out to Morris the fallacy of '*dog-eat-dog competitiveness*' between the two motor giants. While agreeing, his master had replied: '*There's nothing we can do about it. I'm not going to approach Lord*'.

The late Pauline Pither, Lord's youngest daughter and the most forthcoming on the subject of her father, maintained that such antipathy between Lord and Morris never existed. It is easy to dismiss this as social expediency. But an illustration she cited, that she and Lord met Morris by coincidence in Australia and the two men sat on Bondi Beach chatting and eating ice cream, has the ring of truth. This is particularly so as Pauline was on holiday with her parents in Australia at precisely the time merger machinations would have been at their peak, the Lords having left England on January 17, 1952.

Olive Moore's 'take', which admittedly, and obviously, is yet another variation on Lord's own 'party line', is that '*he never* (before) *had such admiration for Morris; never been so friendly with him*', than after Lord announced he was moving to Austin and Morris famously said: '*I don't see why we shouldn't have a lot of fun cutting each other's throats*'.

Reverting to Graham Turner's account, which is divergent, Morris, who was next door when Kingerlee took the birthday greetings call, refused to speak to Lord. Kingerlee, though, persuaded his boss this was churlish and the two executives exchanged pleasantries.

That very same day, with shades of what had transpired many years before with Lord and the shadow factories scheme, Kingerlee rang the Austin chairman, on his own initiative, and asked for a meeting.

Lord warned him not to come to Longbridge but invited him instead to Halesend. It was in a billiard room, seemingly the venue for some of the most momentous events in the history of the British motor industry, that Kingerlee revealed he believed an Austin-Morris merger would be mutually beneficial and competition, especially in overseas markets, was senseless. It is worth remembering that at the time trade deficit was a critical political and economic issue. Kingerlee would have been very alive to that situation.

He suggested Lord and his wife call on Morris unannounced. One can't help feel that a scenario involving the Lords' Bentley crunching over the gravelled approach to Nuffield Place, with Morris, somewhat bemused, peeping through a window over the winter-gripped shrubbery in a bid to identify his surprise visitors, sounds unlikely.

Suffice to say, a meeting between Lord and Morris took place. This too is enlivened by Turner, who, this time, has the Bentley conveying Lord, in secret, to a rendezvous with Kingerlee in the car park of a pub near Cowley. Lord is then taken to the Morris Works and slips in by a rear entrance. A merger deal was struck.

Lord had only to discuss the plan with a small, malleable, board. Morris, although he was personally convinced after the relevant directors' meeting that the union would be approved, was then thwarted by his deputy, now Reginald Hanks.

Hanks had been at Morris since 1922 and was the abrasive replacement for Miles Thomas when the latter resigned in 1947. As the Nuffield Organization's market share and profits fell, Hanks warned Morris: '*Rome is burning*'. The *raison d'être* for his appointment was to put out the blaze and revitalize the company as Lord had done at Austin, and indeed, had at Morris more than a decade before.

The new vice chairman believed the management structure needed streamlining. Empowered by Morris to undertake a major reorganization, without interference, he began an immediate cull far more severe than anything Lord ever undertook. One of the casualties among about seven senior executives was 'Old' George Harriman, father of Lord's protégé and Austin works director, 'Young George'. It was an unwise move.

It is true, Hanks markedly improved the Nuffield Organization's performance—from a profit of £1.5 million in 1948 to eight in 1950. Neither was he opposed, in principle, to a merger with Austin, merely hoping to strengthen his own company's position before it took place. Yet, as Morris had realized almost immediately he had elevated Hanks, it was an unhappy choice; particularly in the circumstances now unfolding.

To make another analogy between Lord, Swinton and the shadow factories from years before; it was now Morris who had to make the embarrassing phone call. It was to tell Austin's chairman the amalgamation was stalled. Perhaps retaliated is too strong a word. But Lord certainly had a practical response—the A30. This was the car I described as confronting the post-War Morris Minor, launched in 1948.

Lord had long been an advocate of chassis-less construction having moved in this direction for the pre-War Austin Eight and Ten. He had gathered round him Ken Garrett from the aircraft industry, who had already solved the structural problem on the Atlantic, and another brilliant aeronautical engineer, Ian Duncan, who was fulfilling a three-year contract with Austin. With the backing of Lord, and flying in the face of the accepted wisdom, Garrett and Duncan developed what was one the first chassis-less cars in volume production in the world[*].

Holden Koto was a disciple of Edsel Ford, worked at Dearborn on the pre-War Ford Eight that Lord admired so much and, at the time of the Austin A30, was a designer working for Austin's American consultant, Raymond Loewy. It was Koto who styled the new baby Austin—in clay, for one of the first times. Dick Burzi reworked it to provide a more traditional Longbridge look. As a point of passing interest, Koto bought the now abandoned Pinin Farina Alfa Romeo—the inspiration for Lord's A90 Atlantic—around 1950, and eventually took it to America.

Eric Bareham developed the A30's zippy overhead valve engine from the A40 unit, while Harry Weslake improved the cylinder head. As the BMC A Series it became one of the finest

---

[*]   The Saab 92 of 1950 beat it by just a few months and the Lancia Lambda beat them both by almost three decades! Some writers describe the Morris Minor as chassis-less. This is incorrect. The Morris needed a sub-frame to anchor its torsion bar suspension.

small capacity motors of all time and it is estimated that between 1951 and the year 2000 some 14 million were made.

Probably wisely, Lord spurned the novelty of chassis-less construction in marketing the A30 and traded on the esteem and affection for the pre-War Seven, selling the fresh model for some years as '*the new* Austin Seven'. It received instant acclaim and it would be fair to say that apart from the suspension and road holding characteristics the A30 was superior to the contemporary Morris Minor. A better engine, obviously, than the obsolescent pre-War side valve, transplanted from the Morris Eight and, of course, a much more advanced build method.

William Morris would have been no more impressed with the new small Austin than he was with his own Morris Minor. It was the departed Miles Thomas who had been the champion of the Alec Issigonis-conceived Minor. Morris had little respect for its designer—'*Issi-wassi-what's his bloody name*'—and described the car as '*like a poached egg*'.

Nothing progressed on the Austin-Morris merger for about a year. It was Lord who reopened the negotiations. Whether he did so 'cold' or whether he was 'given the nod' by Kingerlee, again, we will never know. But it is interesting that Morris moved quickly and presented the board with a *fait d'accompli*. Hanks, predictably, was furious. The news had come from Wilfred Hobbs, slipping, as we have seen him so many times before, through the wings: '*telling all that was necessary to be heard*'.

Hanks caught up with Morris in the nursing home where, we can only conclude, he was resting following the stress of the *coup d'etat*. In outpourings worthy of Lady Nuffield he told the demigod that if he wanted to lose prestige and standing he was on the appropriate course and Lord would keep him out of his factory as he had done Herbert Austin.

Whether or not we accept Lord's version of his replacing Austin, and we suspect other, far broader, issues obfuscate the story, there is no evidence whatsoever that Austin was excluded other than voluntarily. '*He* (Austin) *put his cards on the table. He was getting beyond it and wanted someone he could trust to succeed him and with complete confidence hand over the great factory that had been his life's work*', recalled Lord, somewhat immodestly.

Despite Hanks's protestations, the merger stood. The British Motor Corporation came into being in early 1952. The new organization was the fourth largest motor company in the world behind America's Chrysler Corporation, General Motors and Ford. It had assets worth £66,000,000, employed 42,000 people and the constituent companies were responsible for about half the country's vehicle output. William Morris was chairman, Lord, managing director and Hanks his deputy.

Eventually, BMC, having been renamed British Motor Holdings and in a parlous financial state, was taken over by British Leyland in 1968. Naturally, the reasons for the Corporation's failure are complex and varied. In recent times, and in our culture of blame, it has become fashionable to find the roots of that ultimate ignominy in Leonard's Lord cultivation of this empire during the first decade.

This, of course, is extremely convenient. It avoids some unpalatable truths: the appalling standard of workmanship that came to typify the British car of the 1960s; a workforce in whose motives it is hard to find any purpose other than the destruction of the nation's manufacturing industries and of the social fabric itself. While along the way we may need to debunk some popular icons that were not as praiseworthy as we wish to believe.

If we hark back to the suggested union between Herbert Austin, the Wolseley company and William Morris in 1924, the latter had demurred on the basis: '*the organization would be so great that it would be difficult to control and might tend to strangle itself*'. Similar things have been claimed of BMC. But Martin Adeney in *The Motor Makers* says the argument that the Corporation was so large as to be unmanageable is invalid. It was only too big for the kind of methods employed by '*the idiosyncratic individualists who had built the industry up between the wars*'.

Broadly speaking, he is correct. Let us begin from the premise that we have a chairman who actively disliked and denigrated one of the keynote products—the Morris Minor—and a deputy managing director, Hanks, who immediately said, apropos the new entity: '*We have been in competition with Austins for a long time and we will remain in competition*'. These are disastrous attitudes.

For his part, Lord, perhaps predictably, *does* seem to have found the organization difficult to manage in these early months. He wanted supreme command but William Morris continued to meddle, or as his biographers, Andrews and Brunner put it: '*an elder statesman giving his counsel if asked*'.

Giving that often debilitating 'counsel', usually *without* being asked, was, of course one of his cardinal traits. Lord found the approach so claustrophobic that almost before this flagship of British industrial prowess had left the berth, he sent his chauffeur, Dennis Bush, to Nuffield Place with a letter of resignation.

Morris quickly changed tack but he was a broken man. His last annual meeting took little more than six minutes. Some formal business was processed then he handed the helm to Lord. Morris did not wait for the speeches. He rose, gathered his papers, said good-bye and walked out. Although he was given the courtesy title of president, it was all over. It could be argued that this was the denouement of '*brick by bloody brick*' or perhaps, merely the opening scene. But on the evidence we have seen so far, from a wide variety of sources, I don't think it was either.

It is beyond question there were inherent resentments of Austin within the former Nuffield Organization. As head of their old rival, Lord had manipulated the wartime scene to be first into the marketplace when hostilities ended. Austin had had the accolade of being the only shadow factory participant allowed final assembly of engines, whereas not only were Morris excluded from the scheme, when they were subsequently allocated the Castle Bromwich Spitfire factory, the initial period was rancorous and they were spectacularly relieved of its control. Austin and Lord were stars of the dollar drive, while Morris made virtually no contribution. Finally, Longbridge achieved the coup of making the first new, volume produced British car of the peace.

Yet never let us forget the observation of Dan Warren, an executive in BMC's service structure of the time: '*Believe me, there were Austin bastards and Morris bastards*'. Whether or not Lord did actually refer to Morris personnel as '*those buggers on the farm*' he *is* culpable of failing to make a serious or professional attempt to integrate the two workforces. This did have a detrimental effect on the early life of the Corporation.

We have to accept, of course, that team building seminars and highly paid consultants in these strategies, so familiar to us now, did not exist in Britain in Lord's day. Even if they had, it is doubtful he would have been temperamentally suited to taking advantage of them! We shall return to these issues later but for the moment it is important to consider some of Lord's other major undertakings at this time.

An investment of £300,000 was made to modernize the Works and create a new car assembly building (CAB). The initial contract for the latter was placed with W J Whittall and Sons Ltd on February 15, 1949. Whittall typified the solidarity of Austin. Established as early as 1796 they had operated from the same offices in Lancaster Street, Birmingham, since 1802. They were specialists in the construction of public buildings and factories and went on to contribute to the Jodrell Bank Observatory complex. They also had a branch in London.

The CAB site was the old airfield (always called the flying ground) to the south of the main Works and at the rear of the general offices, built in 1948 and facing Lickey Road, and the administration block*. The *'flying ground'* constituted a low convex hillock. One of the attractions for Lord was that topographically it was directly to the south of the Trentham** building, where bodies were finished, and also the cluster of shops that made chassis components, including engines and gearboxes.

Whittall's first job was to further level the area. Work of this sort had already been undertaken in WW1 to create the airfield. Now an additional 280,000 tons of assorted sandstone rock, marls, pebbles and hard core were removed.

Ultimately the plan was to bring all the constituent parts of a car—Austin made 90% in-house—into the assembly building through tunnels. Just as the whole arrangement was the most advanced in Europe the construction methods were highly sophisticated. The latest techniques were used to accurately position the piles, needed in some areas to support the building's foundations, so that they did not obtrude on the tunnels. The latter were created by the well-established cut-and-cover method but had exceptionally thick concrete walls and a roof reinforced by steel columns and beams to support the enormous weight of the conveyors, plant and road traffic above.

The main assembly hall housed three 250-yard-long tracks emerging from a stores containing three quarters-of-a-million chassis parts. It was naturally lit from 60,000 square foot of overhead glass with more set into walls of straw-coloured brick adorned at the northern end by a giant example of Burzi's flying 'A'. The main entrance proudly sported the *'Austin of England'* script over the doorways. Within there was the potential to produce 2,000 A40s a week, even that figure being exceeded in 1953/4.

Labour minister of supply, George Strauss, now in the last few months of his tenure, opened the building on July 19, 1951. His 'ribbon cutting' speech paid tribute to British craftsman, designers and the Austin Motor Company, although not to Lord, whose concept it had been. And just as the chairman may have felt he should have been given some direct credit, those who picked up the celebratory brochure that day must have wondered where *'the flower beds and green lawns'* that helped it blend so confidently into the Lickey Hills that were *'one of Birmingham's most popular summer evening and weekend resorts'*, actually were.

An element that would certainly not have been covered by the booklet was that of the building worker who walked into the tunnels one day and was never seen in tangible form again. His ghostly footsteps, however, are said to have followed individuals through the catacombs when the day's work was done and all was silent; and that his voice could sometimes be heard at one's shoulder, but when the listener turned, nothing but the bodies of cars hung in the void. Lord's view on these stories would be interesting as some sources attribute him with being extremely superstitious!

All that apart, the car assembly building was an incredible manufacturing resource, a remarkable architectural and constructional achievement in its own right and a gleaming jewel for Lord to present at the BMC 'party'.

---

* This was colloquially known as 'the Kremlin'. It is a term conspicuous by its absence in this book. Why? It is claimed the administration building of Accrington red brick resembled the Moscow edifice. I don't subscribe to that explanation. The term is synonymous with the Cold War era and the Communist regimes of Stalin and others. This seems the antithesis of what Lord stood for. I doubt if he used the sobriquet and neither do I.

** Named after the building contractor who constructed it.

Part of what was going to make CAB function so well was the contribution by Austin transfer machines. We have encountered these strange 'beasts' once before. Now is the time to look at and appreciate them in anatomical detail. The philosophy behind the automatic transfer machine is the commercial and competitive need to manufacture articles more cheaply and in ever-greater quantity.

In Chapter Four we saw that it was Herbert Taylor and Frank Woollard, at Morris Engines, who developed what were, by two decades, the most advanced devices of this type in the world; and it was Leonard Lord who made them work. There is no implied criticism of Taylor or Woollard in that remark. Merely the acknowledgement that the pneumatic and electrical technology of the late 1920s did not match the two men's innovativeness. By 1950 the situation was entirely different and furthermore, reorganization and modernization of the Longbridge plant, except for the recent East Works (the shadow factory), was long overdue.

Basic ideas needed to change too. For every three tons of metal processed by stand alone machine tools—lathes, mills, drills, borers etc.—only one ton of finished product emerged. The resulting scrap, when sold for smelting, realized only a little over 10% of the price at which it was bought as raw material.

Yet the accuracy of these standard machines had improved. The former skills of the operator had been built into the equipment and the emphasis at the human level was now in fitting the jigs and cutters and setting the controls. In addition, automation meant that one operator could handle more than one machine.

Lord's concept was Taylor and Woollard-inspired. Build easily constructed standard units and dispense with all the unneeded accoutrements a bought-in machine would include. Then make the equipment easy to adapt for the range of jobs likely to be encountered. Finally provide a high degree of automation.

The name most associated with the implementation of the Austin transfer machines is Horace Holbeche, who was in charge of the jig and tool room. But electronic specialists like Dick Brierley, Les Burrows on hydraulics, other Works engineers and numerous more all had an important role to play.

There are a number of types of transfer machine. The pattern adopted at Longbridge was normally, but by no means exclusively, of the straight-line variety. These in themselves take a number of forms—platen, non-platen or double indexing.

In the first design, the work—typically an A Series engine cylinder block—would be automatically conveyored between the machine's workstations and secured to what might be likened to a base plate (platen). A disadvantage is difficulty locating this platen in exactly the right position at each station and, long-term, that the platens wear.

On non-platen machines (used for B Series motors) the work is held on spigot-like bushes attached to the stations themselves. The bushes are used to pilot the tools—drills and reamers, for example—thus resulting in greater accuracy. The components advance along hardened steel slides.

The double indexed designs were the most ingenious and celebrated of the Austin machines. They address the problem that some operations on a component may take up to twice as long as others. By complex electrical and mechanical means (indexing) a part can be retained at a particular station while such work is carried out without holding up its fellows on the 'fast track'—rather like placing a wagon in a railway siding beside the main line!

All the machines consist of end pieces between which are located a number of cast iron beds or bases. It is these that support the stations necessary to process a component, whether a cylinder head or rear axle casing. Attached to this 'backbone' are branch, or supplementary beds, to which are fitted the unit heads.

The latter came in a variety of sizes and received the drive for the clusters of tools they held—drills, taps, reamers—and would use on each part. Among the many bells and whistles were troughs for swarf and coolant clearance, gauges that monitored the consistency of tolerances, and provision for pre-setting tools before they were fitted to the unit heads, thus speeding changes.

One of the most remarkable aspects of Lord's transfer machine policy was that so many of the intricate mechanisms were made 'on-site', which is almost certainly a unique phenomenon within the industry worldwide. It is also extremely fitting because both before, and during, WWI Herbert Austin designed and manufactured many of his company's machine tools.

It was not Lord's original intention to make so much of the equipment within the Works. He had asked a number of specialists to consider the job and quote, including the Coventry company of Alfred Herbert. As we learned much earlier, the latter were the most prestigious machine tool makers in the country and claimed to be the largest in the world. But, with what was a cipher for the complacency and contempt for the customer of British industry in general, Herbert's directors told Lord they were not interested in cooperating on machines that, effectively, had the potential to revolutionize the motor industry worldwide and would have given them a major share in the subsequent business. Herbert's concern was with selling Lord basics from their existing range. Not surprisingly, this once enormous company, like the enterprises it served, no longer exists.

Lord's response was eminently predictable. '*We'll make the bloody things ourselves*'.

He was fortunate that the Birmingham works of Archdale showed vastly more initiative than their near neighbour. Yorkshireman James Archdale founded his company in 1868 when he was 29-years-old. Like Lord himself, he had an extremely broad mechanical base and as a youth had worked not only for general engineers and machine tool makers but also steam locomotive builders. An added strength was the firm made a point, in its early years, of non-specialisation and their clients ranged from pen manufacturers to those of ammunition and small arms. It now fell to James Archdale & Co Ltd, with their factories in Ledsam Street, Birmingham and the Blackpole area of Worcester, to cast the end supports and beds for Leonard Lord's transfer machines.

Other outside firms undertook the manufacture of specialist equipment like electrical consoles. But no fewer than 1,200 unit heads, plus 1,000 more for independent machines, were made in a self-contained section of the tool shop on the Longbridge site.

The golden age of the transfer machine was from 1952 until 1959 when 68 (32 platen and 36 non-platen types) were made to produce, principally, cylinder blocks, heads and gearbox cases. When production stopped in 1968 100 had been built with between 15 and 35 stations and 35 and 70 unit heads. At their peak they were machining 12,000 engine castings a week.

The hard cash reality of the transfer machine is a capital saving of very approximately £5,000 over the standard drillers, millers, etc., that would do the same work; there is, again very roughly, a 25% saving in floor space; hourly labour costs are reduced by about 80% as only two operators are needed—one to load, one to off-load—and weekly production is increased by around 20%.

The last of the transfer machines—and let us make no mistake over the fact that this was a Leonard Lord innovation—were 'decommissioned' (scrapped) in *2001*. At the time, they were being used on cylinder heads and blocks for the multi-point fuel injection (MPi) 1275 cc Mini Cooper.

Ironically, Longbridge stopped building this incredible equipment partly because the British machine tool industry complained to the government that their territory was being trespassed upon! It is also of note that licences were sold to Donovan Electrical Limited of Birmingham but as far as is known no machines were ever produced.

It was the transfer machines that delivered the components to the engine assembly section and subsequently, through the tunnels, to the CAB. To achieve this a degree of automatic control was provided by a Hollerith punch card system. It helped channel the relevant parts to a given point on the assembly line so that any number of model variants could be made.

Lord would no doubt have wished to exclude from the publicity material that this control technology dated from the late 18th century! Interestingly, it started to appear in the textile industry with which he was once so familiar. Around 1800 Joseph Marie Jacquard improved and adapted the system to program looms.

It subsequently inspired Charles Babbage, credited with being the father of the computer, and later the American, Herman Hollerith. Hollerith's Computing, Tabulating, Recording Corporation eventually became IBM whose unit record machines dominated much of industry by 1950.

The complexity of the exercise and the disruption involved prevented the conversion of Austin production to full computer control but it was clearly within the realms of possibility and it is a credit to Lord's tremendous vision that he brought from America one of the first two computers in Britain. The other was operated by the Lyons Corner House* chain. The Longbridge example was used in the accounts department and had sufficient surplus capacity for there to be an innovative proposal to hire it out although, as far as is known, this never materialized.

For us to understand how Lord's vision for Longbridge functioned in its entirety we can do no better than refer to Frank Woollard in his 1954 book *Principles of Mass and Flow Production* that happens to have an articulate and neatly crafted foreword by Lord himself.

Woollard wrote: '*Although, in effect, the track is continuous it is actually in four sections, the first being devoted to chassis assembly, the second to chassis painting, the third to oiling and body mounting and the fourth to final connections.*

'*The assembly commences in the marshalling area of the individual component stores where the slat conveyor, on which are mounted various fixtures, is loaded with such items as propeller shafts, rear springs, silencers, exhaust pipes and so on—down to nuts and bolts.*

'*As the conveyor emerges from this area, the frames are placed on their fixtures by a Telpher (hoist) drawing from a frame stock. At the next station the rear springs and shackles are attached to the frame which, preceding to the next station, receives the rear axle and front suspension delivered by an elevator from a tunnel 20 feet below the floor of the assembly building. These components are attached to the chassis—propeller shaft, brake mechanism and cable harness being added at succeeding locations.*

'*At another station, the engine assembly elevator drops the power unit into the required position* "within less than half a hole" *so that the fitters, with a minimum of manipulation, bolt it into place. Then the clutch control is added and that portion of the steering mechanism carried by the chassis is coupled up.*

'*At this point the slat conveyor returns to its starting point and the pendulum boxes that hold the nuts and bolts automatically swing under the conveyor so that the contents are not disturbed. The*

---

*   J Lyons & Co was a British food manufacturer. In 1909 it established a chain of extremely large, populist, London restaurants called 'Corner Houses'. In a sense they were the elegant forerunners of 'convenience dining'.

chassis is lifted automatically and suspended on the overhead conveyor which carries it through a chamber containing an electrostatic paint spraying apparatus which covers all the iron and steel parts, except those that are masked, with rust-resisting paint.

'*The chassis continues through a hot-air drying booth to be lowered to another slat conveyor for further operations. It first proceeds to an oil filling station where the appropriate oils are delivered in measured quantities to engine, gearbox, rear axle, steering box and the braking system which is filled and bled at this point.*

'*This is an interesting operation since* the chassis is traveling all the time and the service pipes are trailed along by a linkage, which engages the track and returns in time to pick up the next chassis.*

'*The exhaust system, which by-passed the spray-painting operation, is now fitted, by which time the chassis has arrived at the elevator which deposits the body on the chassis. The road wheels which travelled in the boot are fitted to the hubs—a multi-head nut runner tightens all the nuts at once. Water is now supplied to the radiator and sufficient petrol for test and movement is put in the tank.*

'*The car now enters on to the fourth conveyor—an elevated double strand slat track—which enables work to be carried on all round and underneath the car. The body is securely fastened to the chassis and the steering box which is mounted in the body is coupled to the drag link on the chassis. At the following stations the bumpers are attached, the seats are positioned, the electric wiring is completed, such cleaning as may be necessary to remove the witness of handling is done, the tyres are inflated to the correct pressure and the finished car is driven off the track for final inspection and test. It then proceeds to the dispatch department.*'

'*The whole process, from the first item placed on the track in the marshalling area to the delivery of the car to dispatch, takes less than four-and-a-half-hours*'.

In this chapter we have devoted a great deal of time to the principles Leonard Lord was applying at Longbridge to create one of the largest and most sophisticated car factories in the world.

It is also worth mentioning that around this time the company bought The Manor at Haseley, just to the north of Warwick. The Victorian mansion, built in 1878 on the site of much earlier residences, was converted for use as a staff training centre. This makes a further nonsense of the contention that Lord had no interest in this aspect of the business, although Harriman's suggestion that the grounds be used to teach groups of under-17-year-olds to drive does not seem to have found favour!

Neither should we overlook what was taking place within BMC on a daily basis.

February 1952 saw the introduction of the A40 Somerset. Mechanically it was very similar to its predecessor, the Devon, and physically a scaled down version of the A70 Hereford, which the Devon had been of the Hampshire. It could have been much more revolutionary and is indicative of how seriously Lord took the need to earn dollars in that he commissioned the American, Raymond Loewy, to style this car.

Loewy is an icon of 20th century industrial design. As he said himself: '*I can claim to have made the daily life of the 20th century more beautiful*'. To do so he gave the world the Coca-Cola bottle—'*its shape is aggressively female*'—the *Lucky Strike* cigarette packet, the 1950s Greyhound bus and the Shell logo.

At face value he had much in common with Lord who said of American cars: '*They are swollen and fat nosed, with grinning chromium mouth organs underneath*'. Loewy said: '*I'd kill*

---

*   This section of the line was known as the 'cake stand' because the rolling chassis was elevated to allow work underneath, and resembled, (loosely!) sweetmeats on the special plates seen in confectioner's windows.

chrome for ever' then described the products of Detroit as '*jukeboxes on wheels, aesthetic aberrations that mask the workings of the machine beneath layers of tawdry flash*'.

His broader views may also have struck a cord with Lord: '*The most beautiful curve is a rising sales graph*' and '*a designer must always think about the unfortunate production engineer who will have to manufacture what you have designed*'.

It was Tucker Madawick, from Loewy's London office, and Holden Koto who actually worked on the Somerset; from around the summer of 1950. But although Lord clearly appreciated the need to revitalize the appearance of Austins and the importance of appealing to a global audience, and was taking visionary steps in that direction, reticence and conservatism held him back. Madawick was certainly aware of this. '*Austin mainly went "in-house" rather than use much of our stuff*' (Sharratt. *Men and Motors of the Austin*).

Maybe Lord was still trammelled by the disappointment of the A90 Atlantic. Arguably, that failed, at least in part, because of its flamboyance. Ultimately it was Lord himself and the ultra dependable Dick Burzi, who crafted the Somerset and the resultant appearance, albeit highly appealing, was not that much different from either the Hereford or Devon. There was also an attractive Somerset convertible with coachwork by Carbodies that rendered the A40 Sports superfluous.

Rather more imaginative than the styling itself were some of the promotions applied to this and other current models. At home the Accession of Princess Elizabeth, and her Coronation in 1953, were skillfully exploited with 'royalist' colours for the Somerset—Buckingham green, Balmoral blue, Windsor grey, Sandringham fawn and, the mysterious, though alliterating hue, coronet cream.

'*See the old country in a new Austin*' offered American visitors the chance of ordering a car before they left for Britain, collecting it on arrival, and having the vehicle stowed aboard the liner that took them home.

The few British citizens who could afford a holiday in South Africa had the option of an Austin from dealer Robbs of Cape Town on a guaranteed buy-back deal. While predictably, Hess was involved with a stunt to drive a Somerset from Ecuador to the Arctic Circle.

This proved even more disappointing than his adventures in the A40 Sports. In the first instance the route was amended to Entebbe, in Uganda, to Jokkmokk in Sweden on the basis, and not altogether in a do-or-die spirit, that there were no through roads across Panama and Costa Rica. Once again the Somerset ended up in an aeroplane that took it from Cairo to Marseilles, to save time. At the end of the 'epic' it had little more than 7,500 miles 'on the clock'.

It was George Harriman who actually dismissed Hess. On this occasion Lord was conveniently absent. The chairman may even have had pangs of regret. Rumour has it that the discarded publicist received a personal Christmas card not to mention an Austin Hereford! But both Lord and Hess must have realized that as the car became more and more commonplace and reliable, and overseas travel increasingly popular, the epics of the 1930s and late '40s had become *non sequiturs*.

1951 was a significant year for Lord in his private life. His two elder daughters both got married. Joan, at Bromyard, into the Breeden family, well known as manufacturers of motor accessories, and Patricia at Upton-on-Severn to Commander M J Howard-Smith.

CHAPTER NINETEEN
OPERATION OVERLORD

'*That 803cc engine was the biggest load of rubbish we ever had*' was Cowley tester Joe Gomm's comment on the Austin A Series engine, quoted by Barney Sharratt in *Men and Motors of the Austin*. The observation is patently absurd.

The A type is generally acknowledged as being one of the finest small petrol engines ever designed, saw some 14 million produced over nearly half a century and was the basis for the power units in more than a score of BMC, British Leyland and Austin Rover core models including the legendary Mini. Sharratt acknowledges the unsoundness of Gomm's remark, and others, such as: '*Morris people expected cars to do 100,000 miles not 3,000*'.

Yet the dialogue illustrates to perfection the blind, irrational prejudice that existed on the Morris side of the BMC partnership without Lord doing anything at all to poison the well. Geoffrey Rose, who we last encountered in the Ministry of Supply dealing with steel allocations, but who had started his career at Wolseley, then returned to the motor industry and moved to Longbridge in 1953 as Works manager—'*a tinge of Morris*'—told this author that Lord did not have a 'down' on Morris. '*He chose the best design; Austin or Morris*'. And, we might argue; the best people.

This is born out, to an extent, by Sharratt, who writes: '*Whether Lord fully cashed in on the merger or not he certainly could not be accused of lacking commitment to the success of both Austin and BMC*'. And that leads us back to the issue of the 803 cc A Series engine which was installed in the Morris Minor from 1952.

When Alec Issigonis designed the car he intended it to have a flat-four (i.e. four cylinder, horizontally opposed) engine, which owed something to a design developed by the German Steyr company in the late 1930s. How well this would have worked we shall never know.

However, there is some evidence the execution was flawed* and it is accepted Issigonis was notoriously weak at designing engines. One of the Minor's principal champions and one of Issigonis's, Miles Thomas, resigned in November 1947, following the inevitable 'difference' with William Morris. Those who had been advocating the use of the pre-War Morris Eight engine now held sway. As someone at Longbridge, other than Lord, said: '*Whoever decided on using that engine buggered the first Minor up for four or five years*'. Issigonis himself was only slightly less graphic: '*A terrible old thing, but we had no option*'.

The observations are correct. Not only did the outdated engine go a long way to negating the outstanding handling characteristics with which the designer had imbued the Minor, it

---

* Two engines to this design survived within British Leyland until circa 1984 when they were scrapped. But it is said crankshaft deflection was sufficiently severe to allow the flywheel to strike the engine end plate.

emaciated the performance and nullified the car's appeal in America at the exact point when Volkswagen was establishing cult status.

The installation of the A Series engine, designed for the A30, and although still needing much refinement, transformed the Minor to the extent it never looked back. Its sales increased by some 50 per cent in the first year of the Austin-powered Mark II and it eventually outsold its Longbridge rival by not very far short of a million vehicles.

Joe Gomm has suggested that the Minor would have been equally well served by the Wolseley Eight unit—'*a beautiful engine*'—and that it was about to replace the side valve motor when the engineering planning committee specified the A Series. Lord had established the committee and included Longbridge works manager Joe Edwards, Harriman and representatives of the Nuffield companies.

That the Wolseley engine could have been used in the Morris Minor is largely wishful thinking. Although an overhead valve unit it was another outdated pre-War design that represented little more than a top end re-work of the old Morris Eight motor. The Austin offering, on the other hand, broke new ground in a number of respects. Designed by Eric Bareham, it had the crankcase portion of the cylinder block split along the crankshaft's centre line. This saved metal, although a very self-deprecating Bareham was always of the view that even then too much '*iron had been poured*' and was getting a free ride! The layout also meant that a deeper than usual sump was needed and included semi-circular cutouts front and rear to accommodate the bottom halves of the front and rear main bearings. These were sealed with cork inserts while the joint washer, between pan and block was, of necessity, in two pieces.

It was not the most elegant arrangement but by what we can only assume was total coincidence, a spin-off of this approach was that when the Mini and its descendants arrived, nearly a decade later, the shallow or 'centre line' block facilitated the revolutionary and all-important phenomenon of accommodating the gearbox in the sump!

Harry Weslake shaped the A Series combustion chambers and valve ports and, as Eric Bareham freely admits, this was instrumental in providing its peppy, free-revving characteristics—a peak of between 5-6,000 rpm whereas the side valve Morris managed 'four'. The engine had been much improved—and enlarged to 948 cc—by the time the Austin A35 and Morris 1000 were introduced in 1956, but the validity of Lord's original decision to adopt the Austin engine and not continue with the Morris is beyond question.

It also illustrates how he was both alive to the need for, and an advocate of, rationalization. This was the first example within BMC. Yet the pre-War 'Lord-look' side valves were very much a rationalized range as were those first four and six cylinder ohv engines. Rear doors common to both the Hereford and Somerset paid lip service to the same principle. Although to be fair, and by then, Lord had wanted to go much further. Overall though, it is unfortunate that he did not now continue the policy with more determination regardless of whether the component emanated from Cowley or Longbridge.

The extremely harsh reality is that to do so would have been impossible. An ingredient of rationalization, then, as much later, would have been factory closures with consequent job losses. Neither the government nor the increasingly powerful trade unions would have countenanced that. Neither would the 'gnomes' from Threadneedle Street have tolerated a blip in their dividends caused by such an upheaval, however temporary, or beneficial in the long-term it may have been.

Nonetheless, there were some sensible consolidations. The Austin B Series engine that was derived from the excellent, and by now well-tried, A40 motor was used in 1954 to replace another obsolete Morris side valve fitted to the MO coded Oxford medium-sized saloon. The B Type developed into the mainstay of the mid range BMC and British Leyland cars and light commercials for nearly 25 years and also had some much more exotic applications, such as a twin overhead camshaft version for the MGA and as an optional power plant for the advanced, but now largely forgotten, Rochdale Olympic sports car.

A Morris engine that Lord took into the fold was an overhead valve six cylinder designated the C Series. It was a departure from Austin tradition in that the camshaft and valve gear were to the right of the block. No bad thing in itself as it avoided the more convoluted Longbridge ploy of siamesed ports to make space for the pushrods. However, the advantages in gas flow were largely negated by having the manifold cast integrally with the cylinder head and some of the holding down studs passing through the ports which is considered bad practice.

From the standpoint of internecine disputes the fact the engine was modified for everyday use rather more than its A and B Series stablemates, and that it had a shorter life than either (1954-1971), is unfortunate. Apart from over-boring in 1959 to increase the capacity from 2639 to 2912 cc, the changes were mainly concerned with the cylinder head. A more conventional type with detachable manifolds was adopted in 1957. Whatever the ramifications surrounding this Morris-derived engine it has the notable distinction of being used in the highly acclaimed Austin Healey 3000.

However, one early project had no such redemption and, by a double misfortune, was a Nuffield flagship. The Riley Pathfinder was the product of the fine mind of that organization's, Gerald Palmer. It was unquestionably an elegant and advanced concept and had evolved before the Austin-Morris merger, when Palmer was chief designer for MG/Riley/Wolseley. His most significant previous achievement was both the body and flat four engine for the aerodynamic and highly promising Javelin for the independent Bradford firm of Jowett.

Lord appointed Palmer as BMC's body and chassis designer almost at the outset making further nonsense of the contention the chairman was prejudiced against Morris men.

The Pathfinder used a four cylinder 2.5 litre twin cam* engine from the RM series Rileys. This had been the first new range produced by the company since Morris took it over in 1939. Unveiled in 1945, the type was among the most stylish and elegant models of the era. The Pathfinder adopted the much less traditional but extremely handsome Palmer-crafted body of the Wolseley 6/90. There was Nuffield torsion bar independent front suspension and the designer's own system at the rear featuring coil springs and Panhard rod location for the axle.

Unfortunately for the newly promoted Palmer the car, destined for launch at the 1953 London motor show, suffered from severe brake judder and excessively heavy steering accompanied by chronic shake at the wheel. The road holding was also unacceptable with a tendency, in some cases, for the Panhard rod to shear when cornering hard. Miraculously, Palmer survived the wrath of Lord, even though Pathfinder production had to be temporarily stopped and the rear suspension system was eventually abandoned in favour of an unsophisticated rigid axle and semi-elliptic leaf spring set-up.

Ironically, it was the seemingly uncontroversial Wolseley 6/90 that toppled Palmer in 1955. An allegedly unfavourable road test of the car in the September 16 issue of *The Autocar* upset Lord to the extent he dismissed the designer. Our spontaneous response must be that it was a gross over-reaction. The more so if we study road test 1574 and take it at face value.

---

* This terminology should not be taken to mean overhead camshafts. The shafts are mounted high on each side of the cylinder block but still operate the valves by pushrods.

In the bland journalistic mode of the day the comments are generally complimentary; flattering even. The areas of difficulty arise over: '*disconcerting lack of grip afforded by the front seats, especially for the passenger*' who was obviously sliding onto the driver and creating a safety issue when the car was cornering at speed. The column gear change comes in for criticism over the length of travel and its sponginess. But worst of all was the observation: '*drivers formed the opinion that the braking system was not in keeping with the rest of the performance. High pedal pressures were required for slowing from speed, and when stopping there was some judder from the front brakes. There were also indications that water was entering the brakes in heavy rain*'. These were further danger points, strongly expressed for the time.

As a talented engineer and a driver of vast experience Lord would have known that 'juddering' brakes on a brand new car, and also a Pathfinder ailment, are most likely to be the result of a design flaw.

Our considered judgement must be, that, once again, Lord had been biding his time to remove Palmer. Yet, it is anomalous that he seems unable to move at the appropriate instant—against, for example, Haefli when the A40 and Sheerline proved so troublesome and Hess when he embarrassed him. The failure to act at the offending moment helped earn him a reputation for unreasonable impetuosity.

There were those, whether from Longbridge or Cowley, who simply signed their own death warrants. Rix and Vic Oak, heading the engineering departments of Longbridge and Cowley respectively, squabbled endlessly about whose component numbering system to adopt. Austin were already well down the road of computerization so the answer was obvious. Foolishly, they took the issue to Lord.

It is Graham Turner in *The Leyland Papers* who writes: '*The fact was that Lord fouled the atmosphere for the most important alliance in the history of the British motor industry to that point and the benefits of the merger were never fully realized.*' Others have quoted the statement and do Lord a similar grave injustice.

Whether historian, journalist or casual observer of the motoring scene, to be realistic, we have to pose the question: What was Lord to do? When the prospects for BMC seemed so bright, and, indeed, for a time, were, was he to accept the sub-standard? Was he, for example, to allow the Morris Minor with its potential as a market leader to continue with an unsuitable engine?

Lord *did* fail to amalgamate the two workforces. Yet there was no magic formula for doing so. When he rose to speak, beneath the tulip shaped, art deco, chandeliers of London's grandiose Grosvenor House Hotel at a Nuffield function, soon after the merger, and quipped that BMC stood for '*Bugger My Competitors*' it is said a stunned silence descended.

But why?

Was the all-male audience, fresh from the production lines and machine shops of Cowley or Adderley Park, so sensitive and prissy as to be shocked by the use of a vernacular verb? And after all, two great companies *should* have had precisely the same competitors to assault. But of course, it was Morris's Reginald Hanks, not Austin's Leonard Lord, who set the tenor for an especially unhelpful disparity on that front. Most likely, any silence was born of hostility towards the new supremo on the simple basis of who he was. A desire to freeze him out. It is a reaction that many of us have succumbed to, or been the victim of, at some stage in our lives.

Yet the corollary is that many in the Nuffield Organization, accustomed to the meddling and indecision of William Morris, applauded Lord for his directness, dynamism and common touch. '*If he stopped at your machine and offered you a cigarette it felt as good as a pay rise!*' If the atmosphere within BMC really was fouled to the extent Turner claims, it certainly was not by the lips of Lord alone. There were many players and some left the cloven print of the Oxford bull.

By the early 1950s the days were long past when drivers of any particular make of car waved to compatriots with sufficient good sense as to have bought the same marque. Yet AA and RAC motor cycle patrols still saluted their members and although the motor car was well on the way to becoming the 'utility' Henry Ford dreamed of, there was still fierce customer loyalty. Austin families. Morris families. Repeat purchases over several generations.

But the duplicated dealer network was to present Lord with another formidable problem. Throughout the UK there were some 3,500 agents representing Austin, Austin Healey and, if you wish to be pedantic, Morrison Electricar. There were a similar number of outlets for Morris with its allied makes MG, Riley and Wolseley. This was of no particular consequence while the brand loyalties prevailed. Or, when there was buoyant demand and the customers expected distinctive ranges of cars. But it was these factors that were the enemy of the rationalization that would eventually be needed.

Each year, at motor show time, many of the agency proprietors bought tickets for a dinner in London. The Morris function was called the 'Nuffield Party' and attracted about 1,000 guests to the Grosvenor House Hotel. About the same number of Austin stalwarts went to The Hyde Park Hotel for what was called, rather more grandiosely, the 'dealers' banquet'. Although Lord saw salesmen as an unnecessary overhead—'*make proper bloody products and they sell themselves*'—he was content to leave the dealer network intact along with their diversity of models.

With hindsight it is clear that action *was* needed. Lord almost certainly appreciated this, and although the maximum number of outlets may have been useful as the new organization found its feet, the plethora of agencies were to become a marketing millstone. Whether Lord could have done anything about the situation, given the economic and political climate of the day, is much more problematical.

In the early '50s the good times were just beginning to roll; for the middle classes, at any rate, and it was they who would have been the customers for what new cars were becoming available. Wartime leader, Winston Churchill, had returned as prime minister in 1951. His Conservative Party's nationalistic manifesto promised to return the country to its '*rightful position*' as a world power.

This would be founded on what Gilles Couderc describes in *British Society and Economy from 1945 to 1990* as: Britain's '*institutions and infrastructure having passed the test of war with flying colours*'. That it was all a total illusion would not be fully realized until the débâcle of the Suez conflict in 1956.

Among the factors that made things feel better were that the rationing of those staples of life, bread and potatoes, and some 'luxuries' like jam, was almost a distant memory. Restrictions had ceased in 1948. Even the petrol allowance had been increased the following year as Harold Wilson at the Board of Trade threw many of the restrictions onto '*a bonfire of controls*'. By 1950 they had gone altogether—to be back, of course, for 'Suez'.

The end of textile rationing came in 1949. Christian Dior's full skirts and generous cut could hold sway on the fashion scene to be worn by those women also fortunate enough to be able to afford, or have bought for them, a Devon or Hampshire, Oxford or Morris Six. At a more serious level, there was full employment, children were better fed, taller and healthier than in the mid-'30s, twice as many of them as in 1939 remained in school until age 17 and beyond, and for many families an annual holiday was becoming the norm.

In society at large something approximating to the '*white heat of technology*', described by Harold Wilson a decade later, was radiating its promise. Nuclear energy was in prospect, infra-red equipment, penicillin, plus a range of new antibiotics developed during the War were being increasingly used in medicine, while plastic, artificial fibres and chemical fertilizers, pesticides and detergents were becoming commonplace.

It was easiest for Lord to swim with this tide of general complacency and perceived increasing well-being. To do anything else would have been extremely difficult. This brings us to several important issues where a number of commentators have questioned his judgment even to the extent of suggesting that Leonard Lord sowed the seeds for the ultimate decline and demise of the British motor industry. This is clearly ridiculous.

Crucial to these criticisms is his supposed inability to cost the cars and ensure profitability. No lesser authorities than Joe Edwards and Geoffrey Rose supported this view. In an interview with Martin Adeney in the late 1980s Edwards said: '*I would say, "this is the ex-Works price; there are all the papers supporting it". He (Lord) would say, "That it, Joe? What's Bill Morris's price on the Oxford and what's it on the Cowley? Well let's put it ten pounds under that." And that at a time when we could sell everything we made*'. Rose told this author, more simply: '*Lord's great failure was cost analysis. But that was common in the industry at the time*'.

Yet are these views justified? It might be helpful to differentiate between 'cost' and 'price'—two financial terms that are sometimes misunderstood. Cost is always the sum involved in making a commodity, whether it be a motor car or a toothbrush, and must include materials, labour, machinery and other overheads. Price is the amount the item can be sold for. The two figures should be as divergent, upwardly, in favour of price, as possible.

We suspect Dickens's Wilkins Micawber would have understood something of costing and pricing. '*Annual income twenty pounds, annual expenditure nineteen nineteen six, result happiness. Annual income twenty pounds, annual expenditure twenty pounds ought and six, result misery*'. We can only surmise that Leonard Lord was familiar with the appealing figure of Mr Micawber in the novel *David Copperfield*. We can be much more certain that he understood both cost and price.

If we again think back to the early days at Morris Engines, Woollard said, concerning the revisions to the transfer machines, that the changes were accurately *costed and explained* in comparison with proprietary equipment to do the same work. Lord's figures never came into question. Similarly, the whole gamut of pricing for the Morris Eight must have been meticulously analysed given the model both saved the company from bankruptcy and became Britain's best-selling pre-War car.

There is further supporting evidence in '*Men and Motors*' where no less a figure than Dick Perry, an Austin ex-apprentice, but also a latter day managing director of Rolls-Royce, says: '*Len Lord could look at an assembly drawing and cost it just like that. If we looked at a particular plan and there was say a door missing or whatever, Len Lord would be the first to spot it*'. The phrasing is not particularly clear and somewhat ambiguous, but the point is, Lord's perception was so sharp that he could spot a door was missing from a factory plan (Perry does not mean from a car!) and that the cost for that detail needed to be included.

That Lord did take costing extremely seriously is born out by his having established a production development department under 'Mad Frank' Griffiths* who had been his chief planning engineer

---

* A nickname born purely of affection and probably earned when Griffiths suggested snaking assembly lines to save floor space!

since the late 1940s. This inspirational move set the innovative Griffiths to work on projects as varied as semi-automatic control for the CAB, advanced paint systems, early robotics and automated machine control, not to mention the plastics technology that would eventually lead the industry to at least a 10% reduction in the metal used in vehicle construction.

The ultimate objective of all this work, of course, was cost reduction. In one typical instance Griffiths's team reduced the production cost of a seat from £3.17s (£3.85p) to 28s (£1.40p) halving the number of parts used and removing the skill from the manufacturing process along the way.

As regards pricing, the best evidence we have of Lord's competency is his move, as the A40 gained popularity in Canada, to hike its tag above that for America. This not only shows his understanding of the customer base but also his recognition of the desirability of extracting as much revenue as the market will tolerate. It is much later that his cost/pricing judgement seems to go seriously awry.

'*What's Bill Morris's price? . . . Let's put it ten pounds under that*' might merely suggest, in the early days of BMC, a cavalier approach. It would, admittedly, have been dangerous, if it was genuinely how he thought. But the market was buoyant and the source of that quote himself says: ' *. . . we could sell everything we made*'. We might suppose, therefore, Lord was '*playing to the gallery*'.

Cost/price did not become a grievous issue until the arrival of the Mini, right at the end of Lord's active tenure and when he was tired and probably ill. And as we shall examine later the situation was far more complicated than a straightforward failure to balance cost and price effectively. Result, misery. There can be no doubt Leonard Lord hoped to dominate the car market and the facility he had created at Longbridge gave him every means to do so. By implication that meant domination by Austin.

Little had been done to modernize Morris since Lord himself had rejuvenated Cowley in the early 1930s. The state-of-the-art plant in Birmingham was a source of jealousy for former Nuffield personnel. They were prone to accuse the chairman of diverting Corporation profits into building a lavish Austin citadel. This, of course, is utterly invalid as the work undertaken at Longbridge very largely pre-dates BMC.

To whatever degree Lord understood cost and price it seems most likely he saw volume as the route to both market dominance and profitability. He had two powerful influences to draw him to that conclusion. Firstly, an awareness of early Morris strategy. William Morris started to achieve a commanding position in the industry after he slashed his prices in February 1921 to sustain and increase demand when the immediate post-WWI boom collapsed.

Secondly, the range of cars Lord had created for Austin—A30, A40, A70, Sheerline/Princess and Austin Healey 100—was better aligned with the market, and more comprehensive, than those of the other BMC constituents. Morris was only strong in the sector for small and medium-sized cars and had no viable luxury model to offer. In the TD, MG had a healthy small sports car but otherwise only the Y and then Z type mid-size saloons dwelling in a customer no-man's land. Wolseley had no small car now that the Eight had disappeared and, unlike in pre-War days, no limousine. Riley had nothing at either the bottom or top and in the middle was in similar doldrums to MG.

Thus, if Lord was trying to arrive at pricing, particularly for family saloons, that would achieve volume and, as a consequence, Austin domination, it follows he may also have been hoping, at this very early stage in the life of BMC, to substantiate an argument for radically rationalizing the model range.

Neither must we overlook that he was already well down that road as regards engines and transmission. The Morris Minor had the Austin A30 (A Series) engine and its gearbox. The Oxford, MG ZA Magnette and a new Austin Cambridge, launched in 1954 all used the B Series motor, while the Morris Isis, Riley Two-point-Six, Wolseley 6/90 and an Austin Westminster that had also appeared in 1954, all adopted the six cylinder C Series unit.

There was also, inevitably, a political dimension. We have already seen the first elements of interventionism on the part of government and the Labour administration's enthusiasm for nationalization. Lord may well have sought to dampen this by pressing for the Austin-Nuffield merger, which, although excluding significant manufacturers (Rootes and Standard) went a long way towards establishing a British-owned 'national' motor industry.

The official announcement of the formation of BMC is extremely bland and speaks of unified control leading to more efficient and economic production. It moves on to the export drive and manufacture and assembly abroad being furthered. The national interest is also said to have been served. A telegram was sent to dealers assuring them, remarkably, that '*the two organizations (Austin/Nuffield) will continue to function as separate entities*'. That seems both contradictory and counter-productive.

The foregoing throws valuable light on what Lord did or did not do in those early years of the Corporation, especially when we look back to the pronouncements of the War Cabinet Ministerial Sub-Committee on Industrial Problems.

Their Inter-Departmental Committee (IDC) on the motor industry had published a paper in 1945 and the BMC press release could have been written—and maybe was—to accord with IDC policy. The committee comprised representatives of The Admiralty, Board of Trade and ministries of aircraft production, labour, production, supply, and war transport but, perhaps significantly, no one with any practical knowledge of the motor industry.

However, the sector was seen as vitally important in providing full employment, contributing to defence and, most important of all, earning foreign revenue. The all consuming final ingredient was to be secured by less fragmentation and economies of scale in the manufacturing process, fewer models, standardized components, less emphasis on home sales coupled to stronger overseas dealer networks and more competitive pricing.

The committee, though, were of the view the industry was reluctant to comply and they proposed intervention with the prime objective of producing a large, powerful 'export' car that benefited from their ideas. Terms like 'forced integration' and 'special assistance' for firms achieving the government's goals, started to be bandied around. It is interesting to note as an aside, that Morris had launched a highly unsuccessful 'empire car' as early as 1927!

The IDC continued to meet considerable resistance from the industry although it has never been explained why this group was more influential than others. It is conceivable it was the result of Lord's vociferousness—and he was certainly that, as evidenced by his *Scope* interview—and the strength of his company. The Committee's difficulties were compounded by internal disputes. Some members believed the intended export car would not match anything from Detroit, others recognized a need to satisfy domestic demand, but with small cars in the variety of makes and models that had always appealed to the British mass-market.

The industry fuelled the dispute by suggesting that focusing on the export car could lead to damage from imported vehicles in the crucial 8-10 horsepower class. The government may have been in the mood for intervention but not controversy, especially if it centred on job losses or a downturn in export revenue.

That it was never wholly committed to the measures being formulated for the motor industry is born out by nothing, or very little, having resulted from an exchange of views between a delegation from the French Ministry of Industrial Affairs and the IDC as early as June 1945. A five-year plan for the French motor industry permitted only the production of government approved models, made from standardized components, in a collaborative manufacturing infrastructure.

In a sense Lord was the victim of the same circumstances as the government. The celebrated historian Correlli Barnett has harshly criticized Westminster between 1945 and 52 for micro-economic policies that resorted to *ad hoc* measures that, by the 1970s, had undermined the industry.

An adversary, the business writer and academic, Nick Tiratsoo, argues that the IDC had '*a comprehensive prescription for the industry's ills*' but was prevented from spooning out the medicine by '*hostile*' and '*conservative*' motor men and like-minded lobbyists. (This is almost exactly the corollary of Lord's stance in *Scope*.)

Timothy Wisler in a paper *The British Motor Industry and the Government, 1944-1952: A Reappraisal* is of the view the government accurately understood the characteristics of the motor industry in 1945 and suggested potentially constructive long term guidelines. But, he says, '*the relationship between the motor industry and the government between 1944 and 1952 was defined by the interaction of risk, uncertainty and time frame objectives*'.

We might equally say that Lord was similarly constrained. Much of what he did in 1952 was bold and ambitious. Perhaps it was not enough. But as we have seen there were hostile, conservative and uncertain presences in his environment too. For the moment the measures did not seem crucial. In any case, Lord had the thorny issue of labour relations with which to contend.

CHAPTER TWENTY
WIND OF CHANGE

In 1947 1,000 non-production Austin workers were made redundant, with barely a murmur, when the old Eight, Ten and Twelve came to the end of their lives. It was as if the old order in industrial relations marched on. 'Hire and fire' as orchestrated by Herbert Austin, and finally by Lord, that led to the demise of the embryo shop stewards' movement between the wars and during the economic depression or 'Devil's Decade'*

Not long after the sackings, Lord launched an inept incentive scheme whereby five cash prizes a week, calculated on the basis of production, could be won in a draw involving Longbridge's 20,000 employees. The injustice is obvious. The failure to appreciate the subtleties of handling a maturing workforce equally so. The best that can be said is that some attempt at dialogue and engagement, however ham-fisted, was being contemplated.

It was five years later events took both a sinister and prescient turn. When production of the ill-starred A90 Atlantic ceased in September, 1952, the 700 workers on that line were made redundant at a week's notice. It was to lead, although not immediately, to a 12-week strike, the longest the industry had ever known.

The stoppage, when it came, in February 1953, was complex and divisive, was arguably more mis-handled by Lord than by his combatants, but had little to do with the A90. Indeed, it is usually referred to in the annals of trade union history as 'the McHugh strike' and, ironically, was essentially an inter-union dispute.

John McHugh was a leading National Union of Vehicle Builders (NUVB) shop steward. In 1951 he had called a one-day strike and would undoubtedly have been construed by management as a troublemaker. When the 'Atlantic' line stopped a year later it was a welcome opportunity to be rid of him. This was interpreted, with some justification, as victimization.

It took place against a backdrop of general NUVB militancy. This was an organization jealous of 'craft' status and anxious to defend its standing in the eyes of bodies like the Transport and General Workers (TGWU) and Amalgamated Engineering Unions (AEU). The latter accommodated lathe and 'mill' operators and skilled fitters. Although representing a relatively small proportion of the workforce, the NUVB's members worked in the body and chassis erection shops and the paint bays and had the means to bring the factory to a standstill. Management, consequently, were game for a showdown.

The strike was unofficial. It began on Tuesday the 17th of the month and pressed for the reinstatement of John McHugh. It involved all but 35 of the 2,300 NUVB members at Longbridge. The rebels worked in the experimental department and saw their work as safeguarding

---

* Broadly the 1930s.

the future. There had been a similar revolt in the same department against McHugh's previous 'down tools'.

Less than a week after the stoppage started the factory closed. It remained shut for three months. The A70 and truck lines had staggered on for a short time but soon 20,000 were out of work and drawing around £2 a week union support plus five shillings (25p) each for any children, instead of receiving an average weekly total of £11. Some sought National Assistance payments but their eligibility was questionable.

Support for the stoppage was unconvincing. Dick Etheridge, a committed Communist and convenor of a Works committee comprising shop stewards from all the unions, believed McHugh's dismissal was unjust. He also saw dangerous precedents surrounding the arbitrary removal of shop stewards. Yet he objected to the unilateral tactics of the NUVB and refused to bring out the remainder of the workforce. In reality he would not have been able to do so. Such a move would have constituted secondary strike action which was prohibited. It would also have provided management with the opportunity to make potentially destructive legal moves against his unions.

Etheridge did, however, negotiate for McHugh's return and in support of the redundant workers having the right to re-employment in preference to newcomers. (There were already 600 jobless in the Midlands motor industry.) None of his arguments held sway with Lord who, perhaps predictably, went so far as to 'blacklist' so-called troublemakers.

Opposition to the strike arose from the seemingly unlikely areas of sections of both the TGWU and AEU. The former's general secretary, Arthur Deakin, wrote a vituperative article in his union's newspaper, *Record*, in the very middle of the strike. He pronounced: '*The Communists in Britain have declared war on the masses of the people. A relatively small section of the labour force is used for the purpose of causing a complete dislocation of the industry concerned.*

'*Strikes which need never have taken place are long drawn out when commonsense discussions would have found the answer to the problems which presented themselves.*

'*In one instance recently* (he is undoubtedly referring to 'Austin') *in a strike concerning only a small number of people, many thousands became involved and there is no shadow of doubt but that the cadre leaders and the hierarchy of the Communist Party moved in to take command*'.

He goes on to lament the effects on productivity and the export drive and concludes that Communists will: '*infiltrate our movement to determine its policy and hamper and hinder the effort we are making in this country to recover and put ourselves in a sound economic position*'.

With his Communist paranoia, and if Lord read the feature at all, it would have been music to his ears. But it was directed more at Etheridge, who firmly believed in shop steward organizations as a model for industry specific unions. These, inevitably, would have undermined the power of a figure like Deakin.

The AEU response to the strike was messier. The Birmingham branch refuted a statement, claimed to be from their Longbridge shop stewards, lending support to the NUVB. Their official, Victor Woodley, told the press: '*To say that the AEU shop stewards at the factory have pledged their support of the strikers is completely wrong.*

'*We union officials have been completely in the dark about this strike all along. It has put many people out of work and is a classic example of the rank and file being forced to do something they don't wish to do.*

'*I am positive that nearly all of the 2,000 strikers have come out unwillingly. The NUVB has acted selfishly and arbitrarily. They made a mistake originally and won't admit it*'.

More music to Lord's ears.

Neither does McHugh seem to have been particularly committed. After his 1952 redundancy he had worked briefly as an insurance agent and had told his NUVB branch that he did not think a strike would succeed because of the time that had elapsed since he lost his Longbridge job. Meanwhile, and as the stoppage gathered momentum, he had the firm offer of a job, at £20 a week, with two assistants and his own office, from a company called Air Industrial Developments Limited.

Cowley did not join the dispute, neither did Pressed Steel, although its workers suffered lay-offs as bodies accumulated at Longbridge. Eventually the McHugh strike petered out. The central figure was never reinstated; negotiations surrounding the re-employment of others lasted until mid-summer; the NUVB eventually (1972) merged with the TGWU; BMC, and the nation, lost, along with the production of thousands of vehicles, £15 million of export revenue alone, and the strike cost the unions about £100,000.

What do we learn of Leonard Lord from this scenario?

Most importantly, that if he could have crushed the unions at this point he would have. The description is emotive. But it reflects a very prevalent mood of the day that I have alluded to before. When WWll started shop floor representation was virtually non-existent and what little negotiation took place was conducted at national level by individual craft unions (like the NUVB and AEU). Such discussions resulted in general agreements between the unions and the Engineering Employers' Federation (EEF) but individual companies were not rigidly bound by them. Lord, in particular, resented any interference and viewed trade unions as an anathema, strenuously resisting any attempts to influence or control Longbridge.

A former lord mayor of Birmingham, Norman Tiptaft, reflecting in June 1953 on the 'McHugh strike', told a lunch of the Dudley branch of the National Union of Manufacturers that those responsible for the stoppage should be kept out of skilled employment.

'*The action of Mr Lord and the Austin company in standing up to the NUVB was a real service to the country*', he said.

Tiptaft took the view, similar to Leonard Lord's, that '*after government interference, the second menace to British industry, is the attitude of a number of workers to production which will enable us to sell our goods overseas*'*.

He went on to describe the Austin dispute as one of the most criminally irresponsible ever foisted on the community and uncompromisingly the fault of the trade union, then concluded with the words: '*the first charge of industry must be decent wages and decent working conditions. But when those are assured agitators that make higher production impossible should be crushed*'.

Effectively, without uttering a word publicly, Lord broke the strike. He held out against what he perceived as disruptive elements and stood by his belief that it was he who should run the factory not the '*man who drove the ambulance or swept the ward*'. When Etheridge refused to bring out the other unions, and it was clear the broad consensus was against the stoppage, Lord knew he had won. Of course, he may not have bargained for the length of the action, or its ultimate consequences.

Later generations may ask, if Lord had done more at this point could the national disgrace of industrial relations at Longbridge in the 1960s and 1970s have been avoided? The reality is there was little more Lord could have done about an inter-union dispute. It is the general intransigence, and all that that implies, which is the true issue. But the problems he faced should not be viewed in isolation.

---

* The semantics of this sentence are poor, but taken in context the meaning is clear.

The French, German and Japanese motor industries were to become major competitors of the British. All three made deep inroads when the domestic industry was mired in labour disputes. In 1953, if ever, Lord would not have been enamoured of German philosophies. However, history would have told him that as early as 1919 the pre-Hitler Weimar Republic (*Deutsches Reich*) began to formulate an industrial relations compromise that could have served him well. Under its terms the government and employers recognized trade unions and the latter accepted, even if they did not embrace, the basic rules of a capitalist economy.

Not surprisingly, the approach was abandoned under Adolf Hitler. But the fundamentals were subsequently refined in the post-War era to include industry-wide collective bargaining, formal structures for employee representation in management decision-making, and pre-employment industrial relations training. It was one of the best models Lord could ever have tested. Coupled with financial investment under the Marshall Plan, and further American backing to create a potent Cold War ally against Russia, Germany turned into a powerful, cohesive commercial challenger.

Lord knew French well enough to speak publicly in the language. If he studied the post-War industrial scene in that country he would have found it chilling reading. Essentially the motor industry was centred on four manufacturers, Citroën, Peugeot, Renault and Simca. Renault, the largest, had been nationalized—a jarring chord in Lord's ears—as a vindictive response to totally unsubstantiated Communist claims that Louis Renault was a Nazi collaborator.

Citroën, now in the hands of the astute Michelin family, rather than that flamboyant, avuncular, *bon viveur*, André Citroën, was showing enormous potential. Peugeot had a customer winning, rationalized, monocoque in their 203 model. By 1951, Simca were ready to build their own star performer, the top selling *Aronde*. As with Lord, Citroën, Peugeot and Renault continued some engineering development with a civilian application during WWII, but that at Javel, Sochaux and Boulogne Billancourt respectively, was rather more advanced. And, as in Germany, Marshall plan money helped considerably in reconstructing France's war ravaged industries.

French industrial relations were not so promising as the overall picture. The violent unrest of the late 1940s, in which Renault workers played a significant part, had its unsavoury roots in the class conflicts of the 1930s. Sizeable numbers of the *haute bourgeoisie*, who controlled the business life of the nation, saw the ascendant Hitler as the means of protecting them from those seeking social reform—principally Communists. However, the political landscape became exceedingly confused after Josef Stalin, general secretary of Russia's Communist Party, entered a non-aggression pact with Nazi Germany in 1939, then changed sides to that of the Allies in 1941.

The problem, in 1947, for 30,000 Renault workers, and subsequently some two million of their compatriots across France, was, broadly, that under the Socialist, Paul Ramadier's tri-partite* government, a considerable increase in production had not only gone unrewarded in terms of wages and improved conditions but was the result of a return to the *status quo* whereby the *bourgeoisie's* capitalist system was being restored at the expense of the worker.

In the early summer the Communists voiced their opposition to the Marshall Plan on the somewhat simplistic Stalinist basis that they were the 'good guys'; capitalists and imperialists, such as Americans, were 'bad guys', and money from those sources was to be rejected.

---

*   It comprised the French Section of the Workers' International (SFIO), Popular Republican Movement and the Communists themselves.

Public servants were the first on the streets, followed by the Renault contingent, then shop and transport workers. Ramadier expelled the Communist ministers from his government when they refused to give a vote of confidence to his economic and social policies. Far worse strikes accompanied by sabotage and loss of life followed. The *Assembly Nationale* (parliament) was paralyzed by its large number of Communist members. Ramadier was replaced on November 22 and his successor, Richard Schuman, needed 80,000 troops to regain control of the country. It could be said the government had been toppled by Communist actions.

Lord must have reflected upon this with much trepidation.

Japan, as we shall soon see, was to play an important role in Longbridge history on a number of planes. When the American occupation began in 1945 under General Douglas MacArthur the objectives were demilitarization to establish a 'peacefully inclined and responsible government', provide industries adequate for peace but with no potential for war, and break the economic stranglehold of the Mitsui, Mitsubishi, Sumitomo and Yasuda companies. It was set against a backdrop of a people still prepared to die for the emperor and an education system that from kindergarten to campus was obsessively nationalistic.

But when 'moderate left' prime minister, Katayama Tetsu, was ousted in 1947 by former diplomat Yoshida Shigeru, things began to look better. Mr Shigeru was prepared to work enthusiastically alongside the Americans who in addition to encouraging a trade union movement were having the schoolbooks rewritten in more liberal and democratic tones.

Nissan had been allowed, since 1948, to make what outmoded cars they had in the plan chest. Then in 1951 the lights turned green for industrial co-operation and expansion. Japan signed a peace treaty with most of its former adversaries effective from April 28, 1952. A tie-up with Austin to make the Somerset followed but was soon soured because the radical changes in working practice, necessary to go from an output of about 250 vehicles in 1948 to full-scale mass production, aggravated the fairly robust unions with their long tradition of fighting over conditions and status rather than money.

The management response was to orchestrate a lock out and a bitter 15-week stand-off ensued. It was resolved when the consultation process was reorganized on the basis of mutual benefit. Because of the Somerset tie-in, Lord would have been acutely aware of the situation and we can recognize some of the ingredients of the McHugh Strike, albeit the negative ones—duration and intractability.

Dick Etheridge learnt more from the McHugh stoppage than Leonard Lord.

His son, also Richard, says: '*It was a celebrated example of how* not *to run a strike and it set the atmosphere for the 1956* (Austin) *redundancy strike that was based on a similar set of circumstances, but conducted by my father, who learnt lessons from this previous single union affair*'.

We now reach a point where we must try to envisage, on the fairly wide-ranging evidence before us, how Lord would have assessed BMC's future industrial relations. This has to be put in the context that, since 1945, production had been irrevocably 'all'. Almost any concession was warranted to keep the lines flowing and infuse the dollar lifeblood that might enable the nation to survive in a cogent form.

Even so, the British industry's productivity still compared favourably with that of France and Germany—about 4.2 cars per employee per year compared with around 3.6 and 3.9 respectively. In addition the home producers were protected by import tariffs that looked destined to continue. All might be well.

Dick Etheridge senior was a devotee of the imaginative and intelligent approach of industry specific trade unions. As the convenor of the shop stewards' joint committee at Longbridge he

195

was also committed to the power of that position. At the end of the McHugh strike he gave an interview to George Sinfield of the Communist *Daily Worker* newspaper. Under the headline: '*This Man Must Be Protected*' and the strap '*The shop steward's status has been challenged*', Etheridge makes a case along the lines of: '*A shop steward has a vital job to do for his fellow trade unionists. This leads him into collisions with the employers. It is unthinkable he should be at their mercy*'.

He goes on to say: '*There are employers who accept our unions on sufferance, and only so long as the unions are strong enough to compel recognition. Trade unionists must always be prepared to exert pressure on the employers to get the best possible conditions of work. That is the reason for organization*'.

Later he deals specifically with Austin. '*The experience at Austin* (the McHugh strike) *shows that even with 100 per cent trade union membership the employers are able to take advantage of disunity*'. The article as a whole was heavy on protection, compulsion and pressure but light on dialogue, mutual understanding and common purpose.

Etheridge expresses similar emotions in his own powerful writing on trade union discipline and unity. When we observe his later relationships with management we cannot help wonder whether the tiny seeds of a broader interchange were present had Lord been more receptive.

Allegedly Etheridge once told a manager that the reason for his politics was his revulsion for the dinner-jacketed customers who would visit his father's coffee stall in the middle of Birmingham in the early hours of the morning. This is no more a mature or constructive viewpoint than that of Lord. Yet the reference is an understatement and, sells Etheridge short.

There was no 'coffee stall'. Etheridge's family's history was rooted in the English 'black country'*. Dick Etheridge (Junior), who has contributed so valuably to this book, says his grandfather (the father of the Dick Etheridge of Lord's day) was set up as a coffee *house* proprietor in John Bright Street, Birmingham, by his mother, who had developed a successful secondhand clothes business.

The surviving Dick Etheridge's account of that business is interesting, and, I would argue, relevant. '*The art deco* (my emphasis) *coffee shop had a daytime clientele of office workers and lower middle class travellers coming from New Street LMS (London Midland Scottish,) station, the access drive to which was opposite and slightly to the left of the shop and facing the Guinness Clock at the corner of Navigation Street. This was where the Longbridge and Rednal trams started from the city centre and many of the unemployed made their way to 'the Austin' from there seeking work. The nighttimes (sic) trade was more diverse as it was made up of middle class theatre goers from the adjacent Alexandra Theatre; the poor and unemployed arriving at New Street station from Wales, Liverpool, Yorkshire and the north east; prostitutes temporarily sheltering from the attention of the police (they were thrown out by dad if they tried to solicit for business in the shop); the political café set; itinerant artists and the destitute who would otherwise be arrested for* "being abroad without a shilling" *under the Vagrancy Act. Many such as the unemployed would stay there all night because they did not have cash and paid for their meal in kind by handing in personal items such as watches and fountain pens*'.

In 1940 the *Luftwaffe*, no doubt aiming for the railway, dropped a 1,000 pound land mine on the pub opposite the Etheridge's coffee shop and destroyed everything in the vicinity. The shop was too badly damaged to be re-opened and after everything useful was salvaged it closed down. It was later reopened further along John Bright Street by two of Dick Etheridge (Senior's) three sisters. Years later there was a divisive Will, the unfairness of which lived with Etheridge for

---

* Loosely defined as the English West Midlands.

the rest of his life and he pledged that he would never make the mistake of discriminating against any of his family again' (*or anyone?* This author's insertion).

It was after the bombing of the coffee shop Etheridge was sent to Austin, as directed labour, under the Emergency Powers Act. There he played a vastly different role and, as Dick Etheridge says of his father: '*The rest is history*', and asks: '*did fate play a forming part in the subsequent history of the British motor industry?*' At the very least, we can see from what direction Dick Etheridge, senior, was coming and how some of his ideas were formulated.

For his part, Lord supposedly said: '*The British workman is a good fellow but a fool when someone gets up on a soapbox*'. The quote is from a vicious attack by John Ennis in the Labour Party funded *Reynolds News* of Sunday, October 29, 1950. It gives Lord no credit for being anything but a vociferous maladroit. Sadly, the quote about British workers used by Ennis is broadly in accord with those revealed in much more sympathetic terms by Olive Moore in the Right wing *Scope* magazine. Yet the comments of Etheridge in *The Daily Worker* and what is attributed to Lord in *Reynolds News* are equally unhelpful.

In truth, what Leonard Lord may have seen of industrial relations in other countries would have been of little value to him. Bevin, as Minister of Labour, had already emaciated British management and neither the Labour governments of 1945 and 1950, nor the Conservatives, newly elected at the time BMC was formed, had the capacity or commitment to create a German style industrial infrastructure.

For these same reasons the Establishment were not going to support the implementation of a Japanese-style structure and the opposite side of the coin was that the British worker would never show the pro-active, effective, militancy of his French counterpart.

Professor Kevin Jeffreys in *Rebuilding Post-war Britain: Conflicting Views of the Attlee Governments 1949-51* argues that '*Labour ministers hoped to turn people into better citizens; values such as duty and responsibility were frequently extolled, and the needs of the community were always to come before the wishes of the individual*'. It is what Peter Hennessy (*Having It So Good* Penguin 2007) calls '*hope and public purpose*'.

Yet the hopes were misplaced. This ethical vision has been cited as a reason for Attlee's defeat in 1951. As Jeffreys says: '*Measures to sustain a wartime sense of community, instead of transforming people into active citizens, foundered in the face of apathy*'.

In *England Arise! The Labour Party and Popular Politics in 1940s Britain* authors Steven Fielding, Peter Thompson and Nick Tiratsoo suggest: '*There were many more responsible than the Labour Party for ensuring that the high ideals of the 1940s were never achieved*'.

At least, Leonard Lord was wise enough to realise it.

Chapter Twenty One
CITIZEN OF THE WORLD

One of the most significant developments in the history of the motor industry was the agreement Leonard Lord reached with the Nissan Motor Company Ltd of Yokohama, Japan, in December, 1952. The significance is not in the licensing deal itself. There are numerous examples[*] of permits being granted to independent companies to build a wide variety of products developed by other concerns. The importance, and the supreme irony, of the pact with Nissan was that BMC—and Austin in particular—taught the very people who were instrumental in annihilating the indigenous British industry how to build a modern motor car.

We touched on the contract in the last chapter. Initially the American and Allied forces, under General MacArthur, occupying Japan from August 1945 until April, 1952, were highly restrictive. By the end of 1947 the policy was becoming more liberal, not least because America felt an increasing need to strengthen Japan as a bulkhead against the Communist threat. However, the all-clear for the empire's industrial rebirth really came with the San Francisco Peace Treaty, signed between Japan and most of its former adversaries on September 8, 1951, but not in force until April 28 the following year.

Nissan had been looking to Volkswagen for a car-building partnership. But to most of their new associates that would have been politically abhorrent. When, wisely, they turned elsewhere, it was to Austin. There could hardly have been a better choice of vehicle for a joint venture than the smart, mechanically sound, A40 Somerset. The Japanese would have been aware of the earlier Devon's success in America and also of the later car's appeal in that country, although rather more limited than that of its predecessor. Furthermore, the A40 with its conventional chassis was going to be easy to put together.

It was Nissan's president, Genshichi Asahara, who came to England in December, 1952, to strike the deal. Somewhat in the mode of the theatre involving Bentleys, pub car parks and back doors surrounding the merger talks between Lord and William Morris, on this occasion Lord and Joe Edwards slipped away with Mr Asahara for lunch at a restaurant in Droitwich. It was not, though, a memorable dining experience as the head waiter had been a Japanese prisoner of war and refused to come out of the kitchen. Mr Asahara was probably accustomed to such

---

[*]   It has often been suggested that Datsun (aka Nissan) built Austin Sevens under licence in the 1930s. This is not correct. Sevens were exported to Japan as complete vehicles, or rolling chassis to be bodied by local coachbuilders. The confusion probably arises because the agent, Nippon Jidosha, built saloons, tourers and vans on the Austin chassis and also bodies for Nissan. But there was no formal link between Longbridge and Yokohama.

198

prejudice and able to put the incident behind him as he returned to the Works and signed the agreement.

It was to last for seven years. Once a nucleus of Japanese personnel had been trained at Longbridge, Yokohama would receive, royalty free for one year, Somerset kits to assemble. Henceforth they were to pay Austin two percent for a year on the retail price of each car and three thereafter. Once the Japanese were accustomed to the procedures they were to get the A50 Cambridge to build from an increasing proportion of locally produced parts.

The first crate was unpacked in March 1953 and the car ready a month later. As we also already know from our brief discussion of industrial relations, the Japanese operation encountered early problems. Yet when these were resolved, Nissan moved steadily towards the entirely locally built Austin. The final, extremely significant, stage in this process was the introduction of transfer machines in August 1956. They were built to Longbridge principles by the Hitachi Seiko company. Although there is no firm evidence, it is possible Frank Woollard acted as a consultant. It has been suggested Woollard was similarly involved with the Longbridge machines but this is definitely not the case, although he may well have been in contact informally with Lord at the time.

When the Nissan agreement expired in 1960 the firm had built about 2,000 Somersets followed by ten times that number of Cambridges. As the Japanese gained confidence there was a home grown estate car and modifications to strengthen the chassis and suspension. The smart, two-tone, paint schemes of the prestige, Longbridge-produced A105, were replicated. Whitewall tyres and spotlamps were fitted and there was even an 'Austin Cambridge' insignia for the front wing to replace the 'Austin of England' script.

To the great credit of all concerned, given the period, the agreement worked with almost total amicability. Admittedly, the Japanese would have been in awe of Austin and its ethos, but they unflinchingly accepted an almost obsessive insistence by their benefactors on the highest manufacturing standards. This went a long way to nullifying their pre-War reputation for inferior goods. As Norman Horwood, the programme co-ordinator, explains in Sharratt's *Men and Motors*: '*Some of the samples were far better than the parts we were using. We were forcing them* (the Japanese) *to work to a higher specification than our own*'.

Although Nissan ceased production of the Cambridge in 1960 they went on to make an estimated two million derivatives of the B Series engine for their own models and were still fitting them in the early '70s. By then the Japanese industry had experienced phenomenal growth, with production increased 700 per cent between 1955 and '60. At the end of the decade car output was the third highest in the world and soon Japan would account for more than half the models imported by its erstwhile overlord—America. By 1980 she had 28 per cent of the global market compared with Britain's 3.4 per cent share. In 1980 the UK's annual output was about one million cars, not even double the figure for the mid-1950s.

It is difficult not to think of ironies. Longbridge's insistence on quality ensured the Japanese could, and eventually would, build world-beating vehicles. Yet the same standards became less and less evident in BMC's own work.

Lack-lustre models and over-lapping specifications were seen as contributing to the decline of Nissan and the whole Japanese motor industry in the 1990s. It was an ailment they could have observed at Longbridge 40 years before. By the end of the 20th century Nissan had, of course, become the flagship *British* motor company after they opened, in 1986, a manufacturing plant on an 800 acre green field site at Washington, in the economically depressed region of Tyne and Wear.

It operated as a single union (AEU) plant almost entirely without industrial dispute and was to become one of the organization's most productive facilities.

In recent years quality issues, and redundancies resulting from an economic downturn, have marred the picture. Nonetheless, and although the firm's president in the early days in Washington, Yutaka Kume, never believed it possible, Nissan achieved their aim of building cars as good as the Austin once was. In the 1990s he said: '*All of us at Nissan are very much indebted. I think we must keep that modest feeling even now*'.

Interestingly, the Nissan Leaf, announced in 2009 and on sale in Britain from about March 2011 as the world's first purpose-designed, mass-produced electric car, will be assembled in Washington from the beginning of 2013.

Ironies apart, we need to ask whether Lord could have exploited the Japanese relationship in a more productive and durable way and whether he showed incredible naïvety in becoming involved at all. Realistically, the answer must be 'no' on both counts. The licensee started with a virtually blank drawing board and, with nothing indigenous to offer, was looking for the best technology it could obtain to build, initially, a domestic motor industry.

At home, Lord was hopelessly constrained. His path lay from an unsupportive government, through thorny labour relations to a corporate model range that was unsatisfactory, becoming increasingly outdated, yet was almost impossible to discard. Also the culture and attitudes in Britain and Japan were entirely different and, certainly at that time, irreconcilable.

As far as naïvety is concerned, the domestic market was still heavily tariff-protected, there were captive outlets in the British empire and Commonwealth and it would have been just as inconceivable in the motor industry, as it was in motor cycle manufacturing and shipbuilding, to conclude the Japanese would one day successfully assault these traditional strongholds.

Lord was contracted to '*use his best endeavours to promote and advance the interests of the company*' and the partnership with Nissan was little more or less than a useful and highly imaginative revenue earner. Even if he had foreseen how the terrain would unfold it does not imply the means to change direction.

While discussing foreign liaisons we should consider the strange phenomenon of the Nash Metropolitan. To a large extent its life-span parallels that of the Nissan project and to a degree vindicates Lord's thinking on the American market in the late 1940s. It was industrialist George Walter Mason who had brought about the mixed marriage of the domestic appliance manufacturer Kelvinator and Nash Motors in 1937. By 1950 Mason had come to the view that the way to increase market share for his corporation's ailing automotive arm was via more compact, economical and, surprisingly, environmentally friendly, cars. '*You don't need a* Queen Mary *to cross the Delaware, nor a two ton car to go shopping for hairpins*'.

The original idea had come from freelance designer, William Flajole, who then worked with another 'independent', Rhyss Miller, to produce a prototype (NXI for Nash Experimental International) that could use either a Fiat or British Standard engine. Some 250,000 people across America attended what were inventively termed 'surviews' and gave their opinion on the model. The consensus was the vehicle was too small. However, Mason was heartened. He had another car, the Rambler, under wraps and that matched the specification his survey told him the public saw as a 'compact'.

Within a year of the Rambler's launch in 1950, 30 per cent of Nash's capacity was devoted to it. Gladdened still further, and increasingly aware of the de-urbanization of the population and the growth in both multi-car families and women drivers, Mason decided to proceed with a very small car—a 'sub compact' or 'metropolitan' as he would have known it and a breed that had fascinated this physical giant of a man for years.

Flajole and Miller's design was extraordinarily innovative and in its original form used just one basic die for all four wings and the two doors. Other pressings also had a dual role. However, most of this had fallen by the wayside by the time the car was ready for production.

By then, Mason realized that even had he been prepared to fund the, admittedly limited, tooling his Nash Metropolitan required, he did not want to reduce manufacturing capacity for the Rambler at the Kenosha, Wisconsin, plant. Yet it was unlikely he would find a partner to build a 'sub compact' among the domestic producers of what he increasingly viewed as pretentious, wasteful, dinosaurs.

It was Leonard Lord, having already been some way down the American small car road, who had the vision to compete against both Fiat and Standard and take on the project. Whether he had already established an *entrée* on one of his frequent trips to America we have no way of knowing. The Metropolitan received the A40's lively B Series engine and also its gearbox, downgraded to a three speed. The front suspension and rear axle came from the A30.

Lord's imaginative, and no doubt personally reassuring deal, signed in October 1952, was extremely straightforward. The Metropolitan's coachwork was to be built by Castle Bromwich body builder Fisher and Ludlow, who BMC acquired in 1953. Final assembly would take place at Longbridge. The marketing was undertaken exclusively by Nash to the extent that, until early 1957, the car was only available in Britain to US Service personnel.

The contract represented the first time an American-designed car, intended solely for the United States market, had been built entirely in Europe—in world trade terminology, it was a 'captive import'.

Neva Langley, from Lakeland, Florida, the daughter of a successful citrus fruit grower, former cheer-leader, talented musician and 1953's Miss America, unveiled the Metropolitan, the career girl's car, in the spring of 1954*. It is doubtful whether, on this occasion, she attracted the 27 million-strong following that were wont to follow the exploits of their country's beauty queen, but the car was another 'Austin' that enjoyed a respectable level of acclaim in America; and still does.

Three thousand were produced in advance of the launch. Over its eight year life, sporting such jaunty and very un-Longbridge-like colours as cream paired with 'custard' yellow, turquoise, and candy floss pink, riding like a motorized water bed, the Metropolitan wooed around 104,000 of those 'career girls'. They followed the advice of the advertisements and '*drove their men folk crazy*' by asking for one.

Arguably, the Metropolitan could have achieved much better results. Mason merged Nash with Hudson to form the American Motors Corporation (AMC) almost at the same moment as the drapes were being drawn from the Metropolitan. But he died of acute pancreatitis on October 9, that same year, aged 63. His second in command and protégé, George Wilcken Romney, later to be a prominent politician and unsuccessful presidential candidate, took over. Like Mason he was committed to 'compacts' but not so firmly to the Metropolitan as the Rambler. In addition, the dealer network preferred to promote the domestic product and there was never a vigorous publicity campaign to support the imported car.

On a broader front, the Metropolitan had to compete with the much less *avant garde* looking Volkswagen and it has also been said the Americans were nervous about continuity of supply from

---

* The beauty queens' 'reign' was from September to September.

Longbridge. Nonetheless, the Metropolitan had been a creditable performer and an initiative that once again highlights Lord's astuteness as a businessman with an extremely sound global perspective.

Other geographies with which Lord was concerned were Australia and South Africa. The former's Victoria Park site had its origins in a typically rancorous enterprise that involved William Morris, the Australian government and the Sydney Turf Club. Simplified as far as possible, Morris, who had an unexplained passion for Australia, decided, in 1945, that ultimately he would like to produce a car locally and to set the process in train, build a body plant.

The site chosen was a former horse racing course, opened in 1908 on the partially drained Waterloo Swamp. One of its more interesting claims to fame was as the venue for escapades by pioneer aviators. These included Colin Defries, an English pilot. In 1909 he made the first, albeit very short, flight in a powered machine over Australian soil then crash-landed while attempting to snatch back his cap, which was on the point of blowing off his pate.

The turf club held the lease on Victoria Park until 1947 but by then used it primarily for training. They read the small print and despite the prospect of jobs and government backed new industry, decided to test in law a clause that gave them the option of continuing to operate a racecourse. The case went to New South Wales's premier, William McKell. While he prevaricated, Morris, in a fit of pique, signed an agreement with Richards Industries who were already making some of his bodies in the far less convenient city of Adelaide.

By the time McKell decided to allow Morris to proceed the ink was dry in Adelaide. Nonetheless, Richards were left in the lurch, but soon negotiated with Chrysler Dodge giving the American firm a valuable *entrée* to the Australian market. Work on Morris's Victoria Park scheme did not get underway until 1948. As the press observed: '*What a McKell of a mess*'.

From 1950 until its closure in 1975, Victoria Park employed an average of around 5,000 people, peaking at 7,000. They were mostly migrants from other regions of Australia, or much further afield, and spoke some 35 different languages. Harmony was helped by multi-lingual leading hands, work groups assembled on the basis of common language and company-sponsored English classes. Labour relations were generally excellent.

As the years passed, anyone familiar with Longbridge's car assembly buildings (CAB1 and later CAB2) would have found striking similarities in Australia. They may also have been impressed by the delightfully period touch of the inclusion, within the plant's boundaries, of the beautifully preserved racecourse administration building. Historic charm apart, a car rolled off the lines every four minutes—50,000 a year from a two-shift structure.

There was a significant model range. At first, both under Morris and BMC, core models like the Minor and Oxford and some Wolseley and MG variants were manufactured followed by the A30, A50 and A95. However, there were at least seven basic types exclusive to Victoria Park.

Leonard Lord was a frequent visitor to Australia. His first trip, in January 1952, was officially described as 'private'. He sailed from Tilbury to Adelaide on the stately, pre-War P & O liner *RMS Stratheden* and was accompanied by Ethel and his youngest daughter Pauline. Although this visit is after Morris's involvement with Adelaide-based Richards Industries, it is the occasion, alluded to by Pauline, when her father ate ice cream on Bondi Beach with William Morris. Whether the encounter was coincidental we cannot be certain, but in view of the timing, just prior to the formation of BMC, probably not.

In any event, the Lord's returned via New York which, given the distances involved and their disembarkation from the *Queen Mary*, in Southampton, as late as May 5, rates the venture as more of a cruise.

A similar, slightly shorter, trip for just Lord and his wife took place in January, 1954, when they visited Cape Town but took in Melbourne on the way back to Tilbury, arriving in April in time for Pauline's forthcoming wedding. The only time Lord seems to have travelled directly between London and Sydney in those far-off days when executives did not 'commute' between world centres by aeroplane, was in 1956—the prestigious, and almost new, *RMS Arcadia* out; the rather less elegant *Orsova* home. Again, he was accompanied by Ethel.

This is probably the visit when Lord addressed Victoria Park executives and other key figures from the industry at a formal luncheon. Whether Lord had quite the affinity with Australia as Morris is uncertain, but his humour, humility and forthrightness certainly appealed to the population and made him a potent ambassador for BMC in their country. As a guest at the lunch put it: *'Len might have been a "limey" when he got up to talk among those "cobbers". He was "dinkum" when he sat down'*.

Whatever the depth of his affection for Australia, Lord certainly had a devotion to South Africa and developed an affinity with the man who was the architect of Austin's most significant interests in that country. John Berryman was a pre-War Longbridge apprentice who went on to serve with the 'Desert Rats'* rising to the rank of Colonel. On his way home from the numerous battles in which the regiment fought he decided to settle in Cape Town, where he became Austin's South African representative.

In 1947 it was Berryman who chose the Alpha Farm at Blackheath in the Stellenbosch area for a proposed Austin factory. It has been suggested, rather ungenerously, that the selection was made because it halved Berryman's journey from his house on the eastern seaboard, to his office in Cape Town. More likely, the reason was the site had water and electricity laid on and superb transport facilities including railway sidings and a spur to the main line.

Lord and Berryman shared a similar forthrightness and they were to travel extensively together in South Africa and Rhodesia (later Zimbabwe). Berryman retired in 1968.

Building operations for the Blackheath plant were put on hold when priority was given to the Austin factory in Canada and again when, in 1949, the South African government imposed financial restraints. The first stage of construction eventually took place in 1953 and the Works was completed in 1955.

From the early 1950s Lord owned an impressive, white painted, house in an elite suburb on the southern coastal fringe of Cape Town. Called 'Lancarty', it had colonnaded terraces on both its floors and was bordered with palms. Lord had it extended to include detached accommodation for his household staff. The property was subsequently rented by Dr Christiaan Barnard, famed for conducting the world's first successful heart transplant operation and was another individual who could be as flamboyant and bombastic as Lord himself!

The market for English manufacturers in South Africa was difficult. American cars were preferred for covering the rugged, expansive, terrain and when Standard had tried to enter the field with the Vanguard it proved not only incapable of excluding the customary clouds of dust from unmade roads, but also structurally incapable of dealing with them. Lord was probably unsympathetic, although he had once quipped, in a slightly different context, that: *'if the cars don't stand up to the roads the customer should build better roads'*! This is precisely what the South African government undertook and it helped BMC.

---

* The nick-name for the Seventh Armoured Division of the British Army. It was coined when the unit fought in North Africa in 1940 but the regiment was subsequently involved in practically every major arena of WWII. Its equipment, incidentally, included the Austin K6 lorry!

Until 1947, Austins for South Africa had been exported fully assembled. However, with the launch of the A40 and prior to the Blackheath Works being established, they were shipped in kit form and built by South African Motor Assembly and Distribution (SAMAD). Even though BMC had been formed in 1952 the title Austin Motor Company was retained at Blackheath until 1958.

The first locally produced car was the A50 Cambridge. As with the initial Somersets for Japan, and continuing the policy adopted with SAMAD, they were sent from Longbridge as kits. The policy continued even for the 1959 Mini and then the 1100. But by 1960 the government was offering financial support and the plant was expanded for conventional production. The project was given added impetus by a world trend towards smaller cars.

Ralph Clarke ended his career with Austin, BMC and ultimately Leyland South Africa, as a divisional managing director. He trained in the country's public transport industry before taking an engineering degree at Cape Town University. He joined Austin in 1955 as plant engineer and was responsible for all capital planning and established most of the South African site's additional facilities. These included the first automotive engine factory in that country. He also worked on product development and became technical director. Naturally he was closely involved with Leonard Lord even to the extent of looking after 'Lancarty' and Lord's cars.

One of the aspects of the chairman's character that most impressed Mr Clarke was his famed decisiveness. '*He came to South Africa at most, once a year,*' he explained. '*On one occasion I had to present a capital expense budget to the local board for approval. Included was the estimate for a new engine plant. Lord studied the report and said: "That seems okay", and turning to George Tuck, the managing director, added: "Send a note to young George* (Harriman) *in the UK telling him I have agreed the project".* 'There was no hesitation, or, "We'll get back to you". Decision made; now get on with it! That was very much his style*', recalls Mr Clarke.

The only, extremely logical, proviso made, demonstrating Lord's eye for planning, was that the new building should be to exactly the same specification as the original assembly plant and that it be placed to facilitate joining the two using matching modules. Mr Clarke remembers with wry humour some other incidents. For example, whenever Leonard Lord was due at Blackheath on a formal visit the board members would assemble in the office foyer. When Lord got out of his car he used to take off his hat, turn it upside down and hold it out to the directors saying: '*I've come for my money*'. It was a standing joke.

On one occasion in 1957 he arrived at the factory outside working hours. Understandably, the security guard, not familiar with UK executives, refused Lord entry. After a brief exchange the officer, now a little fazed, phoned his superior, declaring: '*There is a man here who says he is the Lord and owns this place, must I let him in?*' Naturally the issue was quickly resolved but Lord took it in good part and commended the guard for his diligence. This anecdote is somewhat apocryphal. It has parallels in Rolls-Royce lore. However, if it is true, it reveals the common touch and Lord's humility.

Another time when he arrived unannounced the assembly jigs were being manufactured to switch production from the A50 to A55. Lord walked into the toolroom, watched for a while, and commented on the design of the frames. He then wandered into the rest of the plant but returned half an hour later to mention that a vehicle interior light was on and needed attending to. The story illustrates perfectly, not only the extent to which Lord was interested in the product and the work involved in producing it, but also his meticulous eye for detail, and, if you like, the *cost* implications of the smallest detail!

When Lord visited Blackheath he drove successively an A105, Vanden Plas Three Litre and, later, the Rolls-Royce engined 'R' versions of the latter model. They were shipped from England then received minor modifications at Blackheath to conform with local construction and use regulations. However, Mr Clarke remembers preparing a locally assembled Princess R prior to a 1964 visit. The first 'R' though was one of the two British prototypes. Crewe was somewhat agitated when they discovered Lord had shipped his to South Africa to try it out personally. Finished in 'steel dust grey' it later returned to the UK and was used by the chairman. All these cars carried the UK registration mark BMC 1.

The Blackheath site closed, and was sold, in 1989.

Not all of Lord's commercial activities were as positive as the Australian and South African enterprises. The acquisition of Fisher and Ludlow was crucial to the success of the Nash Metropolitan venture, but Lord took a very hard, although understandable, line with the Standard Motor Company, who were intending to use this formerly independent company to produce the bodywork for the Phase II Vanguard and a new Standard Eight.

Expansion would have been needed at Castle Bromwich to cope with both Longbridge's needs and those of the Coventry firm and as Lord put it to the latter's managing director, Alick Dick: '*I don't see why the hell I should put money into your company*'. Standard arranged for three different alternative suppliers and, needless to say, it was not a happy arrangement. Perhaps Lord had learned the trick from William Morris, one of whose fortes was to squeeze out the opposition by eliminating their supply chain or making it prohibitively expensive.

Ford did the same to Jowett when they took Briggs Motor Bodies of Dagenham around the same time as Lord bought Fisher and Ludlow. They refused to allow the continued supply of coachwork for the Jowett Javelin to the Bradford firm and contributed to a large extent to that historic company's collapse.

Much earlier in the story we encountered the female racing driver Kay Petre. It was during the development of the A40 (1,200cc) and A50 (1,500 cc) Cambridge that Lord took the ground breaking step of appointing Petre as his colour stylist. Perhaps the 'plot' was hatched on the basis of Nash Metropolitan experience.

But why Kay Petre; now a freelance journalist?

We can only speculate. Hess almost certainly knew her from their days racing at Brooklands and, subsequently, as public relations guru, he may have provided a profile for her at Longbridge, and with Lord.

There is also a suggestion Petre was paid a stipend from the time of her accident as a Works racing driver, in which case she would already have been, in a sense, 'on the payroll'.

More noteworthy are the insights that emerge from the appointment and take us back a very long way in Lord's life. Joe Edwards, quoted by Sharratt, says: '*Kay's ideas were too advanced for the day. As a lady she got a rough ride*'.

We need have no fear that Kay Petre could deal with sexism. Vigorously involved in the pre-War international motor racing scene, she was one of the key motivators in forcing the Brooklands authorities to recognize women drivers as equal to their male counterparts. What is worth embracing is the endemic jealousy, prejudice and insensitivity implicit in Edwards's words, of which, in a different context, I have argued, Lord himself could have been, and still was, the butt.

One of the most valuable exercises Petre undertook, and should have benefited the organization to a much greater extent, concerned trim texture and colour coordination. As a light-hearted aside, it is worth reporting that, a full decade before the arrival of the miniskirt, one fibrous upholstery material she chose had the ability to attach itself to the much more decorous '50s garment and raise it to quite unseemly heights. Cars so equipped were known to the apprentices that Petre called on to drive them around for her inspection as '*knicker pickers*'.

Reputedly, the role of the 'colour stylist' was dispensed with when an exterior shade that could be likened to 'rust' was suggested.

In 1953 Lord received his long overdue knighthood. No one was more deserving.

It is not the intention of this book to chart or examine in detail the many models that emanated from BMC during Lord's tenure but a further summary may be helpful. We have already seen that the Austin Cambridge supplanted the Somerset. Similarly at Cowley there was a re-shaped, B Series-engined, Morris Oxford to replace the version so redolent of the Minor.

Austin then launched an enlarged Cambridge, designated the A90 Westminster, or A95 in uprated form. Both used the six-cylinder C Series motor. The Morris equivalent was the unpopular Isis. Until 1956 Wolseley had the 4/44, then the 15/50 and finally, in 1958, the 15/60. The last two were B-Series engined cars as was a Wolseley 1500, derived, fundamentally, from the Morris Minor. The six cylinder range was represented until 1954 by the 6/80 with its old and overly complex overhead camshaft engine, then by the 6/90 and 6/99 with their C Series power.

Riley preserved, until 1955, some RM Series types, with their old and highly individualistic engines, then produced clones of the Wolseleys—One-Point-Five, 4/68 and 4/72. Their larger car was the Pathfinder of 1953 with the old Riley motor. But from 1957 it was called the Two-Point-Six and paralleled the C Series-engined Wolseley 6/90 until the demise of both models in 1959.

From 1950-1955 MG were represented by the TD and TF Midget sports cars with an Abingdon-designed engine, then, until 1962, by the B Series powered MGA. When the 'Midget' motored Y Type saloon ended in 1953 that class was covered by 'Magnettes' designated ZA, ZB and, more prosaically, Series III. All were B Series engine based.

By the late 1950s, Lord was taking a less hands on approach to design and Burzi's considerable talent was coming to full flower. It manifested itself, especially, in the development of the six cylinder Austin models that culminated in the handsome A105 with a softer boot line than its predecessors plus other embellishments.

It is interesting that *Motor Sport* editor Bill Boddy had some extremely complimentary things to say about the latter. This was unusual in that magazine whenever a British car was tested. He even claimed the ticking of the clock could be heard at moderate speed in top gear. However, we might suspect that, rather than a tribute to Austin, this was a jibe at his *bête noire* of the day, Rolls-Royce, who advertised, in rather more extravagant terms, a similar phenomenon for their cars! All that apart, Boddy couldn't resist: '*Whoever designed the Austin gearbox together with its gear linkage, should be quickly found other employment*'. These were dangerous words, of course, to fall before Lord, in the light of what had happened to Palmer.

Fortunately for this particular designer, and whether or not the chairman could hear the clock, he found the car very much to his liking. Lord's Bentleys were soon to be relegated to the country and private use (his last would be S2 Standard Steel Saloon chassis B 301 AA of 1960). Driving personally, or chauffeured, he delighted in an A105 enhanced by Vanden Plas.

Car number BS8 HCO 68371, one of those registered BMC 1, was finished in Carlton grey with extravagant amounts of interior burr walnut, complimented by wool cloth, shag pile carpets from specialists Firth Ltd, and Connolly hide for the upholstery. Lord was so pleased with it he suggested Vanden Plas made 'replicas' and about 500 were built. A niche market had been identified. It was later served by a successful three litre 'Princess' version with the front styled by the north London firm and, from 1960, branded by them. The mechanically and commercially catastrophic four litre with a Rolls-Royce engine followed. There were also 'Vanden Plas' 1100s and Allegros.

A final vehicle from this period that should be mentioned, not least for reasons that will become obvious later, is the Austin Champ of 1952. Those governments that had been so impressed with wartime Willys and Ford Jeeps, themselves Austin derived via the American Bantam, wanted something similar of their own.

The British had attempted a rear wheel drive field car while hostilities were still underway and it was probably for this that Lord had provided the 2.2 litre overhead valve engine. But project FV1800 was a new undertaking for a 4 x 4 of five hundredweight capacity. It first landed on Nuffield desks in 1947. They came up with a pair of prototypes using the highly unappealing name of Gutty and powered by the flat four petrol engine Alec Issigonis had contemplated for the Morris Minor.

The Gutty was not progressed, but in 1948 a contract was placed with Wolseley for twelve 4 x 4s called the Mudlark. Except for the company's famous illuminated radiator badge these looked decidedly like the vehicle that would evolve as the Austin Champ. They were powered by a Rolls-Royce B40 four cylinder petrol engine straight from Crewe's new rationalized range that found its most famous manifestation as the six cylinder, overhead inlet/side exhaust valve motor in Bentley and Rolls-Royce cars of the day. It also lent some features to the engine, coded FB60, just mentioned apropos the four litre Vanden Plas Princess R.

Meanwhile, a designer called Charles Sewell was developing the concept of what was now called 'Car Light, Five Hundredweight, 4 x 4, Open, for Various Roles'.

Luckily Sewell, or someone else, devised the alternative title, 'Champ', and from 1950, through early '51, Austin, because of their manufacturing capacity, built about 30 pre-production versions. Only one contract was ever placed—on August 1, 1951—for 15,000 units. However, the quantities were soon amended and when production ceased in May 1956, just under 13,000 had been built.

The main customer was the British Army, who took it with the Rolls-Royce engine, often made at Longbridge to an equally high standard as those from Crewe and required to be tested underwater—a process remembered by Works tour guides of the day as a great 'crowd puller'. Very occasionally the army Champ appeared with the four cylinder Austin A90 Atlantic power plant. There was also a civilian version of the vehicle that used the same A90 engine.

Almost universally the military design had a poor reputation. At around £1,200 it was expensive, much more complicated than the Land Rover and inaccessible to work on. The latter gradually took over its role. Nonetheless, the Champ was a quality job, the equal of any vehicle of its type as regards performance, and usually preferred by those who also had experience of the Jeep and Land Rover. The knowledge gained producing the Champ stood BMC in good stead when they launched the world-class Gipsy in 1958.

CHAPTER TWENTY TWO
FACT, FANTASY, FICTION

Nineteen-fifty-five was a good year for Leonard Lord. At Longbridge, it saw the festivities for Austin's golden jubilee and, on a broader plane, events that would not only change the form of BMC cars for evermore but also sow the seeds for a global motoring revolution.

A plethora of in-house publications with the themes of technical progress and Austin reliability marked 50 years of the company's existence, but the main event for employees and their guests took place at the Works on Saturday, July 9. It was inspired by Lord who, as well as a highly developed sense of showmanship, could display a tremendous sense of fun, although, until now, that side of his character had been largely private.

There can be little doubt that the Veteran Car Club rally of 1948 was a dress rehearsals for the 1955 Austin celebrations, when Lord was still magnanimously disposed to provide '*pleasure and entertainment for his company's many thousands of workpeople and their families*'. Interestingly, the Longbridge event coincided with the VCC's own silver jubilee celebrations. The club took in the Austin jamboree as part of a five day round-Britain rally and provided more than 200 veterans from eight countries to supplement the local contingent and take part in such high-jinks as a potatoe race and blindfold driving.

The Austin event proper centred around grandstands with seating capacity for 16,000 guests, some of whom had been flown in especially. They were built alongside and directly opposite, the car assembly building. There was a less formal viewing area on the grassed reservation between the service dual carriageway in front of the building.

The VIP accommodation was constructed outside the entrance to the assembly building and draped with panels depicting, alternately, Burzi's 'Flying 'A'' and a 1930s version of the winged wheel motif Herbert Austin had designed for the very first cars. Above, set between a banner reading 'Fifty Years of Dependability', was a 25 foot diameter roundel portraying the founder's face. Directly opposite, on the other side of the grass, an elevated bandstand had been positioned.

The proceedings were opened by Lord who, with the inadvertent gaucheness of which he was sometimes capable, invited the rapidly expanding crowds to blow a raspberry at Birmingham's lord mayor, Arthur Lummis Gibson, on the basis he had not arrived in an Austin. It is totally irrelevant I am sure, but wearing another badge of office, Alderman Gibson was the Midlands secretary of the Central Amalgamated Workers Union!

Kenneth Horne, an extremely popular radio personality of the day, and, incidentally, chairman of automotive glass-maker, Triplex, had been engaged to compère the event. As the audience's mirth, and responses, to Lord's invitation concerning the lord mayor swelled, Horne stormed to the fore driving the 100 hp Austin of 1908 French Grand Prix fame to take up the baton from the chairman.

The balding broadcaster's polished English accent introduced events that ranged from lighthearted driving tests for a variety of veteran vehicles, through a parade of historic Austins that included the turbine powered Sheerline making more noise than Horne's racer, to a pedal car 'grand prix'. Naturally, the latter used J40s and the competitors participated in a 'Le Mans start'* before racing around the road in front of the grandstands egged on by an animated Kenneth Horne. Lord and his wife presented the winner with the car he had pedalled.

Peripheral attractions for the estimated 35,000 people who attended, some of whom had been so enthusiastic as to buy 'black market' tickets at £4 a time, included a set of steam powered fairground gallopers that never actually performed after they were overturned by the first rush of 'customers', and an ox-roast to provide succour at the end of this happy Lord's day.

Permanent reminders of the occasion were medals presented by Irene Waite, Lord Austin's daughter, to employees with 46 or more years service. Lord and 79-year-old Harry Austin, Herbert's brother, still working as a supervisor at the plant, unveiled a commemorative plaque on the wall of the car assembly building. A rather more exotic fixture was a stained glass panel provided by Emil Frey, a dealer from Switzerland. It featured an ancient warrior from that country and was later installed above the entrance to the administration building.

The junior grands prix were replicated many times at other venues and, as well as earning invaluable publicity for Austin at race circuits as diverse as Silverstone and Crystal Palace, saw the children of some automotive notables cutting their 'motoring' teeth. They included Adrian Hamilton, son of Duncan, of Jaguar and Le Mans acclaim, racing car designer John Cooper's daughter, and Jeremy Rivers-Fletcher, son of Alec Francis Rivers-Fletcher, much loved motoring writer and raconteur.

Not surprisingly, perhaps, it was in 1955 that Longbridge received one of a number of visits from His Royal Highness, the motoring inclined Duke of Edinburgh. The occasion has given rise to one of the most snide stories of all concerning Lord. Yet it has been cited as an authentic account of the circumstances surrounding the enormously significant decision to hire the Farinas as BMC's styling consultants.

The duke came to call on the morning of December 8, and, predictably, was taken on an extensive tour of the Works by the chairman, Harriman and Joe Edwards, now group production director. If the account is to be believed, Lord soon broke away to attend to other business. This in itself, if taken at face value, seems inconceivably discourteous and exclusivist behaviour from a man who had been accustomed to dealing with royal visits and the associated protocol for more than 15 years.

Harriman and Edwards, relieved of the supposedly socially inept Lord, are then able to establish what amounts to a back slapping rapport with the visitor that endures until pre-lunch cocktails when this atmosphere of extreme conviviality is again soured by the reappearance of Lord. This remarkable tale climaxes during lunch when Lord tells the Duke of Edinburgh that he and Queen Elizabeth ought to use an Austin Champ rather than a Land Rover on suitable State occasions.

---

* For many years the start of the famous French endurance race involved the drivers sprinting across the track to their cars that were parked, with dead engines, at an angle to the pits. Running to the cars was abandoned for the 1970 race and the traditional 'Le Mans start' abolished altogether a year later.

Coloured by the observation that his highness's fingers are 'very long' the story goes on to reveal how an '*obviously very annoyed Duke points at Lord and tells him to "be careful what you say".*' (Careful of what? This writer's insertion).

The lunch is now hurriedly finished and at Lord's invitation the guest is taken to see Burzi's models of projected cars whereupon Lord is told: '*I think you ought to have another look at things because I'm not sure these are up to the foreign competition*'. Or, if you believe an abridged version: '*They're no good. You will never sell them*'. Allegedly, it was the next day Lord sent for Farina or, alternatively, it was the *next day* the Italian flew to Birmingham.

The story emanates from Edwards. It is used without question in Martin Adeney's *The Motor Makers* and at length in '*Men and Motors*' although, to his credit, Sharratt does raise a very mildly quizzical eyebrow. For this author the far-reaching anecdote has always lacked the ring of truth.

In a first attempt to establish its veracity—a difficult prospect 50 years distant, with everyone who was present, except the duke and possibly an unnamed equerry dead—I contacted his royal highness's office. The initial response was that there was no record of any comments made to Lord. However, the duke's staff confirmed that shortly after the visit a telegram was sent to the chairman thanking him for the excellent arrangements and stating that his royal highness was '*very impressed by the up to date ideas shown and the spirit and obvious enthusiasm of your workpeople*'.

Such a reply was to be expected on the grounds of diplomacy and privacy.

Yet it seemed to me that even if Lord was agitated, suffering from his much vaunted inferiority complex and overly anxious to 'get in on the action', as Edwards said, it is highly improbable that a public figure with such vast experience of putting people from all walks of life at ease as the Duke of Edinburgh, would have displayed annoyance or allowed any embarrassment. More likely to have defused such a situation by suggesting a Champ was delivered to the royal mews for assessment!

The remarks about the proposed models are equally difficult to countenance. It seems inconceivable that a member of the royal family, with no detailed technical knowledge or executive authority, would be as crassly insulting to Burzi and his team, in front of the company's chairman, as to say their work was 'no good' and unsaleable. Even when wrapped in the more flowery prose chosen by Sharratt, the likelihood that the comment was ever uttered, at least in anything like this form, seems doubtful.

Finally, the contention that Farina arrived the next day or was even contacted with such indecent haste reads like pure fiction as well as being almost totally impractical. If we are to accept the theory it would imply a name was conjured out of the ether by an irrational, highly prescriptive Lord who had scant regard for, or sensitivity towards, his in-house stylist.

As regards the first count: Lord could be impetuous over seemingly minor matters. We have seen examples. He was also impressively decisive. But these are terms from a different lexicon to that of irrational and prescriptive.

Because Edwards's version is so deprecating to Lord I decided to raise it again with Buckingham Palace. This time, Brigadier Sir Miles Hunt-Davis, private secretary to the Duke of Edinburgh, agreed to ask his majesty for any recollections of that winter's day in 1955. The brigadier discovered that the prince's recall was 'slightly different' to the account I had presented from the oft-quoted Edwards story. Furthermore, he was not conscious of Lord's inferiority complex and had no recollection of him leaving the party at any time.

Rather more importantly, his royal highness remembers nothing about Lord proposing the use of an Austin instead of a Land Rover but added: '*There was no reason why he should not suggest it*'. The duke, who fully understood how a design studio worked, now becomes much more specific in his remarks. During lunch he asked Lord if he could visit the styling department as he did not think the current Austins were particularly 'distinguished'.

'*I got the impression that the Austin directors and their wives would go into the "stylist" shop and give the "chief stylist" their opinions. Since Burzi was employed by the company, he more or less had to do what they suggested. This was one of the problems for "in-house" designers in all companies, whereas a professional "contract" designer was in a much stronger position to have his way,*' said Prince Philip.

While his highness does not remember criticizing the Austin style he clearly recalls asking Lord whether '*he had ever thought of employing an outside designer*'*. Lord asked if his majesty had anyone in mind '*and the first name to come into Prince Philip's head was Pinin Farina*' on the basis that he was establishing a reputation at that time. The Duke of Edinburgh concluded his remarks to me by saying that he was not sure if Sir Leonard (Lord) had heard of Pinin Farina, thought no more about the matter, but heard later that Lord had sent for Farina '*soon afterwards*', that he had designed a new A40 and that it '*turned out to be quite a success for Austin*'.

What part Burzi himself played in the selection process is difficult to gauge because his true relationship with Lord is also hard to judge. There are those who believe Lord's nature was exploitative in achieving his ends, that that was his attitude towards Burzi, but because their paths crossed on a daily basis there is the 'illusion' of a meaningful relationship.

It may be.

But it was Leonard Lord who intervened to free the designer from internment** on the Isle of Man during the early stages of WWII and have him re-installed at Longbridge, when one of the last things he would have needed was a stylist. Furthermore, they had worked closely, and without rancour, on the ill-starred A90 Atlantic. Burzi had been in sympathy with Lord to a brilliant degree over the design of the 'Flying A' bonnet ornament and they had toiled together, very effectively, to 'Austinize' Raymond Loewy's rather-too-transatlantic perception of the Somerset and Holden Koto's similarly flavoured A30.

What seems certain is that Lord had been thinking of a more European than British appearance to the cars for some time. The 'Atlantic' owed some of its elements to a Farina design. Farina had worked for Nash and also with Donald Healey. It is also conceivable that an approach had been discussed with Burzi, someone with strong Italian links and originally recommended to Austin by Vincenzo Lancia who had been closely associated with Farina very many years before.

The Duke of Edinburgh would not have known that Lord knew Farina's work intimately, but at the end of the day the Italian was the obvious choice for an external consultant.

There was something of the Bugatti about Battista Farina; something of an André Citroën. That desire to blend in an automobile, art and architecture; culture with convenience. Stylists for the Somerset, Loewy and Madawick, had not been the perfect bedfellows for Lord and Burzi. Battista 'Pinin' Farina and his son Sergio were more compatible and certainly had more influence. They would shape a whole line of BMC cars, large and small, for a decade and have an influence for much longer.

---

* He had, of course; at least twice.

** Burzi's Italian background meant he would have been classed as an 'enemy' at the outbreak of WWll. About 8,000 British residents, mostly Germans and Italians, were actually 'interned' (effectively, imprisoned), principally on the Isle of Man, although many more thousands of various nationalities and political persuasions were rounded up. The latter appeared before tribunals and most were subsequently classed as 'friendly aliens'.

Being the second youngest of 11 children earned Battista his nick name—young one—and also a job, at just 11 years of age, when brother Giovanni needed help in the body shop he opened in 1905 after completing a coachbuilding apprenticeship. Battista swiftly took to the world of wood frame and fabric and during WWI was in charge of the construction of a trainer aircraft called the *Aviatic*. But his passion was for cars. With the war over, and aged 27, he went, in 1920, to America to experience the automotive dream at first hand. Ford offered him a job, but with appealing warmth he returned home, to marry his Rosa Copasso.

He worked for Giovanni, alongside two other brothers, for the next 10 years, then decided to strike out on his own with Carrozzeria Pinin Farina. None other than Vincenzo Lancia was a partner. The idea was to build special bodies for popular makes. Perhaps, as someone said later—to '*bring Italian style in architecture to the automobile.*' At first, most of the output was on Italian chassis but there was some interest from elsewhere and by the time war began again, he was in contact with both Renault and General Motors.

Quickly back at the drawing board when hostilities ceased, Farina styled the 1946 Fiat-based Cisitalia for entrepreneur Piero Dusio. It was so stunningly beautiful that it went on display in New York's Museum of Modern Art, was heralded as one of eight outstanding cars of the age, and was adopted as the trend-setter for Ferraris for years to come.

Work then came from Nash, for the Ambassador, and around 1952, the Nash-Healey, the familiar British sports car but with the American manufacturer's engine. All this time, it was becoming increasingly apparent at Longbridge that the shapes and styles of Austins that might still appeal at home and in the Commonwealth were not particularly attractive on a broader stage—were not 'distinguished'. Thus there is a logical and progressive process that led to the signing of an £84,000 contract with Carrosserie Pinin Farina.

The first car on which the Italian genius worked his magic was the A35 transforming it into a slant backed, slightly slab sided, little two-door saloon called the A40 'Farina' and released at the Paris Salon in September 1958. There were imaginatively 'trendy' touches like black roofs for all the colour options and an elegant re-work of the 'Austin A' bonnet ornament. Although it was fashionable in some circles to denigrate the car as looking like a-van-with-windows, the customers continued to come back for more until the slightly softer-lined, slightly more powerful Mark II, was finally discontinued a decade later.

Perhaps the archetypal Farina Austin though, is the Mark II A55 Cambridge, which appeared in 1959. This more than any other was the model to take the quintessentially 'Englishness' out of Austin. With its angular tail fins and aggressively grinning grille, this was no longer the Austin of conservative, reliable family men. As the publicity portrayed, this could be the car of racy girls (by British standards, anyway)—'*marvellously harmonious, pure in line, distinctive in décor*', to quote a tribute to Farina style from the University of Turin.

The basic look was extended to other BMC models in the same category—what was to become known as 'badge engineering'—and then to larger cars like the Austin Westminster, Wolseley 6/99 and Vanden Plas Princess. It would be an exaggeration to suggest Farina's work matured as a result of the involvement with Lord and BMC. Yet it is true that over 10 years a 'certain Englishness' returned to the styles. It is typified best, perhaps, by the A60 Cambridge announced in 1961 and powered by an enlarged version of the A55's B-Series engine. The lines are less brash and the understatement creates an elegant vehicle that was deservedly popular with Austin's traditional clientele.

Simplistically, the converse of badge engineering is rationalization. We saw earlier how advantageous the deleting, not just of models, but marques, could have been when BMC was formed in 1952. Lord failed to do either for the reasons I have suggested. The merger was conducted against the backdrop of the government's full employment policy, a market more buoyant than ever before with irrational brand loyalty, financial interests that would not have tolerated even a temporary hiccup in share prices and a top heavy dealer network that was overly powerful.

Lord may have quipped, somewhat hypocritically, when a Scottish agent arrived in a Bentley for a company-sponsored golf tournament: *'Don't we make a car good enough for you?'* But at ground level it was impossible to devise a battle plan to vanquish this arrogant and complacent force. And that was just one of the issues.

When, with the Austin Cambridge of 1959, the Farina style came fully on stream there was another opportunity to rationalize. A Morris Oxford and a series of clones badged as Wolseley, MG and Riley, each of which seemed uglier than the last, duplicated the A55. In the case of the MG and Riley there were minor modifications to the engines and, in all three, a multiplicity of costly-to-execute trim variations for little better reason than a Wolseley customer would buy a car with that insignia because they also made dependable underpants (sic)!

Again Lord failed to rationalize. Again it was partially because of the strength of the dealer network and because of the apparent strength of the market. Motor manufacturers' profits had multiplied four-fold between 1947 and 1955. Profits per vehicle went up by 70% over roughly the same period with a rise in price of only 30% compared with 50% for most other goods. No one really noticed that in spite of excessive investment encouraged by tax credits, by 1954, British exports had reached a plateau and those of France and Germany were rising sharply.

It was that very situation that would have been partly responsible for one of the most respected motoring journalists of his generation, Laurence Pomeroy, berating Lord at the 1955 London motor show about the lack of imagination displayed by BMC's cars. Pomeroy's father, another Laurence, was the designer of that iconic Edwardian sports car, the Prince Henry Vauxhall and the subsequent E Type 30/98 model of the same make. The son ardently promoted his father's engineering by racing one of the cars over many years. He had also held the post of *Motor* magazine's technical editor since 1937 and wrote with immense authority on automotive technology.

His criticisms to Lord hinged on the more technically innovative cars being developed in continental Europe, pointed up at that very motor show by the presence of the Flaminio Bertoni styled DS 19 Citroën. It featured self-leveling, hydropneumatic suspension, disc brakes on the driven front wheels, power steering and semi-automatic transmission.

Pomeroy's remarks only echoed those of others. Bill Boddy of *Motor Sport*, for example, was in an almost constant state of adoration of the air cooled Volkswagen and he regarded the Mercedes as the best car in the world. There is an air of desperation in Lord's voice when he tells Pomeroy: *'Tell us what you want and we'll build the bloody things'*. Yet Lord knew it would be the height of folly to offer the conservative British customer a car like the Citroën, known in the British motor trade as *'the plumber's nightmare'*! On the other hand he was sufficiently open minded, flexible and alive to the situation to commission, as soon after the motor show as January, 1956, research into an advanced vehicle. It was undertaken by Pomeroy himself and David Hodkin of the firm ERA* and produced two mid-engined prototypes, dubbed 'Maximin'. The project ran in parallel

---

*   ERA was originally a racing car manufacturer, established in 1934 by the competition driver Raymond Mays and a number of fellow enthusiasts. Car making had largely petered out by the start of WWll and the company

with much of Issigonis's work on what actually became the Mini and the ERA design was still being tested in June, 1959, as stocks of the Mini were being accumulated for its launch.

It was in this period, the government begun to use the motor industry as an economic 'throttle'. Between 1952 and 1973 the rates for hire purchase and purchase tax were changed 29 times and in just two years, between June 1965 and November 1967, were altered on seven occasions.

George Turnbull, who was production director at Standard in 1956 and went on to become managing director of British Leyland's car division and eventually chief executive of the British arm of Peugeot-Talbot, said of the situation: '*If the economy was overheated* (they) *put some more purchase tax on motor cars. The government was totally oblivious and if I was ever going to apportion blame for the parlous state the British motor industry got into, you have got to put it at the door of the government . . . The reality is that they didn't handle the industry in a sensitive way. It was the main primer for so many service industries; it was the main employer of labour; it was the biggest manufacturing industry by a mile and they treated it with derision. There's no other word for it. From one day of virtually full employment, I had got to sack 3,000 men which I did with great reluctance. It drove more and more men into militant unions for protection*'.

Just as it is absurd to blame Lord for sowing the seeds of the industry's failure, and much as we might like to view Turnbull's comments as confirmation that it *is* ridiculous, he is overly partisan. Both Labour and Conservative governments were still battling with the dire economic aftermath of the war, inflation was an issue of paramount concern, and although forward planning in the motor industry was made impossible by constant changes to the monetary regulations, it was understandable ministers should use them in an attempt to control consumer spending.

Of far more significance as regards Leonard Lord is Turnbull's point about labour relations. We shall soon see the effects of militant union action, but must again bear in mind that Conservative treasury officials were mainly of the opinion that unemployment was acceptable if it helped contain inflation. That was most definitely not the position of their chancellor (1955-57) and subsequently prime minister, Harold MacMillan.

All these factors have a bearing on what it was feasible for Lord to undertake; and what it was not. It is all very well to criticize the situation in the 1960s where the Corporation still had a network of competing dealers selling vehicles that duplicated each other. But the only effective solution would have been to start with a blank map. Yet we have already seen that in the UK alone there were 3,500 Austin outlets and about the same for Morris. Each would have needed to be bought out, or compensated, for the loss of their agency, then invited to apply for what was tantamount to their own job, but now as sole BMC dealer. Lord could have weathered the outrage and acrimony but the costs would have been astronomical.

By way of example—one main Austin dealership in a country town of 10,000 population was sold in 1957 for around £80,000, which we can assume was the going rate for such a desirable business. The arithmetic is thus self-explanatory.

Rationalization by type or make, as the Farina cars were planned, did not hinge on resolving the problem of an excessively large dealer structure. Lord side-stepped trimming the range because the political and economic climate meant he didn't need to. It may even have helped, temporarily, to keep open as many model options as possible. The tragedy is, the need *would* arise, and the moment had passed.

---

subsequently became, principally, engineering consultants to the motor industry. The name was changed to Engineering Research Applications to reflect this.

Alexander Arnold Constantine Issigonis was born in 1906 to affluent, naturalized British parents of Greek and German origin. They lived in the Turkish port of Smyrna within the Ottoman Empire. This complicated mix brought its own complications. When WWI began the Turks sided with the Germans and the Graeco-British family found themselves living in a hostile environment. When the Germans actually arrived in force, to avail themselves of the dockyard facilities, the Issigonises were interned.

The war progressed through the disastrous 1915/16 offensive on Turkey's Gallipoli peninsular where British, French, Australian and New Zealand troops failed to repress the Turks and open a supply route to Russian and the Eastern Front, but lost some 44,000 lives in sub-human conditions. Eventually General Edmund Allenby, nicknamed the 'Bloody Bull', drove the Turks, extremely rapidly, in the opposite direction from their strongholds in Syria. The Ottoman forces then surrendered on October 30, 1918.

It was now the turn of the Greeks. Promised, principally by British prime minister, David Lloyd George, *'important territorial concessions on the coast of Asia Minor'* in return for a military alliance, Greece took Smyrna on May 15, 1919. There followed, throughout Turkey, three years of fighting between the occupying forces and local revolutionaries. It culminated, certainly as far as the Issigonises were concerned, in the Great Fire of Smyrna. This horror, which ravaged the city from September 13-17, 1922, 'celebrated' the repossession by the Turks of the ancient city, with its cobbled streets and priceless architecture. As part of the process they set fire to the Christian districts.

Perhaps as many as 100,000 Greeks and Armenians lost their lives—burned, hacked to pieces, or drowned in the harbour as they tried to escape while Turkish military bands played loud music to drown the screams. A Royal Navy flotilla arrived from Malta on September 15 to evacuate British nationals. Alec Issigonis, aged 16, and his parents, Constantine and Hulda, boarded the battleship *HMS Iron Duke*, a veteran of Jutland, the great WWI naval set piece.

The tangible life the teenager had known had been erased from the face of the earth. Constantine Issigonis's action in taking British citizenship had almost certainly saved the lives of his family. But the man who was prone to cry, in moment's of duress: *'God bless the Queen'*, adored Britain, and wanted more than anything for his son to be an 'Englishman', never saw the shores of his dreamland again. He died, aged 50, a few months after reaching the sanctuary of Malta.

Alec, and the mother to whom he was obsessively attached, continued their sad journey to London. Once they arrived, Hulda recovered at least part of the family fortune fairly rapidly by suing the British government for what had happened. This facilitated a European motor tour in the Singer Ten she had bought her son and afterwards his engineering studies at Battersea Polytechnic.

His first job, in 1928, was as a draughtsman—significantly, perhaps—to the Willesden, north London, company of Reduction Gears Ltd who built an easy-change clutch mechanism. While at 'Reduction Gears' Issigonis started *'messing around with cars'*, as one of his biographers puts it. They came from Jack Duller's stock of new and used Austin Sevens at a garage in West End Lane, West Hampstead.

The young draughtsman started modifying the cars he bought and indulged in spirited competition at venues like Shelsley Walsh hillclimb and Brighton, where there were speed trials along Madeira Drive. In 1934 he took a job in the drawing office of the Coventry car-maker Humber. It was while there he built himself a racing car known as the Lightweight Special.

It 'devoured' his current Austin piece by piece to become one of the most sophisticated and competent sprint cars of the immediate pre—and post-War eras.

The engine was 'Works' Austin, provided by Issigonis's friend and motor industry contact Murray Jamieson. The chassis was a total departure from the Longbridge car, having as its backbone a stressed box section made from aluminium-faced plywood boards. The major components were fitted into this structure, while the independent springing relied on rubber rings inside a front cross tube. They linked two suspension assemblies contained in load-bearing sponsons just aft of the radiator. At the rear, the movement of swing axles was controlled by tensioned rubber loops similar to large elastic bands.

The set-up owed much to a number of sources—French Voisins of the early '20s, the formidable W25 Mercedes racers of the mid-'30s, some very obscure cars like the German Imperia and British Rover Scarab and, of course, Citroën's *Traction Avant*. By the same token, Issigonis's two greatest achievements, the post-War Morris Minor and the BMC Mini, probably borrowed from the Lightweight Special although the designer always denied this.

In 1936, following a management change at Humber that was not to his liking, Issigonis moved to Morris. It was here he would encounter, by reputation rather than contact, as their tenures did not quite overlap, the dynamic Leonard Lord. Indirectly, it was the latter who was responsible for Issigonis's appointment.

Lord had taken on a Rover designer named Robert Boyle and sent him to America to study procedures at General Motors. There Boyle encountered a British-born titan among American automotive engineers, Maurice Olley. He was a protégé of Royce, had been transferred to America by Rolls-Royce in 1917 to oversee aircraft engine manufacture and stayed on as chief engineer when the Derby firm established a car manufacturing facility in Springfield, Massachusetts.

Olley became deeply concerned about the poor ride qualities of both the Silver Ghost and Phantom models they were making, saw as a solution independent front suspension and in 1930, three years before Rolls-Royce of America failed, shifted his loyalties to General Motors. He was seconded, with his ground-breaking thoughts, to the Cadillac division. '*The first man here to spend a quarter of a million bucks on two experimental cars!*'

Although Olley's contribution to suspension technology is enormous, and this generous spirited engineer's influence on Issigonis was considerable, he had another key role with his Detroit employer. In 1934 a post was created for him as engineer in charge of product study and as such he developed a concept known as 'sectionalisation' whereby groups of engineers dealt with specific areas of a car's design. It was this Boyle studied. When he returned to Cowley, among many he recruited to implement sectionalisation was Issigonis, whom he already knew. He placed Issigonis with the suspension team but from 1937 onwards he became the mainstay of a design and development group, having been up-graded by Boyle's replacement, Vic Oak.

Issigonis was assigned the draughtsman Jack Daniels, a survivor of Lord's closure of the MG drawing office, to interpret his ideas. Daniels worked with Issigonis for most of the next 40 years and gave an insight into his character that will be of value to us later, when we try to take a realistic view of the decline of BMC. In his book *The Development of the Mini* (Breedon Books 1997) Daniels says the little freehand sketches he was given (by Issigonis) '*were quite accurate. You would see a clear outline of what he wanted, the detail you had to sort out yourself afterwards*'. This is endorsed by Charles Griffin, Morris's chief experimental engineer in the 1960s and a colleague from the early front wheel drive period at BMC: '*He was a great sketcher. He didn't do any calculations. It was all in his eye. But if you went through something stress-wise, you'd find it was a beautifully balanced piece of engineering*'.

At Morris, Daniels and Issigonis first worked together on a unitary construction body for the Morris Ten, and an independent front suspension system for the same car. The second project was passed over but saw the light of day on a vehicle that became the MG Y Type of 1947.

During the War Issigonis tackled a variety of ventures that drew on his experience of unitary construction and independent suspension, but it was not until after the armistice that his most successful, though not his most famous, project came to fruition. The design of the Morris Minor, code named Mosquito, had begun as early as 1941 and as we already know was championed by Miles Thomas. Jack Daniels rejoined Issigonis and an expanded team in 1945 to drive the work forward.

Ironically, it was Reginald Hanks who saw the 'Minor' into production. The model was unveiled at the 1948 London motor show and could have been the best small car the world had ever seen. Yet, as explained earlier, the advantage was lost.

Alec Issigonis had missed the departure of Leonard Lord from Morris by a few months, he was to miss his arrival as managing director of BMC by an even shorter period. It has been argued that the designer left to avoid Lord, but such drastic action is not entirely credible. Well before the formation of the Corporation, Issigonis would have been sagging under the weight of William Morris's dead hand, while the purge of directors had done little to lighten the general atmosphere.

Issigonis, who seems to have had an affinity with Hanks, sought his advice about a future career path and the vice-chairman recommended he leave. Whether this was wise counsel is debatable, proffered, as it was, by a man who was unenthusiastic about the forthcoming Austin-Morris merger and was no friend of Lord. Nonetheless, a post with a prestige car manufacturer, Alvis, must have appealed to Issigonis and in the opening months of 1952 he began negotiating a move to the factory of this famous make based on Holyhead Road, Coventry.

He was hired to produce a revolutionary sports saloon, designated TA350, to be built alongside the aero-engines and military and specialist vehicles that were the firm's staple. But it was an unhappy association.

Issigonis's shortcomings as a power plant designer soon became apparent. The Alvis directors may well have been frightened by the complexity of his overhead camshaft V8, but that was as nothing to their fear when they saw the escalating costs of the whole project as it proceeded towards the intended launch at the 1956 British motor show. As early as 1954, mentally at least, the board had decided to abandon the exercise, although they allowed development work to continue. The balance was finally tipped against the TA350 in the summer of 1955 when Pressed Steel considerably increased their quote for making the body.

One positive outcome of Issigonis's period at Alvis was the consolidation of his relationship with Alex Moulton. The latter was born in 1920 and came from a wealthy West Country family. As early as the immediate post-War era his pedigree was impressive. He had studied engineering, first as an apprentice with commercial vehicle builder Sentinel, then at Cambridge University. Mid-way through his degree in wartime Britain he was seconded, as personal assistant to Roy Fedden, chief engineer at the Bristol Aeroplane Company and responsible for the Pegasus and Mercury engines with which we are now so familiar.

When Fedden left Bristol, Moulton joined him to work on a highly unsuccessful 'people's car' before finally completing his studies. Armed with all this know-how he entered the family rubber component business in Bradford-on-Avon and concentrated on the development of the medium for use in trailer, and later car, suspension systems.

Apart from the rubber suspension on his own car, Issigonis was helping the Fry family (of chocolate fame) with the springing of their own hillclimb special and as both machines were hitting the motor sport headlines throughout the late 1940s it was almost inevitable that the paths of Issigonis and Moulton would cross. The two men first met informally at Cowley, and, if the pun can be forgiven, bonded immediately.

Their first official liaison was at Alvis where Issigonis commissioned Moulton to produce all-independent suspension for the TA350. It was loosely based on Citroën's inter-connected layout for the 2CV, but instead of wheel movement being transmitted to horizontal coil springs mounted longitudinally along the sides of the floor pan, the Alvis was to have had conical rubber cones at each wheel that when compressed by wishbones at the front and semi-trailing arms at the rear, would displace fluid (water) front to back. Clearly this was the precursor of the advanced systems that eventually appeared as Hydrolastic on the BMC 1100s and Hydragas on the Austin Allegro and Metro.

Not long before Issigonis found himself at a loose end at Alvis, the impressionable and simplistic British population of the day, Lord among them, was cast into mourning by the 'death' of Grace Archer. On the night of Tuesday, September 22, 1955, BBC radio's everyday story of country folk shocked listeners with a scenario whereby the headstrong rich girl, recently married to an ambitious farmer's son, was struck down by a falling beam as she tried to release her sister-in-law's horse from their village's blazing livery stable.

Lord was among those who helped jam the Home Service's switchboard for 48 hours. Whether to protest at Grace's demise or seek an amended script on the 23rd is unclear. But given Lord's impetuosity we can well believe he leapt from his chair before *The Archers'* closing theme of *Barwick Green* jangled through the ether of his Halesend sitting room and he had heard the fateful words: '*she died in my arms*'.

Controversy has always surrounded the Grace Archer 'death' script. The popular belief is that it was a broadcasting 'spoiler' on the night independent television was launched in Britain. However, the supreme irony, as far as Lord is concerned, is that *'Archers'* creator Godfrey Baseley revealed in 1996, just before he died, that he 'killed' Grace because the actress, Ysanne Churchman, was encouraging other members of the cast to join a trade union!

As an aside it is interesting that BMC cultivated a relationship with the *Archers* team that helped promote the vehicles. Baseley provided a full page advertorial on the Austin Gipsy in the prestigious *Country Life* magazine of April 30, 1959. Around the same time the Milk Marketing Board made a dramatized documentary to promote their product scripted around an Archers' family gathering and involving a variety of Austins. Inevitably, a Gipsy appears, along with an LD milk float and an A105 estate car for the central characters. As a rare and expensive model this last lends credence to the belief that the post-War era was fertile financial territory for many in the farming community!

The Alvis TA350 had died in June 1955. Its departure was announced that November when Issigonis was cast adrift. But Lord had been quick to move. He had already secured the designer's services for BMC, which he would join, at Longbridge, in December. The seal had been set on events that would forever change the world motoring scene. And, some would say, on moves that would lead to the demise of the Corporation.

Chapter Twenty Three
A LONG, DISMAL, SUMMER

If 1955 was a good year for Leonard Lord, 1956 was a momentous one. It was equally so for the nation. But the ingredients were troubling; ugly and the messages grave. As the motor industry approached its annual, two-week, July shutdown, the Standard Motor Company made 3,500 workers redundant and precipitated a 15-day strike. At the Norton motor cycle factory 247 union members were sacked after a 16-week stoppage in protest over redundancy without notice or consultation.

Such actions were at variance with the naïvely held belief that in post-War Britain there would be full employment and was exacerbated by no legal protection against redundancy and no right to consultation. As inflation soared and overseas demand for cars fell, and governments tampered endlessly with hire purchase and purchase tax, Lord would have been heartened by the action at Standard and Norton that left his counterparts in those companies unscathed.

It seemed to mark a return to the ideas he had shared with Herbert Austin and William Morris. Antipathy towards trade unions and socialism, a firm belief that the boss should run the factory as a benign despot and the view that the economics of the sector could be controlled, in part, by summer lay-offs. After all, 1,000 non-productive workers had been shed in 1948, virtually without a murmur, when manufacture of the Austin Eight, Ten and Twelve ceased, and he had emerged in 1953, through a policy of 'no negotiation', the victor of the McHugh Strike.

Thus encouraged, BMC announced 6,000 redundancies, concentrated on Longbridge and Cowley, just one week before the holiday. It was one of the most inept examples of labour relations in the history of British industry. Not only did no one have any idea who was affected until they discovered whether their pay packet of Friday, June 29, was swelled by one week's pay in lieu of notice, but also the dismissals seemed purely arbitrary. No heed was paid to the custom and practice of 'last in first out'. Instead, men and women with 20 or more years' service found themselves as much the victims as those with barely 12 months on the line. The only criteria appeared to be length of time on a specific job.

The management strategy was that the anger and resentment would be dissipated by the shutdown. Indeed, initially very little happened. There was a minor skirmish at Nuffield Metal Products when an additional 750 redundancies were posted, but that was all. However, the Corporation's position was fatally flawed. Works convenor, Dick Etheridge, had learnt the lessons of the McHugh Strike far better than the BMC hierarchy and would not be idle during the vacation. Realising the all-important need for unity and concerted effort, he organized a committee to promote company-wide action, with national backing from the trade unions, and finance from a fighting fund that could sustain a prolonged strike. There was also a plan to involve non-motor industry unions to cut off supplies of raw materials and prevent the movement of finished vehicles.

The opening salvoes were fired in the first days of a July that was to prove one of the most dismally wet and cold on record. Etheridge called a meeting of the 'big six's' (BMC, Ford, Rootes, Rover, Standard and Vauxhall) shop stewards and they pledged to lobby parliament on the ninth of the month. But by July 5, Harold Wilson, now the impressive shadow chancellor of the day, had already been on his feet in Westminster to pose a question to the Tory government that amounted to: '*whatever happened to full employment*'? During the course of the debate the Tories were accused of invoking the law of the jungle.

The analogy appealed to Etheridge. Ever after he was prone to say: '*If the government and employers seek to create a jungle, then they should not be surprised if they find tigers in there*'. A far more important battle cry was: '*Reinstatement without victimization; future consultation; compensation for any made redundant*'—the essence of what the dispute was about.

There was by no means universal commitment, especially among skilled operatives at Longbridge, and a technique was developed to 'persuade' those still in employment and opposed to a strike that they had an obligation to support their less fortunate colleagues. Thus, for the last pre-holiday week, the redundant reported to their workstations. Not surprisingly, the factory police ejected them. Photographs of the expulsions were then sent to the local press along with names of the section leaders and supervisors. However, it was far more malevolent action than this moral blackmail/intimidation, that moved the conflict towards its denouement. Ironically it emanated from the Establishment.

The strike began with the end of the shutdown on July 23. As had happened a fortnight before, the dismissed streamed through the gates with their former workmates. Lord ordered the Works police to again eject them. Dick Etheridge symbolically led those at Longbridge who supported a stoppage from the factory and thus the two protagonists had provoked what was, ultimately, an inevitable strike. The chairman instructed production director, Joe Edwards, to keep a line of communication open and, as most of Etheridge's papers survive, we know he had been given an assurance that he could talk in Edwards's office at any time and not fear dismissal.

At ground level the strategy was to use pickets to prevent raw materials entering the body plants. The focal point was Austin's West Works, but similar tactics were applied outside Pressed Steel at Cowley and Fisher and Ludlow in Castle Bromwich. The theory was that if no bodies, and so cars, could be produced, other components, like engines and transmissions, would clog the system and eventually the plant would grind to a halt. What the unions had not bargained for was the level of violence that would develop, centred on Longbridge's West Gate.

Dr Richard Etheridge, son of the Longbridge Works convenor, has only recently compiled an account of the brutality. It is largely anecdotal and remains fragmented because many of the people who witnessed the ugly events of that cold, wet, summer are now dead. I am, however, extremely grateful to Dr Etheridge for allowing me to publish his research which will appear along with an overview of the dispute in his two volume book: *Walking in the Shadow of a Political Agitator* planned for publication electronically in 2012.

In a bid to supply material to the bodyworks, lorry drivers, many of them members of the Transport and General Workers' Union (TGWU), attempted the highly dangerous practice of taking their vehicles through the gates at speed. This had a dual purpose. It avoided confrontation with the pickets, but was also intended to scatter women strikers seated in rows across the entrance. The latter were equipped with needles on which they knitted scarves in a somewhat macabre parody of the French Revolution's Madame Defarge beside the guillotine.

The speeding lorries were counteracted by the equally hazardous expedient of having small groups of men leap at the cabs, tear open the doors and kill the engine. A number of pickets were themselves almost killed and the approach was modified, so the teams threw themselves in front of the vehicles while compatriots climbed aboard. Once extracted, the keys were tossed down the nearest drain leaving both lorry and driver vulnerable to further abuse. In some cases the tyres would be deflated in a further act of immobilisation.

These actions called for intervention by the regular police who were now on hand to support the factory's own force. The approach was either to use officers mounted on heavy horses and charge directly into the picket line, injuring many beneath the hooves of their mounts, or, to use the animals' flanks to squeeze the strikers against the Works' metal railings. This caused the victims to lose consciousness and/or fall under the beasts. The equally inhumane counter measure was to throw ball bearings under the horses in a bid to make them lose their footing with the risk of terrible injury. This angered the police so much an informal truce was reached.

Mercifully Co-operative Society dray horses, reputedly requisitioned by the strikers, never appeared. The plan had been to arm the riders with wooden poles and joust the lines of mounted constables. The police, as in the miners' strike of 1984, were seen as performing the wholly inappropriate role of supporting management, and by implication, acting as government agents. It is generally held that their violence towards the Longbridge strikers swayed those remaining in work to support the dispute in ever increasing numbers. The leaders and selected pickets were provided with 'minders' from within the union ranks. They were often ex-army men who had been trained in physical combat. Their role was to either intervene if a police officer attempted to manhandle their 'subject' or whisk him into the *mêlée* if arrest seemed imminent.

The stoppage was given a fillip during its first week by a major demonstration. It took place in the pan-shaped expanse of Calthorpe Park, set between Cheddar and Pershore Road in Edgbaston and within a batsman's drive of the famous cricket ground. More significantly, the gathering was in the shadow of the statue of Thomas Attwood*, free trade campaigner, advocate of currency and parliamentary reform, one of a pair of candidates elected as Birmingham's first MPs and distant ancestor of Dick Etheridge.

On the day, Etheridge, standing on the flatbed of a red Austin lorry, was at his oratorical best. But the event was marred by the arrival, in a pick-up truck, of an unidentified Right wing group. Using a hand held loud-hailer the latter began voicing its disapproval of the strike. With considerable skill the convenor kept order but a small contingent broke away and moved to attack the interlopers who used the potentially lethal 'weapon' of a three-foot long monkey wrench to fell one of the demonstrators. As the man lay bleeding from a serious head wound his fellow demonstrators overturned the pick-up. Again the speaker was able to restrain the crowd and resolutions were passed that affirmed the objectives. At the end of the event Etheridge spotted one of his colleagues smashing the loud-speaker of the fled dissidents against a wall as he screamed: '*Bleeding fascists. We just fought a war against these bastards and they are still here*'. With touching compassion the leader embraced the man and said: '*Don't upset yourself. We're going to win this one and they won't matter after that*'. He then took his arm and led him away.

I have dealt with the Calthorpe Park rally, and particularly the final incident, in some detail because it illustrates not only the climate of the times but the entrenchment that had developed. It

---

* After a chequered history in later years, it is now in store.

was Edwards and Harriman who conducted what were ostensibly feeble negotiations between the company, the national representatives of the unions and the Engineering Employers' Federation (EEF). Lord was not present and Etheridge later jibed: '*I understand Mr Lord was recovering in Padstow*'.

What this meant and from what he was 'recovering' in the Cornish town, or why, was not made clear, but we can presume Etheridge was implying that recovery from the shock of the strike was necessary. In truth Lord was on holiday and we may well spring to the conclusion that his absence cannot be absolved. As 'captain of the ship' the overall responsibility for the situation was Lord's and he should have been there.

It *is* a fair point. In the disputes with unions in the troubled print industry of the 1980s no lesser figure than the newspaper baron, Robert Maxwell, spoke directly to Brenda (now baroness) Dean, president and later general secretary, of the Society of Graphical and Allied Trades (SOGAT). And don't we have various examples of prime minister, Harold Wilson, talking to union leaders, most notably Hugh Scanlon, none other than the president of the AEU. '*Hughie, get your tanks off my lawn*'.

However, in this case, 'the captain' had set the course as well as he could and the offer to 'come in', first rendered in the McHugh dispute, was being taken up by Etheridge on a regular basis. Indeed, he and Edwards drafted a deal whereby anyone eventually made redundant, by agreement and following negotiation, was to be awarded two weeks' pay. It was the first time such a formula had been devised in the UK and was subsequently incorporated in the economic legislation of Wilson's 1964 Labour government.

The tripartite talks between BMC, the EEF and trade unions excluded the shop stewards. Neither were they briefed afterwards on the discussions. However, Harriman appears to have been on insipidly amicable terms with Etheridge and passing him in the corridor after one early round of consultation said, 'Hello Dick', while refusing to reveal any information.

As the strike wore on, occupying a significant space in the headlines, the government stance of non-involvement became increasingly untenable, especially as many Conservative back benchers, particularly those with Midlands constituencies, began to voice the same criticisms of BMC management as their Labour counterparts. As a result, minister of labour, Ian McLeod, who had previously been a firm non-interventionist, was instructed to arbitrate. Days of vigorous negotiation between the unions and Corporation followed until the dispute's resolution on August 10.

There was to be reinstatement, negotiation at local level and the compensation package worked out by Etheridge and Edwards if job loss was unavoidable. As the convenor put it: '*Total capitulation*'.

From a union standpoint the struggle had shown how effective organized action could be. The leaders had used cognizance about police tactics, and information on management's plans garnered by sympathetic apprentices, prevented by their indentures from striking themselves, to orchestrate the campaign. They had received support from other trade unionists. Eventually the supply drivers had been pressured by the TGWU to stop running the gauntlet of the pickets at West Gate thus taking 'secondary' strike action. It was a welcome step for all concerned.

Union colleagues from both within and outside the industry had funded the dispute with one hour's pay per head per week. At coachbuilder Panelcraft, the sum was a universal ten shillings (50p), more than seven per cent of the average weekly wage. But above all, unity had won the day. Before Etheridge led the massed ranks back to work, installing them group by group at their allotted posts, the victorious returned to Calthorpe Park on Sunday, August 12.

'*I wonder how my old friend Leonard Lord is feeling today?*' Etheridge pondered to uproarious laughter, before telling the assembled: '*This is the best victory in this area for 50 years. But no individual factory or union will win the fight with the BMC until the Tory government behind them are smashed*'.

Other speakers were more prescient. Les Ambrose, a national executive officer for the AEU told the throng: '*We have started something that must become a pattern, not only for the engineering industry but also for workers everywhere. We must make every employer think twice before discharging any workers*'. Victor Yates, pacifist Labour MP for Birmingham Ladywood for nearly a quarter of a century, said: '*You have struck a blow for trade unionism, but you must make this agreement better and more powerful*'. He went on to attack government policy over Suez, a subject that would soon become as significant as the strike.

It is beyond question that Dick Etheridge was a man of intense conviction. Born in 1909 at Halesowen, a small town in the heart of the Midlands, and subsequently on the railway line to the Austin Works' own station, his family, originally metalworkers and nail-makers, had settled there in the late 18ᵗʰ century.

Dick Etheridge obtained sufficiently impressive qualifications at Handsworth Junior Technical School to have enabled him to pursue a professional career, but the desperate employment conditions of the 1920s and '30s led him to the family coffee shop (whose history was explained earlier) as the only viable option. By the time he joined Austin in 1940 Etheridge was already a Communist Party member. For most of the War he was active in their Works branch while also serving as a shop steward. By 1945 he had risen to factory convenor, representing all the trade unions. He was also secretary of the company's AEU shop stewards' committee.

But for a disastrous showing in the 1950 general election, when he contested, as the Communist candidate, the Birmingham constituency of Northfield, Etheridge would have departed Longbridge by the time of the Nuffield merger. By coincidence Herbert Austin was the Conservative MP for nearby Kings Norton from 1918-24! As it was, Etheridge became chairman of the BMC joint shop stewards' committee in February 1956, just a few months before the strike. When British Leyland was formed in 1968 he took on a similar role with the British Leyland Motor Company's combined trades union committee. In parallel, he had a distinguished career as an officer of the AEU at local and national level and similarly within the Communist Party.

Etheridge could bring an intelligence to negotiation between management and unions that was all-too-frequently lacking in the '50s and '60s. It is apparent in George Sinfield's *Daily Worker* article, quoted earlier, and where he also speaks of the shop steward's desire to see genuinely fair rates on the troubled issue of piecework. It is even more evident on an occasion where the AEU, nationally, asked him to intervene in an unofficial, 120-person pay strike, at Morris Motors Tractors and Transmissions branch on Washwood Heath, Birmingham. After a week, it had caused a total of 3,000 people to be laid off at Longbridge and Cowley. In achieving a solution Etheridge faced a hostile shop floor, something he was quite prepared to do when he believed a fair agreement was being breached, or, '*talk was better than walk*'. This particular success earned him the sobriquet '*olive branch boy*'.

Whatever the reader's political persuasion, Etheridge's commitment to the united front is incontrovertibly sound while his idea for a motor-industry-specific union that fully understood the issues is constructive, logical and was prosecuted in the face of fierce opposition from the established organizations. At the end of the day we have to respect Dick Etheridge's own assessment of the 1956 strike: '*We sowed the seeds of modern industrial law that germinated over the next 10 years and thus gave dignity to workers who for so many years were treated like merchandise on the "commodities market".*

Yet we must also address the Calthorpe Park poser as to Leonard Lord's feelings on that August Sunday morning. One of the most striking and consistent conclusions we should have drawn about Lord is that he was an extremely private individual. It is impossible to judge to what extent he would have felt hurt by the venom, from the shop floor at least, that had been directed towards him, or the criticism of his management style that had extended as far as parliament. It is equally difficult to assess how pragmatic he was about the events of that August.

Dr Richard Etheridge is of the view that his father and the chairman had mutual respect. *'Like boxers who knock hell out of one another in the ring but show a grudging regard outside it'*. A *'gladiatorial relationship'*. Whatever else, we can see clearly it was a very particular association. These judgements are based on personal recollection. The only written evidence is tributes that appeared in the *Birmingham Evening Despatch* and the local *Sunday Mercury* newspapers when Lord retired.

In the '*Despatch*' interview Etheridge says: *'I admire him for his forthrightness. He is no coward. He'd have a go and I'd have a go back at him. I respect him and, I think, he respects me although we have got entirely different outlooks'*. Apart from describing Lord as *'having done a capable job'* and giving him credit for implementing a successful pension scheme, the rest is largely platitudinous padding. It may even be Etheridge uttering what he thought he was expected to say and when it no longer had any relevance. The '*Mercury*' piece is a fantasy from columnist '*Alertus*' in which Lord and Etheridge meet and discuss their 1961 New Year's resolutions one of which is for better industrial relations at *'this little plant of ours'*.

What is far from fantasy is that Lord was in no way vindictive. Etheridge admitted that although there were occasions when he had legitimate grounds to sack the trade unionist, going so far as to add that he never understood why he did not do so, Lord neither dismissed Etheridge nor any other of the factory convenors.

Furthermore, Dr Etheridge, who began his own working life at Longbridge in 1957, happily acknowledges that his subsequent, successful, academic path was, in part, attributable to Lord. He accepted him as an apprentice and sponsored a degree course at Birmingham College of Advanced Technology. The letter to his father begins: *'I see no reason why our personal differences should stop your son Richard from becoming an Austin apprentice . . . '*

Yet there can be no doubt that the strike of 1956 was a watershed in both the life of Leonard Lord and the fortunes of BMC and the British motor industry. It is also arguable that it was the catalyst that helped Lord see the shape of his own future.

Because he disclosed so little it is very hard to reach all the nuances and under-currents of that miserable summer. For example, although we are aware that a significant section of the government welcomed rising unemployment as a means of countering an inflated economy, we do not know to what extent Lord was being manipulated by Westminster—if at all, if tacitly, or if covertly.

We are now extremely familiar with Lord's position on trade unions and it brings us to the conclusion that, at face value at least, he misjudged and mishandled the 1956 situation extremely badly. Probably the best that can be said, is, given there was bound to be a confrontation over redundancies, the strike only lasted three weeks not twelve! On the other hand, and however much he viewed redundancies as a way of coping with recession and market fluctuations, he must have been growing increasingly frustrated by the political thinking that had prevailed since the end of the War. Materials and fuel shortages and controls, then a taxation roller-coaster and now policies that were encouraging a mood of increasing workplace militancy.

As we continue to see, neither the Labour nor Conservative governments were serving him well. When the '56 dispute ended in '*total capitulation*'—Etheridge's choice of words is interesting—Lord must have realized that the landscape had changed, the scenery was not to his liking and although the horizon might be some way distant there were devastating storms upon it. A mild indication of what was to come can be gained from two slightly later disputes—one was a demarcation issue involving electricians working on the transfer machines and was a foretaste of the 'who-does-what' strikes that became a recurring nightmare throughout British industry in the 60s; the other concerned an item as trivial as lockers but managed to halt production for several days.

As always in the story of Leonard Lord there are imponderables. Dick Etheridge was amused by a situation after the strike where, before walking through the machine shop, Lord always phoned the supervisor, none other than Harry Austin, to check whether the convenor was at his workstation. If he was, Lord would make a lengthy detour round the outside of the building. Knowing the two characters as we do there is no obvious reason why there should not have been some brief repartee, and it would not have been Lord's style for that not to have taken place. It is possible, though, Lord felt that an exchange at Etheridge's machine might have compromised the union leader in front of his members. If that was the case, it would be difficult for Etheridge to acknowledge it, but there are hints, from much later, that suggest he could be vulnerable in this respect.

For example, Etheridge's relationship with Donald Stokes, the key industrialist in the formation of British Leyland in 1968, and its chairman until he was replaced in 1977, was entirely different from that with Leonard Lord. Etheridge and Stokes were on first name terms until the former retired in 1975. Etheridge was invited to hear Stokes's maiden speech in the House of Lords when his boss was elevated to the peerage in 1969. He attended the banquet afterwards. Similarly Stokes arranged an exclusive dinner party at Longbridge to mark Etheridge's retirement and the union leader responded later in the year by beginning a lengthy tradition of sending his former chairman a Christmas pudding to his mother's Black Country recipe. Not surprisingly, perhaps, when the press discovered such benefaction they were a little sceptical. And perhaps, some might argue, all those years before, Leonard Lord had judged protocol rather better.

Just as Etheridge had learnt from the McHugh dispute, Lord benefited from the troubles of 1956. Most importantly he began to recognize the need to formulate a workable industrial relations policy. Positive and constructive though that was, the implementation did not work as well as it might have. Lord approached none other than Dick Etheridge and offered him a position as a supervisor—a post that could have involved responsibility for several hundred workers. To say the very least, this was an imaginative move and illustrates once again the stature of Lord and his even-handedness. Also both men could have embarked on a mutually advantageous 'learning curve'.

Rather predictably, given his background and philosophy, Etheridge declined on the grounds he could not join 'the employing classes'. Lord replied: '*It's probably for the best. The nearer the top in this place, the nearer the door*'. Not to be outdone in the bantering stakes, Etheridge returned: '*I know, I saw what you did to my good friend Joe Edwards after the 1956 redundancy strike*'.

There is the potential here to pursue numerous sub-plots but we would probably be unwise to do so. '*Nearer the top, nearer the door*', is a recurring theme with Lord. As regards tautology it's not much better than: '*The higher you get the nearer you are to your hat*', of pre-War Morris days.

Maybe it is indicative of his insecurity, or maybe his own vulnerability—to government, the board, shareholders; colleagues even. While Etheridge, who can't be involved with the 'employing classes', seems always to have 'old' and 'good friends' among them!

If this can be dismissed as harmless banter the exchanges between Lord and Edwards, to which Etheridge alludes, most certainly cannot.

Edwards had been at Longbridge since the early 1930s. At the time of the merger he was works manager and by the time of the 1956 strike had risen to group production director. When Harriman fell seriously ill with a stomach ulcer in 1952, Edwards stood in. He so impressed Lord that the chairman considered him as a possible heir apparent, presumably in the event of Harriman not recovering. Elsewhere, he was respected as a hard negotiator. His strength was that he was far less intransigent than Lord and realized the ineffectiveness of remote, full time, union officials in dealing with day-to-day disputes in a complex industry. There were 39 unions at BMC. Moreover, he appreciated that negotiating with an individual, who could assure both sides of the practicality of an agreement, brought quick settlements.

Some of the measures Edwards and Etheridge thrashed out represented a highly enlightened approach to industrial relations. For example, allowing a convenor to be absent from his work area to resolve an industrial dispute; payment of day work rates (and ultimately average piecework earnings) for the time he was engaged on such duties;* the extension of such principles to designated shop stewards; right of direct access to managers on trade union matters concerning disputes or working practices and even the provision of a company telephone next to the convenor's work space. Creditworthy though all this is, we have to acknowledge that these breakthroughs would have been achieved with Lord's knowledge and had he not agreed he could have vetoed any one of them.

It was to Edwards that Lord now turned to take over labour relations after the 1956 strike. In the light of the way the dispute progressed and its eventual denouement it does not seem a natural choice on the chairman's part, but maybe the broader picture overshadowed the detail of those 19 days. The events that surround the offer are equally puzzling. Once more we find ourselves dealing with a scenario where there are no surviving witnesses. We are dependent on the interpretations of latter day authors, in this case, Turner (*The Leyland Papers*) where the tone is partisan in Edwards's favour and whose account is far from convincing; and Adeney (*The Motor Makers*), where the facts and conclusions are widely at variance with those of Dick Etheridge.

Turner opens with Edwards and Lord having pre-lunch drinks. The environment is similar to that, where, supposedly, things had gone so embarrassingly amiss in the presence of The Duke of Edinburgh. The source of course, is the same. Lord raises the issue of Edwards '*taking charge of labour relations*' and when the latter is unenthusiastic says: '*If you don't like it, you can push off*' (or rather more forceful words to that effect). What is not clear is whether there was to be a new post. Turner is ambivalent; Adeney's view is that the job would be full time, and, vitally important as the role was, that Edwards saw it as demotion. For our part, we simply cannot be sure what Lord was thinking. A downgrade seems unjustified and the suggestion that Edwards took on labour relations at least as part of his 'production' duties, feasible.

In any event, Turner tells us that this man, with '*a company car, a company house, three children at public school*' and who has just signed a five year contract, which turns out to be, allegedly, '*not worth the paper it is written on*', is so grievously offended by being told to '*push off*' that he agrees with his wife, the very same evening, that he should resign. Matters are left in abeyance

---

* Although this did involve some fairly steadfast manipulation of Edwards by Etheridge.

for a few days, after which, in the Turner account, Lord enters Edwards's office and accuses him of '*wanting to take his job*'. At face value this creates the impression that Lord is now paranoid. However, if the chairman *ever did* hold that view, it is interesting. Edwards seems to have been excessively status conscious. If we leap forward by little more than a decade we find him back at BMC, but as managing director. Here his acrimonious relationship with Donald Stokes over their respective future standing in British Leyland genuinely did foul the atmosphere during the formation of that combine and went a long way to ensuring that any benefit from the merger was never realized. Edwards was soon forced out.

To return to Longbridge. The labour relations role was raised again and rejected again. '*Pay him up and get him off the ground today*', Lord told Harriman. A 'brutal' move in Turner's opinion. The reader must judge.

Adeney is more succinct. He explains, as Turner does, how, after a number of offers (14 in 10 days if Turner is to be believed), Edwards becomes head of Pressed Steel. What stems from this level of popularity is redundancies at the body maker that return it to profitability, and the revelation that, with his BMC tally*, Edwards put 15,000 souls out of work in one year. Whether this is an accolade or an embarrassment is not clear, although the author does include Edwards's claim that his actions 'led directly' to government legislation on redundancy payments.

Again, I have analysed the dismissal of Edwards in some detail because it is another excellent illustration of how, in the absence of his own evidence, our judgement of Lord can be coloured and the man diminished by those who have spoken and written of him since his death. And Etheridge is a guilty party here, stating that Edwards was some how made a scapegoat for the strike and commenting after his dismissal: '*Typical Lord—let anybody take the blame except him*'.

The convenor held neither Harriman nor Edwards responsible for the redundancies that lead to the 1956 dispute. '*It* (the sackings) *had the fingerprints of Lord all over it*', he was to tell his son long after the event. And added that the chairman had: '*simply taken the coward's way out* (a direct contradiction of his view in the '*Despatch*' interview) *and ran away leaving Joe Edwards to deal with the day-to-day problems and Harriman the national negotiations*'.

Despite all the manoeuvring, verbiage, insult and counter insult we have ultimately to accept that Leonard Lord, not for the want of trying, failed to establish a robust industrial relations policy. The consequences would be dire.

With hindsight, it is easy to say Lord should have looked outside BMC, perhaps even beyond the industry, maybe even beyond British shores, for the figure he needed.

Not everything about 1956 was dismal for Lord. Indeed the year had started very well when, in March, his daughter, Pauline Pither, had been one of a team of three young ladies who had piloted a four-year-old Austin A40 Sports to victory in the ladies' section of the RAC Rally. Pauline's name though does not appear in the official record of the event. The car was entered by Angela Phipps, then Angela Palfrey, with Aileen Jervis as the co-driver. The Austin sported a small dog where the 'Flying A' bonnet ornament normally stood and too many spot lamps for its battery's health. It was driven at a consistent 80 mph over most of the round-Britain route. After taking the class lead a slip of the slide rule by Aileen, or maybe Pauline, seemingly ruined their chances of victory. None other than Pat Moss, sister of grand prix legend, Stirling, and soon to become one of the most highly acclaimed female rally drivers of all time, was now riding high on her rivals' *faux pas*. Yet, when the final day's driving tests arrived, Moss, having her second BMC Works drive in that pivotal model, the MGA, made an equally simple error to that of the

---

*   Adeney quotes it incorrectly by about 100%. Thus the 15,000 figure is suspect.

A40's crew. She shed decisive points and, ultra-cautious on this occasion, Angela Palfrey seized the prize.

Lord's comments to Ethel when he revealed that his daughter, in a fairly obscure, obsolete, Austin, had beaten a rallying starlet driving his latest curvaceous sports car on which so many marketing hopes rode, are not recorded. However, it had been a good event overall for BMC, or at least Austin—a husband and wife duo in an A90 Westminster finished in the first six, albeit behind a Standard Ten, a mundane A50 had also been in the money, and Austin took the team prize.

Colonel Gamal Abdel Nasser had long prayed to Allah for '*a calamity to overtake the English*'. And so it did, at around the same time as the calamitous strike was overtaking Leonard Lord and BMC. The Suez Crisis began on July 26. It had as much potential to change the course of world history as WWII, 17 years earlier. It prompted America's president Dwight D Eisenhower to remark, when Russia threatened to become involved: '*if those guys start something, we may have to hit 'em—and, if necessary, with everything in the bucket*'. All that apart, it ended forever Britain's pretensions, and those of France, to be a meaningful player on the world stage.

The modern history of Egypt's Suez Canal dates from 1858 with the start of Ferdinand Marie de Lesseps's 11-year project to reconstruct an ancient waterway between the Mediterranean and Red Sea, and thus West and East.

Apart from some interference during the building, British political involvement went back to the time of prime minister, Benjamin Disraeli. There followed a chequered history of administration that also involved the French and the Egyptians themselves.

By the early 1950s and the advent of 'The Cold War', the United Kingdom was seeking to consolidate its position in the Middle East. Simultaneously there was mounting anti-British feeling amongst the Arab nations. The pawn in the game was the canal, through which half the world's oil and two thirds of the petrol needed in Europe now passed. After bouts of violence in the winter and summer of 1952, Colonel Nasser deposed King Farouk of Egypt and formed a republic with himself as president. Harassment of international shipping followed and everything possible was done to frustrate Britain's ambitions in the region. Nasser also caused America considerable anxiety by signing potent arms deals with the Communist bloc.

The British prime minister was the aristocratic Sir Anthony Eden. Like the majority who had served in WWI he had been vehemently anti-war ever since—'*peace comes first, always*'—had been a distinguished diplomat in the second world conflict, but by the time he followed Churchill into the office of prime minister in 1955, had developed an almost obsessive conviction that Nasser was fascism incarnate. It was a catastrophic personality trait.

The crisis was triggered by two events. America and Britain, provoked by Nasser's political machinations, reneged on a promise to provide $270 million dollars to fund the Aswan dam that would have restrained the Nile, generated electricity and provided irrigation for Egypt. Himself provoked, Nasser nationalized the Suez Canal denying free access to many trading nations. Subsequently he blocked the route altogether. Between July and October there were ineffective international negotiations to find an amicable solution while Eden hatched a secret plot with France and Israel.

The Jewish State was to invade Egypt's Sinai Peninsula, the British and French would feign outrage at the conflict, call for a ceasefire, and when it was not forthcoming intervene. This, conveniently, entailed taking control of the Suez Canal. The action took place under cover of darkness on November 5-6; Guy Fawke's night it Britain. Militarily it was a brilliant success. Otherwise, it deeply divided parliament, split national opinion and caused widespread opprobrium in most of the world.

Eisenhower, who opposed armed intervention, was so incensed he threatened to wreck the UK economy and joined other nations in an oil embargo against Britain. Petrol rationing would soon be back.

CHAPTER TWENTY FOUR
BUILD THE BLOODY THING

Sir Anthony Eden called a cease-fire at 5 pm that same November 6, unfortunately without telling his allies. Shortly afterwards he went to Jamaica to recover. While he was away, chancellor Harold MacMillan manoeuvred to oust him from office and on January 9, 1957, the disgraced leader stepped down as head of a humiliated nation. MacMillan, who had been one of the staunchest advocates of military action, replaced him. *'First in, first out'*, the Opposition's Harold Wilson quipped.

What was most important to the car industry about the Suez crisis was it changed public attitudes towards motoring. Petrol rationing was introduced on December 17. Because it was announced in advance there was panic buying, the filling stations ran dry and in some cases cars were stranded at the roadside or in car parks. Restrictions remained until May 1957 by which time the ships Nasser had sunk in the canal had been removed. In the interim, the price of a gallon of petrol reached 6s (30p); a rise of around 25%. Across the motor industry there were lay-offs or short time working as customers pondered whether fuel shortages might be a long-term phenomenon.

There was a short term, although not particularly viable, answer to the petrol drought—the bubble car. They came mainly from continental Europe and if we note the contemporary description of one, the Isetta, that appeared in *The Observer's Book of Automobiles (Frederick Warne, 1956)* we gain an impression of these weird machines. *'Small car with almost identical front and rear contours. Front of car hinges sideways to give access to front seats. Side lamps in upswept ends of front bumper, headlamps faired into straight through "wings" also long side windows. Almost flat tail panel has three short rows of louvres and is flanked by prominent tail lamps. Plain wrap-around rear bumper and tiny disc wheels'*. The Isetta was the progenitor of the genre and originated in 1953 with scooter and motorcycle maker Iso Span in Milan. V.E.L.A.M. took up the cudgels in France. But it was BMW who promoted the vehicle most seriously, to the extent of establishing a British offshoot in a former locomotive works on New England Road, Brighton.

Originally the rear-mounted engine was a 236 cc two-stroke twin but BMW adopted their own four-stroke single. All the cars had independent suspension, hydraulic brakes and a four speed, plus reverse, gearbox. Some models had two rear wheels, others one. Other bubble cars included the 1955 Heinkel from the German WWll aircraft-turned-scooter manufacturer. Very similar to the egg-shaped Isetta, it also used an air-cooled four stroke, single cylinder engine that came in 175 or 198 cc form. The wheel options were also comparable. In 1958 the rights were sold to Dundalk Engineering in Ireland and then to the Trojan company of Croydon who had been building utility vehicles since the 1920s and now applied the name to this bubble car.

The best looking of these cars and the strangest of them were probably the Goggomobil and the Messerschmitt respectively. The first was built in the Bavarian town of Dingolfing and came as either a conventional, but tiny, saloon or an extremely smart sports model. The air cooled, twin cylinder, two stroke engine was placed at the rear and coupled via a manual clutch to an electric pre-selector gearbox. There was all-independent suspension from coil springs and swing axles. They were made from 1955 until 1969 when the factory was taken over by BMW.

The Messerschmitt was a tandem two-seater designed as an invalid carriage by the Fendt company of Rossenheim in Germany, but adopted by the former aeroplane maker in 1953. Again, it was rear engined with, at first, a 175 cc single cylinder two stroke Sachs engine and then a '200'. There was a single wheel at the rear and access to the seating was via a lift-up Perspex 'lid', hinged down one side of the hull. A four-wheel version with a 500 cc twin cylinder motor was made from 1958 until 1960. The obvious attractions of bubble cars were that their diminutive engines used very little fuel (about a gallon per 75 miles) and, in the UK, they could be driven on a motor cycle licence.

Leonard Lord would have been sufficiently shrewd to appreciate that there was no sustainable future, beyond the trauma of Suez, for these creations. Whether they offended his engineering sensibilities, or his patriotic sentiments were outraged by part of the car market being under attack from German marques called Heinkel and Messerschmitt, is less easy to define. Yet it is beyond doubt that he found them inspirational.

What, specifically, was the quote to Issigonis we shall never know. It was the nub of one of the designer's favourite stories and he was notorious for his sense of theatre. A highly protracted version that sounds extremely 'unLord-like' is: '*God damn these bloody awful bubble cars. We must drive them off the streets by designing a proper miniature car*'. The essence was '*design a proper small car to knock the bubble cars off the road*'.

It was, of course, just what a committed 'small car man' wanted to hear. But we should not forget that Lord was, himself, no stranger to the concept of economy vehicles, or fail to appreciate that it is Leonard Lord, not Alec Issigonis and his team, who is the true father of what became the Mini. This, almost totally ignored accolade, was confirmed as recently as 2009, by Bill Davis, who had a distinguished, life-long, career at Longbridge and was a BMC director in the 1960s. '*The Mini wasn't Issigonis's idea. The concept was the idea of Sir Leonard Lord. He told Issigonis precisely what he wanted*', says Davis.

As far as is known Lord first used the term 'mini' in 1947 when he told Austin shareholders that he '*was not yet* (my emphasis) *proposing to make a "mini-car".*'

Long before this, though, and even longer before his tirade against bubble cars, he had experimented with engines that would have been eminently suitable for a 'mini-car'. The first was developed as early as 1941 and took the form of a three cylinder two stroke producing around six horsepower. It was tried in an Austin Eight and then given its own body that was similar in appearance to the Fiat *Topolino* (Little Mouse) of 1936. Interestingly, the latter was close to a genuine 'mini' car with its tiny 570 cc side valve engine and two-seat 'roll-top' convertible coachwork. It also had hydraulic brakes, independent front suspension and a synchromesh gearbox and would be around as both a Fiat and French Simca to inspire (or haunt) Lord until 1948.

Another engine that carried Lord along the mini car road was a two-cylinder version of the A Series. This was tried in a mid-engined bubble car he had told the Morris experimental department to build in early 1957. It was too rough running for passenger car use but is significant in that it was configured for transverse mounting. Around the same time a Goggomobil, Heinkel and Messerschmitt were acquired. Quite apart from the thoughts he had about engines, Lord had a holistic view of miniature cars and broad concepts were running through his mind. There had been the *'Topolino'* experiment of the early 1940s, of course, but of far greater importance was the Duncan Dragonfly.

Ian Duncan, as we already know, was one of the men Lord hired to design his first, new, post-War small car, the A30. The Austin Eight pre-dates it but was merely a resurrected 1939 model. Much earlier, Duncan had worked for Sir Roy Fedden on the 'people's car' we have already also briefly encountered. When they quarrelled, the younger man joined his brother in a business making canning equipment at North Walsham in Norfolk and gained a springboard from which to start experimenting with a car of his own.

From premises nearby the design for a coupé with seating for three abreast was to emerge. It was powered by a torquey, pre-War, parallel twin, BSA motorcycle engine that later became the Birmingham firm's 'A7' motor. One of the attractions of this 500 cc overhead valve unit was that its four-speed gearbox was integral with the crankcase, which meant there were no alignment problems when mounting it *transversely* to drive the front wheels. Hardy Spicer universal joints were used at the inboard ends of the car's drive shafts while the more complex outboard requirements—drive, suspension, steering—were dealt with by the French Tracta company's constant velocity system, by then licensed to Girling who also provided the hydro-mechanical brakes.

Front suspension was by double wishbones and because running on 12-inch diameter wheels constricted space, the drive shafts passed through their lower members. The swivel axle was located in the top arm by ball joint and the actual springing handled by Moulton rubber struts. Steering was of the Burman type. At the rear, the axle was carried on trailing arms with a Panhard rod for sideways location and more Moulton struts for the suspension. All these features are worth noting very carefully.

Not all the technical innovation was the work of Ian Duncan. Frank Hamblin walked out on Fedden at the same time as Duncan. He had been the chassis expert. Before that, in 1937, he was involved in a privately funded, stillborn, venture to produce a car based on the pre-War Morris Minor, but fitted with a rear engine of 'flat four' configuration. It is interesting that not long after, a 'flat four', albeit located at the front, was Issigonis's preference for what was to become his own post-War 'Minor'.

Another refugee from the Fedden camp was William Renwick. He had had a varied career inside and outside the motor industry. It included a spell with MG working on the independent torsion bar suspension of the R Type racer. He was now to look after steering and springing for what had formalized into Duncan Industries (Engineers) Ltd. Alan Lamburn came from the aircraft industry after reading a premature press report about the Dragonfly. He was particularly interested in light alloys and monocoque construction and handled these aspects for Duncan.

The prototype was built in accommodation at Swannington airfield, a wartime RAF base to the north west of Norwich that flew Mosquito aircraft in support of Bomber Command during the last years of conflict. Duncan Industries had moved there to obtain space to develop a revenue-earning coachbuilding business. Unfortunately, the activity attracted the attention of the Inland Revenue and the company was forced to dispose of their most valuable asset.

Duncan hawked the Dragonfly, now clothed in an attractive aluminium body, round the motor industry until he reached Leonard Lord's door towards the end of 1948. The latter was sufficiently impressed to take a ride up Lickey Hill and astonished to find the nimble, sure-footed, little car could ascend the gradient faster than an A40. He bought the machine on the spot, plus an unbodied second chassis, enough parts to build six more examples with Duncan himself thrown in for good measure. The entrepreneur was contracted to Longbridge for three years but an immediate problem that winter's day, was getting back to Norfolk. Lord, who would not relinquish his sleek blue Dragonfly, was persuaded to loan an Austin.

In the material sense it was the end of an ambitious and imaginative project. However, Alan Lamburn retained his interest in economy cars and continued to design one privately. Of particular interest to us is his proposed engine. It would have been an air-cooled twin cylinder of 600 cc but with its gearbox in the sump. The concept became common knowledge when it was described in a feature for *The Autocar* of September 5, 1952. Even if Issigonis, toiling away on a much more prestigious car at Alvis, had missed the magazine article, which is unlikely, he would have been familiarized with the layout by Lamburn himself. He wrote to every motor manufacturer he could think of to try and arouse interest in the approach. It did, of course, become a core element of the Mini and was patented by Issigonis and Austin in 1957.

The parameters Lord set for his small car were very simple. It had to carry four people seated comfortably, be economical, completely different from anything before and use an existing BMC engine. Otherwise Issigonis had a free hand. As the designer walked back to his office after that decisive briefing he had his own, detailed formula in mind.

By now Issigonis had gathered a select team, of what were largely former colleagues, around him. They included Alex Moulton. He had left the Spencer Moulton company and been approached by Lord, who then installed him in a new undertaking, part-owned by Austin, called Moulton Developments. Draughtsman, Jack Daniels, whose association dated back to pre-War days, transferred from Cowley. Chris Kingham, an engine designer, arrived from Alvis whom he had served for almost a decade. John Sheppard was another draughtsman and another recruit from Holyhead Road where he had lost his job when the TA350 project was abandoned. There were at least half a dozen other figures who helped with the drawing and in fashioning the designs.

When, in March 1957, Lord set this talented band to work Issigonis had already undertaken a number of experiments that would be relevant to the Mini. There had been a medium sized saloon that drew heavily on his Alvis experience as regards the engine and suspension, but also on the remarkable Citroën DS. It revealed for the first time his 'wheel at each corner' philosophy.

It was followed by a smaller car that was seen as a replacement for the Morris Minor that, in reality, still had 14 years of life left in it. However, the significance was this rendition had a transverse motor driving the front wheels. Importantly, the gearbox was in line with the engine, a formula the designer had tried in a 'Minor' even before leaving Cowley. This lends the ultimate lie to the story that it was Lord who chose the transverse engine approach. The essence of the saga is, that as development of the Mini, coded XC9003, (later ADO* 15) was gathering pace, Lord, who followed progress on a daily basis, walked through the department as the fitters struggled to find enough space to install the engine.

'*Why not fit the bloody thing sideways?*' he proclaimed.

There is reliable evidence that he actually said something along these lines. But the words have been taken out of context which is obvious once we discover the 'sideways' layout had already been accepted. What Lord may have said was: '*Why not turn it* round?'

This accords with the established fact the engine *was* rotated through 180° for a number of engineering reasons. For example, to place the manifolding in a safer, warmer, position between

---

*   Austin Drawing Office.

the cylinder head and bulkhead and eliminate a problem with severe carburetter icing, while providing a more convenient position for the exhaust.

Also, as originally designed, and thus positioned, with the carburetter on the grille side, the A Series engine used one large gear wheel (the 'step down' pinion) to transfer the drive from the crankshaft to the 'in-sump' gearbox. The internals of the latter were essentially those of the Austin Eight and had synchromesh so weak that it was incapable of overcoming the inertia of the 'step down' gear. Turning the engine through 180° presented an opportunity to introduce a gear train (albeit a very noisy one) to replace the one large pinion, while maintaining the correct rotational direction at the drive shafts. It is most likely Lord was addressing one of, or all, these issues.

Not surprisingly, the development work was carried out with the strictest secrecy in a self-contained building alongside Longbridge's Bristol Road. There the team struggled against the emerging technical difficulties. For example, the universal joints of the day proved unsuitable. It was the chief engineer at MG, Syd Enever, who alerted Issigonis to an appropriate constant velocity device designed in the mid-'30s by the Czech, Alfred Rzeppa.

Neither was the tyre technology of the late '50s up to the loads the Mini would impose at the diameter and section specified. Research being undertaken in Germany to improve the durability of, ironically, bubble car tyres, saved that particular day. Finally, the original monocoque could not withstand the strain from the rubber cones chosen as the suspension medium. They were mounted vertically at the front and horizontally at the rear. Sub frames had to be added to strengthen the anchorages.

The first of the pre-production cars was ready for Lord to try around the Works in October, 1957. It took him about five minutes before he delivered what is, arguably, one of the most significant masterstrokes in industrial history, combined with what is among his most memorable quotes: '*Build the bloody thing*'.

It is possible, of course, that Lord could be so spectacularly decisive because he had known for some years what the essential ingredients of such a car would be. That brings us to the fundamental thrust of this chapter, which is to acknowledge the true importance of Leonard Lord in the creation of the Mini, as recognized by Bill Davis, and supported by so much of the evidence.

The key pointers to Lord's influence are, firstly, his lines of thought and, secondly, his awareness of the enabling technology. As we have seen, he had the embryo concept for a 'mini-car' in his mind as early as 1941 and used the term, at least once, shortly after WWll. But the seminal ideas go back further than that. In 1939 Laurence Pomeroy, who was a friend of Issigonis, had written a justification of an 'unconventional car'. It appeared in *Motor* on February 7.

The car he described owed much in appearance to the Fiat *Topolino* that was to influence Lord's 600 cc experiment of a few years later. But the Pomeroy vehicle had front wheel drive, torsion bar suspension, rack and pinion steering and a transverse engine with the radiator parallel to it, but between the cylinder block and cabin in the mode of the Fiat. Pomeroy dubbed it his 'Mini Motor' and Lord would undoubtedly have noted the article and all the theories it advanced.

After his involvement with the Duncan Dragonfly and with one actually on site, Lord would also have had access to many of the Mini's subsequent constituents and, of course, he would have been one of the people Alan Lamburn contacted with his ideas for an in-sump gearbox. Naturally, and in much the same way, all this information would have been available to Issigonis.

The latter always denied Pomeroy's 'Mini-Motor' was an influence, even to the extent of saying he had no awareness of it. However, that is extremely hard to believe. In any case, some of the basics, for example front wheel drive and a transverse engine, were repeated and there, for all to see, in the Dragonfly. And the latter's suspension was the work of Alex Moulton, who would be the architect of the Mini's springing.

At Alec Issigonis's memorial service in 1988, his friend, Lord Snowdon, described him as: 'a true engineer, designer and perfectionist'. He went on: *'His genius, for he was a genius, lay in his inventive brain concentrating on pure function and essential truth in engineering design'*. Unfortunately, this is somewhat wide of the mark. If genius Issigonis was, it was because he brought together, in one package and for the first time, a number of innovative ideas others had developed over many years. It was Leonard Lord who was the facilitator. Lord who made it happen; initially and ultimately.

However, if we credit Lord with being the natural parent of the Mini, and it is right we should, we must hold him responsible, to an extent, for its growth into delinquency in the society that was BMC.

Lord is never given credit for the charm and sense of humour he undoubtedly possessed, or for being a raconteur. It is true these attributes were not always conspicuous. Issigonis, by comparison, was an extrovert, exhibitionist and blatant self-publicist. His penchant for sketching on napkins and tablecloths whenever there was a journalist in range is well known and contributed handsomely to what became iconic status. Whether it was deserved is another matter.

ADO 15 was revealed to the motoring press on August 18 and 19, 1959, and went public in a scoop for Pomeroy and Motor on their publication day of Wednesday 26. A week after the unveiling to car writers the non-specialist press were invited to Longbridge to be shown what was termed the 'new Austin Seven' to capitalize on the reputation of Sir Herbert Austin's pre-War masterpiece.* A little later a similar event was staged at Cowley for the 'Morris Mini Minor'. Except for trim details and badges the two cars were identical.

Perhaps predictably, the new baby made little initial impact on the market—barely 20,000 sold that first year. However, two factors that are in some ways linked, gave it increasing impetus. One was the cultural environment in the United Kingdom and the other the patronage of the rich and famous.

Lord Snowdon, a title bestowed on Anthony Armstrong-Jones when he married the Queen of England's sister in 1960, had been a close friend of Issigonis since the mid '50s when they were introduced by a mutual acquaintance. Snowdon ran a Morris Minor and then a succession of Minis. Knock-on effects were that an example was given to his bride-to-be, HRH Princess Margaret, as a pre-nuptial present; the Queen herself tried one and another was subsequently provided for Snowdon to teach the heir to the throne, HRH Prince Charles, to drive.

This high profile gave a lead to the glitterati of the period. Mannequin and actress, Twiggy, bought one as did dress designer Mary Quant. They were followed into the driving seat by other actors and actresses including Peter Sellers, Peter Ustinov, Britt Eckland (married at the time to Sellers), Marianne Faithfull and the prima ballerina Margot Fontaine. At least three of The Beatles owned Minis, as did the singer, Harry Secombe, while the world champion racing driver, Graham Hill, was also a devotee.

It was not quite what Issigonis had intended. He wanted to build what he called *'charwomen's cars'*. Or, as he put it, even less elegantly apropos the Mini, and in somewhat muddled and

---

* A similar sobriquet was applied to early A30s for the same reason.

contradictory terms: '*To our horror we discovered that rich and intelligent people bought it first. What could be worse than a suburban housewife with money. They are so stupid, they buy Fords. Some are intelligent—they buy Minis*'.

The radically changing cultural atmosphere that fuelled the growing popularity of the Mini can be described as part of the 'Never had it so good' decade. Prime minister, Harold MacMillan, had uttered the phrase at a Conservative Party rally in Bedford in 1957. It is one of his most memorable quotes and alluded to a rise in wages, increased export earnings and heightened investment based on a global boom. When he said: '*Go around the country, go to the industrial towns, go to the farms and you will see a level of prosperity such as we have never had in my lifetime, nor indeed in the history of this country*', he was, in part, correct.

As the post-War shortages and gloom had eased, many people were enjoying a standard of living far in advance of what their parents and grandparents would have endured in the 1920s and '30s. It manifested itself in everyday life in a multiplicity of ways. Designer Mary Quant set women's hemlines at a provocative minimum of eight inches above the knee erasing the modesty and prudishness of bygone trends.

It was the dawning of the age of rock 'n' roll when small groups of animated British performers first began to 'cover' Americans like Elvis Preseley, Buddy Holly, and Bill Hayley's 'white' interpretation of 'black' music. With parental consent (or without) there could be unchaperoned stays at a Butlin's holiday camp, and the good times rolled that much the better for the arrival of oral contraception. Most families would have a television—the market was close to saturation by 1963. They watched programmes that dared to satirize the Establishment. That parodied the life style from which they had escaped, or promoted 'do-it-yourself' that had become a national passion in the homes many were beginning to buy. Many of those who owned a tv set would also own a car.

Perhaps it was put most succinctly by the poet, Philip Larkin, ironically, a Coventry boy educated at an institution that had vied for status with Lord's Bablake—King Henry Vlll Grammar School:

> *Sexual intercourse began*
> *In nineteen sixty three*
> *(Which was rather late for me)—*
> *Between the end of the Chatterley ban*
> *And the Beatles' first LP.*
>
> *Up till then there'd only been*
> *A sort of bargaining*
> *A wrangle for a ring*
> *A shame that started at sixteen*
> *And spread to everything.*
>
> *Then all at once the quarrel sank:*
> *Everyone felt the same,*
> *And every life became*
> *A brilliant breaking of the bank,*
> *A quite unlosable game.*

So life was never better than
In nineteen sixty three
(Though just too late for me)—
Between the end of the Chatterley ban
And the Beatles' first LP.

It was a different world.

The Mini, for all its enormous success—it was outselling BMC's winner, the Morris Minor, as early as 1960, had reached total sales of 500,000 in 1962, two million in 1969, and would continue in production until 2000—was both inappropriately engineered and a commercial disaster. Terence Beckett (later Sir) was responsible for Ford's top selling, and highly profitable, Cortina. He later became chairman of that company in Britain and went as far as to say of the Mini: *'You can track the decline of BMC from that single product . . . it was a pretty disastrous venture'.*

So what was wrong? Let us look at the engineering first. However innovative front wheel drive and the in-sump gearbox might have seemed it was a complex solution, difficult and expensive to manufacture and a nightmare to repair. A 'cheaper' and simpler location for an engine is at the rear of a car driving wheels that do not also need to be steered. The Volkswagen 'Beetle' is a classic example as, indeed, is Britain's Hillman Imp that appeared in 1963 and was the only 'home grown' rival for the Mini. The Imp used an all-aluminium, overhead camshaft engine derived from a Coventry Climax unit. This was placed longitudinally, but canted over at an angle of 45 degrees so it could be fitted in the 'boot' of bodywork slightly larger than that of BMC's car.

Admittedly, abandoning front wheel drive would have robbed the Mini of the legendary handling characteristics. These were essential elements in turning it into a world beating track and rally car. This aspect was developed, principally, by Issigonis's friend, the iconic grand prix racing car designer, John Cooper. Yet, initially, Issigonis had no intention of providing high performance. In fact, at Lord's behest, he downgraded the engine from 948 to 848 cc to slow the car down.

In any case, the cost of front wheel drive, which was escalated by the complexity of having it integral with an in-sump gearbox, could have been considerably reduced if the basic engine had been shorter (in this context, 'less wide'), the engine bay itself broader, or Issigonis's measurements for the car less dogmatically imposed. In other words, a wider bay would have permitted the use of the A Series motor but with the gearbox fitted to the end of the crankshaft, via the clutch, in the conventional way. It was the route adopted by virtually every other manufacturer in the world when they followed Fiat in recognizing the merits, displayed by Issigonis, of transverse engine/front wheel drive.

The Italian approach, crafted by Dante Giacosa, was initially marketed in 1964 as the Primula by Fiat's subsidiary, Autobianchi. It used simple, unequal drive shafts to compensate for the sideways protuberance of the gearbox. Suspension by steel assemblies was also employed and all other major manufacturers, except Citroën, adopted this material too. With his brilliance as a production engineer, Lord must have recognized the benefits of a more straightforward layout.

Moreover, there was another 'in line' option for the engine and gearbox open to Issigonis and still loosely in the spirit of Lord's insistence on the use of an existing BMC engine. He could have refined the experimental two cylinder 'A' Type the chairman had sent to Cowley for the bubble car project. Surely its successful development would not have been beyond the technical know-how within the Corporation, although Issigonis himself was weak on engine design. In truth, Lord had placed too much confidence in Issigonis; and on too many fronts.

Part of that confidence was reflected in a colossal monetary investment and the scale Lord lent to the venture by demanding 4,000 cars a week. Bill Davis was charged with organizing production and confirms the enormity of the undertaking. '*I doubt if any other vehicle had been produced in those quantities, ever. Certainly not in Europe,*' he said recently.

The development costs amounted to some £5 million and Lord authorized the expenditure of at least £10 million on the necessary tooling. He then displayed his genius for production by extending the principle of the transfer machines, that had been such a feature of the modernization of Longbridge, to body presses. Ford of America had already progressed in this direction and to follow their example he needed an entirely new plant. Quite clearly this should have been located, at best, on the Longbridge or Cowley sites, but at the very least, in the Midlands.

Government policy was that company expansion could only take place in areas of high unemployment. As a consequence, the factory was sited in the heavily Welsh-speaking, former tin plate producing, community of Llanelli, known in the latter half of the nineteenth century as 'Tinopolis'. Another, even less successful example of MacMillan's strategy, was the location of BMC's truck and tractor production at Bathgate, in West Lothian, Scotland, amidst a work force who had no experience in the field and distant from essential suppliers. As we have observed before, governments and their interventionist policies were not serving Lord well.

In Llanelli the Corporation replicated, in half scale, and alongside the Steel Company of Wales's rolling mill, a Ford plant from the suburbs of Chicago. Strip steel arrived at one end of the facility and emerged, after a flow line process, as enough floors and doors for 6,000 cars a week; once they had been railed to the Midlands. The rest of the body parts were made by Fisher and Ludlow, the standard engines with their transmissions came from Longbridge, although Morris Engines in Coventry produced some of the later, more exotic, units. Wolseley in Birmingham made the suspension.

Although the cars were assembled, on a non-marque-specific basis, at both Longbridge and Cowley, overall, it was 'scatter gun' manufacturing and that would be intrinsic to the ultimate failure of BMC and its successors.

The basic construction technique for the monocoque was to spot weld the structure along external seams. It was cheap and it leaked. Not that a severe ingress of water was the only problem with the early Mini.

Even before production began there was a dramatic and extremely costly *volte-face* on the material for the gearbox and clutch casings. Super-light electron was to have been used but normal testing failed to reveal the material's propensity for corroding in damp environments. However, after 1,000 engine units had been built, last minute trials in the Indian monsoons showed the castings did, indeed, crumble. A switch to aluminium resulted.

When the cars themselves emerged there was difficulty disengaging the clutch and with the gear change itself. The distributor was prone to being drenched in road water splashing through the grille, the coolant pump squealed and there was a myriad of rattles and minor faults. The most significant shortcoming though was the flooding of the passenger compartment. Motoring correspondents who had whinged for years about BMC's lack of imagination were now on a different tack. *The Autocar's* writer complained bitterly of floor wells awash with rainwater that was also trapped inside the doors.

Bill Boddy, editor of Motor Sport and one of the most vituperative critics of the British industry and all its works, had, on this occasion, a lighter touch: '*When driving the "world's most exciting car" I found it to live up to its reputation—part of the excitement being to see which foot got wet first'.* The design inadequacies were so severe that solving the problem of leakage was extremely difficult, but the most damning aspect was that Issigonis had been warned repeatedly, prior to production, that water ingress was an issue.

Martin Adeney, with massive understatement in *'The Motor Makers'*, describes the situation as bespeaking Issigonis's 'carelessness'. It was not 'carelessness' but incompetence; both as an engineer and a senior executive. BMC would pay dearly for it. As a whole, the story of Issigonis and the Mini reveals the contempt with which Issigonis regarded the customer and his, and particularly 'her', views. This too was to cost the Corporation dear.

Why Lord did not curb the designer is a mystery. It is hard to believe he was overawed by the camp charm and the self generated mantle of genius. Less so that he was impressed by Issigonis's coterie of influential and aristocratic friends and the way he manipulated and fawned over them. We could argue that after Pomeroy's tirade at the 1955 motor show, and the opportunity presented by a revised post-Suez market, Lord imposed a debilitating urgency on the Mini project.

It is also possible that having given the green light to the Mini he relied too heavily on the judgment of Harriman, who was himself in awe of Issigonis; or simply, to coin a popular expression, he didn't want *'to keep a dog and bark himself'*. It could even be, we are witnessing the first signs of a decline in Lord's health and a lessening in his hyper-activity.

If Issigonis's personality dogged the execution of the Mini, that of others did likewise for its marketing. Harriman would have set the price. It was he who, when presented with the original costing (about £600 on the road), scrawled across the bottom of the memo: *'Knock a hundred quid off.'* Yet once again we cannot absolve Lord from responsibility. As the man in charge all the decisions were ultimately his.

At first the basic model cost £350, the de luxe £390 with purchase tax adding £147 to both. Three years later, the prices were reduced to totals of £448 and £535 respectively. The figures meant that in the worst cases—basic car, discounted, and with no extras such as a heater or radio added—each Mini sold lost the company about £30. It is thought that under the most favourable circumstances the model may have earned a profit of around £15 per vehicle. But this estimate is extremely questionable because of the inadequacies of BMC's accounting systems.

There are a number of reasons why the costing was so disastrously wide of the mark. The traditional accounting approach at Longbridge was on a historical basis that costed the product at the end of the build process, rather than, and as at Ford, by calculating the charge for the various elements and working towards an adjustable, and thus viable, target cost. Even the Nuffield Organization's cost analysis, imbued as it was with the financial astuteness of William Morris, is generally regarded as being superior to that at Austin.

It was Frank Griffiths, Lord's long term head of manufacturing planning and subsequently the production development department, who said: *'Accountants are just bloody historians. They can't tell you what anything costs, but after you've made it they will record it for posterity'.* But irrespective of historical costing, Lord believed, and therefore so would Harriman, that low prices produced volume and high output would, in itself, achieve profitability.

He may have based this philosophy on Morris's actions shortly after WW1 and which we have already considered—slashing the prices of the Cowley and Oxford models to stimulate phenomenal sales. But the circumstances were radically different from those facing Lord in 1959. Morris had few competitors who could offer a car as practical and reliable as his own. He was ruthless in driving down his suppliers' prices and he had accommodating dealers prepared to take a cut in commission. Lord was confronted by competitors who had cars on a par with, if not superior to, BMC's, a haphazard, inefficient, supply chain and a dealer network that lacked confidence in the new model. In a nutshell, albeit a simplification, the more he made the more money he would lose.

Another idea he may have had was part of Herbert Austin's approach, and undoubtedly that of Morris also. Austin believed that the man or woman who bought a 'Seven' ought to 'graduate' to, or be 'inherited by', an Austin Ten and subsequently the larger types. While there was a great deal of such loyalty still around in the 1950s and '60s, after Lord's day the range became increasingly contradictory and divorced from what the market demanded. This was compounded, of course, by appalling build quality. Thus, and particularly as regards the larger cars where the margins were better, there were not the correct models for those customers who were actually committed to BMC marques.

In addition, there was little understanding of marketing techniques. No research into what the customers wanted or what they were prepared to pay. Issigonis would have seen to that: '*A designer has only to make a good car that satisfies* him *and if he is a practical man it will satisfy the world. I have never had any ambition in my life except to satisfy myself and never think of a new car in terms of the people who are going to buy it*'.

One further, highly cynical, view is that quite apart from the lack of an intelligent approach to marketing that involved customer consultation, an overly large sales force was too concerned with spectacular stunts for dealers and providing itself with an easy time. To that end the sales team insisted on a price tag below £500 for the Mini and thus under Ford's base line, and a malleable Harriman bowed to the pressure. To do justice to Lord, it should be said that he would not have priced the Mini at just below £500 solely in the ill-conceived belief that volume could achieve profitability, or, to accommodate salesmen. It was more complicated than that.

Ford, whose Popular was one of Britain's, if not the world's, cheapest cars had been encroaching on the Corporation's market for some time. For example, a 14% share of all sales at the end of the war doubled in less than a decade with an even more impressive rise in profit. The Popular, and its slightly more up-market close relatives, were extremely basic, if not primitive cars. But at almost exactly the same time as the Mini was being unveiled, Dagenham launched an extremely attractive, but mechanically conventional—and that is an important point—small saloon.

The wraps were taken off the Anglia 105E at the 1959 London motor show. It had a new, and what was to become an extremely successful, 997 cc overhead valve, four-cylinder, engine placed, longitudinally, at the front. It was attached to British Ford's first four-speed gearbox and drove the rear wheels. There was independent front suspension by MacPherson strut with traditional semi-elliptic leaf springs supporting an equally time-honoured live back axle. Of equal note was a stylish body, characterized by a reverse rake to the rear window and a continuation of the 'three box' (engine bay, passenger compartment, boot) approach that featured on the previous series. BMC were, of course, following Farina's 'two box' theme for the new A40, to be continued by Issigonis.

The new Ford cost £589 in basic form.

Clearly, Lord had to seize this market for extremely basic, but practical, personal transport in the vein of the original Austin Seven, if he was to achieve the overall volume he needed, even if it meant making a 'loss leader'. It is of interest, but of no particular relevance, because their day was rapidly passing, and import duties enter the equation, that the Mini was cheaper by as much as £140 than some bubble cars!

Another important point relating to pricing is, for all its innovaton, the Mini looked as if it was going to be extremely hard to sell. A pre-production example had been taken to the British Grand Prix on the Aintree circuit, near Liverpool, in July 1959. It aroused little or no interest, only some amusement. At the launch of the 'Seven' to the non-specialist press the journalists were reluctant to take a drive, while dealers were decidedly unenthusiastic. One wrote: '*Mr Issigonis has had applause in the British auto press for his work on the chassis (sic) and engine but if he is also responsible for the body then it is impossible to see how one designer can succeed in one direction and be so lamentable in another*'.

So what was the problem in this case? The lack of refinement in the finish was off-putting. To be fair to Harriman, he had raised this very point and been put down by Issigonis with the arrogant and intimidating words: '*If you do anything to that car, I'm leaving*'. The public, who were used to solid, if unimaginatively engineered, British cars, also seemed concerned that they would be vulnerable in a crash. To a large extent they were correct. Issigonis's stance that he didn't design cars to have accidents was scant comfort.

But perhaps most importantly, the customers were deeply suspicious of front wheel drive, although there was nothing particularly new about it. In pre-War America, prestigious manufacturers Cord and Ruxton had been firmly committed, while in the same era and same country, the Miller was a spectacular racer that used this transmission. At home, BSA, who owned Daimler, had offered a pleasant little three-wheeled car of this type from 1929. It gained an additional wheel in 1931 and endured alongside rear wheel drive cousins throughout the '30s. Although BSA can claim to be the world's first volume producer of fwd cars, the volumes were not very great, which reflects the general prejudice.

Undoubtedly the most high profile British front wheel drive car was the F series 12/50 Alvis of 1928-30. This was a controversial machine to say the least. Highly innovative, fast and complex, it initially had favourable reviews. Montagu Tombs for *The Autocar* spoke of '*absolutely no new vices*' for ordinary drivers under ordinary conditions, '*wonderful comfort*', a '*billiard table*' ride and an ability to corner 20% faster than in conventional cars. However, Jean-Albert Gregoire, the world-renowned French fwd pioneer, felt Alvis had applied orthodox technology to a new concept, while in 1989 the *Bulletin* of The Alvis Register was more brutal: '*The rear suspension is terrible . . . the suspension tends to "wind up" with extremely sudden onset. The first you know is when the car hits you violently in the backside. Then the car hops and judders along with its tail in the air until the whole outfit grinds to a halt or the driver takes the brakes off*'.

In truth, Tombs's ordinary motorists found they needed an entirely different driving technique and in the year motor insurance became compulsory in Britain (1928), brokers were swift to penalize front wheel drive owners. Naturally, the reputation endured and was prevalent, even as late as 1959, amongst many of those with an interest in automotive matters.

It is all these issues Lord was forced to address. Whether he did so realistically is for the reader to assess. Suffice to say that when the Mini alone took 19% of the market for BMC, over just one month, in 1960, Terence Beckett, then heading the planning department at Ford, had the company buy the model and strip it. It was this well qualified economist and engineer who calculated the Corporation was losing £30 per car and felt it could have added that sum to the price and not lost a single sale. Furthermore, there were opportunities to reduce the build cost.

These stark impressions were actually conveyed to Harriman by Ford assistant managing director, Allan Barke. Yet, and no doubt buoyed by the growing success of the Mini, the Corporation's deputy chief adhered to the view that sooner or later volume would lead to profitability. This was unquestionably also Lord's opinion.

Such was Dagenham's understandable fascination with BMC's affairs that in 1963, after Lord had retired, Beckett's successor, Frank Harris, wrote a paper on their rival's finances. When the then Ford chairman, Sir Patrick Hennessy, read it he took the almost unbelievable step of again contacting Harriman and warning him that the Mini was so under-priced that, not only was BMC heading for bankruptcy, but the profits of the whole of the mass production motor industry was suffering as it tried to compete.

The Mini continued to thrill and delight, even if it didn't make any money. There was a multiplicity of variants. When production ceased a total of five-and-a-half million had been built. It had been, and still is, a symbol of many things.

Chapter Twenty Five

A SMASHING TIME

When Leonard Lord retired in 1961, the British Motor Corporation went into terminal decline. This says a great deal about the two key figures that succeeded him, George Harriman and Alec Issigonis. But it is not the whole picture. The legacy left by Lord contained both positive and negative elements.

On his departure, Lord assumed the honorary title of vice-president. Lord Nuffield had a similar position, designated president. When Morris died, on August 22, 1963, Lord took over that role in the October. By then, driven by the patronage of celebrities and the cultural environment within the nation, the Mini was gaining in popularity. The last new car of Lord's tenure was to be almost as successful. Code named ADO 16 the '1100' was launched on August 15, 1962. It was badged first as a Morris then, in October, as a more sporting MG. A year later an Austin and up-market Vanden Plas version arrived in September and October respectively. 1100 clones of the remaining makes from the BMC portfolio—Riley and Wolseley—followed in 1965.

In essence the cars were enlarged Minis but pleasantly styled by Farina and with a revolutionary inter-connected suspension system from Alex Moulton called Hydrolastic that used fluid as the operating medium. In its 12-year life the 1100 was consistently Britain's top-selling small saloon and was a major contributor to the Corporation becoming Europe's third largest motor manufacturer with 35% of the domestic market. But many of the issues that bedeviled BMC remained. The margins were too small to maintain profitability. Some of the vehicles, because of their complexity, were too expensive to make, and the arrogance of Issigonis and the ineptitude of Harriman meant that a model like the 1100 was not revised and up-dated sufficiently to preserve its competitiveness.

The sum result was that in 1967 BMC recorded a deficit. Ironically it was the year Leonard Lord died.

He had closed his Longbridge office door for the last time in November, 1961. As a mark of respect, Harriman kept the room completely intact until after Lord's death. A further expression of his affection for his former mentor and protector came some seven months after Lord's retirement when he arranged an appreciation dinner. This event was prompted by Lord having been elevated to the peerage in May 1962. It took place at the Jacobean-style Welcombe Hotel standing in 157 lush acres near Stratford-upon-Avon. The evening was 'hosted' by all the Corporation's board members on the basis that Harriman made them pay £11 10s (£11.50p) to be so defined. Among those arrayed in the oak panelled dining room, looking over the Italian garden, was Issigonis. Harriman, now chairman, had made the latter technical director with a seat on the Austin board almost as soon as Lord left. He became a BMC board member in 1963.

As the company got into its stride after these upheavals Harriman and Issigonis proved themselves to be just as autocratic as Lord. But the former lacked both the skill and decisiveness of his predecessor and the latter had no idea as to how a business should be run. As we already know, George William Harriman, the 23-shillings-a-week apprentice, first encountered Lord at Hotchkiss.

He was born on March 3, 1908, and by coincidence, like Lord, had been a pupil at Bablake School. Quite unlike Lord, he was suave, good looking, and had a passion for rugby. He captained both the Coventry and Warwickshire teams and turned out for England against 'The Rest' at Twickenham in 1933. All these swoon-inducing attributes, combined with the mellow Coventry lilt of his voice, endeared him to young women but at least one of his liaisons was not particularly wholesome.

From very early on he was Lord's protégé. The tragedy was that in commercial and industrial terms Harriman was 'ever the bridesmaid . . . '. His misfortune was that he was an excellent deputy but never the calibre of the chief he became. His personality though, was useful. His subtlety and gentler manner often proved a palliative for his hero's directness and, what could be bruising, approach. They were the perfect pair; a winning combination.

Like Herbert Austin before him, and indeed, William Morris, Lord was a man who 'walked the job'. Harriman's style was different, infuriating men like Etheridge by talking of 'emoluments' instead of wages. Yet, we should not under-estimate him. When Harriman arrived at Longbridge he was placed in charge of the tool room, a skilled and important job. He was a well-trained and sound engineer, qualities he managed to combine with boardroom charm.

Issigonis for his part was increasingly distancing himself from the customers, their expectations and market trends; sitting in meetings doodling on a note pad, deaf to all that was said. To reiterate the jist of Hanks's comment to William Morris—fiddling while Rome burned. Harriman, hanging on almost every syllable the technical director uttered, was now divorcing himself from an increasingly militant work force and the realities that would place ever-greater pressure on the business.

One disastrous model began to follow another. Not conceptually catastrophic. That would be unfair to Issigonis. But calamitous in their execution and, thereafter, in the eyes of observers whether they be customers or the press.

The Austin 1800 of 1964 was potentially a world-beater. The monocoque was so rigid it achieved the kind of technical breakthrough only equalled when designers had moved from ladder to cruciform braced frames or abandoned the bolt-on body. Mathematically the structure was about three times stronger, torsionally, than the equivalent Ford.

The 1800 had its roots in the quest for a car that could replace BMC's Farina-styled, medium-sized saloons—the Mark II A55 and then A60 Cambridge. The original thinking had centred on another rear wheel drive, but with fwd becoming the preferred format, Lord, who was still very much in command in the planning stages, wanted to proceed in that direction. Of two prototypes, it was decided to opt for the in-house, rather than Farina, design, but finely tuned by the Italian.

Six inches more wheelbase was achieved in a car that at 13ft 8ins overall was 10 inches shorter than the Austin Cambridge and at 5ft 7ins was nearly four inches wider. Meanwhile the bored out (80.26 x 88.9mm) B Series engine, used in the MGB sports car, was revamped to the extent of making room for five main bearings. This was possible because of an earlier expedient of siamesing the cylinders, which meant one water space could be wrapped around two bores thus saving the space of individual water jackets. The overall result was a smoother running motor that, even with just one SU carburettor, delivered 85 bhp at 5,300 rpm. It translated into a sparkling 90 mph backed by the confidence provided by disc brakes at the front and servo assistance.

Suspension was Alex Moulton's Hydrolastic system, but with the units in transverse tubes. The forward one was welded to the bulkhead and it was this arrangement that so greatly helped rigidity. The subframes necessary on the Mini and 1100 could be deleted and with the body strengthened appropriately, the stresses from the springing were transmitted into an immensely stiff cell formed by the centre portion of the whole car.

Stable, sure-footed and intrinsically safe; lively, yet refined with brilliant handling; remarkably commodious and revolutionary looking—was this just too much car for the money; or not enough? Issigonis had moved the 1800 away from what was accepted as the realm of the medium saloon—about 1600 cc and a 100-inch wheelbase—that it was intended to replace. Yet it had not, in the customer's view, ascended into Westminster territory, although the 1800 had almost as much space. Worse, the car was nearly 15% more expensive than the worthy, if a trifle uninspiring, Cambridge. (Mid-term about £883 for a basic model as opposed to £768 for the A60).

The 1800, now often called the 'land crab'* after a remark by an Australian photo-journalist who, from a helicopter, saw one cornering sideways on a rally and thought it looked like the crustacean, was heading for an identity crisis. BMC could not now drop the Cambridge. To do so would have left a revenue-haemorrhaging gap in the model range between the successful 1100 and the astonishing but much less populist 1800. So the A60 was kept on after the launch of the 1800 in August 1964 and left its new stablemate feeling like a spare crab at a clambake.

The Austin dealers, however, were confident. Their Morris colleagues had received the 1100 exclusively for a year and the Austin network was now allowed the 1800 to themselves for two, emphasizing that debilitating philosophy of maintaining two separate structures. They told Harriman they could sell 4,000 of the new model a year. This was to be far from the case. From day one they had difficulty moving the new Austin.

Unfortunately there were issues concerning build quality. The model suffered from profligate oil consumption. Perhaps because the dipsticks had the full mark too high, or, according to an alternative version, the marker was reversible but only calibrated on one side, so an over-diligent owner could readily add an excess of lubricant. There were also electrical problems and the wishy-washy, cable-operated, gear change never worked properly.

The agents estimated that about 15% of the selling price on 50% of the cars was absorbed in pre-sale rectification. Even so, the 1800 was voted 1965 European Car of the Year and it was tragic that many of the barriers to its market success were not removed at source. These included a steering column that replicated the very upright, canted, poise of the Mini. This gave the impression, at least, of an uncomfortable driving position, unacceptable to customers prepared to pay a lot of money for a vehicle for long distance motoring. It was compounded by the heaviness of the action itself despite gearing which necessitated nearly four turns of the wheel, lock-to-lock.

Some of the minor controls were not well designed either. The handbrake, for example, tucked away under the centre of the commendable, full width, parcel shelf; the heater controls

---

* This was never BMC terminology and only became common later.

a grope away near the passenger's knee and the cold start pull nestling forgettably low down, alongside the steering column.

But as Issigonis was to point out when it was suggested that the fascia looked like a washing machine and female motorists may not wish to be reminded of domestic chores when driving: *'I don't want bloody women driving my cars'*. The technical director had a similar contempt for his colleagues. Just one example concerns the stock of 1,000 front seats being accumulated for the ADO 16 (Morris 1100) launch cars. Surreptitiously, overnight and without any consultation with Frank Griffiths's production planning department, Issigonis added a pelmet to conceal the frame on the outer side of the squab on the press preview cars. Griffiths discovered the change by accident and production chaos ensued. The seats that had previously been a universal design were now 'handed'. Those in stock at Cowley had to be retrieved and modified and the moulds and machines altered. This is one of many instances of lack of forethought, followed by high-handedness, and is estimated to have added 0.5% to what would already have been considerable development expenses, and a further £25,000 to the tooling costs. It is reputed Griffiths was 'incandescent' with rage!

The market-place disappointment of the 1800 was trumped, in 1967, by a three-litre saloon. This was a 'pet project' of Harriman that produced not only an ugly, highly unpopular car, but also an illogical one, at odds with the Issigonis philosophy. It used the 1800's central section with a boot and bonnet designed jointly by Farina and Burzi. Power came from a longitudinally mounted version of the C Series engine and there was Hydrolastic suspension. Although the model handled and rode well, there were few takers in the large, luxury saloon, market and it was dropped when British Leyland was formed.

The Austin Maxi that followed in 1969 was much more likely to succeed than the Three Litre. It was one of the very first 'tailgated' saloons in the world with tremendous potential amongst customers seeking a moderately priced, highly versatile load carrier or leisure vehicle. Basically it was a scaled down 1800 driven by a four cylinder, overhead camshaft engine of, at first, 1500cc, then 1750 and defined as the E Series. The motor had originally been developed with the Australian, New Zealand and South African markets also in mind and with the potential for a six cylinder from the same tooling. In the Maxi it drove a trend-setting five-speed gearbox that relied on the disastrous cable change technology of the 1800.

When released, the car proved under-powered with extremely unsatisfactory and troublesome gear selection. Although subsequently improved, it never recovered from the initial public disillusionment.

It is interesting to digress at this point and consider another engine that was a candidate for the Maxi. It was secretly developed under Lord in 1956, was far superior to the 'E' but was subsequently rejected by Issigonis with the complicity of Harriman. It was the work of Dr Duncan Stuart, a colleague of John Weaving of gas turbine fame, in East Works Research. Laid out as a 1,200 cc V4 of equal bore and stroke ('square') it had twin overhead camshafts driven by rubber belts. The gearbox casing was cast integrally with the crankcase and the engine bay 'footprint' was little more than 16 inches square. Free revving and smooth running, power output was around 75 brake horsepower as opposed to about 69 for the 1500 'E'.

More importantly, Stuart's design avoided the major problems that were to bedevil the engine Issigonis chose. Pivotal among these was the need to fit the unit transversely with room for a radiator mounted at the side. The E Series, and indeed the 1800's B Type-derived motor, were shortened by siamesing the cylinders so eliminating two of the water spaces. It worked on the gutsy 1800 but when the 1,500 cc Maxi proved gutless there was insufficient metal in the block to enlarge the bores and increase the capacity—and so power—by any worthwhile amount. Furthermore, that other *bête noire*, the in-sump gearbox, impeded any plan to 'up' the cubic capacity by lengthening the stroke. These problems were compounded, of course, on the six-cylinder engine used later in the Austin and Morris 2200 and Wolseley 'Six'. However, the rather obvious solution in this case was to reposition the radiator at the front of the car!

Why none of these cars made a proper contribution to a viable future for BMC goes far beyond their mechanical and styling shortcomings. Essentially, all the familiar malaises were still present. An excess of makes, models and market outlets; a failure to commit to one type of technology—fwd or conventional rear axle transmission; disregard for rivals' strengths, most notably the Ford Cortina's suitability in the burgeoning and lucrative fleet sector; an over-staffed, inefficient, manufacturing structure and, of course, lamentable quality.

Martin Adeney might regard incidents like the profusion of leaks in the Mini's 'hull' as carelessness on Issigonis's part. But, I repeat, it was the product of outright incompetence and his ineffective management. While the faults themselves may not be catastrophic, the effect on the public image is disproportionately serious. Just how badly built BMC's, and then British Leyland's, cars were in the 1960s and '70s is often overlooked now that the classic car movement has embraced and lent a roseate tint to the proportionally few survivors.

As a young motoring correspondent I tested many of these vehicles. They developed electrical problems, the ancillaries fell apart and in one case a camshaft detached itself from its drive mechanism. It is also worth noting that these were the vehicles presented to showcase the range, and although it maybe coincidence, such shortcomings did not generally afflict Fords, Vauxhalls or the Continental competition. Meanwhile, I was bombarded by complaints from my readership who, having made one of the largest financial outlays of their life, found themselves owning a sub-standard product and receiving little interest or sympathy from the manufacturer.

It is debatable whether Leonard Lord could be described as marketing orientated in the accepted sense: '*Make proper bloody products and you don't need salesman*'. But he certainly respected the customers. This is typified by the care expended over a letter received in 1945 suggesting Arnhem and Alamein as model names. He dictated a charming response, included £10 in the envelope and, according to protocol, recorded the proposals with the Society of Motor Manufacturers and Traders (SMMT).

But when Lord left, and with Harriman displaying little control, Issigonis was free to show his deep-seated contempt for the clients both at home and abroad. An excellent indication of the attitude that was allowed to permeate the Corporation is given by Jean-Pierre de Vries, whose family were Austin agents for the whole of France for more than 50 years. Mr de Vries and his brother, François, both did a year's training at Longbridge in the 1950s. '*It was the best part of my life*', says Jean-Pierre.

Their father, Charles, was a veteran of the horrific First World War Verdun campaign, then became a flier and motor trade entrepreneur, before being copiously decorated by General de Gaulle for his heroism in WWII. I mentioned him earlier in connection with Alan Hess and 'The Seven Capitals' run. Jean-Pierre describes Charles's enlightened business philosophy: '*He used to say that he would rather sell just 10 cars a year at a profit than 100 at a loss. In addition, he was very concerned about customer care and the relationship with his clients and conscious of being vulnerable to unscrupulous staff*'.

By 1927 his business had become centred on the French capital and that year, while running a stand for Rootes at the Paris Salon, he met fellow exhibitor Herbert Austin. A deal was struck whereby de Vries became the Austin dealer for France. In the mid-'50s the business was based in the fashionable Parisien suburb of Neuilly trading as Afiva (*Association Française de l'Importation Vehicules Austin*). The elegant street where the garage still stands links a corner of the Bois de Boulogne to the smart shopping district. At its peak Afiva employed 85 people. There were workshops on Avenue Charles de Gaulle, the main thoroughfare from the city centre to what is now the prestige business development of La Défense. Charles de Vries used to like to claim that in Paris he *was* 'Mr Austin'.

Says Jean-Pierre: '*He was enormously proud of the marque and described the Austin company as his third son. He was passionate to a fault in his loyalty, as subsequent events would prove. He actually liked everything to have an "A" on it and joked that his wife's name was Alice for that reason. There was an "A" on his watch and on the carpets at Neuilly'*. Interestingly, Charles de Vries was a great admirer of Lord who made a gift of a blue and white Austin Sheerline to the dealer's wife.

Jean-Pierre, who always travelled to Longbridge with his father to act as interpreter, describes one encounter: '*We had been at the Works all day, but couldn't get an appointment to see Leonard Lord. My father had his suitcase in his hand and we were ready to leave when the great man suddenly emerged from his office. He insisted we came home with him and stayed overnight'*.

Contact with the cars themselves though, was not so amicable. '*We had another Sheerline for the Paris Salon with coachwork by Sauochik. We liked to raise at least one of the models off the floor with the in-built hydraulic jacks. But on this example, rather than lift off the ground it simply flooded the parquet with fluid'*, continues Jean-Pierre. '*That was the first year we took the Sauochik car, but because it failed to sell we did a respray to make it look like a fresh example and took it back next time. We did that for a couple of years and eventually it did find a home. It featured an electric roof and unfortunately the first time it rained and the new owner tried to get the top closed the mechanism jammed it half way'*.

Even today, mention the name Austin in France and just one model out of the multiplicity of types is recalled—the Mini. Jean-Pierre is swift to confirm it was also the de Vries's favourite. '*A lot of Parisien celebrities either lived near the garage or knew us so it was easy to place a car with people like the manager of Maxim's or the actress Michèle Morgan. When it was seen in these glamorous circles it boosted sales to more ordinary customers'*.

Jean-Pierre's revelations about both his tutelage at Longbridge and his subsequent dealings with the company are worth noting. Training first. '*There were some "ups and downs". On a light note, I went in one day wearing a red tie and my immediate managers said: "Pierre, why do you wear such a bright red tie?"* I replied, jokingly, that it was because I was a Communist. '*The next day they were not speaking to me and I asked the supervisor for the explanation. When he told me I went and explained: "I am not a Communist. I would not speak to Communists. I am a Trotskyite."* That seemed to satisfy them!

'*On another occasion management wanted to establish how many components of different types could reasonably be made in an hour, so they asked the apprentices to turn out the different parts. In every case the engineering apprentices' output was considerably up on what the ordinary worker was achieving. There would have been a walk-out if it had not been conceded that the apprentices could make more because they were doing it "for fun" and the lower figure was acceptable if you were engaged on serious production'*.

The conclusions that can be drawn from these comments are obvious. But Jean-Pierre also has some astonishing disclosures about the company as it metamorphosed from BMC to British Leyland and then to Austin Rover. '*You got the impression no one at Longbridge really understood the French scene. A simple example is that one August we were asked to provide 59 drivers to deliver some Minis around France. Where do you get 59 drivers in France in August? The country is "closed"* *for the vacation! Much more serious was the cars we were being sent and the state they were in. The design of most of the models was 15 years out of date. They would arrive on the transporter with, typically, a card on the dashboard—"no reverse gear". At one point you would be lucky to get a new Jaguar* from Neuilly to the Arc de Triomphe (about 1.5 miles) without it breaking down.*

'*We would be told by Longbridge not to worry, because any work needed was covered by the guarantee. Of course, it never was. There would be up to nine hours labour in some of those rectifications. The allowance for warranty work on an Austin was about £50 and on a Jaguar around £200. On a Toyota it was just £3 because all you need do was change the oil and set the distributor points. Even if we could have endured the labour costs though, the parts were not available. Fourteen weeks for an Austin clutch would be the norm, throughout which we would be providing the customer with a car*'.

The relationship grew increasingly onerous. '*You seemed to be forever changing the signage; the contracts were becoming increasingly intricate whereas my father had been used to working on what was almost a "gentleman's agreement". We were often close to bankruptcy,*' continues Jean-Pierre. Because of Charles de Vries's devotion to Longbridge he continued as the distributor, but matters were to deteriorate further.

'*Eventually the whole of France was divided into four sectors and Paris itself split into another two. In addition, other franchisees were brought in and it really became unviable. Soon after, the Morris distributor pulled out and signed with the Japanese*'. While the de Vries brothers' father was alive they kept their dealership but by 1985 even they had had enough and Afiva closed.

Along with Emil Frey in Switzerland, the de Vries family had been the longest serving overseas Austin distributors in the world. It is interesting that Frey has been quoted as saying many of the same things as Jean-Pierre—that reliability and finish was not comparable with the competition; 10-15% of the retail price was absorbed in pre-delivery work and he could have used a squad of Longbridge mechanics to rectify the cars.

It is a tragic story. It reveals in striking terms the lack of awareness within BMC and its successors of the growing importance of Europe. In addition, the lack of concern for, or empathy with, their 'front line troops' who, in many cases, were amongst the most loyal. '*If they had built and marketed the Mini as it is produced today (by BMW, my insertion), we would have made a fortune*', says Jean-Pierre.

By the 1960s the situation at home was now so bad that even Lord decided to have the registration mark BMC 1 removed from his Vanden Plas Princess R on the grounds that it constantly attracted irate customers.

It is quite impossible to ignore the fact that disastrous labour relations through the 1960s and '70s went hand in hand with atrocious quality and all the other issues to bring about the demise of what had been BMC. When British prime minister, Clement Attlee, took office in 1945 he was an idealist. By the time he was ousted in 1951 he had almost certainly come to realize that, in the main, the British working class did not share his ethical vision. To return to Correlli Barnett's quote: '*Measures to sustain a wartime sense of community, instead of transforming people into active citizens, foundered in the face of apathy*'.

Long before this, the Socialist and trade union firebrand, Ernest Bevin, must have been acutely embarrassed, as wartime coalition minister of labour, to discover that 79,000 days lost

---

*   Jaguar and its allied companies, Daimler, Coventry Climax and commercial vehicle maker Guy merged with BMC and Pressed Steel in 1966 to form British Motor Holdings.

to industrial action in engineering alone, when he took office in 1940, rose to 318,000 in 1941, peaked at 600,000 in 1944 and returned to about 318,000 the following year.

We can be in no doubt that Dick Etheridge, who did not retire as Longbridge Works convenor until 1975, was a highly principled idealist. Others were not of the same calibre. Another Communist, Derek Robinson, succeeded Etheridge. He was eventually dubbed 'Red Robbo' by the press on account of his militancy.

According to Etheridge's son, Robinson first came to his father's notice as a young, fiery, shop steward in his late 20s or early 30s. '*Dad told me that he (*Robinson*) had potential but needed to be given responsibility within the collective. He took him under his wing and guided and trained him. They had something of a father/son relationship and Dad was determined to calm some of the wild ways.*

'*Dad certainly groomed him for succession by giving him early responsibility within the shop stewards' committee and it became obvious that there were few others who had similar natural leadership qualities. Whilst Derek had his detractors in management he also had his admirers and at least one stated publicly that he was misunderstood and that he was a skilled negotiator.*

'*His rise to fame—and infamy—after Dad retired was partly accident and partly self-inflicted. He was heavily criticised by the extreme Left for losing touch with the workforce and this was in no small part due to his failure to "keep his friends close and his enemies closer", something Dad instilled into the shop stewards at Longbridge and elsewhere*'.

Robinson's reign had promising beginnings. With a sympathetic, Harold Wilson-led, Labour government in power, the National Enterprise Board (NEB) was established with the fundamental and very positive belief that for British industry to perform effectively, the energy and enthusiasm of workers needed to be harnessed through the co-operation of trade unions. Soon after the formation of the NEB its president, a paper company executive called Sir Don Ryder, led an investigation into the future of BMC, by now the British Leyland Motor Corporation (BLMC).

In effect, the Ryder Report recommended nationalization brought about by a major investment of government money. More than £1,200m over eight years was to be devoted to capital expenditure and a further £260m provided as working capital. The only condition for the funding was there should be tangible evidence of increased productivity and an improvement in industrial relations. At the time strikes were costing the company an average of 7.5 million man-hours a year and around 15% of its production.

However, the report was also wildly over-optimistic over BLMC's prospects. It foresaw it capturing at least a third share of the British market when, in reality, its holding was already declining. It also expected it to expand its stake in the Western European market from three to four per cent, which would have called for the considerable increase in production of 200,000 cars a year. Nonetheless, Robinson and other trade unionists were included in the deliberations of the NEB. It was the most important advance towards participative management the movement had ever witnessed.

Tragically for an industry that was capitalist, and continues to be so in the western world, Robinson's interest was in destroying that system, not being constructively involved in what was one of his country's core activities. '*I was quite prepared to lead a mighty orchestration of workers so we could smash the social contract*', he said, in 1977. He was alluding to a policy that was very much part of Harold Wilson's ethos of decency, and intended to restrain union wage claims, often in excess of 30%, when inflation ran at 25%.

What Robinson achieved between 1978-9, supported by a hard core of like-minded shop stewards, was 523 stoppages and an estimated loss of £200m worth of production. In general terms, he created a situation where the shop floor could not be controlled by the unions themselves, certainly not by a Left-leaning head of BLMC like Donald Stokes; not even by government.

More specifically, Robinson played a major part in destroying the Corporation. Ironically, he also had a key role in emaciating and rendering ineffective the trade union movement in Great Britain. Eventually, under Michael Edwardes, who took over the chairmanship of the floundering behemoth in 1977, Robinson was sacked. Men who had followed him through the gates over grievances they were not even aware existed, expressed their deep felt view of the convenor in the inevitable furore that followed his dismissal. In the ballot for a strike in support of their leader 600 approved, *14,000* demurred.

The public at large reflected the sentiments. Men and women who wanted BLMC cars and had been exposed to the attitude from striking workers— *'let the buggers wait'*—had not waited. They had gone down the high street to a Japanese or continental European dealer and bought a model that suited them, in the colour they chose, and which was available virtually the same day.

In areas of high unemployment—Northern Ireland, South Wales, North East England—the rank and file were incredulous as to why fellow citizens who had highly paid work, would *not* work. The reputation of British industry, or that of the trade union movement ever recovered. Sociologically, that is more unfortunate than the tyranny of Robinson. But let us not forget, very little of this scenario should be attributed to Leonard Lord. As well as being laid at the door of Derek Robinson, it has to be said, that originally and by implication, it was the work of Dick Etheridge, while Harriman's ineffective management in the previous decade is also considerably to blame.

Yet, to be fair, and as Dick Etheridge junior has emphasised to me, Robinson was elected by ballot amongst the Works committee, who in turn were elected by shop floor ballot. Their influence was the 'will of the people' (or at least some of them). Harriman and Issigonis emerged through the undemocratic 'king making' process. Etheridge, as interpreted by his son, has a more generous assessment of Robinson than mine.

'During the Austin-Rover period it was believed by many, including my father, that Derek had allowed too many of his friends from the Communist Party to surround him on the Works committee and the broader shop stewards' committee. Dad believed that it was this that clouded his judgment at times because he had too narrow a view of the collective thinking amongst the workforce. Dad was never critical of Derek in public or the press and during the week of the sacking he issued a public declaration of support for him as a man and a shop steward. He also confided to me that if he had been in Derek's shoes he would have organised a major strike to prevent Harold Wilson appointing Edwardes as chief executive'.

Chapter Twenty Six
POLITICAL FOOTBALL

Just as it has been relevant to examine how the industrial relations scene at Longbridge grew still darker after Lord's era it is appropriate to summarize the structural developments that took place in the 1960s and afterwards. One of the crucial players is Donald Stokes. As the son of Plymouth's 1930s transport manager he developed an obsession with the Leyland buses the city ran. At an early age he decided he wanted to work for the Lancashire company. As described by Graham Turner in *The Leyland Papers*, it was '*almost a sense of calling*'.

This destiny was fulfilled just before the outbreak of War. After service in the Royal North Lancashire Regiment he rejoined the firm to become, in 1946, its first export manager. His performance at selling buses was spectacular, most notably in Cuba but also across Europe, in the Middle East, Africa and even America. It earned him a seat on the board in 1953.

Throughout the 1950s Leyland took an expansionist view of life, considering a move into the manufacture of locomotive transmissions and oil well equipment as well as, at one point, a merger with Rolls-Royce. Although the latter deal fell through, Leyland took over Standard in 1961 after an abortive attempt by the Coventry firm to form a partnership with Rover.

Meanwhile, at Longbridge, Harriman was considering taking over Associated Commercial Vehicles (ACV), which was the parent company for various lorry and bus builders including AEC, Crossley and Maudslay. The approach was described, in rather poor taste, by one of ACV's directors, as: '*the best news since Hitler invaded Russia*'. What Harriman envisaged in the summer of 1961, at least as a subterfuge, was only an exchange of cab pressings plus collaboration in export markets. Maudslays were, by now, almost indistinguishable from AECs and Crossley had faded from the scene altogether. It was now that the waters were muddied by the hand of none other than BMC's vice president, Leonard Lord.

Lord was still very much in the picture. He attended important meetings and when the press were present chided them from his seat at the oaken table with having nothing more interesting to report. As it happened, there was much of interest for their shorthand to record. Lord was created a baron in 1962 and introduced to the House of Lords as Baron Lambury of Northfield on May 17. His sponsors were Lord Brabazon of Tara and Lord Kindersley. Lord Brabazon was chairman of ACV and the banker, Kindersley, held a similar position at Rolls-Royce. No doubt flushed with *bon homie* on the occasion of Lord's investiture, the three men formulated, in the noble corridors of the Palace of Westminster, a revised and much more ambitious deal than that being considered at Longbridge.

Rolls-Royce came back into the picture and Harriman was forced to present a proposal whereby Rolls-Royce's motor car division would be turned into an independent company with BMC as the majority shareholder; the Rolls-Royce oil engine plant at Shrewsbury would be similarly hived off with ACV, BMC and Rolls-Royce itself each taking a stake of one third. Finally BMC was to acquire from ACV their lorry designs, thus providing a range of trucks that covered not only the light/medium commercial market, but the more rewarding heavy sector as well. Whether or not the scheme was realistic is debatable. Sir William Black, managing director of ACV (not to be confused with John Black in a similar role at Standard) was dubious. '*Oh for Christ's sake, give me 24 hours to think about this or you'll start a terrible gamble in ACV shares*'.

Having thought, he felt Rolls-Royce's car costs were '*frightening*' and an allegiance '*not on*'. Harriman himself concluded the figures '*just didn't look right*' and '*there was very little in it for the shareholders*'. Nonetheless, the concept was placed before the BMC board who would probably have proceeded. An as-yet unheard of non-executive member from the insurance industry called Alec Layborn torpedoed the arrangement. He counselled postponement on the grounds that BMC's figures, nine months into the financial year, were decidedly unimpressive and it would be advantageous to wait for the full term results. This created a 'window of opportunity' for Leyland, recently frustrated in a bid to align themselves with Chrysler. They moved quickly to take ACV.

Harriman, when told the news by Black, expressed his disappointment. What Lord said to Layborn when he next encountered him is not recorded, but the tenor, tone and colour is vividly imaginable.

Had the ACV/BMC/Rolls-Royce amalgamation taken place it would almost certainly have created an organization that could have resisted Leyland's later overtures and possibly averted the disastrous consequences that followed. The intervention of Layborn, who was later joined by another non-executive director, R A Stormonth Darling, points up an important issue that bedevilled industry at the time and continues to do so to this day. It is that, however sound the judgement of an experienced and qualified practitioner in any discipline may be, and Lord is the classic example, those whose métier is the nebulous, mumbo-jumbo, of the stock exchange can thwart their bedrock assessments. It was one of the reasons why Lord could not rationalize BMC in the early years and it had again blighted the Corporation's future. Layborn admitted as much and Harriman commented it was '*a legitimate mistake on our part. It might well have paid to take the risk*'.

By now BMC had acquired Pressed Steel, which meant Joe Edwards had returned to the fold. This spawns another of those stories, presumably from Edwards's lips, and recounted by Graham Turner, that are extremely difficult to accept. On the day of his return, Lord is said to have been waiting for Edwards in the *arriviste's* former office, although it is not clear why Lord should have been there, five years after resigning his executive position, apart from on the grounds of friendship and respect.

Others are present because Lord now supposedly says to Edwards: '*There is only one man in this office today whose hand I want to shake*'. This, of course, would be tantamount to an insult to everyone else. If he said, '*need to shake*' it would make much more sense as Edwards was the only newcomer. Lord is now reported as uttering the words: '*I should never have done what I did and I'm delighted to see you back*'. The first part of the sentence, again, seems unlikely given the circumstances of Edwards's dismissal.

A little later, a further exchange between the two men takes place, now in Lord's former office and in the presence of Alec Layborn. It shows Edwards in a particularly graceless light. '*Shall we tell him what we want to do about his salary, Alec?*' Lord reputedly says, innocuously enough, one would have thought. However, Turner interprets this, undoubtedly steered by Edwards, as the latter being patronized by Lord. Edwards replies, '*if there's any money in it share it between you'*—a ridiculous statement in itself. Turner interprets the episode as the 'old wounds' not having healed.

Edwards was soon installed as managing director with Harriman taking on the role of executive chairman. But, to quote Turner again: '*The joy of* (Edwards's) *homecoming soon turned sour. Harriman told Edwards that he had been talking to Stokes about a merger. Edwards, with a sinking heart, replied that he was not playing but that they had better continue to talk. To him, Stokes was a second Lord looming over the horizon: if a merger were* (sic) *arranged Stokes would clearly expect to be number two* (to Harriman) *in the new organization. Having been ousted once, Edwards was determined that the dose should not be repeated*'.

It seems quite remarkable that, as the former head of one of the leading car body makers in the industry, Edwards had no inkling as to what was afoot as regards mergers and alliances until he finds himself compromised, apparently, by Harriman. His attitude though leaves us in little doubt that any union that did take place would be an unhappy one and its possible benefits negated as a consequence. To be fair to Edwards, he took a number of long overdue steps to strengthen BMC. In the autumn of 1966 he cut 14,000 jobs. New talent from companies like Ford was hired to rejuvenate the management and he approached—unsuccessfully as it happened—the talented industrial conciliator, Jack Scamp, to take charge of industrial relations. In 1967 he laid plans to close Morris Bodies and Morris Radiators in Coventry and Oxford respectively, MG at Abingdon and Fisher and Ludlow in Castle Bromwich with the loss of a further 8,000 jobs.

At a more esoteric level, merger talks continued. Now with prime minister Harold Wilson, involved and 'batting' for Leyland on the grounds he felt Stokes best able to consolidate the British motor industry and revitalize the Corporation. Wilson asked Sir (later Lord) Frank Kearton to facilitate. Kearton was a prominent academic and industrialist but also chairman of the Industrial Reorganization Corporation (IRC) who had carried out an informal investigation into the financial affairs of both BMC and Leyland in the early summer of 1967. As Christmas approached and the share prices of the two companies drifted apart—BMC's down, Leyland's up—with the former's market share shrinking, proposals and counter proposals sped between Westminster and a variety of meeting rooms where the protagonists met or deliberated.

However, one of the major barriers had now become Edwards' refusal to work under Stokes. A take-over of BMC by Leyland, instead of an amicable union, was a possibility and both Kearton and Harriman prevailed upon Edwards to adopt a more accommodating stance. Well past midnight on the Sunday night of January 14, 1968, the interested parties gathered at Stokes's London flat in fashionable St James's. Edwards, deeply unhappy with the situation, shook hands on an arrangement where the Leyland supremo would be chief executive and managing director and Edwards joint managing director. He said he would, '*give it a go*'.

Still the wrangling continued as more worrying details of BMC's situation emerged. Late on the Monday, when the deal was almost finalized, Stokes spoke privately to Edwards. He explained that he was a 'salesman' and needed the Longbridge executive's input to run the new company. '*I'll never forgive you for what you did last night*', returned Edwards and turned away. It was another dark augury.

The planned merger was announced in the early afternoon of January 16, although it had yet to be ratified by the shareholders. There was a flurry of media optimism. British Leyland would be the second largest European motor manufacturer—Volkswagen was the biggest—Britain's fifth largest private company with a 40% share of the domestic car market and 35% of that for commercial vehicles. It aspired to £1,000m worth of annual sales, a £50m pre-tax profit and nearly half of overall market share.

'*Donald Stokes you are a bloody fool. In last Sunday's press you had more publicity than any king or queen in my time, but you ought to know that there are scores of executives at BMC who hate the sight of you even though they've never met you*'. These were the none-too-promising outpourings of Edwards at a trial joint board meeting on February 12. To an extent Harriman had goaded him. The latter had suggested that Leyland was moving inappropriately fast and that Stokes was being unjustly acclaimed as the hero of the hour. Three things were becoming increasingly apparent—Edwards could never work with Stokes, the financial and production forecasts BMC were providing were wildly optimistic and Edwards, in that experimental board meeting, had signed his own death warrant.

By mid-March supine, ill-informed, shareholders on both sides had approved the union. Edwards maintained his adverse position until, on April 18, he was removed to a consultative role. He continued for a few weeks more before telling Stokes: '*It's all yours now, the bloody lot*'. Harriman, his health destroyed by the strain of the negotiations, resigned in September.

The popular analysis is that if Joe Edwards had stayed and used his knowledge and experience of the industry in liaison with Stokes's entrepreneurial talents, the marriage of the two organizations might have worked. That may be the case. But perhaps we should cast our minds back to his dealings with Lord, in the mid-'50s and those of a decade later. The volatility, the sensitivity about hierarchy and the swiftness to take offence. In essence, the Stokes scenario is not that much different from that with Lord.

It maybe that here, and elsewhere, I judge Edwards harshly. It is certainly true that Dick Etheridge, along with many others, respected him and believed that if Lord had staid his hand in 1956, and Edwards remained, the industrial relations problems of the 60s may have been avoided and BMC escaped the clutches of Leyland.

The basis for this is that Edwards understood the Corporation, but perhaps more importantly, as someone who had graduated from the shop floor in Longbridge's South Works, understood the psyche of the workforce.

Dr Richard Etheridge's perceptive assessment is that Lord could not adjust to post-War political change nor the transfer of power to the worker. As a consequence he was incapable of undoing the damage caused by his entrenched attitudes towards trade unionism. Edwards, ever the pragmatist, could have been the catalyst for change. And we have seen examples.

The dreams of British Leyland's early months soon became troubled and would eventually turn to nightmare. Stokes had become what was popularly known as a 'captain of industry' but his hands were on the wheel of a sinking ship. By vocation he *was* 'a salesman' and to help him run his new empire he selected Sir William Lyons of Jaguar as his deputy, an insurance executive, and John Barber, an experienced top manager from Ford. Unfortunately, with Edwards and Harriman out of the picture, it was only Barber who knew anything about running a vehicle maker of this size.

To add to the problems Stokes discovered that the organization's two flagship plants—Longbridge and Cowley—were extremely leaky indeed and he borrowed £25m simply to repair the fabric. Elsewhere in the country there were no fewer than 20 sizeable BMC factories and as many more involved in Leyland's operations. The troubles were compounded by the government expressing growing concern about over-manning, poor productivity and continuing industrial relations issues.

Like Lord before him, (and certainly Harriman), Stokes refused to grasp any of the nettles including that of reducing his 190,000 workforce by the 25% required, seeming to believe he could sell sufficient vehicles to fund the excesses. To this end there was an influx of new talent. This time it was from Triumph, in the guise of Harry Webster, to revamp the range. Issigonis was the inevitable Longbridge casualty who continued, as Stokes would have it, '*designing cars on the backs of dirty envelopes*'.

A plethora of planning and design followed. Off-on-off activity on a replacement for the Mini; something for the Cortina customer—the Marina; something like the long-lived 1100/1300—the Allegro. The problem was, unlike the policies of Lord, this lacked vision. None of the cars were trend-setters. Also, diametrically opposed to Lord's thinking, was bringing in the colourfully named American, Filmer Paradise, to divest the company of many of its dealers. The quote: '*If the bastards can't sell 150 cars a year, cancel their franchises right now and let them fold up their tents and disappear into the night*', has some infamy.

Unfortunately for BLMC, their proverbial 'camels' carried them, not into the wilderness, but into the camps of the opposition, principally Datsun. And they took most of their customers with them. Meanwhile, industrial relations continued to deteriorate in spite of the appointment, in 1970, of a director with responsibility for this area. The vexed system of piecework was replaced with a daily rate and productivity and quality declined still further. Production costs per car could be as much as 80% above the calculated sum.

Stokes embarked on further reorganization that centred on transferring his command, well behind the battle lines, to a 14-storey tower on London's Marylebone Road, not that far from the unreal waxen world of Madame Tussaud. This cost him further talent in the person of embattled Austin-Morris chief, George Turnbull. He believed car factories could not be run from afar and departed to make Hyundai for the Koreans. With Turnbull gone, Barber became more powerful. As deputy chairman and managing director he did succeed in reducing the labour force by natural wastage and in 1973 showed profits of £53m.

But British Leyland continued to crumble. Because of continuing strikes, the type and quality of the very products themselves, an oil crisis in the Middle East that reduced the sales of many of the models and, it has to be said, Stokes's own inabilities. The Ryder Report, already mentioned, appeared in March 1975. The government accepted its recommendations. In summary they provided for factory modernization to make a rationalized range of properly developed cars, produced by workers who spent less time on strike, plus—the removal of Stokes.

The outcome was that Westminster took a larger stake in the company, called it British Leyland Limited and had the National Enterprise Board (NEB) supervise its running. By now industrial relations were at an all-time low, alongside quality. Furthermore, little was done to address the illogicality of the model range.

In 1976, Eric Varley took over from Tony Benn as secretary of state for industry and tried to rein in the organization as strikes continued—most notably a four-month stoppage by toolmakers in 1977. This jeopardized a number of potentially successful models, particularly a new Rover that was awarded the accolade of European Car of the Year but then could not be delivered. When it eventually arrived the potential buyers had largely lost interest and build quality was unacceptable anyway.

South African, Michael Edwardes, left the NEB to become chairman and managing director of British Leyland in November 1977, he was given one very simple instruction by the Labour administration: '*Make British Leyland work; or close it*'. It hinged on one of his own equally simple axiom's and one extremely familiar to students of Leonard Lord: '*Management's right to manage*'.

He could not prevent the stoppages at a stroke. At the Triumph plant in Speke, near Liverpool, the unions tried to face down Edwardes over a partial closure. He held firm and shut the entire factory. Soon after, as we have seen, he sacked Derek Robinson and survived.

But the battle was not quite over, politically motivated factions, with little or no involvement with the British motor industry and less with BL Ltd, were at work. Edwardes was forced to continue his struggle on the industrial relations front when all his energies should have been directed towards the viability of the product range. The snap assessment still had to be—too many factories, producing too many cars that too few people wanted. A rolling programme of closures was implemented and 90,000 jobs shed as the 1980s dawned.

At the same time Edwardes made a seemingly much less significant move but one that was of immense historical importance. He removed the brand 'Leyland' from the cars, returned it to its rightful place on lorries and buses, then created a volume division from Austin, Morris and MG and a prestige unit embodying Jaguar, Rover and Triumph. Sadly though, immeasurable damage had been done to the images of Austin and Morris.

With well under 40% of his time available to create motor cars—most, as we can imagine, still went on labour relations—Edwardes set about the model range. The Mini was to stay and the Metro, which was originally intended to replace it, was to have a life of its own badged as an Austin. It was launched in 1980 when market share, at below 18%, was a record low. The Metro fought its corner, and while stealing some sales from the Mini and Allegro, also attracted buyers from the Ford Fiesta and other true competitors. The Maestro and Montego were also being prepared, but not quickly enough. Edwardes took the dramatic step of signing a deal with Honda to place a medium-sized saloon in the showrooms. Their Ballade became first the Triumph Acclaim in 1981, and subsequently the Rover 200 of 1984.

Margaret Thatcher had come to power in 1979 and was now anxious to sell British Leyland to the private sector, not least because it had already cost the British tax payer £2bn to support. Edwardes resisted any uncoordinated disposal, while pointing out, in terms as unpalatable to Austin enthusiasts as they would have been to Leonard Lord, that that part of the company would remain an '*unsaleable rump*'.

The Maestro came on stream in 1982 as Edwardes' contract fell due for renewal. Thatcher, conducting a crazed policy of privatization and the abandonment of productive industry, failed to re-engage the man who had broken the debilitating power of the trade unions, created the first viable range of cars for nearly 20 years and scaled production to market share. Although the surgery by Edwardes had been a success the patient was still going to die. He left in his wake a fairly complex structure that included a sector called Austin Rover. By the middle of the decade some of the divisions were sufficiently viable to be candidates for privatization but overall the figures were not good—a £73.3 million loss in 1984, six million up on the year before.

Furthermore, and it has to be conceded, as a result of the Edwardes treatment, Austin-Rover did not now have the production capacity to achieve profitability and there was going to be no government funding to correct this. Moreover, moves to be rid of the company had begun. There were talks with Ford where there were mutual attractions in both terms of increased market share and technical exchange.

As the political ramifications of trying to sell a British company to a foreign one became increasingly uncomfortable, Thatcher installed her own man to run BL, and, of course, to lead it or its elements, back into the private sector. The individual chosen was a Canadian, Graham

Day, fresh from British Shipbuilding. He established his headquarters in the City of London with some functions performed from Uxbridge! There was also a change of name to Rover Group.

The Rover 800—another Honda—appeared in 1986, around the time of Day's appointment, and got away to a hesitant start. By the end of the year market share was down to 16%. Not that Day was particularly concerned about this aspect. His prime objective was profitability with one end in view. A huge market research programme was undertaken and found the Mini should continue with the Metro, Maestro and Montego 'de-badged' and known simply by model name. This was partly because Rover was as established a name as Austin, seen to be 'up-market', and already applied to a wide selection of the company's products—cars, the Land Rover of course, and the Range Rover. Also, in part, because the Austin image had suffered disastrously in the 1970s. To all intents and purposes that day in 1987 saw the end of Austin.

In March 1988 Rover were sold to British Aerospace (BAe) for the giveaway price of £152m, had its debts of £400m written-off and received an injection of at least £547m working capital from the government. It was a nice deal for someone, if not the British taxpayer who by now had contributed, at a very conservative estimate, £2.6bn sustaining the car firm in all its incarnations.

At face value BAe had acquired a going concern. The balance sheet for 1987 showed a profit of nearly £28m. However the model range still needed attention particularly in respect of Metro and Montego replacements. The new owners, though, were reluctant to invest. They relied increasingly on the excellent Honda technology with the intention of selling their cars at a premium, and profitably, in each market sector. Honda soon dominated design policy and by the early 1990s, with nothing in the pipeline for later in the decade, BAe sold the company to BMW in 1994. At first the prospects for Rover having an important role in the German firm's product range looked excellent. But managerial disagreements in Munich, coupled with Rover's poor performance both financially and in the market place, soon queered the pitch.

The script on that long-running saga, Mini replacement, was now reaching the final technical scenes, while on the administrative front BMW were working on a major tie-in with Chrysler. Although the 'new Mini' project still looked promising Mercedes-Benz thwarted the other plan by snatching the American for itself. BMW grew increasingly nervous and their anxieties deepened as the pound strengthened in the late 1990s. Rovers were now being sold at a loss in Europe. The future of Longbridge itself came increasingly under threat. Once again the scenario was one of a quest for state aid from Britain's, now Labour, government.

With an astonishing lack of understanding, trade and industry secretary Peter Mandelson turned BMW down. The equally inept British prime minister, Tony Blair, wanted to pull matters back. Mandelson left after an entirely unrelated débâcle, and a new secretary of state, Stephen Byers, was sent in to repair the damage. But the machinations in the boardroom at Munich were outside his control. On February 5, 1999, Bernd Pischetsrieder, BMW chief executive officer and arch advocate of Longbridge and Rover's role in his company, resigned.

Werner Sämann now became the top man at Rover, armed with proposals for an attractive premium model range for Longbridge. New chief executive, Joachim Milberg, went back to the UK government for money. Byers was supportive but chancellor Gordon Brown intervened and only sanctioned aid insufficient for the projects. Meanwhile, recently announced Rover losses stood at close on £650m and were even threatening its parent.

Further tinkering with the state aid figures took place but, in the event, a venture capital company arrived on the scene and gave BMW a secret exit route. In simple terms, the plan was to sell Land Rover, let the financiers build an MG and for BMW to make the new Mini. Faced with 'money men' again dabbling in car manufacture and precipitating unspecified job losses, in mid-March, 2000, a group of businessmen and politicians formed a consortium named Phoenix to put together a counter bid. Eventually, with funding from an American bank, it was successful and Rover passed to Phoenix for the nominal sum of £10 on May 8, that year.

Even this did not represent salvation. What was now called MG Rover, and produced a version of the famous sports car, went into receivership in 2005 and was sold to the Chinese. In 2008 production of an MG restarted in the former South Works using kits made in China. Most of the rest of the site was demolished in readiness for redevelopment unrelated to the motor industry. At the time of writing, to what extent this will take place, is uncertain.

What Leonard Lord would have thought and said is not quite so uncertain. Whether his policies of more than half a century before triggered the events just described is a matter of conjecture. However, it is totally unrealistic to attempt to lay the terminal ills of the British motor industry at the door of Lord, given the ineptitude, incompetence and Machiavellian political manoeuvring we have just seen.

CHAPTER TWENTY SEVEN
KIND HEART AND CORONET

Why Leonard Lord retired, in 1961, when he was 64 years of age is not entirely clear. It would not have been unusual for a company chief of his calibre to continue for at least another decade. In the run up to his departure he was apt to say: '*I'll paddle on for a few more years then let young George* (Harriman) *take over*'. The 'young', you will remember, was an allusion that dated right back to their Morris Engines days when Harriman's father, the dapper 'old' George, also worked for the firm.

There are a number of possibilities that may have prompted Lord's standing down. The most obvious, and probable, was health. Certainly, by the time he retired that face, vaguely reminiscent of Eire's president, Eamon de Valera, had a wearied and worn look. Without doubt Lord was already suffering from a number of bronchial and associated complaints, some more obvious than others. In 1960 he had a bout of illness, very likely of a respiratory or cardiovascular nature. It kept him away from the factory for several weeks and provided a foretaste of what was to come, prompting the quip: '*it gives "young George" a chance to learn the ropes*'.

What was happening to Leonard Lord was the inevitable legacy of a lifetime's unrestrained smoking, a trait adopted not only by Ethel but his children. However unfashionable it might seem to us, to have a cigarette almost perpetually on your lips would have been commonplace among both sexes of all classes through most of Lord's life. It maybe Lord handed over to Harriman, by now not of the most robust constitution himself, because he was, quite simply, exhausted—physically and mentally.

Until about 1938 Lord had displayed his brilliance as both a production engineer and plant manager. But it was not a great deal more than we might expect from a vigorous, dynamic and ambitious young executive. However, once he joined Austin his energy reached spectacular levels. Not only was Longbridge turned into the most prolific and voluminous producer of war materials in the country, virtually under Lord's sole direction, but he was engaged in demanding government activity, under extremely trying circumstances, associated with aircraft production.

Neither was there a respite when hostilities ended. The financial plight of the nation was such that he was forced to drive Austin, with unflinching determination, to earn dollars. Admittedly, his own skill, maybe his manipulative powers, had manoeuvred the company into a position where this would be the case. Even so, the reluctance of others to support him, particularly from outside the factory, where he had little control, must have been frustrating and stressful for someone of Lord's temperament.

The mid-1950s saw an upsurge in trade union power born of a radical change in workplace attitudes. The major strike of 1956 could not have been anything but an extremely unpleasant experience for Lord. To what extent it affected him personally is impossible to know, but it was certainly prescient. A man of Lord's perception and intelligence would have seen the shape of things to come.

To recall the AEU's Les Ambrose at the Calthorpe Park victory rally of August 12: '*We have started something that must become a pattern, not only for the engineering industry but for workers everywhere . . .* 'or the MP Victor Yates: '*You have struck a blow for trade unionism but you must make this agreement better and more powerful*'. Perhaps Lord wanted no part of all this.

That said he was never one to just 'paddle along'. The Mini arrived at the very end of his career. It could have turned 'Sir Len Lord' into a household name, yet, by accident or design—probably the latter—the public never knew the parent, only the mid-wife. Lord was never enamoured of politicians. He actively disliked those on the Left and, whether he would have admitted it or not, was little better served by those of the opposite persuasion. The Establishment, though, honoured him handsomely in 1962 with elevation to the peerage. His somewhat belated knighthood for services to the motor industry had come eight years before. The later accolade was timelier.

The family home on Lord's retirement was an imposing property at East Portlemouth. This tiny village lies to the north east of Limebury Point, a rock in the Kingsbridge Estuary in South Devon and the most southerly of a series of topographical features along the eastern side of Salcombe Harbour. The outlet is formed by a web of rivulets that wriggle together before pouring out to sea. Lord's house, actually called Lambury, not Limebury (corrupted perhaps by the local accent) looked out across the water to the resort of Salcombe itself. It was double fronted with the local stone rendered then painted cream on the upper parts. A garret snuggled between the two end structures before the roof rose again towards the woods standing behind. At the front there were low ramparts partly obscured by a thicket of shrubs and small trees. A stone stairway led down to the smooth seaweed strewn sands of Mill Bay and what is now a private beach. The latter may not have been so formally defined in Lord's day.

It was from this house and the Point that Lord took his title—Lord Lambury of Northfield. As he said: '*Lord Lord would sound bloody stupid!*' Northfield, of course, is the district of Birmingham in which the ward of Longbridge, home to Austin, stood. As we saw in the last chapter the sponsors for Lord's elevation to the peerage were Lord Brabazon of Tara and Lord Kindersley. Lord Brabazon is the better-known. Among many other things, he was a pioneer aviator and balloonist, supposedly the first person to take a pig for a flight in an aeroplane, and a one-time Austin racing driver. Kindersley was a prominent banker and at this point the chairman of Rolls-Royce.

We know the events that took place on the afternoon of Lord's investiture could have been momentous for the motor industry although not relevant to the particular occasion. The evening was more relaxed, with an informal meal at the Hyde Park Hotel in London's West End. It is interesting because it throws some light on Lord's relationship with Harriman. It is clear the two men were close. Why is not so apparent. Naturally, one assessment is that at Morris Engines Lord identified in his junior a malleable, supine, character he would find it useful to have around ever after. That said, he must have had a liking and some respect for Harriman. He attended Lord's middle daughter, Patricia's, 21st birthday party; not, we would suspect, at the behest of the young lady. However, Harriman was not similarly honoured at the Hyde Park Hotel celebration as George and his wife*, Stella, were suddenly sent on their way.

---

* This was Harriman's second wife. His first, Selma, died in the 1950s. There was one daughter from that marriage and no children from the second.

This has given rise to the suggestion that Lord was deeply superstitious and having done the mental arithmetic realised that the presence of the Harrimans would bring the total at table to an unlucky 13. There is no substantive evidence he read his tea leaves or was concerned with any other pagan rituals. The most plausible explanation for Sir George and Lady Harriman missing their supper is that, on this occasion, Lord wanted to preserve a strictly family atmosphere. But that is not wholly convincing either, because Lord's secretary, Ruth Bailey, attended, but perhaps because she had organized the event.

Just as he never delivered a paper to the Institution of Mechanical Engineers, Lord Lambury neither made a maiden speech in the House of Lords nor subsequently addressed the chamber. His presence, though, was still very much felt at Longbridge. Elsewhere he maintained a lower profile in what were to be the last few years of his life.

Even his private passions were beginning to be set aside or curtailed. He had joined the Hereford Cattle Society in 1943 and continued to breed the species, with some success, until 1959, when his membership lapsed. Lord was then living at Bibsworth House, in Worcestershire's 'chocolate-box' village of Broadway where he and Ethel moved from Halesend in 1955. The automotive significance of his cattle is, of course, that when the board were endlessly prevaricating over a logo for BMC and Lord had better things to do, he tossed a rosette awarded to one of his bulls onto the table and said: '*Use that*'. Alongside the Rolls-Royce badge the red, white and blue insignia that evolved is probably the most famous from one of the classic eras of British motoring. It was a stroke of genius, hinging, like so many moves of brilliance, on simplicity; and typical of Lord.

Whether or not the cattle themselves achieved the distinction they have been given credit for in some circles, is questionable. The Hereford Cattle Society have no record of any major trophies won by either L P, or Sir Leonard, Lord and neither have the Royal Smithfield Club recorded the accolade 'supreme champion' to any beasts he raised. However, his bull, Fenhampton Broadside, did win the senior male championship at the prestigious, but local, Three Counties Show of 1949.

'Fenhampon' was sold to Raymond Reynolds of Hobartville Stud, in Richmond, New South Wales and was acclaimed as one of the finest Hereford bulls ever brought to Australia. No doubt he sired generations of imposing cattle. Whether he was the inoffensive and huggable beast known in the family as 'Ferdinand' is not clear. Neither can it be ascertained whether he received as much petting from his master as family photo albums confirm he enjoyed from the rest of the clan!

At this time Lord was also a fruit grower. Herefordshire and the adjoining counties are the garden of England with regard to perry pears. This, usually inedible, fruit is used to produce a long-established alcoholic drink made famous by the once-popular commercial brand, Babycham. Lord cultivated pears and other fruit at his various Midlands homes but whether any were noteworthy, as has been claimed, is, again, doubtful.

By now Leonard Lord's involvement with the extended family that had consumed so much of his emotional energy had ceased. His daughters were married and there were no longer pouting teenage 'waifs' to stumble upon in the corridors at Halesend or drive to pony rides on the estate. David Blundstone, the nephew he had funded through medical school, had qualified as a doctor and like all the family members, except Lord himself, were dutifully driving BMC cars. The Bentley was now an early S2 Standard Steel Saloon and Lord's only basic, as opposed to coachbuilt, Crewe model. To be fair, his 'official car' was that personal favourite, a Vanden Plas Princess; first in BMC three litre form and then with the Rolls-Royce four litre engine.

His paternal instincts were largely directed towards his grandson, Guy Breeden, who was the son of eldest daughter Joan's first marriage, to Miles Breeden of the car accessory empire. Guy still recalls with enormous affection the time spent with his grandfather. '*He was a lovely man. I fondly remember sitting on his knees and "driving" the Vanden Plas Princess R, BMC 1.*' The drives Guy Breeden, who was born in 1953, would best remember would have been at Warren's Gorse, in Daglingworth, near Cirencester. Lord and Ethel had moved back to the Midlands and that village in the Duntisbourne Valley, beside the A417 Gloucester to Cirencester road, in 1962. Not even an S2 Bentley had been capable of wafting Lord swiftly enough over the 200 miles between Salcombe and Longbridge to allow him to exchange the chug of the fishing boats, and the smell of the sea, for the occasional therapeutic whiff of machine oil he prized so highly.

Life was even calmer now. There was more time for Lord's long term hobby of photography and the allied artistic pursuit of painting in oils. His pictures are not readily available although at least one survives in private hands. More prolific are his caricatures of himself. Drawn with all the deftness of an accomplished draughtsman they suggest Lord was more relaxed with himself than he is given credit for. Often taking the form of an autograph executed on the dinner menus of the ocean liners on which he travelled, a single-stroke, stylized 'L' parodies that enormous nose, then has his steel-rimmed glasses perched on top.

To an extent he enjoyed ball games. He was associated with Daglingworth cricket club but we can reasonably assume that this reflected most Englishmen's endemic enthusiasm for the game rather than any active participation. He was known also at Cirencester Golf Club and, as golf was a traditional promotional activity within the motor industry, Lord would have had some competency on the greens. Some weight is added to this belief by the existence, in South Africa, of a Sir Leonard Lord Trophy, donated to the Blackheath Works golf team.

Overall, however, he kept a low profile in Daglingworth, only occasionally being seen at village events. Yet, those who remember him, speak of warmth and generosity. The poorer children who, perhaps, did not have the price of a shy at coconuts or a spin of a tombola, could look to Leonard Lord for their sixpences.

It was at Warren's Gorse, on Wednesday, September 13, 1967, Leonard Percy Lord's life came to a sudden end. He suffered a fatal coronary thrombosis at the relatively early age of 70. Just as his father had drunk himself to death, his son had, effectively, smoked himself to death. Carbon monoxide and other toxins inhaled from cigarettes cause hardening and thus restricted blood flow in the arteries around the heart. This, in turn, not only damages the heart itself and causes it to fail, but injures other major organs. Lord was under attack on two fronts. He smoked almost continuously himself for most of his life but suffered the secondary effects of living in a domestic environment where everyone else smoked.

Secondary causes of death, and ones that come as no surprise when they appear on the death certificate, were chronic emphysema and bronchitis. The first is a condition often directly related to smoking. The heart is strained as it tries to pump oxygenated blood through air passages in lungs constricted by the carbon deposits from cigarette smoke. Bronchitis is, of course, an allied condition that further restricts the flow of air to the lungs. Lord had destroyed both his lungs and his heart. He would have been in considerable discomfort and physically wracked. He almost certainly knew at the time of his retirement, stress factors and perceptions of an unpleasant future for the industry apart, that the pay-off for his smoking was not too far distant. In the lead up to his death Lord had been treated by his physician, Dr Grove-White, for a pulmonary infarction which in lay terms is an obstruction in a branch of the pulmonary artery, a clear portent of what was soon to follow. He had also suffered bronchopneumonia.

It was George Harriman who was first to pay tribute in a statement that was unquestionably from the heart and undeniably accurate. '*I hardly know how to express my sense of loss at the sudden passing of Lord Lambury. I cannot, from a personal point of view, do justice to all he has meant to me in my business career, and indeed my whole life, in the 40 years we have been ever more closely associated. He was my guide and mentor during many difficult as well as good times.*

'*With his natural gift of leadership he was always a man of decision—indeed, a top-line man if ever there was one—who directed his team in such a way that whatever the problem, or however great the project in hand, he cleared their path, dispelled their doubts and inspired them with enthusiasm. Because he was so often forthright and outspoken the world may have regarded him as tough, but with his abundant qualities went a heart of gold which conditioned all his plans and decisions, however swift and penetrating they might be*'.

Naturally, and especially in the 1960s, one would expect to find a lack of objectivity in anything written or broadcast about the dead. However, the outpourings on Lord—and there were many—followed Harriman's lead in not only reflecting respect for the deceased's talents but, in no small measure, an affection for him. The reports appeared not only in the specialist press, but both in Midlands provincial newspapers and nationally. The obituaries were peppered with adjectives and phrases such as 'genius', 'man of decision', 'one of the greatest', 'a tiger'. *The Birmingham Post* spoke of that city, the Midlands and Britain itself '*having reason to be immensely grateful to a man who did so much for the prosperity of the motor industry on which so many depend*'; *The Motor Trader* reflected on Lord's life being '*a monument which we can admire and to which future generations well might look as an example*'.

There is, however, one tribute I intend to reproduce in full. It comes from the *Cambrian* column in the last named journal of September 27, 1967, and although it does border on hagiography, gives a particularly broad and telling portrait of its subject.

'*This is not an easy column to write this week. I find the going slow, with pauses between the sentences and odd thoughts creeping between the lines. I want to talk about "Len" Lord (he will never be Sir Leonard or Lord Lambury to me) and every time I tap a key I have to remind myself that he isn't here with us, at least not physically, any more. I don't like using the past tense about him. It seems to put a finality on the man and on his work, but that finality isn't there. When I look at what he created, and when I think of the thousands of workpeople, shareholders, executives, dealers and users of motor transport who have benefited from him, and the future that spreads out, I just find it impossible to write finis. What a wonderful thing it must be to have lived a life of which the benefits to one's fellows go on even when the progenitor has departed. You can have all your carvings on tombstones, but the whole lot won't add up to this.*

'*De mortuis nil nisi bonum. Is that the way to write? I don't think so. We all have our faults and, no doubt, Len had his, but one does not sit, one dare not sit, in judgement on either the living or the dead, although we are still inclined to do so. So what I have to write is neither sycophancy nor sentiment, neither adulation nor judgement. What I think I must do, to begin with, is to put the man in perspective against a world background and here he shines as a guiding light to this great country of which I, for one, am proud to be a citizen. With more men like Len Lord and fewer politicians and theorists this nation would be in a far better position than it is today. Len was a Britisher and he flew the Union Jack (sic), and he wasn't ashamed to have it at his masthead.*

'*Len told me once that he had toyed with the idea of up-ending his headquarters from Longbridge and transferring it to the States but he knew, and I knew, that he couldn't do it. So, more than any other man, he built the British answer to America and to Europe and when the country conferred his barony on him it gave him no more, and probably less than was his due.*

'I liked him. He was blunt and one of "Birmingham's own", although he was not born there. It was as I detected something of a pose, but he was right to build his image. It was one that worked. I think it was because each of us recognised this that we got on so famously. I have known occasions when we have punched away at each other and have thoroughly enjoyed the scrap because all the time we knew it was "friendly".

'I don't think Len had an ounce of malice in him. He was straight-talking, true, but he could be straight-talked back to, and loved it. This was part of the joy of life to him.

'Another great asset was his ability to shed formality. I well remember an occasion on which he was entertaining some Australasians at London's formal Savoy (Hotel). It was hot. The room was stuffy. Len rose from the table, shed his coat (jacket) and took his lunch in his shirt sleeves. So, with a vast relief, did everyone else. The initial horror on the face of the toastmaster was swept aside as a thing of no account, and of course, these chaps from "down under" just loved him.

'I remember some acrimonious words with him about spare parts. "All right. You only know half the story. You can go to BMC Service and see what it really is all about, and you can print just what you find. I shan't want to vet it." So I did and I understood more then than I did before. That was Len. You could deal with a man like that.

'I was in Australia when he made a luncheon speech before an enormous and influential assembly. No flannel, no fuss, the whole lot straight from the shoulder and I think that did a great deal to get the new BMC set-up "off the dock" among those tough "cobbers". Len might have been a "limey" when he got up to talk. He was dinkum when he sat down.

'With all that he found time to build Britain's answer to the overseas and Continental giants. Yes, he was a man among men. Now at last I have written it, and I haven't said all I wanted to say by any means, but what I did want to get off my chest was a feeling of personal debt. A trade journalist in a highly competitive, cantankerous, sensitive and querulous industry like this one of ours needs just a few points of reference in which he can place absolute trust. Len Lord to me, was one of those. I shall not forget'.

Perhaps *Cambrian*, the magazine's editor Brian Cambray, is verbose, sentimental, the sycophant he denies, a hagiographer. The first two elements may be the product of his Welsh descent, the latter two are irrelevant as Lord is dead. Yet, surely, the columnist encapsulates to a very considerable degree the esteem in which Leonard Lord was regarded at the time of his death.

It is interesting too, that Lord's former colleague and enduring friend, Frank Woollard, writes in almost identical, although much more measured terms, in his *Motor* article of more than a decade earlier. '. . . *it took 40 years to produce the first million Austin cars, the second million were made in seven-and-a-half years during Sir Leonard's chairmanship of the company . . . . He has the supreme gift of reducing difficult situations and involved problems to elementary terms without falling into the trap of over-simplification. He is frank and direct in all his dealings and is able to give clear directions to his executives. He is completely honest in thought, he does not deceive others and, more important perhaps, he does not deceive himself.*

'He has the ability to pick the right men and to inspire and maintain their enthusiasm because of his own faith and belief in the work he is doing. He realizes that business is not static but dynamic, sometimes violently so, and he is not afraid of changing course if that should be necessary. Though holding positive opinions he will generously admit if he is mistaken. He sets great store by loyalty but believes that it should be given as well as accepted: thus he is loyal to those who serve him'.

In the next and final chapter we will look at why the image of such an industrial titan can have become so tarnished, why the memory poisoned to the point where he now seems a pariah. We will consider also who might be responsible.

Leonard Lord rode to his funeral service and subsequent interment in the Vanden Plas Princess hearse of Cirencester undertaker, Cowley and Son. The vehicle was appropriate as Lord had been the initiator of these fine and dignified vehicles. On that cold, dismal Saturday, when the rain was apt to come in blustery scuds, some 150 mourners filed into Cirencester's 12th century Parish Church of St John. The Rev Edger Landen played "Abide With Me" on the Willis organ housed in a case designed by the celebrated Victorian architect Sir George Gilbert Scott.

Those who listened to the Rev Rowland Hill conduct the service were from all walks of life and included Ford chief Sir Patrick Hennessy, Jaguar's 'Lofty' England and Donald, Geoffrey and Brian Healey as well as Alfred Emmence, Lord's chef, representing the other staff of Warren's Gorse. There was also his secretary, Ruth Bailey. But there were many others who came to say farewell. People who knew the man only casually or simply by reputation.

All heard the minister say that Lord, '*despite his great achievements, great powers and business ability, was no hard-headed, ruthless businessman but someone of great sympathy and a very warm heart*'.

In due course the hearse, carrying the family's contribution to the 94 wreaths followed by Cowley and Son's Vanden Plas limousine, moved away. Leonard Lord's last resting place would be the cemetery of the Saxon church in Daglingworth. As the rector, the Rev J B Hall, concluded the service in the presence of close family members the messages on the floral tributes spread around the grave were more personal and intimate. Once more they emphasised Lord's warmth. Pauline had written, lovingly: '*In memory of the best dad in the world*'. Joan: '*To my dear dad*', and Patricia: '*Dad—always in my thoughts*'.

Ethel Lily Lord—Len's Lil—was laid beside him in July 1978. She died of a brain haemorrhage on July 13, 1978, aged 81, at Patricia's home in Loudwater Lane, Rickmansworth.

A month after Lord's funeral, with the intrusiveness of the age, his Will was published. The estate amounted to £155,000 after tax. His secretary and all the members of staff at Warren's Gorse were generously provided for. It was the last of many unrecorded acts of kindness.

As the simple inscription at the foot of the grave noted, Leonard Percy Lord was 'At Peace'.

CHAPTER TWENTY EIGHT
WHO POISONED THE WELL?

'Lord had fouled the atmosphere for the most important alliance in the history of the British motor industry to that point . . . The benefits of the merger (Austin and Morris) were indeed, never fully realised'.

The Concise Oxford Dictionary defines the verb foul as: *'Offensive to the senses, loathsome, stinking, dirty, soiled, filthy, charged with noxious matter, clogged, choked'*. Collins's equivalent volume adds: *'Revolting, charged with or full of dirt or offensive matter, putrid, rotten, morally or spiritually offensive, obscene, vulgar, unfair'*.

It is ugly language.

There seems little doubt it was first applied to the actions of Leonard Lord by a newspaper journalist and one-time BBC economics correspondent called Graham Turner, when he wrote the book entitled *The Leyland Papers*, circa 1970 and published in 1971. What is truly offensive, morally and spiritually; what is obnoxious and unfair, is not only that the statement is patently untrue when considered by any informed or intelligent observer, but that it has been repeated and propagated many times and even described as a 'brilliant' assessment.

In this work I have tried to make a balanced appraisal of Leonard Lord. In common with every other human being, his character was flawed. I have not tried to escape that fact. There are examples of it being clearly so. However, it is also inescapable that Lord was, as Cambrian says in that *Motor Trader* tribute, a *'man among men'*. Not just a brilliant production engineer and extraordinary plant manager, but arguably, one of the most significant industrialists, in *any* field, of the second half of the 20th century.

It would be tedious, and only reiterate much of what has appeared in previous chapters, if we re-examined, or even summarized, the detail of Lord's life. However, if we distance ourselves from most of that detail and look at the bedrock on which his life and personality were based, we will be aided in placing the character and achievements in their true perspective. I intend to do this by a three-phase analysis. It will cover Lord's early life, move on to his periods of prominence with Morris and Austin, his wartime activities and those of the immediate post-War era and conclude, perhaps most importantly, by considering the British Motor Corporation time that he allegedly 'fouled'.

The significance of the formative years is two fold. It contributed enormously to Lord's nature. But it has given rise to the foolish populist view that he was *'a bitter man with a huge inferiority complex'*. It is certainly true that Leonard Lord's childhood and adolescence were extremely hard. The frivolous ambitions of a drunken father had put the family out of one comfortable home and then, because of his untimely and unnecessary death, made a second residence—Coventry's *Hope and Anchor* public house—untenable. It was compounded by relative, and it was only relative by the standards of the day, poverty, and the circumstance whereby what was high quality and broad-based schooling, had, nonetheless, to be funded by charity.

This could have been an embittering experience. But I suggest it was not. The mother to whom Leonard Lord was so closely attached was of Irish descent. Her own mother came from the small community of Blackrock on the coast of the Republic, just to the south east of Dublin. Whatever her religious persuasion, and while Leonard Lord the chorister certainly never sang from anything other than the Anglican hymn book, Emma Swain (Lord's mother) would have been a resilient, strong willed girl. Moreover, she was likely to have had a deep sense of morality and after her marriage would have imparted all her principles and values to her two children.

This is evidenced by Lord's concern for, and kindness towards, his widowed mother. And while the elder child, Annie, does not feature in what we know of her brother's early life, there is no reason to suppose he was not equally caring towards her. Indeed, his later generosity, after she was widowed and had a son to raise and educate, far exceeds what might have been expected. Thus, we already have a kind, thoughtful youth.

Did he have a *'huge inferiority complex'*? One of the main disseminators of this piece of information (or misinformation) is Joe Edwards. It is based, certainly in part, on impressions still being gleaned in the mid-1950s. It seems extremely unlikely that a man with the status of Lord, by then overwhelmingly successful and extremely wealthy into the bargain, would be debilitated in this way.

Was he still festering over the fact that in the distant past he could not afford to attend university? This, too, must be questionable. He had already recorded an impressive trawl of qualifications—*'I mopped up every sort of scholarship as it came along'*—without undergoing higher education. In any case, the Austin Motor Company, and subsequently BMC, did not, in the main, have a university-trained hierarchy. If Lord did seem acerbic on this front it could well have been that he resented those who had advanced their careers by privilege and social influence rather than hard work. There would be those around him who fell into that category.

On the other hand, does that claim of a *'huge inferiority complex'* stem from the impression that he seemed ashamed of his background and upbringing? Lord was a very, very private man. It is what has made this book so challenging to write. Certainly, and understandably, he did not want to talk in any depth about his early years. The single facet that his father had been—at one time—a Coventry public baths superintendent was sufficient information for the public domain. It was true, and acceptable. He was also apt to reveal: *'He died too young'* which was bland, but also true. No one need, or did, know more. It is only recently that a fuller picture has been revealed, but never in as much detail as in this book.

It is also remotely possible that Lord had an issue over his failure to appear at the Front in WWI. Again he would encounter many who had been involved, even if, in some cases, the value of their contribution was questionable. I avoided using the unpleasant expression 'draft dodger' in the relevant chapter, yet Lord's move from Courtaulds to a reserved occupation at 'Coventry Ordnance' was certainly opportune. How one judges him in this context can only be from a personal, moralistic, view. Seventy million men and women worldwide donned uniforms in The Great War. Nine million perished leaving three million women and 10 million children in the formerly combatant world largely at the mercy of harsh, or barely adequate, support structures. This was especially so in Great Britain. A generation had been lost. The pointlessness of the waste was indescribable. Leonard Lord was not only a loving and caring son he was extremely sensitive. Clearly, he took the view that his first duty lay at home.

What Lord achieved in his life was the result of phenomenally hard work and determination. The *Motor Trader* may have eulogised his whole life as being *'a monument which we can admire and to which future generations well might look as an example'*, but the early years are inspiring in their own right.

His energy, commitment and ambition were almost super-human. As we have seen, between the ages of 12 and 14 he studied to the dawn. In adolescence it was 6 am to 6.30 pm at Courtaulds, with a night class to teach after that, before more of his own studies lasting into the early hours. It was very much a part of Lord's ethos of advancement by nothing other than hard work—in his case, incredible application and dedication. *'They (youngsters) don't do that these days'* he said in later life. Yet, ironically, it was the expectation of commitment and a work ethic that came so naturally to Lord that was to be one of his problems, if not his nemesis.

For all his hard work, a part of the picture that should not be underplayed is Lord's brilliance. And we ought never to accept a lesser term. In the first instance he was an extremely gifted draughtsman. It is disingenuous, as has been written in recent times, to dismiss his artistic talents as those of a man who *'fancied himself as a stylist'*, or *'considered himself something of an artist'*. From very early on he was capable of producing exquisite isometric projections of machine tools he had often designed himself. In later years he produced innovative styling for whole motor cars.

He was a man who walked the job and embodied that characteristic, often so revered and respected by the shopfloor worker—the ability to use the equipment as competently as the person employed to do so. It was also present in men of the calibre of Royce and Herbert Austin. There is little purpose in describing again the time spent with various machine tool makers or what were probably days of frustration and impatience during the brief stay at Daimler. Suffice to say, it was the experience gained in these environments that gave Lord such a superb understanding of the day-to-day operation of an engineering works, and indeed, how to build motor cars.

But it is certainly worth re-emphasising that when he arrived at Hotchkiss (soon to be Morris Engines), *'knocking on the door and saying he had come to take any job going'*, the transfer machines were among the most advanced in the world, but of little use. It was Leonard Lord, not yet 30, who got them to work.

By then he was almost handsome. The crinkled red hair swept over his pate, but the brow was already high. The eyes penetrating yet mischievous behind those perpetual wire framed glasses. The voice revealed a subdued Midlands accent. Whether self-consciousness over the nose had yet diminished is uncertain. It has been described as 'hypnotic'. *'A nose that once seen is never forgotten. That stops at nothing, that brooks no interference. A witty unsentimental nose, a gimlet of a nose for ferreting out weakness and hypocrisy; a nose that loves free speech and free men. An aristocratic and impertinent nose. A nose that could grow only on an English face. Nothing a man with a nose like this could say or do could surprise you'*.

Whether or not Oliver Boden had an opinion about Leonard Lord's nose is not known but much the man had to say probably surprised the works manager at Morris's newly acquired Wolseley plant. In 1927 Lord was sent from what was now Morris Engines to join Boden in a major reorganization. Arguably it was too much promotion too soon. Lord was 31, Boden, clearly with his own ambitions, only 40. Technically there was no contest. Lord revitalized the factory and had a new engine in production with impressive speed. But we have to concede he displayed here, and elsewhere, what is conveniently termed, arrogance. If it was that, it was probably born of social and workplace immaturity.

It manifested itself most strikingly when William Morris, suitably impressed by Lord's performance at Wolseley, asked him to repeat the process for Cowley. Lord would only go *'with full management control'*. This created the embarrassing situation where the incumbent had to be dispensed with. Soon after Lord arrived, Miles Thomas commented on the former's 'arrogance'. *'He was proud of his new authority, almost to the point of arrogance'.*

All that said, we have to remember, Lord had extremely difficult roles to perform; and quickly. Wolseley was a moribund company, with out-moded methods conducted in too much factory space. Morris itself, remarkably, was heading for bankruptcy. MG, now of course under Lord's control, had a catastrophic balance sheet and a ludicrous portfolio of models. Sales of some barely reached double figures in a year. Leonard Lord returned Wolseley to respectability, he saved Morris and in doing so created Britain's best selling car of the pre-War era, and, much though MG aficionados may like to decry the fact on the basis the drawing office was closed, the cars 'Morris-ized' and racing abandoned, Lord was the saviour of their favoured marque. He may even have interceded with the puritanical Morrises on behalf of Cecil Kimber, whose marital relations were viewed by many as extremely unsavoury. This last point apart, the business achievements by one so young were quite astonishing. Surely it is understandable, that under these circumstances, diplomacy and the niceties of office interchange were sometimes swept aside.

One of the absurdities in what has been recorded of Leonard Lord's life is the importance attached to his supposedly excessive swearing and his smoking. *'Lord foulmouth'* is a frequently used, and particularly offensive, term. I have already attempted to explore this phenomenon in some depth. However, it has not been possible to establish with any certainty that Lord's profane vocabulary was any more extreme or prolific than would have been the norm in any industry at the time, or indeed, today. In fact, some who were there confirm that Lord's swearing was in no way exceptional. Thus, to attach any great significance to it seems no more than a distraction from the man's true worth.

Why someone as articulate as Lord, a person who wrote and spoke well, swore, if indeed he did to any exceptional degree, is a more interesting proposition. My own view is that it was a form of protection; a means of emphasizing the common touch he unquestionably had and a way of concealing his sensitivity and soft heartedness in an environment which would often have been lewd and brutish. I have expressed the opinion that Miles Thomas did very much the same thing, but used different techniques.

If Lord was uncomfortable on the shopfloor on this score it seems likely that he would have been far from at home on the broader Morris scene. Miles Thomas describes a closed clique of smug middle class managers and their prissy wives. That would not have impressed the high-performing Lord, or Ethel. It seems highly probable they felt outsiders. If Lord was embittered at all, or embittered about Morris, it could have been over this.

Marching hand in hand with some of these issues is Lord's smoking. If his swearing was the norm contextually the number of cigarettes consumed was certainly not. His father had been a compulsive drinker. I know of no means of discovering whether Ethel smoked before she met her husband but she was heavily dependent on tobacco afterwards, as were all her daughters. If there are such traits as positive and negative compulsions William Lord had alcohol as a negative and his son cigarettes. It is enormous good fortune that on the positive side the latter had a seemingly compulsive desire for work and in the most effective way. Although Lord was by no means teetotal, his 'gin and frenches' definitely do not appear on the negative side of the slate.

Most commentators on Leonard Lord begin their focus with his sudden and apparently untimely departure from Morris. This is an extremely complex area and I do not intend to revisit it in any detail. For many years the consensus seemed to be that Lord's departure was a relatively unacrimonious dispute with William Morris over money—either Lord's actual salary or royalties on the Morris Eight, for which he had been responsible. As we have seen, recent research suggests that, as the national re-armament programme gathered momentum, Lord and Morris were increasingly at loggerheads over their company's involvement in the shadow factory scheme.

Herbert Austin, as chairman of the committee liaising with the Air Ministry, and Lord Swinton as air minister, were privy to this. It seems probable that one, or both, placed Lord in a strategic position within the scheme through the expedient of engineering his move to Longbridge, as Works director, in 1938. It may not be too extreme to claim that at Austin, Lord was the government 'plant'. If we are to go down the dangerous path of inventing a scenario, it also seems feasible that Lord was told (by Swinton and/or Austin) to bring Morris into the shadow factory programme—which he failed to do—or cut loose, lie low for a period, then become actively involved in the government's plans.

A number of published ideas though do not seem credible. Firstly, that Lord had always intended to retire at 40. Although he was precisely that age when he left Morris, and years later liked to joke that one of his greatest achievements was retiring twice, it is almost inconceivable that a man of his incredible dynamism could have rested on his laurels so early on.

Second, that Lord and Morris parted amicably. It is true that Lord returned to the fold, or the peripherals of it, in 1937, to manage a trust established to help regions with high unemployment. Why Lord took this on is a mystery. He did not need the high salary and had no aspirations about returning to Cowley. Of most interest to us is that his management of the fund illustrates not only an understanding of the broader business scene, but his humanity.

Third, that, as Lord irreverently put it: *'Old Austin said he was getting old and "caught me on one leg". He had had enough and wanted me to manage his Works for him'*. There is, of course, a measure of truth in this, but we suspect it was much less straightforward.

There is a further element that I touched on in the relevant chapter and will now briefly revisit. As a journalist I know that a dash of sexual scandal helps sell a book, or indeed, article. A version of Lord's departure that has been propagated very recently centres on him being dismissed for having a relationship with a young woman tracer at Cowley. It falls, I would suggest, into the category of prurience. If Lord had an affair, at 40, devoted family man as he was, with three young children and a wife who had an extremely attractive personality, was supportive, and a calming influence in all their lives, would have been, as far as all the evidence indicates, totally out of character. It is entirely possible, of course, that a rich and powerful executive, presented with such an opportunity could easily have succumbed. In addition, we know there were ingredients in Lord's personality that were attractive to women. He could be charming, was humorous, outspoken, sharp witted, irreverent and self-confident. Yet, I have never been able to trace anyone who can provide even a Christian name or definitive spelling for his alleged lover's name, nor any documentary confirmation she ever existed. We must remain open-minded. But I am inclined to believe that the story is contemporary invention.

We cannot advance far from Lord's rift with Morris without arriving at what may be his most famous quote. *'I'm going to take that business at Cowley apart, brick by bloody brick'*. It is probably unique among 'Lordisms' because only one other person heard it. Miles Thomas. I do not dispute it was said. Nor, perhaps, at the time, or for a while, meant. For it to have retained any conviction, 16 years later, when BMC was formed, indicates paranoia and Leonard Lord was not paranoid.

There are two important points to note about Lord's arrival at Longbridge in February 1938. Firstly, he proved, again, that he was a brilliant production engineer and local plant manager and extremely able at running a whole factory of the size and complexity of Austin. Secondly, he revitalized and reshaped virtually the whole of the model range with amazing speed and energy. New automobiles of attractive, modern, appearance were designed and in production within 12 months. A range of 'commercials', the introduction of which had been stalled at board level for years, was launched at the same time as the first of the cars. It provided Austin with vehicles that could easily be adapted for military use, lending considerable weight to the argument that Lord had a government 'string to his bow'.

The range and volume of equipment produced by the Works when WWll eventually started was enormous. Some of the statistics appear in the appropriate chapters. That this output was possible was due, in no small measure, to the drive and commitment of Leonard Lord. He was to say of the situation: *'Austin died on my hands, Payton died on my hands. Look at me. Can't die. Can't leave it'*. The last part of his assessment was certainly true. The Works said of Lord he was a man with no eyelids so could never sleep.

Impressive as the contribution to the war effort was, what is even more so is Lord's vision. He manipulated Longbridge's output. I choose the words carefully and, again, let the reader judge the morals. But Lord 'contrived' a situation that ensured Austin was in pole position within the industry when hostilities ceased. In practical terms it meant Lord had cars to market well before anyone else. And by the standards of the day, they were good. One in particular—the Twelve—was metamorphosed into a Sixteen by fitting the brand new overhead valve engine Lord had massaged through the wartime system. It was a conventional but world-class car.

Not surprisingly there was resentment at Lord's and Austin's swiftness off the starting blocks. Yet, in 1945/6 what did the competition have to offer? Morris, potentially, the innovative Minor. But it would be a long time coming (1948) and with the exception of Miles Thomas, management at Cowley, and especially Morris himself, would ensure it was a major disappointment. Ironically, it was not until Lord took it under his wing in the early BMC days that the car developed into the icon it is today. Standard had the Vanguard, destined to become an unmitigated export disaster. Ford nothing but a cheap small car and an enormous, heavily-American-based, gas guzzler. The rest, by and large, what they had offered pre-War, or mildly revamped versions thereof. Proof positive Leonard Lord was head and shoulders above his peer group.

It is now extremely important to appreciate that Great Britain was, quite literally, bankrupt, at the end of WWII. British politicians like to speak of the United Kingdom's 'special relationship' with America. It's a pleasant thought. But the relationship was not sufficiently special to overlook a debt that would take until 2006 to be paid. The process began in 1945 when Leonard Lord, more effectively than any other industrialist, strove to earn dollars. It is possible to criticise Lord on two counts—the cars were uninspired and that he sacrificed all on the alter of production.

Interviewed by Barney Sharratt for *Men and Motors of the Austin* one employee of the time said: *'We didn't worry too much about what the public wanted. We didn't worry about warranty costs. Not until it was too late. If the labour force got a bit uppity and asked for more money, we just paid up to keep the tracks running. It sowed the seeds of future problems'*. Yet this lack of realism extended as far as government. Prime minister Clement Attlee has been attacked for 'squandering' Marshall Plan money on a welfare state, and secretly, it is now admitted, on atomic armament, instead of equipping British industry for future challenges.

Attlee did what he believed needed to be done. After all, Britain was a country that in the 1920s and '30s left thousands of the maimed heroes of The Great War to earn their daily bread by selling matches on streets corners, or, like convicts on Dartmoor, breaking stone for civil engineering projects. Not to mention abandoning large numbers of its ordinary citizens to squalor and deprivation.

Lord did what he knew had to be done. And supremely well. He also created a motor works that was the largest and most modern outside America and on which a strong and healthy British industry should have been based. In simple terms the merger of Austin and Morris was intended to further that prospect with a corporation of such scale it would hold a dominant position in the home market and have the strength to repel increasing competition from overseas.

Already the A40 Devon, and to a lesser extent the Dorset, had been spectacular revenue winners for Britain, or, as Lord had preferred to quantify it: for every car sold, put food into mouths. However it is expressed, Lord was a key figure, possibly the principal player, in turning his country into the world's biggest exporter.

The A40 was the first all new British family-car of the post-War era and while it was far from perfect it was fit for purpose and widely appealing. Also, and although Lord's intent went largely unfulfilled, it made another move in the important direction of constructional rationalization. Was he on the right track? His detractors say not. So where has he already been found lacking?

Certainly he had not reconciled himself to the increasing influence of the trade unions. Most likely he had found this so unpalatable that he chose to under-estimate the seriousness of the situation. But given the depth of the country's financial crisis, it was wholly justifiable, however unwise in the long-term, to maintain production at any price. By his own admission, the dollar-spinning A40 cost more to make than its selling price. To a large extent that was a consequence of the post-War labour and materials market. Yet, while it is untrue that Lord had a poor grasp of finance and was incapable of realistic pricing, it is the case that he, and indeed Harriman, adhered to the false premise that volume would ultimately compensate for an inadequate monetary return on the product, or even, as in the case of the Mini, a deficit. Years later, Donald Stokes was guilty of a much more damaging outlook by believing the scale of the business could somehow off-set colossal over-manning and a profligate, wildly inefficient, manufacturing infrastructure.

Lord's belief was compounded to a degree by his long-standing conviction that the future lay with small cars. The conviction, of course, was correct, although it is only now that it is becoming universally accepted. The problem for Lord was such vehicles, inevitably, offer lower profit margins than their larger counterparts. The explanation is that the same number of basic tasks needs to be performed on a limousine as on a 'mini-car'.

There were also personal issues surrounding Lord's ruling of BMC. He was an autocrat. It is unjust to vilify him on that basis. Austin himself, Royce, Ford were all of that ilk. Men who had a thorough understanding of the job and were prepared to roll up their sleeves and lay hands on the machines. But a further facet of Lord's autocracy is that he never created an effective line of succession. He was prepared to subscribe to the Longbridge culture of promoting from within, whereas a far superior policy would have been to seek fresh blood from other car companies, from outside the industry, or overseas.

It may be a severe judgement but the Austin strategy of 'passing on the baton' tended to create a stultified, non-progressive environment where, to an extent, Lord was surrounded by 'dead wood'. For example, it is hard to see what Hancock, on engine design, and who had been with Herbert Austin at the start, was 'going to bring to the party' in 1940; Rix failed to appreciate the benefits of chassiless construction when they were laid before him and, as a consequence, the prototype BMC Cambridges suffered catastrophic failures. Lord was capable of dealing decisively and, some would say, harshly, with such problems but he did not tackle the root cause.

If we develop this theme we cannot avoid the conclusion that Lord grossly over-rated the ability of Harriman. It is true that at Hotchkiss, where he first encountered him 'young George' was little more than a boy. But Lord had ample opportunity to assess him in later years. It has been said he liked Harriman only because he did what he was told. I give Lord credit for more intelligence and less vanity. However, it is very possible he was sufficiently aware of his own demeanour to appreciate the value of Harriman's ultra-suave approach to roller the turf after the chairman had passed! He was the perfect foil for Lord; an excellent 'number two'. Yet simply not the stuff of a top man.

A related issue to that of succession is training. Turner claims, probably primed by Edwards, that Lord did not believe even in *the simpler forms of training* and was opposed to an apprentice scheme. Quoting Edwards directly in *The Motor Makers*, Martin Adeney writes: *'Lord's view of apprentices was that they were lucky to be allowed in. We had a place up on the old firing* (sic) *ground in an old tin hut, with about four milling machines about 50 years old and a driller. That was their approach'*.

The impression given is at best highly misleading; at worst inaccurate. It is correct that by the 1950s the training programme operated at Longbridge was not as advanced or sophisticated as that at plants such as Ford. But the Austin scheme had been a source of pride within the industry since the 1920s and Lord continued to be highly supportive, take an active interest and attend and fund events. Under his management the apprenticeship scheme was as extensive, if not more so, than the highly acclaimed structure operated by the company pre-War.

The details are set out for aspirants in an attractive, fully illustrated, landscape format, 19-page booklet. The first leaf of text is a foreword from Lord in which he emphasizes the value of training. Career paths were available for both engineers and tradesman, the entry qualifications for the former being particularly high. Trade apprentices had a wide variety of options ranging from carpentry and tool or pattern making to electrical maintenance or coachbuilding. All engineering entrants spent a year divided between the machine shops and foundry (eight and four months respectively) before specializing during their remaining three years in one of three disciplines—automobile engineering, production, or works maintenance. All the fields were supported by study at external colleges to Higher National Certificate (HNC) level.

The 'tin hut' referred to by Edwards was no more, or less, than a Nissan hut on the flying ground. Although the machinery may have been time expired students who worked with it speak of the challenges presented by compensating for liberal tolerances. It equipped them extremely well for their future careers! Neither was the quality of the work lacking. Among many other tasks, engines were sectioned to international display standard.

The most severe criticism of Leonard Lord is the so-called 'fouling' of the atmosphere at BMC by his supposed prejudice against Morris, leading to many of the benefits of the merger being negated. It would be difficult to deny that Lord's memories of Morris, particularly at the end of his period there, were unhappy. But those who are in a much better position to judge than latter day commentators are, in the main, firmly of the view that he was neither vindictive nor malicious.

Moreover, many of his alleged misdeeds do not withstand close examination. For instance, the contention that Lord channelled revenue into a luxurious and state-of-the-art Longbridge, while leaving Nuffield sites in decrepitude, is a fallacy. Austin's car assembly building that Morris personnel looked upon jealously when they visited the site had been completed before the merger took place. Their own accommodation had received little attention since Lord himself reorganized it in the early 1930s. Its dilapidated condition was down to the parsimoniousness of William Morris, who clearly did not believe that charity began at home. When managers asked for structural improvements, such as a roof on the loading bay at Bodies Branch, Morris was apt to say: *'You'll burst the walls; burst the walls'*. Exactly what this weird aphorism means is difficult to interpret, but seems to be a contention that what was in place was adequate and everyone should 'make do' with it.

The charge that Longbridge men held most of the top jobs at BMC is not justified either, though you could argue that it would be human nature for Lord to gather around him the people he knew best and with whom he already worked. In the first instance top management was divided between Austin and Morris but with a slight bias towards the latter. William Morris was chairman, Lord his deputy and managing director. Hanks, who had no Austin associations at all other than he still believed he was in competition with the Birmingham firm, was vice chairman and Harriman, who had been more a Nuffield man than an Austin one, became deputy managing director.

If we take one year at random (1956) J F Bramley and H C Mullens became BMC export sales directors. The first was an Austin man and the second from Morris. In the subsequent departmental reshuffles the promotions were almost equally divided between Austin and Morris (R E M Pratt, J W Bache and E M Gibbs of Austin, J W Malone, L A Beare and F Potter from Morris). In home sales the pattern was exactly the same with a slight bias towards the Nuffield Organization, similarly in the service and finance departments. In manufacturing there was a strong leaning towards former Nuffield employees—seven to two, although, of course, the top man, Edwards, was 'Austin'. Elsewhere the balance was equally even handed.

Leading Morris man Hanks soon faded from the scene, but he was a decidedly inappropriate incumbent. And Lord 'squeezed out' an ageing William Morris, mainly because of his familiar trait of vesting full authority in an executive then constantly interfering. That had infuriated Miles Thomas as much as it did Lord.

The late Geoffrey Rose, who had a Wolseley and Morris background, combined with a usefully relevant dash of experience as assistant director of wheeled vehicle production at the Ministry of Supply, was adamant, that Lord did not favour Austin components in preference to Morris other than on the basis of superiority.

We must remember that the chairman had a comprehensive understanding of engineering matters and could spot design inadequacies. By way of example, and however distasteful it is to Nuffield devotees, we can cite the C Series engine, the Riley Pathfinder and the Wolseley 6/90. When the first materialized from the Morris drawing office its cylinder head was seriously flawed and needed a major re-work before the motor earned distinction in, most notably, the Austin Healey. The Pathfinder's rear suspension bordered on the catastrophic and resulted in the sobriquet 'Ditchfinder' among motoring wags, while the Wolseley clearly had shortcomings in the execution of its brake design. On the other hand the use of the Austin Eight's feeble gearbox innards in the A30 and Morris Minor and, remarkably, the Mini, can be excused, to a degree, on the grounds of expediency and economy rather than Lord's prejudice.

It is also worth noting that at the time BMC was formed, Morris was much less well regulated financially than it had been pre-War. To a large extent this was a result of construction methods moving from chassis-based to the integral body shell. The former method allowed Cowley to receive bodies in major sections—bonnets, wings, doors etc. Transport costs were minimized by movement in bulk of these 'stackable' items, most of the assembly work could be undertaken on site and control generally, especially of cost, was good.

With the move towards monocoque construction, complete bodies, often ready-painted and sometimes already trimmed, were delivered by lorry in batches of between four and six, or by conveyor from the Pressed Steel factory next door. Transport costs rose, of course, and cost regulation generally became much more difficult. Austin was now at an increasing and enviable advantage. Around 90 per cent of parts were made at Longbridge and the car assembly building had been designed to capitalize on unitary construction.

A picture of how the financial balance changed will be gleaned if we consider Mini production. Body shells and panels plus a host of other components being transported over considerable distances, compounded by everything from inclement weather to industrial disputes, helped spell excessive production costs. However, in this case, it was partly due to government intervention (the body component plant being sited in Llanelli) rather than to Lord's stewardship.

We must now move to the unsavoury area of labour relations. Lord's political persuasion would have been strongly Right wing and he had an intense aversion to Communists. *'We are told we must co-operate with the workers. With whom are we going to co-operate—the shop stewards? The shop stewards are Communists'*. There was nothing unusual about the stance, however, it is extremely unfortunate Lord was juxtaposed with such a fervent and committed Communist as Dick Etheridge. Had there been a little less conviction on both sides, a little more flexibility and empathy from Lord, the scene may not have been so troubled in the short term and, perhaps, not even so vexed ultimately.

To his credit, Lord was very much aware that there was a problem and, we suspect, knew he was incapable of resolving it. He tried to find a solution. But, as we know, Edwards left him to his own devices and the fundamental issues remained, and worsened.

Some readers may feel I am clouding the issue of the production director's dismissal. Certainly, it is by no means clear, that it was precipitated by Edward's refusal to take on an industrial relations role. Dick Etheridge was firmly of the view that Lord made his 1956 strike negotiator the scapegoat for the débâcle of that summer. Edwards, quite correctly, mistrusted Issigonis, and, to say the least, was non-plussed by Harriman's total confidence in him. He was also an outspoken critic of Lord's management strategy and, especially, his failure to rationalize. These differences came to a head when Lord returned from his Padstow holiday and, utterly predictably, sided with Harriman. That, many believe, is what led to Edwards's sacking.

At a practical level, Lord has been criticized for the Corporation's lack-lustre cars—vehicles that populist writers like to term 'grey porridge'. They have in mind the Austin Eights and Tens, the Morris Oxfords and Austin Devons, Dorsets and Cambridges, the Hampshires and Herefords and probably many more besides.

Lord had adopted a philosophy that was very much the gospel according to Herbert Austin. It was not that his predecessor could not have designed an overhead camshaft engine, or explored the vagaries of semi-automatic transmission. He had done so. Austin knew that such complications were of no interest to the tens of thousands of his core customers. A farmer in the Welsh mountains or Lowlands of Scotland would not contemplate buying a car that no local garage understood, let alone could fix.

By the same token, Lord was attuned to the conservatism and expectations of the British market and its extended outlets in the Commonwealth and former British Empire. It is all very well to state that the Citroën DS, with its complex, self-leveling suspension, *avant-garde* interior and space age aerodynamics, was the sensation of the 1955 London motor show and imply that the domestic industry should have been similarly positioned. Few in Britain would have put down hard cash for a car like the Citroën. The UK sales figures, even allowing for import duties, subsequently reflected this as they had done for the DS's predecessor, the *Traction Avant*, that was equally revolutionary in 1934.

Yet Lord was forward thinking, open minded and above all decisive. What ever the trigger, the Farina styling he introduced gave the British customer a modern-looking Western European car that moved BMC a considerable distance from any Austin, Morris, MG, Riley or Wolseley that had gone before. Neither did he fail to respond, with equal vision and determination, to implorations from the motoring press—most significantly Pomeroy, but others, notably, Bill Boddy of *Motor Sport* magazine—when they called for technical advancement.

On the negative side, Lord neither rationalized the excessive range of makes and models, reduced the absurd number of plants the Corporation operated, nor trimmed the duplicated dealer network. What can be said in his defence is that preserving marques like Morris, and even Riley and Wolseley still, just about, had some justification on the basis of British traditionalism and customer loyalty.

Shutting factories and shedding jobs would have been a very thorny issue indeed given the level of union militancy and that part of the political mantra was still 'full employment'. The problem only began to be addressed when Edwards returned to BMC in the run-up to the fusion with Leyland.

In addition, government economic policy made both planning types of car and also production levels, and thus rationalization, extremely difficult. A further impediment was the City whose none-too-altruistic interests would have been represented by the non-executive directors on Lord's board.

As regards the dealers, as I have previously suggested, the logistics were extremely complicated and unless some 'magic bullet' could have been found the costs phenomenal. If only marginally, it was all just about sustainable on the strength of what the balance sheets indicated.

I have expressed in the main body of this book my firm belief that it was after Leonard Lord relinquished his executive role that BMC and subsequently British Leyland and the rest, went into progressive, terminal, decline. Also, that most of the seeds for the débâcles to come were not sown by Lord. Neither did he so *'foul the atmosphere'* at BMC that a golden opportunity for British industry was lost. If we wish to be ultra-simplistic and we accept the huge successes that Lord achieved in the post-War era and the potential he created for BMC, it could be claimed that just one error—and one that I have freely admitted on behalf of Leonard Lord—led to the whole series of disastrous events. Namely Lord's failure to implant an effective, competent, line of succession.

Harriman may have been sauve, but he was ineffective, out of touch and unapproachable to almost all the workforce. 'Young George' had not, as Leonard Lord jokingly said, *'learnt the ropes'*. One of his first actions, and perhaps his most disastrous of all, was to appoint Alec Issigonis technical director.

It was Harriman and Issigonis between them, not Leonard Lord, who destroyed the British Motor Corporation.

At face value, its replacement had some chance of success. In *The Leyland Papers* Turner is full of optimism. *'British Leyland now has what at one time seemed unlikely—a fair chance not merely of survival but also of prosperity'*. Many are of the view that if Joe Edwards, with his labour relations and plant management skills, had been prepared to work with the successful marketeer, Donald Stokes, there would, indeed, have been a fair chance of survival. But, as we have seen, and as was the case with Leonard Lord, he refused, in even more acrimonious terms than he displayed to Lord. If ever the atmosphere for success was fouled it was by this hand.

Before coming to an ultimate conclusion as to who 'poisoned the well' I would like to raise one further point. In polite society it is considered taboo to speak ill of the dead. Even so, when we examined the tributes and obituaries written about Leonard Lord, the tide of respect, acknowledgement of his genius and sheer undiluted affection is overwhelming. Members of his family speak of his kindness and warmth, apprentices of his fairness and generosity of spirit, many who only knew him a little tell of how he would manipulate the system to deliver compassionate solutions. One simple example is a 1940s service manager who fell ill and was told he needed a period in a warm climate. Currency restrictions made that impossible for a civilian, so Lord arranged for the man and his wife to be sent on a three-month Mediterranean cruise for the company 'inspecting' distributorships. An engineer was provided at each location to ensure all technical questions could be answered.

Of course, there are those who are eager to present a darker side. Most of what has been written about Leonard Lord, even by Harriman, portray his 'tough and outspoken' side. A 'man's man' we might say. He certainly enjoyed the company of his, entirely male, corps of apprentices and is known to have revelled in the all-male celebration arranged for his retirement. Yet, if Leonard Lord was a 'man's man' he was certainly also a 'ladies man' but most definitely not a 'skirt chaser', unlike some, very close to him. His affinity with women was the almost inescapable consequence of his upbringing and domestic situation. He had had an extremely close relationship with his mother and his only sibling was female. In addition, at home, he was surrounded by women.

It is usually an excellent bellwether of the true temperament of a senior executive if they are liked and respected by their secretary. Ruth Bailey certainly had enormous admiration for Lord, served him loyally for many years, was an active participant in 'the team' and the chairman heavily depended upon her. In similar vein, the interview he gave to Olive Moore of *Scope* magazine is probably his most frank and forthright of all and she is obviously greatly enamoured of every aspect of his personality.

So who *did* poison the well?

Inevitably, in an organisation the size of Austin, and even more so BMC, there is ill-feeling, animosity, jealousies petty or grave, prejudices and resentments. A broad selection of voices, many of them positive, receive a hearing in Barney Sharratt's *Men and Motors of the Austin*. Both a strength and weakness of this work is that Sharratt rarely comments on the views being propounded. Nonetheless Lord is portrayed with objectivity.

Thereafter I must allow the reader to reach his or her own conclusions. Andrews and Brunner's *The Life of Lord Nuffield* appeared in 1955 and is pure hagiography. All references to Lord are mere platitudes to accommodate William Morris, who was still alive and actively involved in the writing. Thus they are totally innocent in the denigration of our subject.

Miles Thomas leapt into print with *Out On A Wing* almost before Morris's corpse was cold. In his genteel way he is fairly critical of his former patron but in 1964 Lord was still very much on the scene and the writer is wary. His criticisms of Lord are either veiled or he 'damns him with faint praise'. Overall the picture he paints of life in the Oxfordshire of Morris—and generally—leads us to the view that he and Lord would have little affinity. Indeed, Wyatt in *The Austin 1905-1952* states forthrightly: *'Lord Thomas of Wolseley** (aka Miles Thomas) *disliked him* (Lord) *sufficiently to reject Payton's invitation to run Austin's* (sic) *jointly with Lord in 1946'*.

---

*   Not his correct title.

Turner's book was published four years after Leonard Lord's death and three beyond the formation of British Leyland. Joe Edwards was still alive and is quoted extensively.

Adeney's *The Motor Makers* appeared in 1988 and broadly repeats what Turner and/or Edwards had to say. As regards Lord specifically he cites Thomas and repeats some of the folklore.

Jonathan Wood is a latter day motoring writer who regularly mentions Lord in his work, wrote a biographical article for *Automobile* magazine in 2008 and, for whatever reason, is generally hostile.

I have argued that Leonard Lord was the most significant British industrialist of the latter half of the 20th century. The basis for this is simple. We have seen how Lord's technical expertise transformed Hotchkiss/Morris Engines and, combined with his dynamism, had a similar effect at Wolseley. It was also the salvation of an ailing Morris Motors—one of the bastions of Britain's manufacturing prestige.

Yet none of this is sufficient to justify the accolade I have bestowed upon him. He worked his 'Morris magic' at Austin—not so much financially but in the sense the company and its products were revitalized, almost overnight. There followed a period of exceptional endeavour to help sustain a nation whose back was to the wall in the face of a monstrous aggressor. But even this is not enough to warrant Lord being acclaimed in my terms.

However, to lead Austin into the late 1940s with imagination, vision and ruthless determination, when the country was starved of the dollars that were a critical means of keeping its economic heart beating, sets him apart from all his peers. That he did so, frustrated by government and impeded by an increasingly recalcitrant workforce, only adds to his stature.

The creation of BMC, on the superb production foundations laid by Leonard Lord, offered the British motor industry unparalleled global opportunities. It was under-pinned by realism, perception and decisiveness when others would have prevaricated for months, if not years, and led to Britain providing the blue-print for the world's small cars for decades to come. As Cambrian said, Leonard Lord was a man among men. Sadly, but as is the case with all mankind, on the broader canvas there were shortcomings and failings.

In his masterly biography, *Charles de Gaulle, The Last Great Frenchman* (John Wiley and Sons, 1993) Charles Williams writes: '*There would have been no argument at all had there been no France, and there would have been no France if there had been no de Gaulle*'.

I leave you with the thought that, after 1945, there would have soon been no British motor industry at all if there had been no Leonard Lord.

This unfamiliar portrait of Leonard Lord was taken by the celebrated
London photographer, Paul Tanqueray. From Lord's age it is probably the
official picture taken around the time he took control of Morris in 1933.
(Courtesy British National Portrait Gallery/Tanqueray Estate.)

Where Leonard Lord began to grow up. The *Hope and Anchor* public House, now demolished, on Whitefriars Lane, Coventry. He later lived on nearby Foleshill Road. (*Photo Paul Fox.*)

Bablake School, Coventry today, much as it would have been when
Leonard Lord attended. (*Courtesy Bablake School.*)

The Morris Eight, introduced by Leonard Lord in 1934, a year
after he had taken command of the ailing Morris empire, became
Britain's best-selling car. It saved Morris from almost certain bankruptcy
and was a technically advanced, quality product, vastly
superior to the Ford Y Type and much better than the Austin Seven.
(*Courtesy the late Geoff Creese.*)

Stylist Dick Burzi at his best. The beautifully proportioned lines of the late
pre-War Austin Light Twelve Four New Ascot saloon appealed to the
conservative, middle class, Austin customer. But inspired by Lord, Burzi
was to give Austins an altogether more dynamic, rather Americanized,
look. (*Photo Tim Legge/Austin Ten Drivers' Club.*)

The first 'Lord-look car' was the Austin Eight (AR1 Series). The model reappeared after WWII (coded AS1) but only as a four-door saloon.
(*Photo Ron Day, New Zealand.*)

After the 'fall of France', General de Gaulle had his headquarters in
Britain. Here Leonard Lord takes him on a tour of Longbridge Works and pauses
on the Stirling bomber line. (*Copyright holder(s) currently unknown*).

Top dollar. Currency earning Devon was Lord's early post-War masterstroke.

Chassisless at last. The A30 of 1951 was the first volume produced,
chassisless car in the world. It was a concept Lord had promoted for many years.
(*Photo David Chaundy.*)

The original Mini continues to give untold pleasure. In its day
it was a commercial catastrophe and the engineering suspect.

APPENDIX

VEHICLES PRODUCED UNDER THE AUSPICES OF LEONARD LORD
(Makes are alphabetical, models in chronological sequence)

Private Cars

AUSTIN

Eight 1939-1942 and variants (e.g. tourer) and four door saloon only 1945-47
Ten 1939-1945 and tourer then saloon only 1945-1947
Twelve 1939-1940 and 1945-1947
Sixteen 1945-1949 and variants (e.g. Countryman)

A40 Dorset 1947-1949
A40 Devon 1947-1952 and variants (e.g. Countryman to 1956)

A110/A125 Sheerline long and short wheelbase* 1947-1953

A120/A135 Princess saloon and touring limousine 1947-1950
A135 Princess ll 1950-1953
A135 Princess lll 1953-1956
Princess IV 1956-1959
Princess Limousine 1952-1968 thus surviving long after Lord's day in control of BMC

A70 Hampshire and variants (e.g. Countryman) 1948-1951
A70 Hereford and variants (e. g. Countryman and coupé) 1950-1954

A90 Atlantic soft top 1948-1950
A90 Atlantic fixed head 1949-1952

Jensen-bodied A40 Sports 1950-1953

A30 1951-1956

---

*   The lwb car was only available from 1949-1953.

A40 Somerset saloon and coupé 1952-1954

Austin Healey 100-4 1953-1955

Nash Metropolitan 1953-1957 (USA and Canada only) 1957-1961 (Europe etc.)

A40/A50/A55 Cambridge 1954-1961 (The Mark ll A55 <1959-1961> was a Farina-styled model).

A35 1956-1958. The Countryman was produced until 1962

Westminster (A90, A95, A105, A99 and Countryman variants of some models) 1954-1961. The A99 was to Farina styling. There was a limited number of Vanden Plas A105s directly inspired by Lord.

Austin Healey 100-6 and 3000 1956-1968*

Austin Healey Sprite Mark l ('Frogeye') 1958-1961

Austin A40 Farina saloon and Countryman 1958-67

Princess (then Vanden Plas Princess) Three Litre 1959-61

Mini 1959-2000

Vanden Plas Princess Four Litre R (in conjunction with Rolls-Royce)**

MORRIS (Independent)

Minor side valve*** 1931-1934
Eight (Series One#) 1934-1937

MORRIS (As part of BMC)

Minor (and variants e.g. Traveller) 1952-1971##

---

* Lord's 'claim' to these cars is slightly tenous. Although the 3000 was made at BMC Abingdon and the 100-6 originally at Longbridge the engine was a pre-BMC Morris derivative.

** This model was never produced when Lord was at the helm of BMC. It did, however, have its genesis when he was still in control (1960) and he was extremely enthusiastic about it, which is why I have included it here.

*** Lord was not responsible for the troublesome overhead camshaft pre-War 'Minor'.

\# The description used from about 1935 but not at launch.

\#\# Although Leonard Lord had absolutely nothing to do with the conception of the Morris Minor, launched in 1948, it was at his instigation, in 1952, that the model was fitted with an Austin overhead valve engine thus turning a rather disappointing and under-performing car into a best-seller.

Oxford (and variants as above) 1954-1961

Isis 1955-1958*

MG

To attribute any pre-War MGs to Leonard Lord is tenuous. It is true, he ran MG, as part of The Nuffield Organization, from 1933-1936 and thus could be said to be ultimately responsible for the cars of that era. In this context we might cite the J, K, L, N and P Type Midgets, Magnas and Magnettes. However, it would be more accurate to say that Lord's greatest impact during this period was to close the prolific, independent, drawing office, rationalize the range and insist that MGs were powered by versions of existing Morris engines. These actions unquestionably preserved the marque for future generations.

MG as part of BMC

TF 1953-1955

Magnette 1953-1961 (ZA, ZB and Mark lll)

MGA 1955-1962

RILEY

Pathfinder 1953-1957

One Point Five 1957-1965

Two Point Six 1958-1959

WOLSELEY

4/44 1952-1956

6/90 1954-1959

15/50 1956-1958

1500 1957-1965

6/99 1959-1961

---

* Although this car's predecessor, the Morris Six, was in production for the first year of BMC it cannot be claimed the model was manufactured under the auspices of Lord as both the engine and bodywork were purely Nuffield creations.

COMMERCIAL VEHICLES

AUSTIN

Eight Van 1939-1940 and 1945-1947
Ten Van 1939-1940 and 1945-1947
Ten WD Utility 1939-1945

K2 Two/Three ton lorry (and military variants)1939-49
K4 Five ton lorry (and military variants) 1939-1949

K5 Three Ton 4x4 military lorry 1941-1945
K6 Three Ton 6x4 military lorry 1941-1945

CXB and K4SL coach 1945*-1950

K8 25 cwt van 1946-1953

A125 Sheerline ambulance and hearse 1947-1955

FX3 Taxi 1948-1958

K2SL Small coach 1948-1949

FL1 Hire Car 1949-1958

Loadstar ** Three and five ton lorry 1949-1954

CXD forward control coach 1950-1955

Austin Champ 1951-1956 (There was a military and civilian version)

K9 4x4 1/1.5 ton lorry# 1952-1955

Austin Gipsy 1959-1967

FX4 Taxi 1958-1971

---

*   It is highly unlikely any Austin coaches were manufactured before 1947.
**   The name was dropped when it was realised an American manufacturer was already using the term. The 'K' designation was subsequently re-adopted!
#   This was primarily a military type but some civilian versions were built.

MORRIS

After the formation of BMC, vehicles that would have been branded as Morris Commercial were badged as simply Morris, sometimes as Austin and even as BMC. Overlapping makes the picture complicated. Listed below are some of the models with which the reader is most likely to be familiar.

J Series 15 cwt van—introduced by Morris in 1949 but progressed through four series until 1974.

LC 25/30 cwt truck 1952-1960.
LD One/one-point-five ton van 1952-1968.

FV and FE Three, five and seven ton lorries 1948-1959.

VA 1958-1976.

WE Three/five ton lorry 1955-1964.

BIBLIOGRAPHY

The Vintage Motor Car Pocket Book (Clutton, Bird, Harding) Batsford 1959.

Bedford Instruction Book 30 CWT and Two Ton (Vauxhall Motors) 1938.

Commer Driver's Instruction Book 15 CWT and 20/25 CWT (Commer Cars Ltd).

The Sports Car (Stanford) Batsford 1957.

Wolseley Radial Aero Engines (Seymour) Tempus Publishing 2006.

Issigonis (Bardsley) Icon Books 2005.

The Motor Makers (Adeney) Collins 1988.

Bentley Mark VI (King) Complete Classics 2007.

Morris Light Vans 1924-34 (Seymour) P & B Publishing 1999.

Bentley The Vintage Years (Hay) Dalton Watson 1986.

Veteran and Vintage Cars (Burgess-Wise) Hamlyn 1970.

The Austin Seven (Wyatt) Macdonald 1986.

The Daimler Tradition (Smith) Transport Bookman Publications 1972.

Monstrous American Car Spotter's Guide (Burness) Motorbooks International 1986.

Philip Larkin Collected Poems Faber and Faber 1988.

Austin Pedal Cars (Whyley) Arthur Southern 1999.

The Observer's Book of Automobiles Frederick Warne 1960 edition.

The Vintage Motor Car (Clutton, Stanford) Batsford 1954.

Gullible's Travels (Hess) Motor Racing Publications 1948.

The Sports Car Pocketbook (Boddy) Batsford 1961.

The Thoroughbred Motor Car 1930-40 (Scott-Moncrieff) Batsford 1963.

Alec Issigonis The Man Who Made The Mini (Wood) Breedon Books 2005.

The Life of Lord Nuffield (Andrews, Brunner) Blackwell 1955.

The Maintenance and Driving of Vintage Cars (Wheatley, Morgan) Batsford 1964.

Walker RN (Robertson) Pan 1958.

Out On A Wing (Thomas) Michael Joseph 1964.

The Leyland Papers (Turner) Eyre and Spottiswoode 1971.

British Cars at Le Mans (Pascal) Haynes 1990.

A History of the World's Sports Cars (Hough) Allen and Unwin 1961.

Men and Motors of the Austin (Sharratt) Haynes 2000.

Austin The Counties Years (Brown, Whyley) Arthur Southern.

Fiftieth Anniversary of the Austin A70 Hereford and Austin A40 Sports (Whyley) Austin Counties Car Club 2000.

Austin 50 Years of Car Progress Austin Motor Company 1955.

Pre-War Austin Seven Club Magazine (October 2005, February 2006, November 2006, November 2007).

Austin Motor Company Minute Books (Various).

Austerity Britain (Kynaston) Bloomsbury 2008.

Having It So Good (Hennessy) Penguin 2007

MGB The Illustrated History (Wood, Burrell) Haynes 1988.

Archdale Machine Tools James Archdale 1948.

Engines and Enterprise (John Reynolds) Haynes

VCC Gazette. Magazine of the Veteran Car Club of Great Britain (Various)

INDEX

❦

Lord, William, Lord's father, 1
    landlord of *Hope and Anchor*
public house 2-3, 267
    death of, 3, 270
Lucas electrics, 105, 106, 107, 108, 162
Luftwaffe, 93, 110, 197
Lyons, Sir William, 255

Macclesfield, Earl of, 52
MacDonald, Ramsay, 64
MacMillan, Harold, 214, 230, 236, 238
Madawick, Tucker, 181, 211
Madresfield Court speed trails, 91-92
Magg machines, 67
Mandelson, Peter, 258
Mann Egerton, 95
Mann Overton, 167
Marne, battle of, 70
Marshall, Cambridge coachbuilder, 95
Marshall, Senator George, 122
    Marshall Plan, the, 122, 145, 194-195, 272

Mason, George Walter, 200-201
Mass Observation movement, 136
Maudslay, 252
Maugham, W. Somerset, 71
Maxim's restaurant, 248
Mays, Raymond, 90, 213
McCahill, Tom, 144
McHugh, John, 191-193
McHugh Strike, 191, 193, 195-196, 219, 222
McKenna Duties, 71
McLeod, Ian, 222
Meadows engine, 163
Mechanix Illustrated, 144
Medina, MV, 60
Mercedes, 88-89, 213, 258
    agency, 72

Merthyr Tydfil, 61
Metropolitan Vickers, 100
MG Car Company Ltd, 34, 48-49, 87, 89, 91, 92, 254, 257, 258, 270, 277
    Charles, Hubert, 115
    Financial losses, 40
    Midget, 38
    Racing 38-40, 143
    (MG) Rover, 259

MG 1100, 243
MGA, 184, 227
MGB, 244
MG R Type racer, 232
MG TD, 188
MG Y Type, 188
MG Z Type, 188
Michelin, 194
Milberg, Joachim, 258
Milch, General Erhard, 93-94
Miles, F.G., 101
Miles Master, 100
Millionth Austin, 12, 128
Millionth Morris, 48, 128
Mills, John, 95
Mini, 148, 183, 204, 214, 216, 231, 233-243, 245, 247-249, 256-258, 261, 275
    Celebrity owners, 235
    Engine, 148, 234
    Early public reaction to, 241
    Experimental, ADO 15, 233, 235
    Experimental, XC9003, 233
    Front wheel drive, 241
    Royal family and, 235

Ministry of Labour and National Service, 147
Ministry of Supply, 126-127, 170, 275
Mons, battle of, 70
Montlhèry track, 89
Moore, John, 149
Moore, Olive, 154-155, 170, 197, 278
Moore-Brabazon, J.T.C. (Lord Brabazon of Tara), 88, 252, 261
Morgan, Michèle, 248
Morris Motors, 58, 60, 66, 72, 74, 76, 127, 257-258, 271, 272, 274, 275, 277-279
    Bodies Branch 254, 275,
    Experimental department, 231
    Financial structure, 34, 270
    Morris Eight, 61, 158, 182-183, 187
    Morris Radiators, 254
    Proposed merger, with Austin/Wolseley, 72

Morris Models (pre-Lord):
    Cowley, 51-52
    Oxford, 51-52, 63
    Oxford MO, 184, 186
    Minor (1928), 31, 232
    Twelve, 21